FOUNDATION SEI

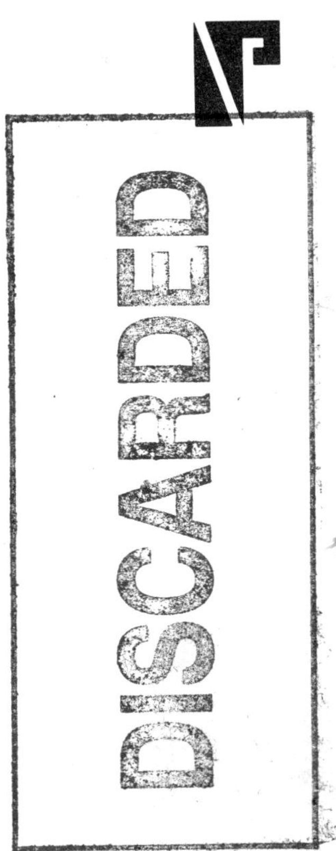

NORTHWICK PUBLISHERS

14, BEVERE CLOSE, WORCESTER, WR3 7QH, ENGLAND

Telephone Number: 0905-56876/56529

FOUNDATION SERIES

Other books in the series:

FINANCIAL ACCOUNTING
AUTHOR W. HARRISON F.C.I.B., Cert.Ed.

COST ACCOUNTING
AUTHOR G. J. WILKINSON-RIDDLE B.A., F.C.A.

ECONOMICS
AUTHOR R. G. WINFIELD B.Sc.(Econ) Hons., F.C.I.B.

FOUNDATION SERIES

LAW

Second Edition

P. GERRARD B.Sc., Ph.D., A.C.I.B.

Senior Lecturer in Banking
Liverpool Polytechnic

NORTHWICK PUBLISHERS

NORTHWICK PUBLISHERS

ISBN 0 907135 57 9

Printed in England by Clays Ltd, St Ives plc

First Impression 1983
Second edition 1987
Reprinted 1988
Reprinted 1990

CONTENTS

PREFACE TO THE FIRST EDITION

It is essential for anyone who wants to pursue a career in business or one of the professions to have a working knowledge of the law. This knowledge may be acquired for the first time while at school, when studying law as either an O-level or A-level subject, but perhaps the majority study law for the first time as part of a professional course, such as Associateship of The Chartered Institute of Bankers or the Institute of Cost and Management Accountants, or on a Business Studies or other Degree course. It is for all of these groups of students that the book has been primarily written – although those who simply want to update their knowledge will find the book just as useful.

ACKNOWLEDGEMENTS

To complete any book of this size and complexity needs the encouragement and assistance of others. In this respect, I would like to give my thanks to the following:

To Mr E. P. Doyle, Principal of the Liverpool School of Banking, for giving me invaluable help and advice. Through his efforts, my draft scripts were converted into the completed book.

To Dr M. A. Hennell, Senior Lecturer in the Department of Statistical and Computational Mathematics at the University of Liverpool, for allowing the book to be stored on his word processor.

To Doctor Hennell's secretary, Mrs H. E. Hallaron, to Mrs M. L. M. Hennell and to Mrs B. Jones who patiently typed the script into the word processor.

To the following professional bodies and academic boards for giving me permission to reproduce some of their past examination questions:

The Chartered Institute of Bankers.
The Institute of Cost and Management Accountants.
The Institute of Chartered Secretaries and Administrators.
The Chartered Institute of Transport.
The Associated Examination Board.
The Joint Matriculation Board.

Finally, I would like to acknowledge that any errors or omissions contained within the text are entirely my responsibility.

Spring 1983 P. GERRARD

PREFACE TO THE SECOND EDITION

Since the first edition of this book was published in 1983, it has become very popular with students because of the simple way in which the content is expressed and the logical way in which the content of each chapter is developed.

The second edition of this book has used the first impression as a base, but added to and/or amended the original text by including:

(1) Up-to-date relevant case law; and,
(2) Relevant sections of recent statutes; and,
(3) New material, such as the section on negligent statements; and,
(4) The development of material which had been briefly described in the first impression, such as that relating to exemption clauses; and,
(5) A law report citation for nearly every quoted legal case; and,
(6) the re-writing of the description of some of the legal cases, thereby making the background detail and the basis of the court's decision easier to understand.

The book has been brought up-to-date as at January 1987 and this should help the book to retain its popularity and ensure good examination pass rates.

January 1987 P. GERRARD

CHAPTER 1

The objective of any student should be to pass the end of session examination and in achieving this objective, enjoy the subject that is being studied. This book, in itself, should help you to achieve this end, while for those of you attending full-time or part-time courses, your lecturers should help make the subject even more enjoyable.

It would be unfair to say that everything will be plain sailing. For, as with any subject, there will always be certain parts to a syllabus which are complicated and therefore difficult to understand. If this happens to you, and I am sure it will, then you should not despair. Almost certainly, many of your colleagues will be in the same position. In these circumstances, you should read the topic over again, and if you still cannot understand it, then, if you are attending a college or are at school, ask your tutor to go over it once more.

Once you have completed the text of each chapter, you should ensure that you can answer all the past examination questions that have been listed at the end of the chapter. If you feel you can answer all of them well, then you are fortunate and can almost certainly look forward to being awarded a distinction when the examination results are published! Where some questions on first reading appear to be difficult, read them a second time and then decide whether or not you can provide a satisfactory answer. If you are still having problems, go back to the relevant part of the text and read the topic over again. This procedure should ensure that you are able to give a good answer, but if you are still uncertain, if you are attending a college or are at school, ask your tutor to go over the problem with you.

With regard to the style of examination questions, certain general points can be made. In the main, GCSE questions require answers that simply test the recall of information. So, if a number of details are missed out in an examination answer, it would still be possible to obtain a very high mark. In contrast, many questions that are set on A-level or professional examinations are in the form of case studies, and therefore they have to be interpreted. So, at this level, there is an emphasis on application of knowledge. As such, students will either interpret a question correctly and gain a high mark or interpret a question incorrectly and get few or no marks. Many students fail law (and other) examinations because they misread such interpretation questions and the only real way of overcoming the problem is to spend at least fifteen minutes at the beginning of each examination in analysing the questions and planning your answer. Only at this stage should you begin to write your answer down.

Over and above this general advice, two further points should be noted with regard to answering questions in a law examination.

The first is that you must always be **Accurate**, **Brief** and **Clear** in your presentation. Secondly, and with particular reference to case study questions, you should always give answers that are logical. The following sequence, which will certainly impress your examiner, is suggested:

Firstly: Identify and state the area of law with which the question is concerned.

Secondly: Quote and describe any relevant statute or judicial precedents. In this context, if you have forgotten the official title of the statute or the names or year of a case precedent, simply quote the details.

Thirdly: Apply the legal principles detailed in the first part of your answer to the case study.

Fourthly: If it is possible to do so, and certainly if asked to do so in the examination, make a decision. This fourth stage will indicate to the examiner whether or not you fully understand the legal principles.

In order to give you a few illustrations of good examination style, several of the questions which appear at the end of the chapters have had model solutions prepared. The appropriate solutions can be found in the "Appendix of Answers" at the back of the book.

By using this style, you will always be in a position to answer examination questions in a logical and flowing manner – but do remember, at the same time (as stated above), to be accurate, brief and clear. Then, provided you have interpreted the question correctly, success is sure to follow.

Before moving to the main text, one final point must be appreciated and this is that the law is continually changing and developing. In order to keep up to date, it is essential that you get into the habit of reading the better quality newspapers and legal journals and that you make notes about any new statutes or precedents. By doing this, then, as a college based or school student, you may even be one step ahead of your tutor! Certainly, if you can quote up-to-date, relevant information in answering your examination questions, then this will create a very good impression upon the examiner.

CHAPTER 2

THE LAW AND THE PEOPLE WHO ADMINISTER IT

INTRODUCTION

As many of you will be studying law for the first time, quite naturally, your first question should be "What is law?" You may be surprised to know that the legal profession has not yet been able to produce a universally or generally acceptable definition of law. But this is not to say that definitions have never been made – for they have. However, the problem has always been that as soon as a definition has been published by one lawyer, others have pointed out its shortcomings.

The problem in English language is aggravated by the fact that there is a major difference between the term "a law" and "the law". (In other languages (e.g. German), there are two different words and so the problem does not exist.)

A law can be described as a rule of conduct which applies to all the people who make up a community. Some of the laws dictate the relationships which the people must have with each other, as private individuals or on a business basis, while others dictate their relationship with the state. The problem immediately arises of whether all rules of conduct are legally enforceable. The answer to this is emphatically "no" and many examples can be quoted to illustrate the point; e.g. Golf Committees impose rules and regulations governing how players should conduct themselves when playing a round of golf on their course: for example, prohibiting the wearing of jeans when playing a round of golf. If one player contravenes this rule, it is not possible for his playing partner or the golf club to take out a legal action in court against him in an attempt to get him to observe the rule: although, clearly, if the committee feels strongly enough about the matter, it could expel him from the club if that was desired. It is more difficult to establish why some rules do become laws which can be enforced in the courts against any of us, while others do not. In general, it can be said that the rules become law when parts of society (particularly Members of Parliament today), feel that rules should be universally applied to the people who make up their community.

These rules are forever changing as communities develop. New laws are introduced for a wide range of reasons. Today, laws are introduced to cope with society's development (e.g. Sex Discrimination Act, 1975), or for economic reasons (e.g. European Communities Act, 1972). In contrast, other rules are relaxed or abolished (e.g. Suicide under the Suicide Act, 1961) because the reason for them originally being necessary is no longer appropriate. Moreover, the court structure and rules are changed from time to time to make legal enforcement more efficient and effective, for example, the Judicature Act, 1873–5 and the Courts Act, 1971.

Finally, the meaning of "the law" is generally considered to be the composition of all the individual laws that have been imposed upon a given community whether by legislation, judgement of the court, etc.

QUOTATION OF LEGAL CASES

When legal cases are quoted in any book, the majority of them are in the form: **Name A *v.* Name B (1983).**

Name A is described as the prosecutor (in a criminal matter) or the plaintiff (in a civil matter).

Name B is described as the defendant, irrespective of whether the case is of a criminal or civil matter.

v. separates the two parties, and, as anyone who fills in a fooball coupon knows, it is the abbreviated form of "versus". When quoting the full title of the case, it is essential to pronounce the letter v either as "v" or "and".

(1983) This is usually the year when the judgement was pronounced. However, on occasions, different books quote different years after the name of the second party (B). The reason for this is that one book has used the date of judgement, whereas the other book has used the date the case was published in the Law Reports, and where there is a significant time lag between the two, clearly, the years will differ. To minimise misunderstandings caused by this duel system, the legal profession has now adopted the custom of quoting the Law Report date.

The above is a general description of how cases are quoted. More specifically, cases styled in the following ways will be seen throughout the book.

R. *v.* Gould (1968)
This indicates that the person bringing the legal action is the monarch and, in this capacity, she is the representative of the state. When quoting cases of this type in books (and in the examinations), it is easier to use just the letter R. It is perhaps better to use either Regina (or Reg) if the

monarch, at the time of the case, was a queen, or Rex, if the monarch at the time of the case was a King – but clearly, you have to know the sex of the monarch at the time of the case!

When such cases are the subject of an appeal, the letter R is always dispensed with and replaced by an official prosecutor such as the Director of Public Prosecutions. The party who appeals (appellant), always has his name quoted first. For this reason, the order of names may be reversed when the quotation relates to the case as heard before the appeal court.

Now, let us examine how a civil case is quoted: e.g.

Cutler *v*. United Dairies (London) Ltd (1933)
These are the respective names of the parties, the plaintiff's name appearing before the letter "v" and the defendant's name after the letter "v". Sometimes, joint actions are taken and when this happens, the name of a second party or simply "another" is quoted as either a joint plaintiff or defendant. Nearly all the cases quoted in this manner relate to civil matters. Very occasionally, the state becomes involved and when this happens, the usual style is to quote "The Queen" or "The King", although R is permissible.

In Re Hall (1871)
Although not universally so, this type of quotation invariably relates to cases which involve the interpretation of a will. Its literal translation means "in the matter of" and may refer to a person or a thing.

In Bonis Steele (1868)
This type of quotation is most frequently seen when a will is being proved. Its literal translation is "in the goods of" and it is sometimes quoted in this English style although it is more usual to see it quoted in the abbreviated style of "In b".

R *v*. Aston University Senate Ex Parte Roffey (1969)
The words ex parte mean "on the application of". Such quotations are frequently seen where the state is acting as prosecutor, at the instigation of a particular person.

The Wagon Mound (1961)
When a legal case involves a shipping vessel, then invariably the case is referred to under the name of the vessel. Thus, the majority of Admiralty cases are styled in this way, although other cases (and several are quoted in the Contract Chapter), are also styled in a like manner.

McAlister (or Donoghue) *v*. Stevenson (1932)
The ultimate Court of Appeal for cases originally heard in Scotland or Northern Ireland is the House of Lords in London. For this reason, the

decisions on cases which originate from outside England will become binding on English courts where they have been the subject of appeal to the House of Lords. The above style of quotation, though, shows a peculiarity of the system in Scotland. For when a married woman is party to a legal action, not only is her married surname quoted (in brackets) but also her maiden name. However, most books simply quote the married name (i.e. Donoghue) for the sake of brevity.

CLASSIFICATION OF LAW

There are various ways of classifying the law, and the one described below is merely a suggestion.

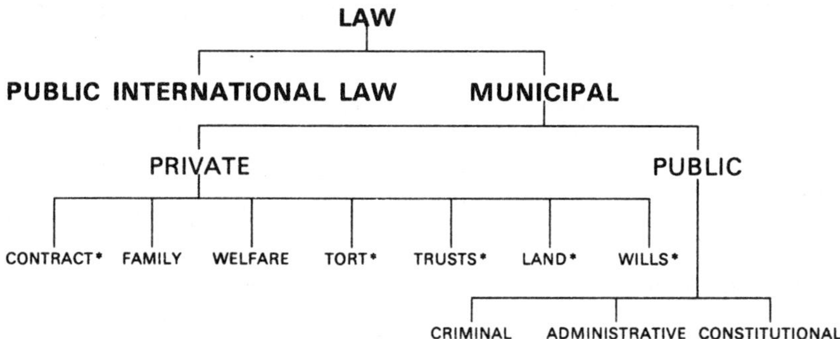

(*In this book there are separate chapters on each of these branches of law.)

A brief-description of each of these branches is:

1. Public International Law – The rules which govern sovereign states in their relationship towards each other.
2. Municipal Law – The law of the state.
3. Public Law – The law which governs the relationship of the individual and the state.
4. Private Law – The law which governs the relationship of individuals to each other.

PRIVATE LAW

5. Contract – The law which determines whether a promise or a set of promises is legally enforceable.

6. Family – The law which concerns marriage, divorce, separation and the responsibilities of parents to each other and their children.

7. Welfare – The law which concerns the rights of individuals to state benefits.

8. Tort – The law which imposes obligations on persons, e.g. not to defame.

9. Trust – The law which governs the relationship which exists between the settlor of property, the trustee who holds it and the beneficiaries for whose benefit it is held.

10. Land – The law which concerns itself with the rights and obligations of the owners and possession of land.

11. Wills – The law which dictates the rules and rights concerning a deceased's estate.

PUBLIC LAW

12. Criminal – A wrong committed against the state, with the state usually bringing the legal action.

13. Constitutional and administrative – The law which determines the relationships between various government bodies and between them and individuals.

This book concentrates on private rather than public law in line with the syllabuses of most professional and other examining bodies.

TITLES OF PARTIES TO A LEGAL ACTION

The titles the respective parties assume depend upon whether civil or criminal proceedings are being pursued.

CIVIL PROCEEDINGS

The person who is bringing the legal action is descibed as the plaintiff and his name always appears to the left of the letter v. The person who is being subjected to the legal action is called the defendant and his name appears to the right of the letter v.

CRIMINAL PROCEEDINGS

The person who is bringing the legal action is described as the prosecutor and the person who is being subjected to the legal action is described as the defendant. Where the action is successful, the result is described as a conviction. This means that the defendant will receive a punishment, which amongst other things, could be a prison sentence or a fine or both.

APPEALS

After the facts of the case have been heard, the Justices of the Peace (in the Magistrates' Court) or the Judge (and perhaps Jury) (in the Civil or Criminal Courts) will have to make a decision. This decision will favour one party to the detriment of the other. Subject to certain conditions, an aggrieved party has the right to appeal against the decision. If the request for an appeal is successful, this involves the facts of the case being presented in front of a court of higher standing. The court will consist of a person or persons who have a greater working knowledge of the law and who consider the finer legal details of the case. This process of appeal may continue as far as the House of Lords as described in Chapter 3. When decisions are appealed against, the parties become known as:

Appellant – The person who is appealing against the earlier decision.
Respondent – The person against whom the appeal is being brought.

Note: As described earlier, this may mean that the names of the parties become reversed when quoted in text books. For the student, this may be confusing, as when reading an appeal case which is being reported in a newspaper, it is often difficult to understand who was the original plaintiff and who was the original defendant.

PURSUING A LEGAL ACTION

A legal action may be pursued for many reasons. It may be to:

(a) Enforce someone to do something he should have done but has not.
(b) Prevent someone from doing something he intends to do.
(c) Stop someone doing something he is already doing.
(d) Punish someone for a wrong they have done.
(e) Obtain compensation.

In England and Wales (Scotland has its own system), the majority of legal cases are tried in Magistrates' Courts. (In fact, 97% of all criminal cases are tried before and dealt with by Magistrates). This system has evolved over the years and it has resulted in the majority of the less serious wrongs being dealt with in a speedy and inexpensive way. However, this system does have its critics, for it is frequently pointed out that the Magistrates (also known as Justices of the Peace), are "unpaid amateurs" who often hold no legal qualification and may have only been given two days' training before sitting on the bench for the first time. As a consequence, decisions could be made without legal foundation – but this criticism is not wholly justifiable as the Magistrates can refer matters of law to a legally qualified "clerk" who is always in attendance, even though this person's main task is to administer the court. The other major problem of the Magistrates system is that its powers are limited. Thus, crimes or civil wrongs of a more serious nature immediately by-pass this court and are initially heard before the County Court or Crown Court. Also, with certain types of wrong (e.g. theft from a shop), if a defendant does not want the matter to be decided there and then by Magistrates, he can elect to be tried by Judge and Jury in one of these higher courts.

When a person is taking a legal action against another or being subjected to legal action, it is possible for this person to act on his own behalf. But, because the law is so vast and complex, it is almost certainly inadvisable to proceed in this way. It is far better to seek the assistance of a legal adviser, and, although this will be costly, the court case will at least be dealt with in a professional way. Furthermore, depending on a person's means, it may be possible for him to qualify for legal aid – a fund from which legal expenses can be paid in whole or in part. The extent of the aid depends upon a person's income and capital.

Also, where a professional adviser is employed, a system of plea bargaining may be used, whereby the legal advisers of the parties to the case come to some agreement with the Judge in private. This often results in a defendant's plea being changed from Not Guilty to Guilty and with, perhaps, certain charges being dropped and thereafter a judgement quickly follows. Many such examples can be found in the newspapers, for example, in the celebrated Ipswich rape case reported in the "Sunday Times" on 11th July 1982, where plea bargaining resulted in the accused receiving only a £2,000 fine instead of the usual prison sentence.

THE LEGAL PROFESSION

In England and Wales, the legal profession can be divided up under two main headings – namely, solicitors and barristers. Each group has its own duties and functions and its own controlling body. Although the growth in numbers of these professional advisers was for many years quite steady, over the past decade the numbers have risen dramatically and there is some cause for concern – particularly for barristers who are finding it impossible to get "chambers" after they have completed their year's pupilage.

In addition, there are some duties of a legal nature which may be carried out by legal excutives who work as assistants to solicitors.

SOLICITORS

At 31/12/85, there was just over 61,500 solicitors compared with 26,000 in 1973. Their duties and functions are wide and varied and most of their income is derived from:

1. Conveyancing
   To a large extent, solicitors had a monoply over this type of work due to certain provisions contained within the Solicitors Act 1974. For, the Act provided that only a solicitor, or barrister or notary public was allowed to prepare a final conveyancing document for a fee. In 1983, the Law Society commenced a series of legal actions against a range of conveyancing agents who, it was alleged, were providing a full conveyancing package for a fee, while they had no legal authority to do so. However, the actions were dismissed because it could not be proved by the Law Society that the conveyancing agent had prepared the final conveyancing document for a fee.
   Various members of Parliament considered the monopoly position not to be in the best possible interests of the general public and so took up the plight of the conveyancing agents – partly arguing that by increasing competition, fees would be reduced. Ultimately, this has led to a provision being made in the Administration of Justice Act 1985 which allows licensed conveyancers, who are not qualified solicitors, to carry out conveyancing work for a fee.
2. Drawing up wills.
3. Acting as the personal representatives of deceased persons.
4. Attending to the formalities necessary to incorporate a company.
5. Attending to divorce settlements.
6. Giving general legal advice (e.g. say where a client has been threatened with dismissal by his employer).
7. Acting as trustees (see Chapter 7).
8. Advising clients when they are considering commencing a legal action or are having one brought against them in the lower court.
9. Representing clients in the lower courts. e.g. where a client is being tried on a drink-driving offence in the Magistrates' court.

In the main, the above are duties that can be carried out from his own office and thus court appearances tend to be infrequent. When they do occur, they are in the lower courts, particularly the Magistrates' Court but also occasionally in the County or Crown Court.

By law, solicitors are not permitted to incorporate themselves. As a solicitor rarely wants to work for himself, by himself, then the majority of solicitor practices operate as partnerships. This has the advantage that each partner can specialise in one branch of the law and thus expert advice is immediately available when a client asks for assistance in, say, a trust, will or company matter. Where a solicitor is operating by himself, it may be quite some time before the necessary advice is given to the client especially as the sole practitioner may have to look the matter up in his reference books (if he has copies) or seek advice elsewhere.

QUALIFYING

For a person to become qualified as a solicitor, the following requirements must be satisfied:

(a) The "student" must be articled with a solicitor of at least five years standing.

(b) The period for serving articles will vary between two years for a law graduate and five years for a non-graduate.

(c) A series of courses must be attended. The number and duration of these depends upon prior educational qualifcations of the student.

(d) The professional examinations must be passed.

Furthermore, all solicitors, who are admitted to the Law Society after 1/8/85, must attend a compulsory continuing education scheme, which is of three years duration, otherwise they will not be given a practising certificate. The scheme obliges a solicitor to accumulate a stated number of points over the three year period by attending a range of recognised courses.

NEGLIGENCE

If a solicitor has been negligent or has made an honest mistake, his client or any third party injured by the negligence may sue him. Clearly, any competent solicitor would never wish to find himself in this position, but if he did so and an action against him was successful, he would have to settle the claim. In turn, he would make a claim on his professional indemnity insurance policy. For, all solicitors have been obliged to take out such cover since 1975, and in January 1987 the minimum cover which had to be effected was half a million pounds.

When embezzlement of clients' funds has taken place (e.g. misappropriating balances on clients' account), then a client can recover from the Law Society. A legal case reported in *The Times* on 16/2/83 established that if a client's claim becomes statute barred in law as a result of a solicitor's negligence, the client has a right to sue his solicitor. **Davis *v.* Soltenpur (1983).**

Finally, the only time a solicitor can sue his client is for non-payment of his professional fee.

BARRISTERS

Today, there are approximately 5,000 barristers compared with 2,900 in 1973. Their main function is to represent clients in court. Whereas solicitors act on behalf of clients in the lower courts, barristers tend to act in the higher courts and have almost exclusive rights to do so at this level. For this reason, there are times when barrister representation is essential and such representations form the bulk of their work. Their other main duties are:

1. To draft legal pleadings.
2. To draft legal documents.
3. To provide "counsel's opinion", i.e. to give advice to solicitors who have been presented with a complicated legal problem by one of their clients.

It is not permissible for a private individual to approacn a barrister directly. What must happen is that a solicitor must introduce the client to the barrister. In a way, this works to the client's advantage, for he does not have to search around for a barrister who specialises in the particular area upon which he needs advice.

By law, barristers are not permitted to incorporate themselves, nor may they enter into a partnership. Thus, they work by themselves and for themselves and for this reason, specialise in a limited branch of the law.

QUALIFYING

For a person to become qualified as a barrister, the following requirements must be satisfied.

1. An application must be submitted to become a student at one of the four Inns of Court – Lincoln's Inn, Gray's Inn, Inner Temple and Middle Temple.
2. A student must "keep terms" – i.e. dine at the hall of his Inn a set number of times.
3. Attend a vocational course at the Inn for a period of one year.
4. Pass the necessary examinations set by the Council of Legal Education. From Autumn 1983, the Bar's professional examinations have only been available to those applicants who hold a second class Honours Degree or better.
5. For a period of one year, after satisfying the above, become a student of a barrister of at least five years' standing.
6. Find chambers – it is this requirement which is causing grave concern today.

NEGLIGENCE

Because of the principle of "public policy", a barrister cannot be held liable in negligence for the manner in which he conducts a court case or for any matters connected with a case before it reaches the court. However, on matters of a non-litigious nature, liability could attach. **Rondel *v*. Worsley (1967)**, and **Saif Ali *v*. Sydney Mitchell and Co. (1978)**.

When a solicitor introduces one of his clients to a barrister, once the task has been completed, the reimbursement procedure is for the client to pay the solicitor, who, in turn, pays the barrister. Because solicitors are notoriously slow to invoice clients and clients are then notoriously slow to pay up, it is usually a considerable time before a barrister is paid for the service he has given. It is still not possible for a barrister to sue a solicitor for unpaid fees (even though a solicitor can sue his client), but the method of payment has been subject to a great deal of debate recently and is currently under review.

Finally, the advantage of becoming a barrister is that, it is possible at a later stage to be considered for higher judiciary office, e.g. Queen's Council.

LEGAL EXECUTIVES

Many solicitor practices, especially the larger ones, have employees called legal executives, who essentially act as assistants to the senior or junior partners. Legal executives attend to a wide range of the more routine day-to-day legal duties including, for example, some of the more basic procedures involved in buying or selling properties (e.g. the carrying out of local and official searches). Although their duties are less onerous than those of a solicitor, it is still necessary for them to have a good working knowledge of the law.

They have a separate controlling body which was established in 1963 and is called The Institute of Legal Executives. The Institute also acts as an examining body. Subject to a member of at least three years standing passing the first level of examinations, he will qualify as an associate member. Then, subject to him continuing to act as a legal executive for a further period of five years and passing a second level of examinations, he will qualify as a fellow. The majority of duties undertaken by legal excutives are carried out from a solicitor's office. However, fellows have limited rights to audiences in the County Court. Also, a fellow may qualify as a solicitor and to achieve this status he would have to pass along the same qualifying route as a non-law graduate.

JUDICIAL OFFICERS

Here, reference is not being made to Judges, but specific people who have been appointed senior Judicial Officers. These include:

1. The Lord Chancellor

This is the highest legal office in England and Wales. The appointment is a political one, whereby the Prime Minister submits the name of one of her Cabinet to the Queen for her approval. Thus, there is no permanency of office – change may occur due to change of government or loss of favour. The appointed person has many functions to perform. As a Judge, he is head of the House of Lords, the Court of Appeal, etc. As an adviser, he puts forward names to the Crown for potential High Court or Circuit Judges.

2. The Lord Chief Justice of England and Wales

Again, this is an appointment made by the Queen on the advice of the Prime Minister. Upon appointment, he automatically becomes a Peer (i.e. Member of the House of Lords). Although this entitles him to sit in the House of Lords, he rarely does so. Instead, he attends to his own duties as head of the following:

(a) Queens Bench Division and
(b) Court of Appeal – Criminal Division, and
(c) Queen's Bench Divisional Court.

3. The Master of the Rolls

Again, this is an appointment made by the Queen on the advice of the Prime Minister. Upon appointment, he automatically becomes a Peer. His main duties are:

(a) Organising the work of the Court Appeal, Civil Division,
(b) Supervising the admission of qualified solicitors to the Rolls.

4. The Law Officers

There are two law officers – the Attorney General and Solicitor General. Both are political appointments approved by the Queen on the advice of the Prime Minister. They are rarely Cabinet Ministers but are usually experienced barristers. The latter is really an essential requirement because of the complex legal duties that are undertaken.

(a) Attorney-General

He has many wide ranging functions. These include:

(1) Representing the Crown in civil cases.
(2) Acting as Prosecutor in important criminal cases.
(3) Being Head of the English Bar.
(4) Supervising the work of the Director of Public Prosecutions.
(5) Advising the various Government departments on legal matters
(6) Upon a request to do so, initiating certain types of prosecution say, where a person who wishes to commence an action does not

have sufficient interest (locus standi) to bring an action by himself.

(b) Solicitor-General

To all intents and purposes, he is the deputy of the Attorney-General. On occasions, both will jointly give an opinion, say, when a Government Department has asked them to do so. The Solicitor-General may perform all the functions of the Attorney-General. This may be by specific authority of the latter or because the office is vacant, or because the Attorney-General is absent or ill. Authority for this is contained in the Law Officers' Act, 1944.

DIRECTOR OF PUBLIC PROSECUTIONS

The office of Director of Public Prosecutions (D.P.P.) has been in existence for over one hundred years. To be considered for this post, a person must have worked as a solicitor or barrister for at least ten years and his appointment is made by the Home Secretary. In the main, the D.P.P. will prosecute through his own staff, although, occasionally, it must be carried out through the Treasury Council.

Certain types of offence must be referred to him before a legal action can commence (e.g. an offence punishable by death). In other circumstances, matters may be referred to him for his opinion (e.g. where a police authority cannot decide whether or not sufficient evidence is held to instigate criminal proceedings).

To help him carry out his duties, he is assisted by a number of barristers. As mentioned in 4(a) above, he operates under the supervision of the Attorney-General.

EXAMINATION QUESTIONS

Question 1

(a) Penny seeks your advice on how to qualify as a solicitor or barrister when she leaves school. What advice would you give her?

(b) Explain the work of **EITHER**: (i) a solicitor **OR**: (ii) a barrister.

(A.E.B. O-Level)

Question 2

Explain the position in the English legal system of each of the following;

(a) the Lord Chancellor;

(b) the Master of the Rolls;

(c) The Lord Chief Justice;

(d) Attorney-General.

(A.E.B. O-Level)

CHAPTER 3

SOURCES OF ENGLISH LAW AND THE COURT STRUCTURE

SOURCES OF ENGLISH LAW

The term "sources of English law" can be interpreted in several ways as would be concluded if a range of books on the subject matter was read. But here it is suggested that the term sources of the law can be classified in accordance with the diagram below. The constituent elements being fully outlined in this chapter.

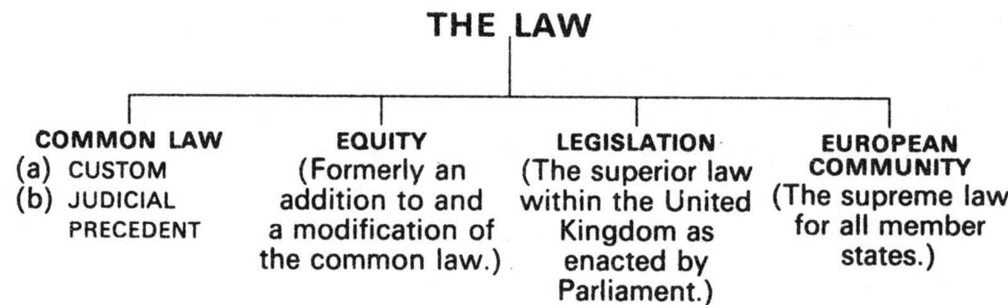

THE NATURE OF COMMON LAW

The term "common law" is generally considered to have four meanings and to understand which applies to a given set of circumstances the words need to be interpreted in the context of the whole. Thus, the term can be used to describe the law:

1. Which is common to the whole of England – because of this, it excludes local law.
2. Which is not legislation. Thus, it means all law which is created by the customs of people and by judicial precedent (see below).
3. Which is not equity (see below). Thus, it refers to law which developed from the old common law courts as opposed to the Courts of Chancery.
4. Which is applied to the whole of England and thus excludes foreign laws.

The origins of common law date back to Norman times. During that period, local customary laws differed widely from one area to another and were also not always fairly applied. So there started an evolutionary process which eventually resulted in fairness and uniformity.

The initial stage was the appointment of Royal Commissions which toured the country. There were different types of Commission and, depending upon their status, would either:

(a) Try people held in local gaols, with the objective of clearing the gaols. These were known as the Commissions of Gaol Delivery.
(b) Hear and determine major criminal cases which had arisen in the locality since their last visit. These were known as Commissions of Oyer and Terminer.
(c) Try civil cases. These were known as the Commissions of Assize.

Originally, most of the Commissioners were church officials (ecclesiastics), but this position slowly changed over the years. Eventually, they were nearly all lawyers by education and prior to their appointment, had held high judicial office.

After completing their circuit, they would return to London and together discuss the cases they had heard. They would place particular importance upon the local customs which had been used as evidence in court, the decision they reached and the reason for reaching the given decision. Following a full discussion, they were able to decide which customs were good and which were bad. Then, when on future circuits, all the judges would apply only those customs which collectively they had decided were good. This system of adopting good customs and abolishing bad customs eventually resulted in a much more uniform legal system.

To begin an action in such a court, a plaintiff would have to obtain a writ. The type of remedy the court could grant depended upon the type of writ that had to be obtained. This procedure caused problems from time to time because plaintiffs occasionally obtained the wrong kind of writ. In these circumstances the commission would throw the case out. Thus, the plaintiff would have to get the correct type of writ and wait until the Commission came to the area again before the legal action could be pursued.

Later, there came a time when the court would only hear a case where the writ had been based on an earlier judicial precedent. This caused problems for plaintiffs, particularly if they could not find an identical precedent. However, the ruling was not over rigid – for if a plaintiff could find a similar precedent, then a writ would still be issued. It became evident, however, that a new type of law was needed whereby a plaintiff could pursue a legal action even though no precedent existed. This new law became known as equity (see later).

From this brief outline, it is clear that "common law of the land", as it is known, developed from the earlier general customs and case law decisions. The common law is thus different from local laws, statute, equity and foreign laws.

CUSTOMS

Customs can be described as social habits or patterns of behaviour. All societies tend to evolve these customs without either consciously creating them or expressly forming them.

This is the oldest form of law in England and was the foundation of the Common Law – in fact, its origins can be traced back to pre-Norman times. However, as development took place, the scope for new customs to evolve became less and less. Thus, today, it is true to say that customary law (as a new source), is almost non-existent, for it has been superseded by legislation.

There are two main types of custom – those which apply throughout the country and are known as general customs, and those which apply throughout a limited part of the country and are known as local or particular customs.

1. GENERAL CUSTOMS

Today, most general customs have either been absorbed into legislation or judicial precedent or fallen into disuse, and for this reason, they are no longer an important source. Historically, many of the early rules laid down by judges had their origins in general customs which the courts subsequently adopted. A good example of such an application is the fact that Mercantile Law has mainly originated from the customs of merchants.

Although there are few general customs in existence today, occasionally, it is still necessary for the Court to decide whether a given situation is or is not a general custom. To aid courts in such matters, a general set of rules has been formulated. These are described in 3 below.

2. LOCAL CUSTOMS

A local custom is one which only applies through a limited locality, e.g. a parish, manor, borough or county. Most of these customs have been abolished over the years for the reasons described in the Common Law section above, and, as a consequence, few exist today.

3. TESTS FOR CUSTOMS

The principal rules which the Courts use in order to decide whether a custom exists or not are:

(a) TIME IMMEMORIAL

To be valid, a custom must have existed since time immemorial. In English law, this has been fixed as the year 1189. In theory, a party claiming custom must prove that it continuously existed back to 1189, but, in practice, the Courts do not rigidly exercise this rule. What tends to happen is that proof is given that it had existed for as far back as living memory goes and if that can be established to the satisfaction of the Court, a presumption can be made for the remaining period. To rebut such claims, a disputing party must prove that the custom could not or did not exist as far back as 1189.

Mercer *v*. Denne (1905)

Denne owned part of a beach and proposed to build houses on the land. Some local fishermen sought to prevent this from happening, claiming that they had a customary right to dry their fishing nets on the land. Various people gave evidence to show that the custom had existed for at least seventy years and the Courts were then prepared to assume that it had existed since 1189. *Held.* Denne was not allowed to build the houses on his own land, because the Courts were prepared to accept that this local custom had existed since time immemorial.

Simpson *v*. Wells (1872)

Wells was convicted of obstructing a public footpath and he set up a defence that he was exercising a customary right. As part of his evidence, he indicated that his legal right originated in the Statute of Labourers 1361. *Held.* This defence failed as the custom had its origins after 1189. (In fact, he gave rebutting evidence against himself.)

Note. This test only applies to local customs and not to general customs: **Goodwin *v*. Robarts (1875).**

(b) CONTINUITY

The custom must have been in continuous operation for the whole period without lawful intervention. Thus, it must have been possible at all times to exercise it lawfully. If it were not always in operation, even for a very short period, it would not be recognised as a valid custom.

(c) NEC VI, NEC CLAM, NEC PRECARIO

The custom must have been exercised peaceably, openly and as of right. Thus, a right which is exercised by permission will not be considered as a local custom.

(d) REASONABLE
The custom must not be unreasonable within the eyes of the law.

Wolstanton Ltd. and Duchy of Lancaster *v.* Newcastle-Under-Lyme B.C. (1940)
Under an alleged custom, a landowner authorised mining under a tenant's house which later caused it to subside. When the tenant brought the landlord to Court, the landlord further alleged that there was a customary right not to pay compensation. *Held.* The landlord's defence failed as his action was held to be unreasonable.

(e) CERTAIN
The custom must be certain and relate to a defined subject matter, beneficiaries, and locality.

Wilson *v.* Willes (1806)
It was alleged that tenants of a particular manor had a customary right to take as much turf for their lawns as they liked from the village green. *Held.* The alleged custom was invalid. Not only was it unreasonable, it was also uncertain.
(f) It must not be contrary to statute.
(g) It must be consistent with other customs.
(h) It must apply to a definite locality which is legally recognised, e.g. parish.
(i) It must be compulsory and legally effective.

4. CONVENTIONAL USAGE
Local customs need to be distinguished from conventional usage, which tends to be found in certain trades or professions. Conventional usage only binds by agreement, irrespective of whether this is express or implied, and, as such, can be expressly excluded. This, it is optional, in contrast with local customs which are compulsory.

Smith *v.* Wilson (1832)
An agreement was entered into which permitted the shooting of up to one thousand rabbits on a particular piece of land. A dispute arose concerning the meaning of "one thousand" in the context of the agreement and a legal action was commenced to resolve the point. To help it to make its decision the court found it necessary to make reference to local custom usage. Having done that, it was held that the term "one thousand rabbits", in fact, meant "one thousand two hundred rabbits".

JUDICIAL PRECEDENT

The literal meaning of precedent is that it is a pattern upon which future conduct is based. In law, the same interpretation applies. This is so not only in England but also in other countries, as the earlier decisions made by Courts are treated with respect. More importantly, the decisions are sometimes treated as a precedent and when a future case arises where the circumstances are of the same or a similar nature, the Court will usually follow the decision made previously, even if it was made by a different Court. There are two principal reasons for this:

1. There is a natural preference for a person making a decision to justify it by reference to what has been done in the past rather than to take the entire responsibility himself.
2. The procedure would eventually result in the law becoming more uniform and certain.

Most legal systems make use of precedent for guidance purposes, but in English law, certain types of precedent are of a binding nature.

Historically, it was as far back as the thirteenth century that English Courts had started to cite earlier cases, but in these times, there was no binding decision. The doctrine of binding precedent (*Stare Decisis*) originated in **Mirehouse *v.* Rennel (1883)**. In this case, Baron Parke said that "Precedent must be regarded in subsequent cases and it was not for the Courts to reject them or to abandon all analogy to them." In fact, it has been said that binding precedent would have developed earlier if there had been an adequate system of law reporting and a well defined hierarchy of Courts. After remedying these defects in the nineteenth century, the doctrine of binding precendent has evolved rapidly.

LAW REPORTING

A system of precedent depends upon the availability of accurate reports of all the important decisions of superior Courts. Today, this now runs into many thousands of volumes, and although lawyers may wish to tell you that they are familiar with all legal decisions, in reality, they know how to find out if there is a precedent for a given set of conditions. A few years ago, this would have been a time-consuming process. But, because computers are now used, it is possible to store massive quantities of information which can be recalled very quickly by asking the computer to search in its data files. The reports themselves are prepared and published by private enterprise – not the Government. Furthermore, it should be noted that the reports themselves are not the law, but a record of the law as established in a legal decision. It is essential to appreciate this point, for not all legal decisions are reported and a question arises as to whether such unreported decisions are law or not. The answer is that they are law and can be vouched for by a barrister who was present at the hearing of the case.

Law reporting had its origins in the thirteenth century and the historical development divides into three periods.

1. THE YEARBOOKS

This was the system from 1283 to 1535. The books were written in Anglo-French and are a compilation of notes taken by students of law who were present at cases which were of interest to them and upon which they recorded the key details. Today, they are of greater interest to legal historians rather than to practising lawyers. They are, to a certain extent, of dubious value as there is no consistency to their form or content – and some of them – from a legal viewpoint – contain a great deal of irrelevant information.

2. PRIVATE REPORTING

These are alternatively known as "named reports" and are related to the period 1535 to 1865. They were produced and published by individuals, (Judges, Barristers, etc.) under the name of the reporter, and, as with the Yearbooks, are of varying quality. There are some which are treated with great respect (e.g. Sir Edward Coke), while others are treated with suspicion (e.g. Espinass – of whom it is said that he only ever heard half of what went on and reported the other half!)

The better quality reports were published in the same format. Viz:

(a) A statement of the facts in issue; then,
(b) The general nature of the pleadings on either side; then,
(c) A brief statement of the arguments of counsel; then
(d) The judgement of the Court.

There was a range of criticisms directed at the private reports because many were inaccurate, some were expensive and all took a considerable length of time to be published.

3. MODERN PERIOD

In 1865, the General Council of Law reporting was created. This Council has continued through until today and is responsible for the publication of official reports known as the "Law Reports". These relate to the important decisions of superior Courts and they use a reference system which relates to the year and the Court that has made the decision. All the reports are "authorised" in the sense that the Barrister who writes the report has to submit his report, prior to publication, to the Judge who presided over the Court. This ensures that the report is accurate. Since 1953, these reports have been published weekly.

Although the "Law Reports" are described as official, other types of "non-official" reports are published by commercial concerns. These are highly popular among practising lawyers and include:

(1) All England Law Reports – published since 1936 on a weekly basis.

(2) A range of special reports such as:

(a) Lloyds Law Reports – relating to insurance, shipping, aircraft, etc.
(b) Common Market Reports.
(c) Industrial Reports.
(d) Tax Reports.

HIERARCHY OF COURTS

Prior to the Judicature Acts, 1873–5 and the Appellate Jurisdiction Act, 1876, there were various Courts whose jurisdiction overlapped. As there was a certain amount of rivalry between them, this situation led to the law being uncertain, because situations developed where two Courts of equal standing made conflicting decisions.

Then, towards the end of the nineteenth century, the above Acts sought to establish an hierarchical structure. The general rule was and still is that the decision (Stare Decisis) of a higher Court binds itself and any lower Court and, as the highest Court is the House of Lords, its decisions bind all other Courts. Diagramatically, the hierarchy is illustrated as follows:

COURTS MAKING THE DECISION	COURTS BOUND BY THE DECISION
A. HOUSE OF LORDS.	ALL COURTS
B. COURT OF APPEAL – CIVIL DIVISION.	ITSELF & D, E & F.
C. COURT OF APPEAL – CRIMINAL DIVISION.	ITSELF & D, E & F.
D. DIVISIONAL COURTS OF THE HIGH COURT.	ITSELF & E & F.
E. HIGH COURT – WHICH INCLUDES QUEEN'S BENCH DIVISION, CHANCERY DIVISION, AND FAMILY DIVISION – AND CROWN COURTS.	F.
F. COUNTY COURTS AND MAGISTRATES' COURTS.	NONE.

BINDING POWER OF THE COURTS

HOUSE OF LORDS

In the legal decision taken in **London Street Tramways *v.* London County Council (1898)**, it was stated that the House of Lords was bound by its own decisions unless the previous decision was made without full details being brought to its attention. However, in 1966, the Lord Chancellor made an announcement that in exceptional circumstances, the House would not be bound by its previous decision. This power was widely discussed in **Chancery Lane Safe Deposit and Office Co. Ltd *v.* Inland**

Revenue Commissioners (1966) and first exercised in **Conway *v.* Rimmer (1968)**. In all other respects, all lower Courts are bound by the decisions of the House of Lords.

COURT OF APPEAL

(a) CIVIL DIVISION

The decisions of the Civil Division are binding on itself and all lower Courts and are subject only to the exceptions laid down in **Young *v.* Bristol Aeroplane Co. (1944)**.

(1) Previous decisions will not be followed where they have been given "per incuria" – where the Court's attention was not brought to relevant, binding decisions.
(2) If there are two conflicting decisions, the Court must decide which of the two it will follow.
(3) An earlier decision cannot be followed if it conflicts with a subsequent decision of the House of Lords.

(b) CRIMINAL DIVISION

This division binds all lower Courts and normally itself. The occasions when the Criminal Division will not be bound by its own previous decisions occur when:

(1) injustice would be caused to the appellant: **R *v.* Gould (1968)**; or
(2) the previous decision was wrong in law: **Williams *v.* Fawcett (1985)**. In fact, Denning had suggested that this course of action would be available when giving his judgement in **Davis *v.* Johnson (1978)**, although he received no general support from his fellow judges concerning his comment.
(3) A full Court of five judges is sitting on the present case, whereas the earlier decision was arrived at by the normal sitting of three judges.

The general reason why the Court may not follow a previous decision is that the objective of a decision in a criminal hearing is justice rather than certainty.

It should be noted that a decision of the Criminal Division is not binding on the Civil Division and vice versa.

JUDICIAL COMMITTEE OF THE PRIVY COUNCIL

The function of the Court is to hear final civil and criminal appeals which emanate from some Commonwealth and Colonial countries that wish to continue using the Privy Council as their Supreme Court. For example, Australia, Hong Kong and Gibraltar still make use of the Privy Council.

It has been established that the Court is not strictly bound by its own decisions or those of the House of Lords.

Furthermore, their decisions are not binding on any English Court, although they are of a strong, persuasive nature, particularly in the County Courts and High Courts. The reason for this is that the Council is composed of highly respected judicial officers, including the Lord Chancellor, the Lords of Appeal in Ordinary and certain Privy Councillors.

BINDING ELEMENT OF A PRECEDENT

It has been seen above that the decisions of superior Courts are binding on lower Courts – but it is essential for the lower Courts to know exactly what they are bound by. For a judgement is made up of three distinct parts:

1. A statement of facts as found by the Judge.
2. An account of the Judge's reasoning and a consideration of the relevant law.
3. The actual decision between the parties.

The binding element of the decision is the item which appears second on the list and is known as the **"ratio decidendi"**. Simply stated, this means the legal principle or reason behind the decision.

The facts, as found by the Judge, can be interpreted at various levels of generality. The following example illustrates this point.

A father induces his daughter to break her contract of marriage with her boy friend. The boy friend subsequently sues the father and fails. From these simple facts and the decision, a series of interpretations may result, viz.:

Fathers are allowed to induce daughters to break contracts of marriage.
Parents are allowed to induce daughters to break contracts of marriage.
Parents are allowed to induce all children to break contracts of marriage.
All people are allowed to induce all children to break contracts of marriage.
All people are allowed to induce all children to break all promises.
All people are allowed to induce anyone to break all promises.

The ratio of any case will have to be decided by a Judge in a similar, later case. It will be up to the Judge to decide whether the ratio is to be restricted to, say, one alternative in a whole list of possibilities or widened to all of them. Thus, a Judge has a certain amount of flexibility by being able to widen or restrict a "ratio".

Besides the element of the judgement which is binding, there are also groups of words or statements which are known as "obiter dictum". These are pronouncements of law which go beyond the limits of the case being considered and, as such, are not strictly binding. Nevertheless, if the obiter is pronounced by a superior Court, a lower Court will certainly make note of it because for them, obiters are of a strong, persuasive nature.

Whether a statement is considered to be a ratio or an obiter will depend upon the subsequent interpretations and preferences of later judges.

RES JUDICATA

Res Judicata means that a matter has finally been dispensed with when the time of appealing has expired. To show how it applies and how it differs from a "ratio", the details of the **Re Waring Dec'd Westminster Bank Ltd *v.* Burton–Butler and Others (1948)**, can be considered. Here, two people had been left sums of money from which tax had not been deducted. One party went to court to establish if a tax liability existed. In 1942, the Court of Appeal held that there was a liability and the amount was duly settled. The other party did not go to Court, nor did he settle the tax element. Then, four years later, in **Berkley *v.* Berkley (1946)**, which was an identical case to that of Waring, the House of Lords decided that there was no tax liability in these circumstances. Upon hearing this decision, the person who had paid the tax some four years previously, attempted to get the earlier decision of the lower Court reversed, and thus, reimbursement for the amount paid. However, the Court held that the matter was "res judicata" and, as a result, nothing could be recovered.

SUBSEQUENT STANDING OF A DECISION

There is a range of terms which can be used to indicate the effect of a later decision on an earlier decision. These are:

REVERSAL. Here, the decision of a case is reversed upon appeal. For the Appellate Court disagrees with the principle laid down by the lower Court, and thus, finds for the other party.

OVERRULE. This occurs when a later, but identical, case is decided by a superior Court in the same way, but is based on a different, legal principle. The previous rule (which was laid down by the lower Court), is described as "overruled".

DISAPPROVAL. This occurs when a Superior Court, during its judgement, expresses doubt about the validity of a previous rule – but does not expressly overrule it.

DISTINGUISHING. This occurs when the Court hearing a later case points out some difference or distinction between the present one and the earlier one. Clearly, this can be used to overcome the problem of an earlier but inconvenient ratio – say, when hardship or injustice would result if the case was decided in an identical manner to the previous one.

TYPES OF PRECEDENT

A suggested classification is as follows:

(a) ABSOLUTELY BINDING

Certain precedents must be strictly followed and the basis for this statement is found in the hierarchical structure of the Courts. Thus, the decisions of the House of Lords have utmost authority and are absolutely binding. After this, the lower Courts are bound by any decisions of those Courts having a higher status.

(b) CONDITIONALLY BINDING

Courts of equal status are not bound by any decisions of their counterparts – these decisions being known as conditional precedents. In practice, today, Courts of equal status tend to follow decisions of their counterparts, unless this action is considered undesirable.

(c) PERSUASIVE

There are some precedents which do not establish binding law. However, Courts may follow these decisions even though not obliged to do so, on the basis that they consider them as good as law. Typical examples are:

(1) Decisions made by the Court of Appeal which have later been adopted by the House of Lords.
(2) Any decision made by the Judicial Committee of the Privy Council.
(3) Statements made by Judges which are "obiter dicta".

(d) DECLARATORY AND ORIGINAL PRECEDENTS

There is a fine distinction between these two terms:

Declaratory – precedents which declare the existing law.
Original – precedents which apply a new rule and thus create or make a new law.

The dividing line is very fine for a Judge is declaring law by making use of an existing precedent, but, as no two cases will be exactly the same, the Judge's decision adds to the previous law. Thus, this type of precedent may be described as both "declaratory" and "original".

(e) EXTENDING PRECEDENTS
Precedents are, to a certain extent, flexible in the sense that even absolutely binding ones can be extended.

EQUITY

The meaning of equity in common usage is "fairness". Not surprisingly, in law, it has a different meaning as explained below. When the country was widely subject to Common Law, it was seen that certain shortcomings existed, for example:

1. As the Common Law did not recognise trusts (see Chapter 7) or interests in land (see Chapter 6), legal actions relating to such matters were unavailable.
2. In certain situations, the Common Law provided an inadequate remedy. For, the usual remedy was to award damages and this was not always the most suitable form of relief.
3. In certain situations, the law treated one of the parties unfairly – say, because one party was a local dignatory and he could unduly influence the court which would result in the decision going in his favour.

To overcome these problems, a system evolved whereby the aggrieved party could petition the King (who, in those days, was known as the "Fountain of Justice") to obtain his decision. Upon receipt of the petition, the king would refer the matter to a member of his "council". This particular member was called the Chancellor. In the early days, he was an ecclesiastic who had a working knowledge of the law. It was the ecclesiastic's responsibility to examine the facts of a case and this would mean that all parties to the case would have to attend a meeting in his presence. Attendance was compulsory and involved the issuing of a writ or subpoena on all necessary parties. The Chancellor did not have any set guidelines or rules to follow – only his conscience – and because of this, the outcome was never certain. Indeed this became evident when a comparison was made of the decisions of different Chancellors where the facts of a case were similar, but different decisions were made.

To remedy such problems, and to cater for the ever increasing number of cases being presented to the Chancellor, a separate Court of Chancery was formed. Furthermore, there was a move from listening to oral evidence to the examination of written statements.

From this time on, statements began to be heard by different judges, rather than just the Chancellor, and to achieve uniformity, a set of rules had to be compiled. This set of rules, which at that time was rigidly applied, became known as Equity and was applied by the Court of Chancery until 1875. Then, following the passing of the Judicature Act, 1873–5, The Court of Chancery and Common Law Courts were joined together to form a single Supreme Court of Judicature. As a result of this merger, judges had to administer both the Common Law and Equity. Even though the two courts had been blended together, the law remained separate. Problems, to some extent, still existed. Over the years, though, many problems had been resolved, not least of all, the position which subsisted when Equity and Common Law conflicted. The position, here, had been established some two hundred and sixty years previously in the Earl of Oxford's case 1615. Here, it was finally resolved that where Equity and Common Law conflict, Equity will prevail. This decision reduced the rivalry between the two separate courts but did not completely eliminate it.

Today, Equity, in the main, is applied to trusts and land.

LEGISLATION

Legislation, which is also known as statute, is the foundation of law by the Monarch in Parliament. It involves three distinct parties – the House of Lords – the House of Commons – and the Monarch (today, Queen Elizabeth II). Historically, legislation began in 1225 with the reissue of Magna Carta. Since then, it has grown to its current massive size.

THE PROCESS OF LEGISLATING

Before an Act of Parliament becomes statute, it is known as a Bill. A Bill may be introduced in either the House of Lords or House of Commons with one exception – money Bills must be introduced in the House of Commons. Wherever it starts, as soon as the Bill has been approved in one House it must be passed to the other. The various stages are:

FIRST READING. An official announces the Bill, giving only its full title and the name of the Member who is introducing it. The Bill is then printed.

SECOND READING. After the Members of the House have received a copy of the Bill and have had a chance to read it, its principles are debated and a vote taken. Where there is a majority in favour of the Bill, it will proceed to its next stage. In fact, a vote is not necessary, provided no more than twenty Members object.

COMMITTEE STAGE. The finer details of the Bill are considered by either a special committee of Members, or the entire House which acts as a committee.

REPORT STAGE. The committee reports back to the House which the Bill is passing through. It provides details of the points it discussed and any proposed amendments. Further amendments can still be made by the House.

THIRD READING. A final debate takes place on the general principles and a vote is then taken. When there is a majority in favour, the Bill passes from one House to the other, where a similar procedure takes place.

If, when it is passed through the other House, it is approved, the Bill is then sent to the Monarch for approval. This is known as "royal assent" although since 1854, the assent has not been given personally, but, in practice, by a committee of three peers, one of whom is always the Lord Chancellor. Following the royal assent, the Bill becomes an Act of Parliament and is immediately enforceable unless a later starting date has been provided for.

COMPARISON OF COMMON LAW (PRECEDENT) AND LEGISLATION (STATUTE)

The fundamental part of English law is Common Law. This evolved out of custom and historically, was always a more important source than legislation. In fact, legislation presupposes the existence of Common Law, adding to it and altering it. In essence, legislation is enacted, while Common Law is unenacted. Furthermore, legislation overrides the Common Law, but, no development of the latter can ever override legislation.

As countries develop, so the life styles of industry, commerce and private individuals grow increasingly more complex, and thus, legislation becomes a major source of law, just as it is today in the United Kingdom.

CLASSIFICATION OF STATUTES

CONSOLIDATING STATUTE. This occurs when a new Act combines existing statute law on a common topic and creates a new statute. It does not add to or amend existing law, but makes it easier to establish the law relating to the common topic. A good example of this type of statute is the **Sale of Goods Act, 1979**.

CODIFYING STATUTE. This occurs when the whole of the previous law on a given branch is re-enacted. The previous law may consist solely of precedents or be a mixture of statute and precedents on a given branch. Codification usually only takes place when the law on that branch is well developed, for to do it too early would result in loss of flexibility and also slow down development. Examples of codified English law are the **Bills of Exchange Act, 1882**, and **Partnership Act, 1890**.

DELEGATED LEGISLATION

Although Parliament has the monopoly of creating legislation in this country, it may delegate its powers to other persons or bodies. Examples of when this occurs in practice are when legislative powers are transferred to specified Ministers, local authorities, or, in some cases, to professional bodies (e.g. eminent accountants providing drafts for what eventually became **The Insolvency Act 1986**). It is necessary for such powers to be occasionally delegated for the following reasons:

1. TIME FOR DISCUSSION/DEBATE IS LIMITED. Available Parliamentary time is very limited. Thus, in certain situations, a Bill containing only the framework of the intended law is passed on to someone else such as a responsible Minister, for his department to complete the details.
2. TECHNICAL LAW. Parliament may not be competent to discuss details of a bill which is of such a highly technical matter that ministers would not be able to understand it.
3. TIME IS OF THE ESSENCE. There will be occasions when the objective is to change the law quickly. To pass such law in the normal way is a cumbersome and time-consuming process, and to overcome the problem, Ministers of State are empowered to introduce new orders.

Since the beginning of the twentieth century, the amount of legislation being delegated has increased tremendously. Some people worry about this trend, as it is taking the making of English Law out of the hands of duly elected representatives and into the hands of the Civil Service. But this worry may be dispelled because:

1. Parliament continues to retain control over delegated legislation through the **Statutory Instruments Act, 1946**. Thus, before becoming operational, most orders made by statutory instrument need to be approved by Parliament. Ultimately, Parliament may revoke or rescind the delegated power.
2. There is also judicial control which can be exercised over delegated legislation. The Courts can question the validity of any piece of delegated legislation and can declare it void for being ultra-vires (beyond the powers of) what was requested.

AG *v*. Fulham Corporation (1921)
The local authority had been given power, under the **Baths and Wash-Houses Acts, 1846–78**, to open a wash-house which would enable the general public to wash their own clothes. Instead, they opened up a laundry in which other people's clothes were washed by employees of the Corporation. *Held.* As the local authority was acting ultra-vires (beyond its powers), an injunction was granted which prevented them from operating in this way.

INTERPRETATION OF STATUTES

When enacting legislation, Parliament is supreme. But this does not mean that the courts cannot influence the development of enacted law as the Courts are the bodies who have to interpret what the legislation means. Where the words are clear, no interpretation will be necessary, but where they are not clear, then guidelines are needed. As the individual parts of a statute are rarely absolutely clear, then it is obvious that the Courts have considerable control over the way in which statutes are applied.

The primary task of the courts is to try to establish the intention of Parliament. In achieving this, the Courts will look at the wording of the appropriate parts of the statute and initially construe them strictly in accordance with their literal and grammatical meaning. (This is based on the assumption that Parliament will always express its intentions perfectly!)

The methods of interpreting statutes can be classified under two different headings:

1. STATUTORY AIDS

(a) The **Interpretation Act, 1889** – a statute which defines statutory terms.

(b) Interpretation of terms within the statute itself.

(c) The preamble (i.e. introductory statement) to the statute. Private Acts always have preambles, whereas Public Acts may have them.

2. GENERAL RULES OF INTERPRETATION

(a) THE LITERAL RULE

The words will be interpreted to give them their literal and grammatical meaning. This will apply even if hardship results. There is an exception to this general rule, for, where the literal or grammatical meaning would lead to absurdity, repugnancy or inconsistency, it will not be followed.

(b) THE GOLDEN RULE

In **Grey *v.* Pearson (1857)**, Lord Wensleydale said, "The grammatical and ordinary sense of the words is to be adhered to, unless this would lead to absurdity or repugnancy or inconsistency with the rest of the instrument, in which case, the grammatical or ordinary sense of the words may be modified so as to avoid such absurdity, repugnancy or inconsistency and no further." What this means, basically, is that even though the words in isolation may be, say, repugnant, when looked at in the context of the whole enactment, they may still be reasonable.

For example, in normal circumstances, the "issue" of a deceased person has a right to benefit from the deceased's estate. But where the "issue" has murdered the deceased, it would be repugnant to allow the person to derive any benefit. **Re Sigsworth (1935)**. Repugnancy, as applied to deceased's estates, has now been expressly provided for in the **Forfeiture Act, 1982**.

(c) THE MISCHIEF RULE

This is alternatively known as Heydon's rule: **Heydon's Case (1584)**. For, in situations where there is an ambiguity, the courts may look at the original law to see what wrong (or mischief) the enactment sought to remedy. With this information available, the words can then be interpreted. **Gorris *v.* Scott (1874), Gardiner *v.* Sevenoaks R.D.C. (1950)**.

(d) THE EJUSDEM GENERIS RULE

This literally means "of the same genus". Where particular words are followed by general words, the general words will be interpreted in relation to the particular words. A good example of how this rule applies can be taken from part of the **Betting Act, 1853**, for it prohibited the keeping of a "house, office or other place for betting purposes". In the light of this, it was questioned in **Powell *v.* Kempton Park Racecourse Co. (1899)**, whether Tattersalls Ring (an open air enclosure at a racecourse which is reserved for certain bookmakers), fell within the statute. If the Court had applied the literal rule, then the ring would have been interpreted as an "other place". However, the Court applied the Ejusdem Generis rule and construed the general words "or other place" in the context of "house or office". Thus, "other place" must mean covered accommodation rather than an open air enclosure.

(e) UT RES MAGIS VALEAT QUAM PEREAT

This literally means "let the thing stand rather than fall". As drafted, it must be presumed that each word in a statute has to have an effect, and thus, words can be neither repetitious nor redundant. If words appear to be either of these, then the Courts must interpret them in such a way to avoid this happening.

(f) EXPRESSUM FACIT CESSARE TACITUM

This literally means "if something is expressed then there is no room for implication". So, if an Act imposed rates on houses, buildings, etc., but made no reference to land, then the Act could not apply to land upon which no properties had been built.

There are many other minor rules. Altogether, though, it is considered that the general and minor rules have many exceptions and are, in some cases, considered to be contradictory. However, all of them are helpful in appropriate circumstances. Various presumptions may also be made by the Courts, e.g.:

1. An Act applies only to England and Wales.
2. The Crown is not bound by a statute unless there is express provision to the contrary.
3. The Act does not have retrospective effect. But there have been one or two exceptions here in respect of taxation enactments.

In addition to the above rules, Courts may use the Oxford dictionary to help them interpret words which are unclear. But they are not permitted to use:

1. Marginal notes.
2. Text books.
3. Reports of committees.
4. Speeches in either the House of Commons or the House of Lords.

With all these aids that are available, one would expect that any part of a statute could be satisfactorily interpreted. But this is not so, for as Lord Read said during his judgement in **O'Brien and Others *v.* Sim-Chem. Ltd (1980)**, "I give up!" The reason for this was that he was attempting to establish the rights of women to equal pay under the provisions of s. 1 **Equal Pay Act, 1970**, as amended by s. 8 **Sex Discrimination Act, 1975**, and he found it impossible to do so.

EUROPEAN ECONOMIC COMMUNITY

As from 1st January 1973, the United Kingdom became a member of the European Community and accepted that Community Law should be applied throughout this country. Unlike many other international agreements which are solely binding on governments, the acceptance of Community Law affects the lives of each and every one of us. Furthermore, where there is a conflict between Community Law and English Law, the former prevails. Cases which are based upon **Articles of the Communities**

Acts are heard not in some Central Court but in the respective members' courts.

The law itself is created by the Council of Ministers which consists of one person from each of the member states. When voting on matters of law, each of the members' voting rights are weighted and so a simple majority in number of votes cast does not automatically mean that the motion has been passed.

The law emanating from the Community may be considered under the following headings:

1. REGULATIONS

These are applied generally throughout the member states and, although they do not need formal recognition by each individual Parliament before they apply, usually it is necessary for some legislative action – if only to repeal an existing statute which would conflict with the regulations.

An example of a regulation where enforcement was necessary in the U.K. was on the matter of tachographs – devices which had to be fitted to road haulage vehicles so that, among other things, they recorded for how long a driver had been at the wheel of his vehicle. Initially, the United Kingdom government decided that they would allow the road haulage industry to introduce the tachographs on a voluntary basis. However, the European Commission took the matter to the European Court of Justice where it was held that as this was a regulation, it had to be adopted by the United Kingdom and thus the policy of voluntary installation was not acceptable. **Re Tachographs: E.C. Commission *v.* United Kingdom (1979).**

2. DIRECTIVES

These indicate that member states should introduce laws to achieve given objectives, but the method of achieving this (i.e. by amendment to existing law or enactment of new law), is left to the individual member states. It is usual for time restraints to be imposed. For example, various sections of the **Companies Act, 1980**, (now consolidated in the **Companies Act, 1985**) were included to satisfy the requirements of the E.E.C. **Second Directive on Company Law.**

3. DECISIONS

These are not of a general nature but are specific, and relate to matters or cases brought before the Council (or the European Commission). They may refer to or be referred to by a member state, a private individual or a corporation (e.g. work of "equal value" should receive equal-ity of payment as illustrated by the claims of Cammell Lairds (Shipbuilders) canteen worker who wished to receive the same hourly pay as skilled shipbuilding workers).

COURT STRUCTURE

The Court structure in England and Wales has developed and will continue to develop. Perhaps the biggest reorganisation took place over a hundred years ago as a result of the **Judicature Acts, 1873–5**. Today, the structure may be classified under two headings – Civil Courts and Criminal Courts.

CIVIL COURTS

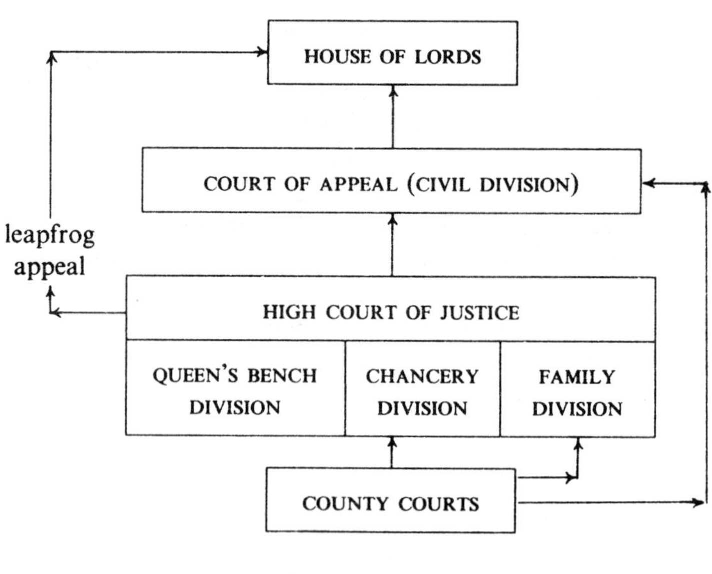

(system of appeal)

CRIMINAL COURTS

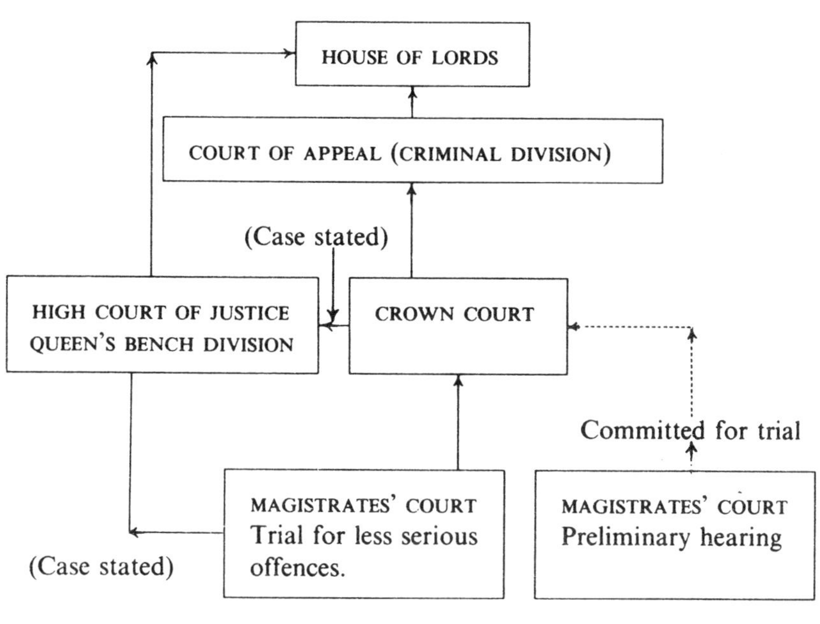

(system of appeal)

Note: The Privy Council (which hears appeals mainly from outside the United Kingdom), and the European Court of Justice (which may be requested to clarify matters on E.E.C. law by any Court), may be incorporated in both diagrams but neither has a direct link with the detailed Courts.

CIVIL COURTS

HOUSE OF LORDS

This is the highest Court in England and is the final court of Appeal in both civil and criminal matters. When hearing an appeal, the Court consists of a committee of not less than three drawn from:

The Lord Chancellor.
The Lords of Appeal in Ordinary – who are known as the Law Lords.
Other peers who have held high judicial office.

Appeals are heard, not only on matters which originate from English Courts, but also from the Courts of Scotland and Northern Ireland. The right to appeal, by either of the parties to the case, is not automatic. It requires either leave of the original Court or the House of Lords.

In normal circumstances, appeals must be made strictly in accordance with the hierarchical structure illustrated in the diagram. However, by a provision in the **Administration of Justice Act, 1969**, certain types of appeal may by-pass the Court of Appeal and go straight to the House of Lords.

Because it is composed of some of the country's most eminent lawyers, one would not expect its decisions to be criticised. However, an article published by Murphy and Rawlings in the Modern Law Review no. 44, November 1981, has criticised a range of judgements under four headings:

Particularisation.
Over-implification.
Unjustified assertions.
Evading the issue.

This article makes interesting reading and it is suggested that you study it in order to fully understand the nature of the criticism and the full meaning of the above four terms.

When the Lords are hearing an appeal, they will only allow transcripts of unreported cases in exceptional circumstances. **Roberts Petroleum Ltd *v.* Bernard Kenny Ltd (1983)**. As the country is now subject to E.E.C. law, then the House of Lords and any lower Court may refer any question of E.E.C. law to the European Court of Justice, Strasbourg.

COURT OF APPEAL (CIVIL DIVISION)

The Court is constituted of Judges currently in office and ex-officio Judges. These are drawn from:

The Master of the Rolls (Lord Justice Donaldson), who usually presides over the Court.
The Lord Chancellor.
The Lord Chief Justice.
The President of the Family Division, and, on occasions, other High Court Judges.

Although, in the past, the quorum has been three (thereby enabling a majority decision), it is now permissible for just two Judges to sit, provided they do not reach conflicting decisions. In the main, it hears appeals which originate from the High Court of Justice, or County Court, on matters of either law or fact brought by the plaintiff or the defendant. Furthermore, it hears a limited number of appeals that originate from either special Courts or Tribunals, e.g. Restrictive Practices Court.

The appeal procedures for this and the Criminal Division changed in 1982 in an attempt to make the system more efficient. Today, Barristers have to submit an outline of their pleadings in writing. Then, when the appeal is actually heard, it concentrates upon the essential and contested points. Finally, after arriving at their judgement, it is no longer necessary for the Judges to read them out aloud and, in their place, a printed version of the judgement is available to all parties who require one.

HIGH COURT OF JUSTICE

1. *Queen's Bench Division* – Presided over by the Lord Chief Justice.
2. *Chancery Division* – Presided over by the Lord Chancellor.
3. *Family Division* – Presided over by the President of the Family Division.

The President of each division is assisted by a team of about seventy five puisne Judges (Judges of lower status), any of whom may be called upon to help the President. It is usual for such Judges to remain within their own Division, and so transfers are rarely seen. Such Courts have original jurisdiction in the sense that they may be the first Court to hear a particular case. Their main duty, though, is to act as an Appellate Court.

QUEEN'S BENCH DIVISION

This is presided over by the Lord Chief Justice who is assisted by approximately 44 puisne Judges. Its jurisdiction may be divided under the following headings:

1. ORIGINAL JURISDICTION

As regards original jurisdiction, the Queen's Bench Division can be considered as operating three quite distinct courts, each dealing with its own specialist areas of law. Since 1970, as described below, it has taken over the jurisdiction of the Admiralty court and, since 1981, it has been given jurisdiction over the new Commercial Court. The third court has jurisdiction over those cases which are not assigned to any other part of the High Court. (e.g. tort, breach of contract, etc.). The Commercial Court deals with cases relating to the commercial matters of merchants and traders (e.g. insurance claims). Finally, the Admiralty Court deals with cases relating to claims and actions involving ships (e.g. salvage). Cases heard in this Division are normally presided over by a single Judge. However, juries sometimes assist (e.g. in defamation cases).

2. APPELLATE JURISDICTION

Here, appeals from Magistrates' Courts (on criminal matters), or Crown Courts, both based on points of law, are heard before two or three Judges. An example of when such an appeal system was used was **R *v.* Marylebone Justices Ex. parte. Jasmin Farrag (1980)**. Here, the defendant's Barrister was allowed to appeal against a Magistrate, who had sentenced her client, because the standard Court proceedings had not been followed – So here, the appeal was based on a point of law. If such an appeal is made, and it is based on a point of law, it is known as a "case stated".

3. SUPERVISORY JURISDICTION

Here, jurisdiction is exercised over inferior Courts whereby, for example, their mistakes are rectified by what are called prerogative orders. These may be of three types:

(a) MANDAMUS. These can be issued to a Court or public body, instructing them to carry out a duty – e.g. to a local authority in order to get it to produce its accounts.

(b) PROHIBITION. These have the objective of preventing an inferior Tribunal from hearing and making a decision on a matter which is beyond the Tribunal's jurisdiction. The order is not available if the Tribunal has already made a decision, because in this instance, a certiorari order (see below) must be applied for.

(c) CERTIORARI. These have the effect of bringing a matter which has been decided upon or is pending in an inferior Court or Tribunal to the High Court. There may be several reasons for this action. For example, to establish that:

(1) The inferior Court or Tribunal has not exceeded its jurisdiction, or,

(2) Natural justice has not been denied.

Where appropriate, the decision of the inferior Court may be quashed.

CHANCERY DIVISION

This is presided over by the Lord Chancellor, who is assisted by eleven puisne Judges. Matters relating to companies, partnerships and the administration of deceased's estates, etc. are dealt with here.

FAMILY DIVISION

This Division came into being at the beginning of October 1972 and is presided over by the President of the Division, who is assisted by sixteen puisne Judges. Matters relating to marriage, family property and children are dealt with here.

COUNTY COURTS

Today, there are about four hundred such Courts in England and Wales which are presided over by about one hundred and twenty-five Circuit Judges, whose responsibility is to hear cases at specified Courts in their Circuit. They sit singly, but there is a provision with some cases (e.g. alleged fraud), for a trial by jury of eight persons. The Judge is assisted by a Registrar who must have been a solicitor for at least seven years.

In general, cases are brought against a defendant in the district where he resides or his place of business is situated – but with land, it is usual for the case to be dealt with in the district where the land is located.

Examples of matters which could be dealt with by the County Courts are:

1. Actions founded on contract or tort. However, the torts of libel and slander are excluded unless both parties agree.
2. Equity matters (such as mortgages or trusts).
3. Bankruptcies – but with some exceptions.
4. Company winding-up.

As regards 1, 2 and 4, the courts jurisdiction is subject to prescribed monetary limits which may be varied from time to time by Order in Council (e.g. at present, winding-up cases may be heard provided the company's share capital does not exceed £120,000).

The prescribed limits may be exceeded where either:

(a) both parties agree, or,
(b) the case has been sent from the High Court.

Appeals against County Court judgements mainly go to the Civil Division of the Court of Appeal

CRIMINAL COURTS

HOUSE OF LORDS

Before an appeal can be heard, leave of the Court of Appeal (Criminal Division), and the House of Lords, is needed – and this must be on a point of law or general public importance. The quorum for the Courts is three and its constitution is as described in the Civil Courts section. Collectively, when the Judges sit in this way, they are known as Lords of Appeal in Ordinary. Each Judge delivers a separate judgement and the verdict is by a majority.

COURT OF APPEAL (CRIMINAL DIVISION)

The quorum for the Court was three, but now two Judges may sit, provided their decisions do not conflict.

It will consist of the Lord Chief Justice, Lords Justices of Appeal, and any Judge requested to sit from the Queen's Bench Division. Only one judgement is given, although separate verdicts on points of law are permitted.

The source of appeals are:

1. By persons convicted on indictment in the Crown Court, or,
2. By persons convicted in Magistrates' Courts but sentenced by the Crown Court.

Where the appeal is based on a matter of law, it is available as a right, but, for any other reason, leave of the Court is required.

The Court will either:

1. Dismiss the appeal, or,
2. Uphold the appeal, thereby quashing (dismissing) the decision of the lower Court, or,
3. Order a new trial, or,
4. Reduce or extend the length of sentence given by the lower Court; or,
5. Where fines have been imposed, to increase or reduce them.

CROWN COURTS

The Crown Courts' responsibilities today relate to hearing cases:

1. Where the offence is punishable with a three month prison term or more – e.g. murder, treason, rape, etc.

2. Where the accused has been found guilty by the Magistrates' Court (see below), but the Magistrates had insufficient power to pass the appropriate sentence.

3. Where there is an appeal against a Magistrates' Court's judgement.

4. Which relate to certain civil matters, e.g. appeals concerning the licensing of premises.

The country (England and Wales), is divided into six Circuits and within these Circuits there are about ninety Crown Court centres. Each of the centres is given a tiering which dictates the type of cases which may be hcard.

FIRST TIER. – Where criminal cases are dealt with by High Court Judges and Circuit Judges. (Civil cases may also be dealt with by High Court Judges.)

SECOND TIER. – Where only criminal cases are dealt with by High Court Judges and Circuit Judges.

THIRD TIER. – Where only criminal cases are dealt with by Circuit Judges and Recorders.

From the above, it is seen that the Courts are presided over by the following parties:

HIGH COURT JUDGE. He is a puisne Judge of the Queen's Bench Division and will be appointed to serve in one of the six circuits.

CIRCUIT JUDGE. He is appointed by the Crown and must previously have been a Barrister for ten years and a Recorder (see below) for three years. He serves both in the County Court and Crown Court.

RECORDER. He is considered as a part-time Judge of the Crown Court who must undertake at least one month's work in this capacity in any period of twelve months. To be appointed, he must have a high standing in the legal profession. While carrying out his task as Recorder, his suitability for higher office will be assessed.

All trials in the Crown Court take place before a jury which will eventually give a verdict of guilty or not guilty. If the jury gives a verdict of guilty, then the Judge will pass sentence.

Note: When hearing appeals, a Judge will sit with not less than two nor more than four Justices of the Peace. So, when acting as a Court of Appeal, there is no jury. This same constitution applies when a person has been committed to the Crown Court for sentencing.

MAGISTRATES' COURTS

Today, there are some nine hundred Magistrates' Courts in England and they deal with a wide variety of criminal and civil cases and also undertake certain administrative duies. Such Courts are presided over by Justices of Peace who are mainly unpaid, part-time lay Magistrates (about 26,000), or full time and paid Magistrates, who are known as Stipendary Magistrates (about 50). Their work may be categorised as follows:

1. COURT OF TRIAL

Although a single Magistrate may hear trivial cases (e.g. drunkenness), it is more usual to have between two and seven Justices who may impose maximum prison sentences of six months and fines of one thousand pounds. Typical cases heard here relate to petty theft, common assault and various traffic offences, drunken driving, driving without insurance, etc. In some cases, an immediate judgement is made, whereas in others, it may be passed on to the Crown Court – i.e. where the defendant elects to be tried by jury.

2. COURT OF PRELIMINARY INVESTIGATION

Here, the Justices are being asked to determine from the evidence presented whether the accused should be tried at the Crown Court. After presentation of the Prosecution evidence, the accused is charged and he may plead "Guilty" or "Not Guilty". At this stage, he may submit a defence, but it is more usual for him to reserve it. If the Justices decide that there is a prima facie case, then a Crown Court hearing will follow. In the meantime, the accused must either remain in police custody (i.e. prison), or be remanded on bail (i.e. freed on condition that when the case is heard, he will attend at the hearing). In contrast, where a prima facie case has not been made out, the accused must be released.

3. MISCELLANEOUS JURISDICTION

These tend to relate to administrative duties, e.g. approving applicants and premises for the sale of intoxicating liquor, betting shops, cinemas and theatres. They also undertake civil duties relating to matrimonial orders for separation and maintenance of spouses, adoption of children and also the recovery of unpaid debts, such as those for tax or electricity.

EXAMINATION QUESTIONS

Question 1

There were many defects in the common law which led to the development of equity.

(a) What were those defects?
(b) How were they remedied by equity?

(A.E.B. O-Level)

Question 2

The common law has been described as "the heart of the legal system". To what extent is this a true statement of English law today?
(J.M.B. A-Level)

Question 3

What do you understand by common law? Distinguish it from the other principal sources of English law.
(Chartered Institute of Bankers)

Question 4
English law has two principal and two subsidiary sources. State and describe them briefly.
(Chartered Institute of Bankers)

Question 5
Describe and explain the tests which a judge applies before recognising an alleged local custom as valid.
(A.E.B. A-Level)

Question 6
Explain what is meant by the doctrine of judicial precedent.
(A.E.B. O-Level)

Question 7
Why is a judicial precedent sometimes referred to as "binding"? Explain your answer by reference to the court structure. How can a binding precedent be avoided?
(A.E.B. O-Level)

Question 8
Explain the extent to which (a) a precedent, and (b) a statutory instrument are binding upon a judge when deciding a case.
(I.C.M.A.)

Question 9
What is meant by the ratio decidendi of a case? Why is it important to identify it?
(A.E.B. A-Level)

Question 10
How do judges approach the interpretation of statutes and to what extent are they prepared to rely on extrinsic materials to assist them?
(A.E.B. A-Level)

Question 11
"Parliament alone makes the law." How far is this true?
(A.E.B. O-Level)

Question 12
"But the judges not only have the duty of declaring the common law, they are frequently called upon to settle disputes as to the meaning of the words or clauses in a statute."

State and comment on the various methods the judges use in their task of interpretation of statute law.
(Chartered Institute of Bankers)*

Question 13

What are the advantages and disadvantages of delegated legislation?
(A.E.B. O-Level)

Question 14

(a) What is delegated legislation and what forms may it take?
(b) What factors have encouraged its development?
(A.E.B. A-Level)

Question 15

(a) Explain how statutes are created.
(b) How far do groups other than the government influence the purpose and content of statutes?
(A.E.B. A-Level)

Question 16

Describe and examine critically the part played by laymen in the administration of the law.
(J.M.B. A-Level)

Question 17

Describe the jurisdiction of Magistrates' Courts and consider the advantages and disadvantages of not using professional lawyers as Justices of the Peace.
(A.E.B. A-Level)

Question 18

Draw a diagram to illustrate the structure of the Civil Courts. Describe the work of one of the civil courts with first instance jurisdiction.
(A.E.B. O-Level)

Question 19

In relation to the High Court explain:
(a) the jurisdiction of the Court;
(b) which judges sit in the Court;
(c) the avenues of appeal from decisions of the Court.
(A.E.B. O-Level)

Question 20

Explain the working of the Crown Court system today.
(A.E.B. O-Level)

CHAPTER 4

CONTRACT

NATURE OF A CONTRACT

The law of contract is part of the Civil Law, and it indicates when a promise or set of promises is legally binding. A brief definition is that it is "an agreement between two or more parties which is intended to have legal consequences".

A more formal definition of a contract is "an agreement, enforceable by law, between two or more persons to do or abstain from doing some act or acts, their intention being to create legal relations and not merely to exchange mutual promises, both having given something, or having promised to give something of value as consideration for any benefit derived from the agreement."

It is noticeable from both definitions that the agreement must be one enforceable at law and this situation should be compared with one where the agreement is a simple one with no binding nature; e.g. where two friends agree to meet in a public house at a particular time. Here, if the agreement is not honoured because either one friend is late or does not turn up at all, there are no legal remedies available to the aggrieved party.

When studying the law of contract, it will be quickly realised that what is actually happening is that you are studying a series of cases which have passed through the Courts.

However, it should be remembered that the number of contracts which result in litigation form an extremely small proportion of the total number of contracts which are entered into daily. For the majority of contracts that the respective parties enter into are simple transactions (e.g. purchasing food or other goods in a shop or paying for services), and these rarely, if ever, result in litigation.

CLASSIFICATION OF CONTRACTS

There are many ways of classifying contracts, but a simple method of doing this is to divide them up into:

(a) SPECIALTY CONTRACTS (CONTRACTS UNDER SEAL)
These are contracts executed in the form of a deed and their validity is derived from the form of deed alone. The deed will always be in the form of a written document which is subsequently signed, sealed and delivered. There are certain features which distinguish this type of contract from a simple contract (see below). Perhaps the most important of these is that a simple contract has to be supported by consideration, whereas it is not necessary for consideration to support a specialty contract.

(b) SIMPLE CONTRACTS
The majority of binding contracts are of this type and may be created orally, in writing, or by implication.

TERMS USED TO DESCRIBE CONTRACTS

Although the above is a method of classifying contracts, there are various terms which are frequently used to describe contracts in this chapter. These are:

VALID CONTRACT. A contract which one party can enforce against the other in a Court of law if the other party, say, does not do what he has agreed to do.

UNENFORCEABLE CONTRACT. A contract which is valid, but, because of certain circumstances, one or both of the parties cannot enforce it against the other, even with a legal action, if that person does not carry out his legal obligations under it, e.g. where someone has agreed to sing at a concert but dies before the date.

VOIDABLE CONTRACT. A contract which is binding but which may be set aside by one of the parties if he wants to do so, e.g. a contract entered into by a minor to buy shares may be repudiated while in minority or within a reasonable time of attaining majority: **Steinberg *v.* Scala (Leeds) Ltd (1923)**. Such contracts, in themselves, are valid, as the minor can proceed to buy in accordance with the contract if he so wishes.

VOID CONTRACT. This is not really a contract at all and as such has no binding effect whatsoever, e.g. where a person buys an annuity (i.e. a right to a continuing payment) on the life of X from a third party, but unknown to either party, X was dead at the date of purchase: **Strickland *v.* Turner (1852)**.

EXECUTED CONTRACT. A contract in thich both parties have carried out all that they were required to do under the terms of the contract.

EXECUTORY CONTRACT. A contract in which one or both parties still have to carry out obligations that they have agreed to do under the terms of the contract.

REQUIREMENTS OF A VALID CONTRACT

The following are the essential requirements of a valid and enforceable contract:

(a) There must be an offer by one party (known as the offeror) and an acceptance of it by another (known as the offeree).
(b) There must be an intention to create legal obligations.
(c) All parties to the contract must have full legal capacity.
(d) All parties to the contract must be genuine in their consent to the terms of the contract.
(e) With the exception of contracts under seal, all contracts need to be supported by consideration.
(f) The contract must be one which is not contrary to public policy, e.g. must not be illegal.
(g) Where special formalities are necessary, these must be carried out, e.g. some contracts must be by deed, while others have to be in writing.

If an agreement does not satisfy all the above points, it could either be described as a void, voidable or unenforceable contract depending upon the circumstances.

It is essential to have a comprehensive understanding of all of these features; consequently, they are fully described below.

OFFER AND ACCEPTANCE

A contract is founded upon an agreement which arises from an offer being accepted. Pollock expanded on this statement by saying that "one party proposes his terms, the other accepts, rejects or meets them with a counter proposal and thus, they go on until there is a final refusal and breaking off, or, until one of them names terms which the other can accept as they stand".

On the rare occasions that litigation results, it is essential for the Court to decide on the facts presented to it, whether a firm offer was made, and, if so, whether it was accepted. The way that the Courts achieve this is considered immediately below.

OFFER

DEFINITE OFFER

In the first instance, it is essential to prove the existence of a definite offer, which may be made orally, in writing, or by implication. Such offers may be made to one person, a group of persons or the whole world – (i.e. a general offer). With regard to acceptance, then only the offeree (or offerees if the offer has been made to more than one person), may accept. However, where the offer is a general one, anyone may accept by complying with the terms of the offer.

OFFER MADE TO A SPECIFIC PERSON

Boulton *v.* Jones (1857)
Boulton bought a business. Jones, who was owed money by the vendor (seller) of the business, ordered some goods from the vendor. These were duly supplied by Boulton (the new owner), but Jones refused to pay for them, saying that his contract was intended to be with the "vendor" because the goods he ordered were to be used in reduction of an outstanding debt. *Held.* Jones was not liable as there was no contract between him and Boulton.

OFFER MADE TO THE GENERAL PUBLIC

An offer, to be legally binding, must be clear and unequivocal and to illustrate this point, the following cases should be compared:
Harvey *v.* Facey (1893). When negotiating the purchase of a property, Harvey asked "Will you sell us Bumper Hall Pen? Telegraph lowest price." The following reply was made: "Lowest cash price for B.H.P. £900." Harvey then replied: "We agree to buy B.H.P. for £900 asked by you." Facey would not sell the property to Harvey, who then commenced an action for specific performance. *Held.* A binding contract had not been formed. For, Facey's statement was not an offer to sell, it was merely a statement of price (i.e. an invitation to treat).

Bigg *v.* Boyd Gibbins Ltd (1971). Here, the following statement was made: "For a quick sale, I would accept £26,000." The reply was as follows: "I accept your offer." As the defendant subsequently decided not to proceed and buy the property, the plaintiff brought an action for specific performance. *Held.* A legally binding contract had been formed, for there was a clear and unequivocal offer which had been accepted.

An example of a general offer is one where a reward is offered to a person who does a particular thing, e.g. finds lost property. A further example of a general offer can be seen by looking at the classic legal case:

Carlill *v*. Carbolic Smoke Ball Co. (1893)

A patent medicine company advertised that it would give a reward of one hundred pounds to anyone who contracted influenza after they had been using one of the special smoke balls for more than a minimum period. Mrs Carlill bought the product, used it as directed, but still caught influenza. *Held.* Mrs Carlill's claim was successful. The offer was shown to have been accepted, and it was not necessary for the offeree (Mrs Carlill) to confirm her acceptance to the offeror for the agreement to be binding.

COMMUNICATION OF OFFER

It is essential for the offer to be communicated to the offeree – because no one can accept an offer of which they are unaware. Thus, if someone finds lost property and returns it to the true owner, the true owner is only legally obliged to pay any offered reward money if the finder was aware of it beforehand.

Taylor *v* Laird (1856)

Taylor, a ship's captain, gave up his post while part way through a voyage. However, he continued to work until the vessel arrived back home and then claimed for full wages. *Held.* Taylor's claim was unsuccessful. He did not communicate his offer to the shipowners, and, therefore, they were not in a position to accept or reject the offer.

INVITATION TO TREAT

The distinction between this and a definite offer has, in the past, caused concern to the Courts and first arose in the interpretation of the law of contract applied to auctions.

An invitation to treat is simply an invitation to others to make offers and may apply to auctions and stickers or displays in shop windows.

AUCTIONS

When someone at an auction bids for a particular lot, he is making an offer to buy at that price. It is not the auctioneer who is offering to sell at that price, and so he is free to accept or reject the offer. **Payne *v*. Cave (1789)**, and **British Car Auctions *v*. Wright (1972)**.

This process of bidding may continue until the auctioneer accepts the final bidder's offer and acceptance is signified by the fall of the auctioneer's hammer, **s. 57 Sale of Goods Act, 1979**.

Harris *v.* Nickerson (1873)
It was held that an advertisement to sell specified goods by auction on a particular day was not a promise to potential bidders that the sale of specified goods would actually take place. Thus, in these circumstances, there is no binding contract between the auctioneers and any person who travels to the auction with the specific intention of bidding for a lot which was withdrawn in the meantime.

ADVERTISEMENT OF GOODS

The issue of a catalogue which advertises goods is considered to be an attempt to induce offers (i.e. invitation to treat) and not an offer in itself: **Partridge *v.* Crittenden (1968)**. This decision was followed in **C. A. Norgren Co. and others *v.* Technomarketing and others (1983)** where certain items had been listed at the back of a brochure but as it was discovered that they were subject to a copyright dispute, it had been agreed that they would`not be sold even though they were retained in the catalogue. This argument also applies to goods advertised at a particular price in a shop window or inside the shop itself. The shopkeeper is not offering to sell at that price, but is inducing offers to buy at that price. This interpretation has been applied in:

Pharmaceutical Society of Great Britain *v.* Boots Cash Chemists (Southern) Ltd (1953)
Here, an action was taken against Boots for selling drugs in a manner which was believed to be a contravention of the **Pharmacy and Poisons Act, 1933**. For, customers were simply able to pick the drugs up from a shelf and place them in a basket prior to taking them to the checkout till and paying for them. Statute provided that the sale of certain drugs had to be supervised and the question arose as to whether this term was contravened by such self-service procedures. *Held.* The contract was completed at the cashier's till and, as supervision took place at this point, Boots had not contravened the statutory provision.

Note: The contract is completed at the cashier's till, not at the moment the customer take the item from the shelf and places it in the basket.

Fisher *v.* Bell (1961)
A shopkeeper displayed a flick knife in his window which was advertised as an "Ejector Knife" 4/- (today 20p). A policeman noticed this and subsequently, the shopkeeper was taken to Court for prosecution under the **Restriction of Offensive Weapons Act, 1959**. *Held.* The display in the window was merely an invitation to treat, and so the prosecution failed.

From the above, it is seen that when a customer picks up an article in a shop, in law, that person is offering to buy. If the shopkeeper wants to sell, the offer will be accepted and the contract completed by the exchange of goods for money. It is also necessary to consider a situation where a shopkeeper has incorrectly priced an article which is on display. If, at the time the customer offers to buy, the shopkeeper realises his mistake and points out what the correct price should be, in reality, the shopper cannot compel the shopkeeper to sell at the incorrect price. *Note.* If the customer has switched labels in an attempt to defraud the shopkeeper, a criminal liability would arise.

ACCEPTANCE

The acceptance of an offer may be made orally, in writing or by implication. The first two are self-explanatory, but an example of the third is illustrated by:

Brogden *v.* Metropolitan Railway Co. (1877)
Brogden had supplied coal to the railway company for a number of years. There had been no formal contract, but Brogden suggested that there should be one. The railway company sent a draft contract which was amended and added to by Brogden, who subsequently returned it after marking it "approved". The contract was not formally executed but the parties acted as though it had been. At a later date, an argument arose and Brogden refused to make further deliveries. He said that there was no valid contract as the railway company had not accepted the amended draft. *Held.* By their conduct, the parties had, by implication, adopted the terms of the amended draft (even though it was not formalised) and were therefore bound by its conditions.

COUNTER OFFER

This is a rejection of the original offer and arises when new terms are introduced by the offeree which the offeror did not have the chance of examining.

Hyde *v.* Wrench (1840)
Wrench offered to sell a farm to Hyde for £1,000 on 6th June. On the 8th June, Hyde offered £950. On 27th June, Wrench refused the offer for £950. Then, two days later, Hyde said that he would be prepared to pay £1,000. Wrench refused this second offer (even though it was equivalent to the original asking price) and Hyde attempted to enforce the contract against him. *Held.* There was no enforceable contract as the counter offer of 8th June was considered as a rejection of the original offer – and without the agreement of Wrench, it was not capable of being

revived. Similar decisions have since been made in **Neale *v.* Merrett (1930)** and **Northland Airlines Limited *v.* Dennis Ferranti Meters Limited (1970)**. It should be noted, though, that such counter offers may be accepted orally or by implication **(Butler Machine Tool Company *v.* Ex.-cell-o Corporation (England) (1977)**.

REQUEST FOR INFORMATION

It is essential to distinguish between this term and "counter offer". For the latter amounts to a rejection of the original offer, whereas the former does not. On occasions, it is difficult to distinguish between the two, but an example of a request is where: A offers B some goods which must be paid for on a strict cash basis. Then B enquiries if A would accept payment over two months, as in **Stevenson *v.* McLean (1880)**. This would be considered as a request for information and not a rejection of the original offer.

CONDITIONAL ACCEPTANCE

This does not amount to acceptance. An example which is frequently encountered is when land is being sold. In the first instance, it is standard practice to submit a draft agreement via solicitors to the purchaser and if this party agrees to the terms, the property is described as being "sold subject to contract". Thus, without evidence to the contrary, as in **Michael Richards Properties *v.* Corporation of St Saviours Parish, Southwark (1975)**, the Courts will interpret the words as meaning that the incidence of liability is postponed until a formal document (i.e. a contract based on the draft) has been completed and signed: **Winn *v.* Bull (1877)** and **Tiverton Estates Limited *v.* Wearwell Limited (1974)**. The draft document is unenforceable at law.

It has now been established that the term "subject to contract" is only appropriate in the early stages of negotiation. For, if negotiations have been taking place for quite some time, the courts may hold that it is not possible for an acceptance to be conditional: **Alpenstow Ltd. *v.* Regalian Properties plc (1985)**. The two parties had been negotiating for the sale of a property for five months. At that advanced stage, very detailed terms of a contract were sent to the defendants (Regalian), but the document still incorporated the term "subject to contract". The terms were acceptable to the defendant, but the plaintiff would not proceed. As a consequence, an action for specific performance was brought by Regalian, while Alpenstow attempted get a caution registered against the underlying land, cancelled. *Held.* A legally binding contract existed and the action for specific performance succeeded. For, although the term "subject to contract" is appropriate in the early stages of negotiating, the term is inappropriate after some four or five months of negotiating. Furthermore, where a detailed and conscientiously drawn document (such as the one here) has been produced, it would be expected that the clause "subject to contract", would no longer be incorporated therein.

TENDERS

A tender can be described as an invitation to suppliers to put in offers to supply goods and/or services. The person who tenders (the tenderer) then awaits the offers from the suppliers, which must be submitted by a specified closing date. After the closing date, the tenderer usually chooses the one which he feels is best suited to his requirements, although he is not legally obliged to choose any: **Spencer *v.* Harding (1870)**. Furthermore, his choice may not necessarily be the cheapest. Any tender must be closely scrutinised by the suppliers, for it may be one of two types, as the following examples show:

(a) A advertises for tenders for the supply of 50 tons of coal for delivery between 1st June and 1st July 1988. B, C and D submit tenders, and, of these, B's is accepted. Upon acceptance by A, the contract is immediately formed.

(b) E, advertises for tenders, indicating he may need up to 80 tons of coal during 1988, and that deliveries are to be made if and when demanded. If F, G and H submit tenders, and H's is accepted, the legal meaning of acceptance here is vastly different from that which prevails in (a). For, although E has accepted H's tender, in the legal sense, acceptance occurs each time a separate order is placed. In the latter situation, if E never ordered any coal (or ordered less than 80 tons within the stipulated period), there is no breach of contract. *Note:* If the agreement had been for E to buy all the coal he needed from H, but subsequently bought from someone else, then the contract is broken. **Kier *v.* Whitehead Iron Company (1938)**.

Further, if orders are placed with a supplier under the terms of the tender, he is obliged to supply the goods: **Great Northern Railway Company *v.* Witham (1873)**.

COMMUNICATION OF ACCEPTANCE

Where the offeree has made up his mind to accept the offer, the agreement is not complete until it has been communicated orally or in writing to the offeror or by the fall of a hammer at an auction. In some instances, acceptance may be proved by conduct: **Carlill *v.* Carbolic Smoke Ball Company Limited (1893)**. (See back.)

For an acceptance to be valid it must be communicated by a duly authorised person: **Powell *v.* Lee (1908)**.

METHOD OF COMMUNICATION

On occasions, the offeror may prescribe the method to be used to communicate acceptance. Thus, by simply complying with the method, the agreement is completed. However, there is some doubt as to whether precise observance is necessary. There are some precedents, though, which support the view that an offer sent by telegram must be accepted by telegram and an offer sent by post must be accepted by post. Where the offeror insists on one method of communication, then only that method will be effective. However, where no particular method is insisted upon, any method that corresponds with the degree of urgency expressed in the offer is sufficient: **Yates Building Company *v.* R. J. Pulleyn and Sons (York) (1975)**.

TIME OF ACCEPTANCE

Today, there are many precedents which can be cited to indicate how the Courts will interpret a given set of circumstances and in whose favour they will decide.

USE OF POST

This has been shown to occur as soon as the letter of acceptance is put in the post, even though it never reaches its destination: **Household Fire Insurance Company *v.* Grant (1879)**. However, the envelope must be correctly addressed and posted: **Re London and Northern Bank, Ex parte Jones (1900)**.

In **Adams *v.* Lindsell (1818)**, the Courts considered a situation where the offeror incorrectly addressed his letter. Briefly, Lindsell wrote to Adams offering him some wool at a particular price and requested a reply by letter. Although the offer letter was sent on 2nd September, because it was wrongly addressed by Lindsell and had to be re-directed, it did not reach Adams until 5th September. An immediate reply (accepting the offer) was given, and this reached Lindsell on 9th September. However, the wool was sold to another party on 8th September because in the normal course of events, a reply should have been received on 7th September. Adams sued for breach of contract. *Held*. An offer is made when it actually reaches the offeree – not when it would have reached him in the normal course of post. However, because the mistake had been made by the offeror, the action for breach of contract succeeded. In any case the letter of acceptance was posted on 5th September, three days before the goods were sold to the other party.

USE OF TELEGRAM

Acceptance takes place at the moment the telegram is handed in at the Post Office by the offeree: **Cowan *v.* O'Connor (1880)**.

USE OF TELEPHONE

Acceptance occurs at the moment the offeror hears that his offer has been accepted. When acting on behalf of clients, solicitors may create binding contracts over the telephone: **Domb and Another *v.* Isoz (1980)**. But, if the line is cut before the offeror hears that the contract has been accepted, there is no binding contract.

USE OF TELEX

This point was considered by the Court of Appeal in **Entores Limited *v.* Miles Far East Corporation (1955)**. As such messages are communicated instantaneously from sender (offeree) to recipient (offeror), then the same rules apply to these as to telephones. Thus, acceptance must be received (seen on a printout) before it can be considered as effective. Here, a London based company offered to buy some goods by telex from Holland. The Dutch company immediately accepted the offer by telex. It was held that the contract had been concluded in London, i.e. the place to where acceptance was returned. A similar situation was the subject of discussion in **Brinkibon Limited *v.* Stahag Stahl Und Stahlwarenhandels Gmbh (1982)**. In arriving at its decision the House of Lords adopted the rule discussed in the 'Entores' case above.

In both of these cases, it was pointed out that the respective contracts had been made in the offeror's country (i.e. where acceptance of the offer had been received). This factor is of particular importance when one party wishes to serve a writ on another and both are located in different countries or, perhaps, negotiations take place with an agent who is a resident of a third country. For, with transactions of an international nature, if litigation is to proceed, the court, which is being asked to judge the action, must be certain that the matter is within its jurisdiction.

KNOWLEDGE OF THE OFFER

English case law supports the view that the acceptor must have knowledge of the offer: **Williams *v.* Carwardine (1833)**. Thus, say X has lost a gold watch and offers a rewards for £50 to the person who finds it. Later, Y finds it, but he can only claim the reward if he was aware of the reward prior to finding the watch.

CROSS OFFERS

An example of how this may arise is where A writes to B, offering his car for sale at one thousand pounds; while at the same time, B writes to A offering to buy the same car for one thousand pounds, and the two letters cross in the post. Do the letters create a valid contract? By a majority decision in **Tinn *v.* Hoffman (1873)**, it was held that there is no contract. However, this rather "strict" decision may not be followed today if it could be clearly established that the two parties intended to create a legally binding agreement.

RECALL OF AN ACCEPTANCE BEFORE IT REACHES THE OFFEROR

A precedent from Scotland, **Dunmore (Countess) *v.* Alexander (1830)**, indicates that this is permitted. Here, the offeree accepted an offer of employment, but then subsequently declined. Both letters reached the offeror on the same day. *Held.* The acceptance was cancelled.

There is no English authority on this matter and so the decision an English Court would make in similar circumstances is uncertain.

TIME AND PLACE CONTRACT IS MADE

The establishment of this point became important because of the increased usage of computers and Telex machines as methods of communication. In **Entores Limited *v.* Miles Far East Corporation (1955)**, it was held by the Court of Appeal that a contract is made when and where the acceptance is received by the offeror.

TERMINATION OF OFFER

An offer terminates either by:

1. Revocation by the offeror before acceptance; or,
2. Lapse of time; or,
3. Failure of any condition, subject to which the offer was made; or,
4. Death of either the offeror or the offeree before acceptance; or,
5. Rejection by offeree; or,
6. Making of a counter-offer by the offeree.

1. REVOCATION BEFORE ACCEPTANCE

It was held in **Payne *v.* Cave (1789)** that revocation is possible and effective at any time before acceptance. This decision would remain the same where the offeror had described himself ready to keep the offer open for a given period, but revoked it before expiry: **Routledge *v.* Grant (1828)**. There are exceptions to this general position and they arise where the offeree gives and the offeror accepts some consideration (e.g. a cash deposit), to keep the offer open to him for a given period. Furthermore, for revocation to be effective, it must be communicated to the offeree. **Byrne v. Van Tienhoven (1880)**. Here, the defendant wrote a letter to Byrne on 1st October offering goods for sale. This reached Byrne on 11th October and he accepted the offer, replying by telegraph. However, the defendant had written to Byrne on 8th October revoking the offer, although this letter was not received by Bryne until 20th October. *Held*. Byrne had accepted the offer and the contract was good. For revocation to be effective, it needed to be received by the offeree before acceptance. It was immaterial whether the revocation had been posted or was on its way.

It should be noted that once an offer has been accepted, it is not possible for the offeror to withdraw the offer if he finds out that he has made a mistake, unless, of course, the offeree was aware of the mistake. This point was discussed by the Court of Appeal in **Centrovincial Estates v. Merchant Investors Assurance (1983)**. Here, a landlord offered to rent some property at a rate of £65,000 p.a. This was accepted, but subsequently, the landlord realised that the rent he should have requested was £126,000 p.a. Although the landlord sought to have the mistake rectified, the Court held that this action was not possible.

2. LAPSE OF TIME

What amounts to lapse of time will vary from situation to situation, and will be a matter for the Court to decide upon. Thus, where an offer is made by telegram, it must be accepted by telegram. An acceptance by letter may be too late and thus unenforceable.

In contrast, other offers may be accepted within a month or even longer, and the contract is still binding.

Ramsgate Victoria Hotel Limited v. Montefiore (1866)

In a letter dater 8th June 1864, the defendant offered to take some shares in a company. The company did not notify the defendant of their acceptance, but, on 23rd November 1864, they alloted some shares to him which he subsequently refused to take up. *Held*. The offer had lapsed because of the company's unreasonable length of time in notifying acceptance. Thus, refusal was justified.

3. FAILURE OF A CONDITION

An offer may be conditional. Where this is so, and the condition fails to be satisfied, the offer will not be capable of acceptance, e.g. where an offer has been left open until midday on Thursday, it will lapse if not accepted by noon on that day.

Conditional offers may be express or implied from circumstances: **Financings Limited *v.* Stimson (1962)**.

4. DEATH

The effect that death has on the continuity of an offer depends upon the circumstances, and certain general rules have been established:

(a) DEATH OF AN OFFEROR

If the offeree knows of this, then he cannot accept. Where the offeree is ignorant of the death, the law is uncertain. In general, it may be stated that death varies the nature of such a contract, and therefore the offer would be terminated, but conflicting decisions were made in **Bradbury *v.* Morgan (1862)** and **Dickinson *v.* Dodds (1876)**.

Where the contract relates to a personal service, then, clearly, upon the offeror's death, a valid acceptance cannot be given, even if the offeree is ignorant of the death.

(b) DEATH OF AN OFFEREE

General principles seem to indicate that the offer terminates upon death, prior to acceptance, irrespective of whether the contract relates to personal service or not: **Re: Cheshire Banking Company, Duff's Executor's Case (1886)**.

After acceptance, if the offeror or offeree dies, then their respective personal representatives can act on behalf of the deceased to enable the agreed contract to be completed.

INTENTION TO CREATE LEGAL OBLIGATIONS

The law recognises that there is no intention with certain agreements, particularly those of a domestic nature, to pursue a legal action if the agreement does not materialise. Thus, if I agree to meet a colleague at Anfield to watch Liverpool slaughter another visiting football team, but I either cannot or do not arrive, my colleague cannot take a legal action against me for breach of contract.

Furthermore, there may be other simple agreements which the parties thereto do not intend to be the subject of legal action. This is so, even if the agreement is in writing. But in these situations, both parties should expressly agree to this, either orally or by making it form part of the written agreement.

In general, the Courts have two main guidelines when deciding if the parties intend to create legal obligations, although in some situations, the position is provided for by Statute:

(a) If the agreement is of a domestic or social nature, then the assumption will be that there was no intention to create legal obligations unless evidence is produced to the contrary.

(b) If the agreement is of a commercial nature, then the assumption will be that there was an intention to create legal obligations, unless evidence is produced to the contrary.

1. DOMESTIC AND SOCIAL AGREEMENTS

When an agreement is of a domestic or social nature there will be a presumption that the parties did not intend to create legal obligations. However, one party may produce evidence to the contrary. Thus, each case has to be judged on its own merits. The following examples, though, should be compared:

(a) **Balfour *v.* Balfour (1919)**

A civil servant came back to England on leave with his wife. Whilst in England, his wife consulted a doctor who advised her for medical reasons not to go back overseas when her husband returned. She took her doctor's advice. Prior to the husband's departure, he had agreed to remit her an allowance of thirty pounds per month. Two years later, the husband suggested that they should separate. She subsequently sued as the promised payments had not materialised. *Held.* By the Court of Appeal, there was no enforceable contract as this was a domestic agreement.

A similar decision was made in **Spellman *v.* Spellman (1961)**, whereby a husband bought his wife a car, partly in an attempt to reconcile a strained marriage. The reconciliation did not work out, and eventually the husband left, taking the car with him. She attempted to recover it. *Held.* This was a domestic agreement in which there was no intention to create legal obligations.

(b) **Merritt *v.* Merritt (1970)**

A husband deserted his wife and certain agreements were made. He agreed to pay her forty pounds per month and she agreed to clear their mortgage debt. The husband also agreed to transfer the title of the house to her name but he did not honour this agreement. *Held.* By the Court of Appeal. The husband's promise to transfer title was legally binding. In circumstances like this, the parties bargain keenly and any agreements that result have legal consequences.

(c) **Jones *v.* Padavatton (1969)**
A mother informally agreed to pay her daughter forty-two pounds per month to read for the Bar, although overall, the exact terms of the agreement were very uncertain, as were the terms for the purchase and rental of a house in which the daughter would reside. *Held.* Although binding agreements could be made between parents and their children, in this situation, the agreement was considered to be a domestic one. Furthermore, as the arrangements were far too vague and uncertain, they were unenforceable. Uncertainty was again the reason for not finding an agreement to be binding in **Gould *v.* Gould (1969)**.

(d) **Simpkins *v.* Pays (1955)**
A lodger and two members of the family with whom he was staying entered newspaper competitions and they agreed that if they ever won a prize, it would be shared equally, even though the entry was submitted in only the defendant's name. On one occasion, a prize of £750 was won, but the defendant refused to share it, saying that the agreement was only a friendly one. *Held.* The agreement was a binding contract as there was an intention to create legal obligations. Thus, the prize had to be shared.

There have been other situations whereby the parties involved in disputes of a family or domestic nature have rebutted the presumption that there was no binding agreement. Examples of such cases are **Parker *v.* Clark (1960)** and **Snelling *v.* John G. Snelling Limited (1972)**.

(e) **Julian *v.* Furby (1982)**
A situation may arise where an agreement was regarded as partly a domestic arrangement and partly a legally binding contract. Here, Julian, an experienced plasterer, helped one of his daughters and her husband to buy, alter and furnish their house. Later on, a domestic argument arose and Julian sought to recover the cost of materials which he had supplied and the cost of his labour. Furby was prepared to pay for the materials, but not the labour, which, he understood, was to be provided free. *Held.* By the Court of Appeal. The parties had never intended to enter into a legally binding agreement as regards the labour, which Julian willingly gave to help out members of his family. Thus, the action failed.

2. COMMERCIAL AND BUSINESS AGREEMENTS

Here, there is a presumption of the intention to create legal obligations. However, it can be rebutted by evidence to the contrary as the following illustrates:

Jones *v*. Vernon's Pools Limited (1938)
Jones had submitted a football coupon on which he had a winning line. However, the Pools company said that they had never received the coupon, and, therefore, they were not obliged to pay him any prize money. *Held.* Because the coupon contained a clause which stated that "the transaction should not give rise to any legal relationship . . . or be legally enforceable . . . but . . . binding in honour only", then this was a bar to legal action.

The same decision was made in **Appleson *v*. H. Littlewood Limited (1939)** for similar reasons.

3. STATUTORY PROVISIONS

Occasionally, an Act of Parliament will be passed which results in certain agreements being unenforceable. An example of this is now found in the interpretation of "engagement to marry" under **s. 1 Law Reform (Miscellaneous Provisions) Act, 1970**. For, although engagement is an agreement between two parties, the proposed marriage cannot be enforced by law as the parties concerned are held not to have intended to create legal obligations.

CAPACITY TO CONTRACT

In general, the law allows binding agreements to be entered into by any person, e.g. private individuals, partnerships and corporations. But there are other groups, e.g. minors, mentally incapacitated persons and those suffering from an excess of alcohol, who, in normal circumstances, cannot enter into a binding agreement. The reason for this is that the law will assume that they are incapable of knowing what they are doing, and so they need to be protected from unscrupulous third parties.

MINORS (INFANTS)

According to **s. 1 Family Law Reform Act, 1969**, any person under the age of 18 is a minor. In law, a minor's contracts are divided into those which are valid, those which are void and those which are voidable.

VALID CONTRACTS

These may be subdivided into contracts for necessaries and contracts for the minor's benefit.

NECESSARIES

Minors are obliged to pay for any necessaries which are supplied to them. The word "necessaries" does not solely relate to items which are essential to support life, but is extended to include any items or services which are needed to maintain that person's station in life. With relation to the supply of goods, than a statutory definition is to be found in **s. 3 Sale Of Goods Act, 1979**, viz. "goods suitable to the condition in life of the minor and to his actual requirements at the time of sale and delivery".

From this, it is seen that it is not only essential to prove that the goods were suitable to a minor's station in life, but also that they were suitable to his actual requirements at the time of delivery. For, if sufficient of the goods in question have already been provided, then any excess is not considered a necessary and thus, a contract to provide it is unenforceable.

Nash *v.* Inman (1908)
A tailor sued a Cambridge undergraduate who had ordered various articles of clothing, including eleven fancy waistcoats, and who had not paid for them. *Held.* Although in normal circumstances, such waistcoats were considered necessaries for Cambridge undergraduates, because Inman had already been supplied with adequate clothing, the plaintiff's action failed.

It is really a question of law and fact as to whether an article is a necessary. So, although food, clothing, lodging, medical attention and educational books are clearly necessaries, Courts have held that uniforms, hiring of cars, asking for legal advice, and using horses as a means of conveyance could also be necessaries, depending upon the circumstances.

Necessaries need to be compared with luxuries. The method of treating the latter was discussed by Alderson B, in **Chapple *v.* Cooper (1844)** – even though this case related to an action for unpaid funeral expenses against a minor. He said . . . "articles of mere luxury are always excluded, though luxurious articles of utility are, in some cases, allowed". Furthermore, in **Ryder *v.* Wombwell (1869)**, it was held that a pair of jewelled solitaires and a silver goblet were not necessaries, even for a minor who moved in the highest circles. In contrast, it was held that a gold watch and chain could be necessaries for a minor who was an undergraduate: **Peters *v.* Fleming (1840)**.

ONEROUS TERMS

If a contract contains onerous terms for the supply of goods, even where the goods are considered suitable for the minor's requirements, then the contract will still be void: **Fawcett *v.* Smethurst (1914)**.

REASONABLE PRICE

By s. 2 **Sale of Goods Act, 1979**, a minor need only pay a reasonable price for necessaries rather than a contract price.

EXECUTORY CONTRACTS

An example of such a contract is when a minor orders necessaries but then cancels the order before delivery. Whether an action would be sustained against such a minor is debateable, but it is believed that an executory contract could not be enforced against a minor.

CONTRACTS FOR A MINOR'S BENEFIT

Where a minor enters a contract from which he obtains an education or training for a trade or profession, or, alternatively, gains experience in a trade or profession, he is bound by it. Occasionally, there will be a dispute and when this happens it is up to the Court to decide whether the contract is really "for the minor's benefit". When deciding this, the Court will look at the contract as a whole. Thus, even if some of the terms of the contract are not directly beneficial to the minor, it does not necessarily mean that the contract is invalidated. Much case law can be quoted here, and the leading cases on the topic are:

Clements *v*. L. & N.W. Railway (1894)
A minor entered his employer's insurance scheme which meant that he had to forgo certain statutory rights. After sustaining an injury, he claimed under the employer's scheme and statute. *Held*. The employer's scheme, as a whole, was for his benefit, and thus he could not also claim under the statute.

De Francesco *v*. Barnum (1890)
Two minors bound themselves for seven years to be taught dancing by the plaintiff. They also agreed only to accept engagements with the plaintiff's approval, but they later accepted invitations from Barnum. Although the original agreements were drawn up for the minor's benefit, the Court found that there were many onerous clauses in the contract. *Held*. Because the contract was unreasonable, it was unenforceable.

Doyle *v*. White City Stadium Ltd (1935)
A minor boxer signed a contract agreeing that if he were disqualified in a bout, any prize money would be withheld. In one fight he was disqualified but still attempted to claim his prize money, contending that, as a minor, he was not bound by the contract. *Held*. His claim failed, as the contract, as a whole, was for his benefit.

Roberts v. Gray (1913)
A young billiards player agreed to go on tour with a well known professional, but, before the tour started, a dispute occurred and the young player refused to go. The professional sued for damages. *Held.* As the contract was for the minor's benefit, he was bound by it. By breaching it, he was liable for damages.

Chaplin v. Leslie Frewin (Publishers) (1965)
The plaintiff entered a contract which allowed the publishers to print a book on his life story. When completed, Chaplin felt that the content was inaccurate and tried to void the contract on those grounds. *Held.* At the time the contract was made, it was for the minor's benefit and thus could not be voided.

Furthermore, it has been established that trading contracts are not enforceable against a minor, however much they are for his benefit. It has also been held that a minor (a) cannot (in the absence of fraud) be compelled to repay monies paid for goods ordered from him which he did not deliver: **Cowern v. Nield (1912)**. and (b), he cannot be liable for instalments due under a hire purchase agreement, even though the money was used in the minor's trade, e.g. the purchase of a lorry: **Mercantile Union Guarantee Corporation v. Ball (1937)**.

Finally, where a minor enters into a contract which is not substantially for his benefit, then it is voidable (see later). He can, therefore, rescind it while still a minor or within a reasonable time of attaining majority.

VOID CONTRACT

By **s. 1 Infants Relief Act, 1874**, the following types of contract are absolutely void and have no legal effect:

1. Contracts for the repayment of money lent or to be lent.
2. Contracts for goods supplied or to be supplied other than necessaries.
3. Accounts stated.

REPAYMENT OF MONEY LENT OR TO BE LENT

If a banker (or other lender) gaves a minor a loan or overdraft, any agreement to repay it while still a minor, or even after attaining majority, is void. Thus, a bank (or other lender) cannot take legal action to recover an advance or realise any security which has been taken to secure the advance. The same applies when a minor fraudulently misstates his age in order to obtain a loan. However, a criminal action is possible against such a minor under the **Theft Act, 1968**, because he will be considered as someone who has "dishonestly obtained the property of another by deception". Clearly, if the minor honours his obligation and repays, then there are no problems for a lender – but, if he does not or will not pay, there is nothing the lender can do, legally, to recover the advance.

The two leading legal cases on this topic are:

Coutts & Company *v.* Browne-Lecky (1947)
An infant was granted an overdraft by his bankers which was supported by the guarantee of two adults. The minor defaulted and the bank claimed from the guarantors. *Held.* By **s. 1 Infants' Relief Act, 1874**, the advance to the minor was void and so he could not legally be compelled to repay. Because, in law, there was no enforceable debt, then the guarantee security given to cover the "debt" was void. So, the guarantors had no liability.

R. Leslie Limited *v.* Sheill (1914)
A minor fraudulently misrepresented his age and obtained a loan from a moneylender. *Held.* The moneylender could not recover this advance because the loan was void. Nor was the claim for tort of deceit successful as this would have been an indirect way of enforcing a void contract.

GOODS SUPPLIED OR TO BE SUPPLIED OTHER THAN NECESSARIES
The legal meaning of the word "necessaries" has been fully described earlier. Thus, any contracts entered into by a minor which are for items which are not necessaries cannot be enforced.

When a minor has obtained goods by fraud, then the Civil Court may compel the minor to return the goods to the rightful owner, but this is only possible where the goods are still in the minor's possession, and are identifiable.

ACCOUNT STATED
The meaning of this term is a promise to pay a past debt. For example, if A sells goods to B for twenty pounds, and B sells the goods to A for five pounds, then, if the amounts are netted, B owes A fifteen pounds. If B acknowledges the debt in writing, it is not necessary to prove the debt related to the two transactions, for A can sue B on the written acknowledgement – which is known as an account stated. However, A cannot use this method of recovery if B is a minor.

VOIDABLE CONTRACTS

These contracts are ones which are valid and binding on a minor unless he repudiates them during minority or within a reasonable time of attaining majority. There are only a limited number of types and these include:

(a) *Contracts which are of a continuing nature.*

(b) *Contracts which enable a minor to acquire interests in property of a permanent kind.*

The latter may be of four types:

1. Contracts concerning land, e.g. leasing premises, or,
2. Contracts to purchase shares in a company, or,
3. Partnership contracts, or,
4. Marriage settlements.

After repudiating a voidable contract, a minor is not liable on future contracts entered into with the same person, but can be sued on contracts entered into before repudiation. The latter contracts are binding upon him, unless (as mentioned above), they are repudiated during minority or within a reasonable time of attaining majority. What the words "reasonable time" mean is up to the Court to decide – and this will depend upon the facts of each case.

Steinberg *v.* Scala (Leeds) Limited (1923)
A minor was allotted some shares and made payment for the allotment and the first call. She was unable to meet the further calls and attempted to repudiate the contract while still a minor – asking for the return of the monies already paid and for her name to be deleted from the register. *Held.* Her name could be removed from the register (thus avoiding future calls), but she was not allowed to recover the amounts paid because there had not been a total failure of consideration.

FURTHER CONSIDERATIONS WITH MINORS

ABILITY TO RECOVER BACK

Although it would appear common sense that a minor can recover money which he has paid for goods under an absolutely void contract, this is not so. The rule is that such money or goods which are delivered by a minor to the other party are only recoverable if there has been total failure of consideration. **Valentini *v.* Canali (1889)** and **Corpe *v.* Overton (1833)**.

SECTION 2 INFANTS RELIEF ACT, 1874

This lengthy section provides "No action shall be brought whereby to charge any person upon any promise made after full age to pay any debt contracted during minority or upon any ratification made after full age of any promise or contract during minority whether there shall or shall not be any new consideration for such promise or ratification after full age."

Although long winded, a brief interpretation of how it applies is:

(a) A mere ratification after attaining majority of any contract coming within section 2 is not actionable: **Coxhead *v.* Mullis (1878)**.

(b) Upon attaining majority, a new promise, supported by new consideration, is valid, provided it relates to an obligation which is not the payment of a debt: **Ditcham *v.* Worrall (1880)**.

LIABILITY IN TORT

An infant cannot be sued in tort if the end product is to make him liable on a contract which is not binding upon him. But where the action is purely one of tort, the minor can be held liable: **Burnard *v.* Haggis (1863)**, and below:

Ballett *v.* Mingay (1943)

Mingay (a minor), borrowed some electrical equipment from Ballett, and, when Ballett requested its return, this request could not be complied with as the equipment had been on-lent. Ballett then sued in detinue (i.e. unlawful retention). *Held.* Mingay's action went beyond that which was expected of him – i.e. he was expected to retain Ballett's goods and return them to him in the same condition that they were received when requested to do so – thus, he was liable.

Fawcett *v.* Smethurst (1914)

Smethurst, a minor, hired a car to collect some baggage from a particular place but in the process he met a friend and they did not directly go and collect the baggage. On the return journey, the hired car caught fire and was damaged beyond repair. The fire could not be attributed to any negligence on the part of Smethurst. *Held.* Smethurst was not liable as the claim against him was one of breach of contract. In making this decision, Atkin J., used the ratio of **Jennings *v.* Rundall (1799)** as a precedent.

QUASI CONTRACTS

A doctrine has evolved which provides a remedy against one person becoming unjustly enriched at the expense of another. It may be applied equally to both minors and adults who have gained from fraudulent action – and where a fraudulent minor is still in possession of the goods, these must be given up.

The doctrine has certain limitations, but there are three separate situations which should be noted:

(a) Where a minor has obtained goods by fraud (e.g. by overstating his age), and is still in possession of them, an order for restitution can be made, thereby enabling the title holder to recover his goods.

(b) Where a minor has obtained goods by fraud but no longer possesses them, then neither the goods nor any money paid to the minor for them can be recovered. Although, in **Stocks *v.* Wilson (1913)**, the doctrine of restitution enabled the true owner to recover such monies from a minor, in **R. Leslie Limited *v.* Sheill (1914)**, it was suggested that the Stocks' case had been wrongly decided.

(c) Where a minor obtains money by fraud, it does not matter whether the same money is still in his possession or has been spent, it is irrecoverable.

MENTALLY INCAPACITATED PERSONS

Contracts entered into by such persons are voidable at the option of the incapacitated person, provided:

(a) At the time the contract was made, he was suffering from this disability and was incapable of understanding what he was signing and,

(b) The other party knew of the disability: **Imperial Loan Co. *v.* Stone (1892)**.

Liability on a contract continues unless, within a reasonable time of returning to sanity, the contract is repudiated. However, the other party is always bound by the contract.

The above needs to be considered in conjunction with s. 2 **Sale of Goods Act, 1979**, for where necessaries are bought by and delivered to such persons, then a reasonable price must be paid for them.

Since the passing of the **Mental Health Act, 1959**, which has now been consolidated into the **Mental Health Act, 1983**, there has been a provision that someone (usually a relative of the incapacitated person), may apply to the Court of Protection for an order which will enable them to act on behalf of the incapacitated person. If the application is successful, the Court will issue a Court of Protection order which indicates the extent to which the appointed persons may bind the incapacitated person.

PERSONS SUFFERING FROM AN EXCESS OF ALCOHOL

When a person enters into a contract and, at the same time, he is in such a state of drunkenness, he does not know what he is doing, then, if this is clearly apparent to the other party, the contract is voidable: **Gore *v.* Gibson (1845)**.

Section 2 of the **Sale Of Goods Act, 1979**, also applies to drunken persons whereby they are obliged to pay a reasonable price for necessaries supplied to them.

Any contract entered into while drunk can later be ratified when the person becomes sober. **Matthews *v.* Baxter (1873).**

COMPANIES

In Chapter 5 it will be seen that a company has a separate legal identity, i.e. it has a personality of its own which is quite distinct from the persons who own it (**Salomon *v.* Salomon & Company Ltd (1897)**), and who manage it. Furthermore, the majority of companies are registered under one of the Companies Acts. To be granted a registration, certain documents have to be submitted to Companies Registry. One of these documents is a Memorandum of Association and, amongst other things, it contains what is called an objects clause which defines what the company has been formed to do. Any actions (including contracts), which the company carries out in accordance with the objects are described as intra-vires (within the powers of) and can be enforced on behalf of and by the company in the event of default.

In contrast, companies occasionally do things which are not provided for by the objects of the Memorandum and, as such, the actions are described as ultra-vires (beyond the powers of) of the company. In these circumstances, it was not normally possible to enforce such actions through the Courts. The position which subsists when a matter has been held as ultra vires has changed dramatically since 1972, as explained in Chapter 5.

FORMALITIES FOR COMPLETING A CONTRACT

Because a company is an artificial person, it needs real people to enter contracts on its behalf. These people are known as directors and prior to binding the company in respect of certain contracts (e.g. the proposed take-over of a competitor), they must attend a meeting to discuss and approve matters. The meeting must be called (i.e. the due period of notice must be given), and conducted in accordance with the requirements of its Articles of Association. It will be essential to establish that a quorum was in attendance and that when a vote was taken, the resolution to enter into the contract was passed by an appropriate majority. However, for general day-to-day business, the Companies Acts provide that a director can enter into contracts which bind the company, unless the company's own articles of association provide otherwise.

Following the passing of the resolution, it is then possible to enter into the contract. The method of completion of the contract (i.e. under hand or under seal), should comply with what the Articles and resolution have provided. Most contracts will be completed under the hand of a duly authorised official (e.g. the company secretary or one director), although occasionally, contracts will be completed under seal. Provision for this is now contained within s. 36(1) Companies Act 1985.

CONSENSUS AD IDEM (AGREEMENT)

If a party is induced to enter a contract by fraud, misrepresentation or mistake, then, depending upon the circumstances, the party may treat the contract as void or voidable. The reason for this is that there has been no real agreement because the document that was signed was based on circumstances which were different from those contemplated. Thus, there was no "meeting of minds".

CONSIDERATION

In any action on a simple contract, it is essential for the plaintiff to show that the defendant's promise upon which he is suing was part of a bargain to which he, personally, contributed. For a mere "moral obligation" or "bare promise" is insufficient – the bargain must be supported by what is called "valuable consideration". Thus, if I promise to give my cousin £50 as a present and subsequently change my mind, my cousin cannot enforce payment against me. For a promise without consideration, as in this example, is a gift and such promises are unenforceable in Courts of Law. In contrast, a promise supported by consideration (e.g. "I promise to pay my cousin £600 for his car"), is described as a bargain, and, as such, is a contract which is legally enforceable in the Courts.

DEFINITION

The definition most often cited is the one found in **Currie *v.* Misa (1875)**, as "some right, interest, profit or benefit accruing to one party or some forbearance, detriment, loss or responsibility given, suffered or undertaken by another".

RULES FOR CONSIDERATION

There is a series of general rules which relates to consideration, viz:

(a) It must be real.
(b) It need not be adequate.
(c) It must be legal.
(d) It must move between promisor and promisee.

(e) It must be capable of performance.
(f) It must not be past.

(a) CONSIDERATION MUST BE REAL

Consideration must have some value. A typical example of value is when a party does more than he is already bound to do. In contrast, where a party's action is carried out simply to discharge a pre-existing obligation, then there is no consideration. The following examples will illustrate what the above means.

1. A PUBLIC DUTY IMPOSED ON THE PLAINTIFF BY LAW

Where a person is simply carrying out his public duty, this will not be regarded as consideration, e.g. Where someone has been subpoenaed to give evidence in a legal action as in **Collins *v.* Godefroy (1831)**, it was not possible for that person to enforce payment of a sum of money which was promised to him for attending the Court and giving evidence, for no consideration had been given as this party was only carrying out his public duty. But where one party renders more than his public duty, then this may be held to be consideration; e.g. the provision of extra policing in order to protect someone's property: **Glasbrook Brothers *v.* Glamorgan County Council (1925)**.

2. EXISTING CONTRACTUAL DUTY

(a) *To the Defendant*

Vanbergen *v.* St Edmunds Properties Limited (1933)

The defendant was in the process of having a bankruptcy notice served on the plaintiff. The latter asked for serving to be delayed and the defendant's solicitors agreed, subject to the debt upon which the notice had been based being paid by a due time on a given day. The defendant paid as promised, but the advice telling the solicitors of the credit went astray. As a consequence, the bankruptcy notice was served and Vanbergen sued for damages and breach of contract. *Held.* The action was unsuccessful as the paying of the debt during the extended period did not amount to consideration.

(b) *To a Third Party*

Scotson *v.* Pegg (1861)

Scotson contracted to deliver coal to a third party (A), or to his order. A then sold the coal to Pegg, asking Scotson to deliver the coal direct to Pegg in accordance with the contract, and Pegg agreed to unload it at a specified rate when delivered. As Pegg did not honour the agreement, Scotson sued for breach. Pegg contended that he was not liable in contract as there was lack of consideration – because the contract between

Scotson and A provided that coal might be delivered to the order of A. *Held.* As the delivery of coal was a benefit to Pegg, there was consideration.

Shadwell *v.* Shadwell (1860)
The plaintiff's uncle, upon hearing his nephew had become engaged, wrote to tell the nephew that he would pay him one hundred and fifty pounds per year – during the uncle's life, or, until the nephew derived an income of six hundred guineas. After the marriage, the uncle lived for eighteen years, paying twelve sums and part of a thirteenth. Upon the uncle's death, the nephew sued the executors for the outstanding amounts. *Held.* The action was successful as marriage was deemed sufficient consideration to support the uncle's promise, for the nephew had incurred responsibilities and had changed his position for life. Almost certainly, the uncle had derived some benefit from seeing his nephew settled.

3. COMPOSITION WITH CREDITORS
It is possible for a group of creditors to accept an arrangement offered by an illiquid debtor for a percentage of the debt owed, and to consider it as full satisfaction. (See point (b) 3 below.)

(b) CONSIDERATION NEED NOT BE ADEQUATE
It is not part of the Courts' duty to assess the relative value of the respective parties' contribution to the contract. Furthermore, if someone makes a bad bargain, the law will not protect him unless he has been induced into the bargain by fraud or misrepresentation: **Haigh *v.* Brooks (1839)**.

Under this heading, the sufficiency of consideration needs to be discussed (although the term "sufficiency" is not synonymous with "adequacy"). The general rule on this matter is laid down in Pinnel's case where it was held that payment of a lesser sum than the amount due cannot be considered as satisfaction for an existing debt.

Pinnel's Case (1602). Pinnel sued Cole in debt for £8.10 shillings which fell due for payment on a bond on 11th November 1600. Cole, in defence, said that at Pinnel's request, he had repaid £5.2 shillings and 6 pence, which had been accepted in full settlement of the debt. *Held.* Pinnel's action was successful, although on a technical point. In the judgement, it was said that the case was particularly important in English legal history for it established that payment of a lesser sum on the day cannot be taken as satisfaction for the whole sum.

There are some exceptions to the rule in Pinnel's case and these arise:

1. Where the debtor, at the creditor's request, makes a lesser payment

at a time earlier than the due date, e.g. if Pinnel had paid £5 2s and 6 pence prior to the 11th November.

2. Where the method of payment is altered with the creditor's agreement. **Goddard *v.* O'Brien (1882)**, where payment of a lesser sum by cheque was held to be good. But the ratio in this case was overruled by the Court of Appeal in **D & C. Builders Limited *v.* Rees (1966)**.

3. Where, a debtor compounds his debts, i.e. offers his creditors a percentage of the debts owed to each of them. An example of this is a Deed of Arrangement, which, to be effective, must conform with the Deeds of Arrangement Act, 1914; e.g. J has debts of £5,000 and assets of only £3,500. Subject to him complying with the above Statute, it is possible for him to pay, say, only 70p for every £1 of debt owed to his creditors and this would fully discharge his debt to each of them.

4. There is also a common law method available where the part payment of one party (say, A), could fully discharge a debt (owed say, to B). This is by the doctrine of Accord and Satisfaction. To use this method, A must:

(a) Obtain the agreement (*accord*) of B, and
(b) Provide B with some consideration (*satisfaction*) because he has accepted a lesser sum – unless the agreement has been made under seal.

It was thought that the common law unfairly treated a party who had not fully repaid his creditor, even though the creditor had agreed to accept the lesser sum. For this reason, equity looked at the matter where such a promise had been made, but from a different viewpoint. From this evolved the *Doctrine of Equitable Promissory Estoppel*.

As an example, if A waives his contractual rights against B, and B then changes his position in reliance of the waiver, A would not be able to take a successful action against B on the original contract. Furthermore, in equity, the party who waives his rights may be estopped from denying that the waiver was intended to be binding.

The essential requirements of this doctrine (which is a defence rather than a cause of action) are:

1. There must have been an agreement between the parties by which the defendant owed an obligation to the plaintiff.

2. The plaintiff must have waived his rights, in whole or in part, against the defendant.

3. The defendant must have given no consideration for the waiver.

4. The defendant must have altered his position in reliance of the waiver.

If this doctrine had been applied, Foakes would have avoided liability for unpaid interest in the following circumstances:

Mrs Beer obtained judgement against Dr Foakes on 11th August 1875 for a debt and costs amounting to £2,090 and 19 shillings. It was agreed that the judgement debt was to be repaid by an immediate amount of £500 and £150 every six months until the debt was cleared. This agreement was honoured, but in June 1882, Mrs Beer brought an action for £360 of accrued interest. *Held*. By the Court of Appeal, her action was successful. For, although in the earlier agreed repayment programme, she had agreed not to take any further action on the judgement, this had not been supported by consideration from Dr Foakes. **Foakes *v*. Beer (1884)**.

(c) CONSIDERATION MUST BE LEGAL

Any contract entered into for immoral or criminal purposes is void, and case law supports this viewpoint.

Pearce *v*. Brooks (1866)

A coach builder hired out one of his coaches to a known prostitute, who refused to pay for the hire of the vehicle. Pearce sued her. *Held*. The vehicle was hired for a known immoral purpose, and the action was unsuccessful.

Foster *v*. Driscoll (1929)

At the time of prohibition, a United Kingdom exporter contracted to send a shipment of whisky to the United States of America. *Held*. (At that time). The import of whisky was illegal and the contract void and unenforceable.

(d) CONSIDERATION MUST MOVE BETWEEN PROMISOR AND PROMISEE

A stranger to a contract may not, by himself, sue on a contract. Thus any action for a breach of contract must be brought by a party who gave consideration.

From this statement, the doctrine of privity of contract (see later) arises.

Tweddle *v*. Atkinson (1861)

William Guy's daughter was married to Tweddle. Guy promised to pay Tweddle £200 in consideration of Tweddle's father paying £100. However Guy died before making the payment, and Tweddle sued his executor's for the payment. *Held*. No consideration had been given by Tweddle, but only between his father and his father-in-law. As only parties to the contract could sue, and Tweddle was not one of them, the action failed.

Price *v*. Easton (1833)
Easton promised that if W. Price did certain work for him, he would make a payment of £13 to J. Price. The work was carried out but the sum of money was not paid, and so J. Price sued for it. *Held.* As no consideration passed from J. Price to Easton, the action failed.

(e) CONSIDERATION MUST BE POSSIBLE OF PERFORMANCE
A promise to do something which is impossible is not legally binding and will be held to be something lacking the intention to create legal obligations.

(f) CONSIDERATION MUST NOT BE PAST
When one party performs an act before the other party makes a promise, the earlier act is not consideration in support of the promise.

Roscorla *v*. Thomas (1842)
After the sale of a horse to Roscorla, Thomas stated that the horse was sound and free from vice. However the horse proved to be vicious, and as a consequence Roscorla sued Thomas. *Held.* The sale had been completed before the promise was given. Thus Roscorla could recover nothing on the promise that the horse was not vicious.

There are a few exceptions to this past consideration rule. One of these is that consideration for a bill of exchange may (and usually does) relate to an antecedent debt or liability.

LEGALITY

It is a rule of law, that any court action which is brought by a person who has acted illegally, or who wants to compel someone else to commit an illegal act, will not be successful. Illegality in this context means either something forbidden by statute or something contrary to public policy.

1. FORBIDDEN BY STATUTE

A simple illustration is if I enter into a contract with someone so that I will pay them £50,000 if they will steal a valuable painting from an art gallery. I cannot take a legal action against them for breach of contract if they do not fulfil their obligation – for the underlying contract is illegal as it is a contravention of the Theft Act, 1968.

2. PUBLIC POLICY

Various examples could be quoted under this heading.

(a) IMMORAL CONTRACTS. These are contracts considered to be against public morals (see **Pearce *v*. Brooks (1866)**) or the sanctity of marriage.

(b) CORRUPTION OF PUBLIC LIFE. It is illegal to attempt to purchase a public honour, say, by making a charitable contribution on the condition of being knighted. If the honour does not follow, the contribution cannot be recovered. **Parkinson *v.* College of Ambulances (1925).**

(c) DEFRAUDING THE INLAND REVENUE. Any agreement which has the objective of evading tax payments is illegal. **Napier *v.* National Business Agency (1951).**

(d) CRIMINAL INVOLVEMENT. If someone kills another during a struggle and then agrees to pay damages to the deceased's widow, it is not possible for the person to claim indemnity on an insurance policy even though the policy covered such risks as "bodily injury to any person . . . caused by accidents" – for it would be contrary to public policy. **Gray *v.* Barr (1971).**

(e) JUSTICE. When a person is granted bail, one or several third parties must act as a surety for him. Effectively, if the bailed person defaults, the sureties will be asked to pay over the amounts they have agreed to be liable for. Thus they will suffer a personal financial loss in the event of default. Clearly this loss would be eliminated if the bailed person paid an equivalent sum to the surety. If such a payment was made and the accused failed to attend court, it would not be possible for him to recover his payment by legal action. **Herman *v.* Jeuchner (1885).**

(f) RESTRAINT OF TRADE. There are many examples which can be quoted under this heading. The majority are of a business nature. Some relate to the sale of a business where the purchaser writes unreasonable terms into the contract – For instance, one which prohibits the vendor from setting up a similar business within say fifty miles of the original place of business within a period of, say, ten years or agreements made between large companies (recognised as the stronger party) and small businesses (recognised as the weaker party), whereby the latter binds itself, by way of a solus agreement, to sell only the products of the large companies. The relationship between major oil companies and petrol stations can be used to illustrate the point:

Esso Petroleum Co. Ltd. *v.* Harper's Garage (Stourport) Ltd. (1967). The defendant owned two garages with attached petrol stations, called, say A and B. For each, there was a solus agreement containing various covenants which related to the plaintiff's products, selling prices, etc. With regards to garage A, the agreement was for a period of just under four and a half years, but for B, it was for twenty one years. Furthermore, the plaintiff advanced £7,000 to Harper's to help it to buy and improve B and, in so doing, took a mortgage over the site. Some thirteen months after taking the advance, Harper's indicated that it wanted to fully repay the loan, but Esso refused. Subsequently, Harper's began to sell V.I.P.

petrol at the two sites and Esso sought an injunction. *Held.* By the House of Lords. The two solus agreements were subjected to the test of "public policy" as related to unreasonable restraints of trade. Although the agreement with regards to garage A was reasonable, with regards to B it was unreasonable – because of the twenty one year time scale. So the agreement relating to B and the accompanying mortgage were invalid.

Cleveland Petroleum Co. Ltd. *v.* Darstone Ltd. (1969)
A garage and petrol station were leased to Cleveland. Cleveland then underleased the site and eventually there was an assignment to the defendant. At the time the assignment was entered into, the defendant challenged the covenant obliging it to sell Cleveland products and Cleveland, in turn, sought an injunction to enforce the company to observe the covenants. *Held.* By the Court of Appeal. The injunction was granted. Denning, in arriving at his decision made the following comment: 'it seems plain to me that in three at least of the speeches of their Lordships, a distinction is taken between a man who is already in possession of the land before he ties himself to an oil company and a man who is out of possession and is let into it by an oil company. If an owner in possession ties himself for more than five years (Note: This time period was quoted in the Monopolies Commission Report on the Supply of Petrol (1965)) to take all his supplies from one company, that is an unreasonable restraint of trade and is invalid. But, if a man, who is out of possession, is let into possession by the oil company on the terms that he is to tie himself to that company, such a tie is good.

Alec Lobb (Garages) Ltd. *v.* Total Oil G.B. Ltd (1985)
Total provided an advance to Lobb to enable it to develop a site and, as part of the overall agreement, Lobb agreed to sell Total products for twenty one years. As the company was already in occupation of the site, the agreement was subject to the rules relating to restraint of trade. *Held.* By the High Court. The agreement was unenforceable because it exceeded the time period of five years (see above case). The Court of Appeal rejected this decision, saying each case must be judged on its own merits (rather than on a policy basis) and, in any case, the House of Lords, in the Esso Petroleum case, had said that the five year restriction could be extended provided there was "economic necessity" for an extended duration. In the current circumstances, Lobb had benefitted from Total's financial injection in the sense that it could continue to trade. Also, the agreement had provided for reviews after seven and fourteen years. In view of the consideration afforded by Total, the twenty one year period was considered to be reasonable.

Finally, further examples can be seen in the employer/employee relationship, and two of a sporting nature are:

Eastham *v*. Newcastle United (1964)
At the time of the case, the soccer club, in accordance with Football Association rules, operated a "retain and transfer" system. The essence of the system was that:

1. A player could be retained by a club, even though his contract had been determined.
2. Following determination, a player could be debarred from playing for another club whilst at the same time, there was no obligation on the existing club to retain him.
3. Although the player could be put on the transfer list, he could only be released if the purchasing club were prepared to pay a stipulated fee for him.

George Eastham took the club to court as these rules were strictly being applied against him and he believed them to be unreasonable. *Held.* The clauses represented an unreasonable restraint of trade, and were therefore legally invalid and unenforceable.

> *Note:* The aftermath of this decision was that players were given the freedom to negotiate new contracts as soon as the previous ones expired. This eventually led to exhorbitant transfer fees and high wages and almost certainly is one of the main reasons why many clubs in the lower divisions are in a precarious financial position.

A similar, but not identical problem arose in the late 1970s in cricket. At that time, many of the world's leading players agreed to compete in a series for Kerry Packer (who owned a T.V. station) in Australia. The players who took part in the series were subsequently banned from representing their countries in test cricket by the International Cricket Committee – but this action was held to be unreasonable and illegal. **Greig *v*.Insole (1978)**.

FORM OF A CONTRACT

As a general rule, there are no set formalities needed to create a valid contract in English Law. However, certain contracts are unenforceable unless created in a particular way. The various methods of creation are:

(a) *Execution by Deed; or*
(b) *Execution in writing; or*
(c) *Evidenced by writing; or*

(d) *Orally*.

Types a, b and c have the benefit of greater certainty and are less likely to lead to disputes.

(a) EXECUTION BY DEED

The following contracts, if they are to be valid, must be executed by Deed, i.e. they must be signed, sealed and delivered.

1. The creation of a lease where the term of years exceeds three years.
2. The transfer of all or some of the shares in a British ship.
3. The transfer of title to land.

(b) EXECUTION IN WRITING

Unless executed in writing, the following contracts will be void.

1. Bills of Exchange, cheques and promissory notes (Bills of Exchange Act, 1882).
2. Contracts of marine insurance: s. 22 Marine Insurance Act, 1906.
3. Acknowledgements of statute barred debts: Limitation Act, 1980.
4. Transfer of shares in a public company: Companies Act, 1985.
5. Assignment of copyright: Copyright Act, 1956.
6. Hire purchase agreements: originally by the Hire Purchase Act,1965.
7. Money lending transactions: originally by the Moneylenders Act, 1927.

For items 6 and 7, and any consumer credit-transaction, the contract is unenforceable against the debtor or hirer without a court order unless it is evidenced in writing and properly executed – s. 61 and s. 189(4) Consumer Credit Act, 1974.

It can be seen that all the above are provided for by statute.

(c) EVIDENCED IN WRITING

Some contracts are unenforceable if they cannot be proved by written evidence. This evidence may take the form of a simple note or memorandum which has been signed by the person giving it or his agent. The extent to which written evidence is needed is provided for by statute. The following are two examples.

1. Contracts of Guarantee – s. 4 Statute of Frauds, 1677.
2. Contracts for the sale or other disposition of land – s. 40 Law of Property Act, 1925.

GUARANTEES

When originally written, s. 4 Statute of Frauds, 1677, provided that no action could be bright on six types of contract unless they had been evidenced in writing and signed by the party giving it, or his agent. Today the only type of contract to which this rule applies is a guarantee.

DEFINITION

A guarantee is defined as "a written promise by one person (guarantor) to be responsible for the debt, default or miscarriage of another person (principal debtor) incurred to a third party (creditor)": s. 4 Statute of Frauds, 1677.

Note: The words in brackets are for guidance only and do not form part of the statutory definition.

FORM

Guarantees, like any other types of contract, do not have to be in any particular form but they are unenforceable in law unless evidenced in writing and signed by the guarantor (the giver of the promise) or a duly appointed agent.

Note: To ensure that a guarantee is enforceable, a creditor should insist that the guarantor or duly appointed agent signs one of his own written forms in the presence of the creditor.

DISTINCTIONS BETWEEN GUARANTEES AND INDEMNITIES

1. By signing a guarantee, a guarantor promises to be collatorally answerable for the debt, default or miscarriage which the principal debtor owes to the creditor. From this statement it is seen that there are three parties to a guarantee. If the principal debtor, who has primary liability, does not perform what he has agreed to, the guarantor, who has secondary liability, will be requested to do so on his behalf. Effectively, if a guarantor is being responsible for a debt, he is saying "If he (as debtor) does not pay, I (as guarantor) will."

This should be compared with an indemnity where there are only two parties. Here, the person giving the indemnity (the indemnifier) assumes primary liability at the onset. Thus, the indemnifier undertakes immediate liability himself, rather than becoming liable only if the debtor defaults. Effectively, when an indemnifier says he is being responsible for a debt, he is saying "I (as indemnifier) will see that you (as creditor) are paid."

2. As a guarantee is provided for in s. 4 Statute of Frauds, 1677, it must be evidenced in writing to make it enforceable. Indemnities are not provided for by this statute and as such need not necessarily be in writing – although often they are because the indemnifier wants to expressly know the nature and extent of his liability.

It is for this reason that an oral guarantee is not enforceable, but an oral indemnity is. If an oral promise results in litigation, then the courts must decide whether the promise given was a guarantee or indemnity, for only in the latter case will there be a legally enforceable liability. **Mountstephen *v.* Lakeman (1871)**.

SALE OR OTHER DISPOSITIONS OF LAND

Although originally provided for by s. 4 Statute of Frauds, this is now regulated by s. 40 Law of Property Act, 1925, which states "no action may be brought upon any contract for the sale or other disposition of land or any other interest in land, unless the agreement upon which such an action is brought or some memorandum or note thereof is in writing and signed by the party to be charged, or some other person thereunto by him lawfully authorised".

This updated provision is a wide one, covering not only the transfer of freehold or leasehold estates (see Property chapter) but also the letting of sporting rights and taking of water from wells.

REQUIREMENTS OF A MEMORANDUM (OR NOTE)

Although the written memorandum need not be completed at the time the contract is made it must have been brought into existence by the time any legal action is initiated. The essential requirements are:

1. CONTENT

Although it is not essential for the full agreement to be set down in writing, it is essential to have a note or memorandum of the agreement, which contains all the material terms of the contract: **Hawkins *v.* Price (1947)**. As a minimum the requirements are:

(a) The names or adequate descriptions of the parties. For the latter oral evidence may be needed to establish the true identity of the party. **Carr *v.* Lynch (1900)**.

(b) A description of the subject matter together with the material terms. It should be remembered that each individual set of circumstances needs to be carefully examined in order to decide which terms are material and which are immaterial – thus which should be included in the memorandum and those which need not.

(c) A consideration clause must appear – although, for guarantees, it is not essential for such a clause to be contained in the memorandum, s. 3 Mercantile Law Amendment Act, 1856.

2. SIGNATURE

It is essential for the person who is agreeing to be liable, or his duly appointed agent to sign the memorandum. Signature in this context has a very wide interpretation – which may include printing, typing, stamping or initials and need not appear at the foot of the document.

Furthermore, the document actually relied upon as a memorandum need not have been specifically prepared as a memorandum. For, in the past, the courts have accepted the following for the purposes of evidence:

(a) A telegram,
(b) A recital in a will,
(c) A letter written to a third party.

THE JOINDER OF SEVERAL DOCUMENTS

It is not necessary for the note of memorandum to be contained in a single document. Oral evidence may be admitted to connect separate documents provided:

(a) There is sufficient reference, express or implied, that there is more than one document and one refers to the other.

(b) A sufficiently clear memorandum results when the separate documents are read together.

(c) The memorandum contains the signature of the party being charged (or his agent).

Pearce *v.* Gardner (1897)

The defendant agreed to sell Pearce some gravel, but the contract was breached. In court Pearce produced a letter signed by Gardner which evidenced a contract. However nowhere in the letter was Pearce's name specifically mentioned and, furthermore the letter began "Dear Sir". Fortunately Pearce had retained the envelope which had contained the letter clearly showing that it had been addressed to him. *Held.* The letter and envelope were considered as a memorandum within the provisions of the Statute of Frauds, 1677.

Timmins *v.* Moreland Street Property Limited (1958)

The defendant agreed to buy a property from the plaintiff and gave him a 10% deposit in the form of a cheque payable to the plaintiff's solicitors. The plaintiff gave a receipt for the cheque, but the cheque was subsequently stopped and the contract repudiated by the defendant. Timmins sued for breach of contract claiming that the deposit receipt and cheque signed by the defendant was a sufficient memorandum – in the absence of the contract having been reduced to a memorandum in accordance with s. 40 Law of Property Act, 1925. *Held.* The action failed because the Court of Appeal decided that there was nothing to connect the receipt issued by the plaintiff to the cheque made payable to the firm of solicitors.

In contrast, the Privy Council in **Elias *v.* George Sahely & Co. (1982)** decided that, in the circumstances of this case, two separate documents could be linked together to form an adequate memorandum. The separate documents consisted of:

(a) a letter, containing all material terms of the underlying transaction – but, unfortunately, it had not been signed by the defendant; and,

(b) a deposit receipt, which although it did not bear a cross-reference to the letter, made provision as follows: "Received from Fauzi Elias, the sum of $39,000 being deposit on property at Swan St., Bridgetown agreed to be sold be George Sahely & Co. Barbados to Fauzi Elias and/or his nominees.'

CONTRACTS NOT EVIDENCED IN WRITING WHICH SHOULD BE

THE DOCTRINE OF PART PERFORMANCE

This is a doctrine which applies only to contracts relating to land. It evolved in equity and is used by the courts to prevent one party to a contract using the Statute of Frauds as a basis of fraud, e.g. by saying a contract is unenforceable because it was not evidenced in writing although it should have been. For by s. 40(2), Law of Property Act, 1925, if one party has performed his part of an agreement, the other party can be forced to perform his, even if the agreement has not been evidenced in writing.

This provision also applies if the one party has only performed part of what he has agreed to do. In these circumstances, the court, at its discretion, may order specific performance against the other. This order will only be made when:

(a) The contract is one for which specific performance can be granted.

(b) Adequate oral evidence is available to establish that a contract had been entered into and what its terms were.

(c) The act of part performance was carried out by the plaintiff – not by a third party.

(d) It would amount to fraud if the defendant was allowed to take advantage of the fact that the contract had not been reduced to writing: **Rawlinson *v.* Ames (1925)**.

(e) The act of part performance exclusively relates to the contract to be enforced: **Chaproniere *v.* Lambert (1917)**. In some situations, if this strict rule was applied it could lead to injustice – which would thus conflict with this equitable remedy. Today a more flexible approach is used and it has been sufficient to establish that part performance related to some contract which was consistent with the contract the plaintiff claimed existed: **Kingswood Estate Co. Limited *v.* Anderson (1962)** and **Steadman *v.* Steadman (1973)**.

Notes: (1) The payment of money is never a sufficient act of part performance.

(2) Where an agreement has been made which is subject to contract, an action for specific performance will fail: **Cohen *v.* Nessdale Ltd (1981)**. Here, someone agreed to take a lease by way of assignment. At that time, even though the agreement was subject to contract, a ground rent payment was made. *Held.* Although the payment of the ground rent was an act of part performance, the remedy of specific performance was unavailable because the agreement at that time was subject to contract.

These principles may be applied to the facts of the following cases:

Wakeham *v.* Mackenzie (1968)
Mrs Wakeham, a widow, gave up her council house to look after Mr Ball an elderly person, who was in poor health. He promised orally to give her his house upon his death. While Mr Ball was alive, the widow made payments for household expenses, and was paid no remuneration. *Held.* She acted in accordance with the agreement even though it had not been evidenced in writing. As this was considered to be an act of part performance she was entitled to have the property conveyed into her name following Ball's death.

Dickinson *v.* Barrow (1904)
An oral contract was agreed for the purchase of a house. In the process of its construction, the purchaser requested various alterations and additions, but following the completion of the work, he refused to buy the house. *Held.* His actions constituted part performance and thus he was compelled to buy.

Maddison *v.* Alderson (1883)
A farmer promised to leave his housekeeper a life interest in his farm upon his death, provided she would continue to work for him without wages. He later made a will along these lines, but after his death, his will was declared void. The woman looked to the doctrine of part perform-

ance as a remedy. *Held.* There were many reasons why a housekeeper might work without wages (e.g. if she was destitute, or a mistress, etc.), and thus her claim for part performance was unsuccessful.

Note: In view of the decision in **Williams & Glyn's Bank *v.* Boland (1981)** and **Williams & Glyn's Bank *v.* Brown (1981)** see page 205, this case would no doubt be decided differently today.

UBERRIMAE FIDEI

The literal translation of these latin words is "of the utmost good faith" and is a highly relevant consideration in the law of contract. For as explained below, certain types of contract are uberrimae fidei (e.g. contracts of insurance), whilst others are not (e.g. contracts of guarantee). The distinction is important, for non-disclosure of a material fact will render the former category of contract void at the option of the injured party (because non-disclosure is considered to be bad faith). In contrast with the latter group, such contracts will not be rendered void by non-disclosure (because non-disclosure, here, is not considered to be bad faith).

CONTRACTS UBERRIMAE FIDEI

(a) INSURANCE

Non-disclosure by the insured of a material fact will enable the insurer to void the contract if he so desires. This situation is rarely met in practice because when someone applies for any type of insurance (e.g. for a car, house or life policy), he is usually asked to complete a comprehensive proposal form, and then sign the form as confirmation of its accuracy. The questions on such proposal forms are wide ranging and usually include a general question such as "is there any other information which may affect the validity of the policy?" Because of this, it is usually as the result of a lie by the proposer rather than silence by him that an insurer will attempt to void the contract, e.g. a person who has been banned from driving, when completing a car insurance proposal form states that he has a clean driving licence. This is a clear example of bad faith. But in other situations, the occurrence of bad faith is not so obvious – for by silence or answering no, an act of bad faith could be committed:

Locker and Woolf Ltd *v.* Western Australian Insurance Co. Ltd (1936)
In answering the question "has this or any other insurance of yours been declined by any other company?", relating to an application for fire insurance, the answer given was "no". In actual fact, the same insurance

company had previously declined to insure some of the plaintiff's cars. *Held*. By the Court of Appeal. This was non-disclosure of a material fact and entitled the insurance company to void the fire insurance policy. A similar decision was made in **Woolcott *v*. Excess Insurance Company Ltd and others (1978)** where an applicant failed to advise the insurance company that he had a criminal record.

Finally, if the assured disregards the terms of the contract of insurance after it has been agreed, this will amount to bad faith and thus the contract can be avoided: **London Assurance *v*. Mansel (1879)**.

There are other situations in which the doctrine of uberrimae fidei may be applied and these are summarised below.

(b) ISSUING SHARES IN A COMPANY UNDER A PROSPECTUS

Under the provisions of the Companies Act, 1985, a company (or its promoters) are obliged to disclose certain details when issuing shares by prospectus. Where this information is not provided, or is inaccurate, those responsible will be liable in damages. However, if the reason for non-disclosure was an honest mistake, or it was immaterial, there will be no liability.

(c) SALE OF LAND

When a sale is being effected, the vendor is obliged to advise the purchaser of any known defects in title and also the existence of any restrictive covenants.

(d) PARTNERSHIPS

If one partner becomes aware of any matter which will affect the operation of the partnership business, he should immediately make it known to his fellow partners.

EXAMPLES OF CONTRACTS NOT UBERRIMAE FIDEI

The majority of contracts cannot be avoided even though one party has failed to advise the other of certain details. This rule applies even if it is known or suspected that the other party is under a misapprehension, e.g. A jeweller offers to sell Mrs B a ring. Mrs B is under a misapprehension (although Mrs B does not communicate this to the jeweller) that it contains a high quality diamond and is set in gold and as a consequence offers £400 for it. In fact it is a ring which is of plate gold and contains a low grade diamond and has an approximate value of £50. At one time, such a contract would be binding on the purchaser (unless the seller had made statements which were misrepresentations) because the maxim of "caveat emptor" would be applied. However, today private consumers are given certain statutory protections against transactions like this – Supply of Goods (Implied Terms) Act, 1973, and Sale of Goods Act, 1979, and redress would normally be available.

Besides such consumer transactions, guarantees are also contracts which are not uberrimae fidei. This was established many years ago and many precedents can be used to support this viewpoint: **Hamilton *v.* Watson (1845), Westminster Bank *v.* Cond (1940), National Provincial Bank Ltd *v.* Glanusk (1913), Royal Bank of Scotland *v.* Greenshields (1914)** and finally **Cooper *v.* National Provincial Bank Ltd (1945)**.

In the final case, Cooper gave two guarantees to secure a customer's bank account. When the bank, at a later date attempted to enforce the guarantee against him he said that a guarantee was a contract uberrimae fidei and so the bank, at the time it was being taken, should have disclosed to him that:

(a) The account holder's husband was an undischarged bankrupt.

(b) The husband had authority to draw on the account holder's account. *Held*. These were "normal" happenings which fall within the banker/customer relationship and, as such, the bank was under no duty to disclose them – unless specifically asked a question on the matter.

DURESS AND UNDUE INFLUENCE

When a person is induced into entering a contract through the pressure of another, the court will refuse to enforce the contract. Pressure in the context of this statement may be divided into:

DURESS

Here, pressure is in the form of violence or threat of violence or the seizure of property. Such pressure may be directed at the party who is entering into the contract or someone so close to him (e.g. his spouse) that it is considered to be equivalent to the party himself: **Welch *v.* Cheesman (1974)**.

It is debateable whether contracts entered into under duress are void or merely voidable. The later interpretation appears to be the most widely acceptable one, and this is particularly so, in view of the Privy Council's decision in **Barton *v.* Armstrong (1975)** – Here it was held that dispositions under duress were considered to be the equivalent to dispositions under fraudulent misrepresentation – and, as the latter type are voidable contracts, so must the former be.

More recently, the courts have stated that contracts can be voidable because of the economic duress: **North Ocean Shipping Co. Ltd. *v.* Hyundai Construction Co. Ltd (1979)**. The defendant agreed to build a shipping vessel for the plaintiff for just under thirty one million U.S. dollars, the sum to be paid in five instalments. After the first instalment had been paid, the value of the dollar fell and the defendant indicated that it would only proceed with the construction if the plaintiff agreed to pay a further ten per cent on the four outstanding instalments. The increase was agreed, but about eight months after the vessel had been delivered to it, the plaintiff sought to recover the additional ten per cent that had been paid. *Held.* Although the increase had originally been voidable because of economic duress, the right to rescission was lost because:

(a) The price increase had been supported by consideration (because instructions were given to increase the stage payments of the documentary credit through which the instalments fell due for payment. This action constituted something which was over and above the provisions in the original contractual agreement and was, thus, consideration); and,

(b) The contract had been affirmed due to the long time delay in commencing an action for reimbursement.

UNDUE INFLUENCE

This is a less strong form of pressure whereby one party has the power to mentally guide or subtly influence the other, thereby preventing him from exercising his own free will. In law, there are certain relationships where it will be presumed (parent/child, solicitor/client, guardian/ward, trustee/beneficiary, religious adviser/disciple and doctor/patient), even though this may not actually occur. In any of these relationships, the second named party, as the weaker person, may consider such contracts voidable at his option. If a legal action results, the onus of responsibility falls on the first named party, as the stronger one, to show that he did not influence the other in order to get him to enter into the contract. This could be proved, if say the stronger party had ensured that the weaker party took independent legal advice before signing the contract and the weaker party had consulted his own solicitor.

With regard to the parent/child relationship, then it is usual for the presumption of undue influence to be terminated when either the child attains the age of eighteen, or becomes married. In special circumstances (e.g. where a child provides security for advances to a parent even though taking legal advice from either the parent's or the finance company's solicitor), undue influence can still apply: **Lancashire Loans Ltd *v.* Black (1934).**

There are other types of relationship for which undue influence will not be presumed, e.g. husband/wife. However, it could be proved as a matter of fact, but the onus of responsibility is on the weaker party to prove that he or she had been influenced: **Williams *v* Bayley (1866)**.

When assessing the facts of a case in a legal action, the court will attempt to establish if the transaction resulted in one party gaining an unfair advantage over another, a principle discussed many years ago in **Allcard *v.* Skinner (1887)**. Where this cannot be established, a claim for undue influence will fail: **National Westminster Bank *v.* Morgan (1985)**. But, where undue influence is proved, the underlying contract can be voided: **Kingsnorth Trust Ltd *v.* Bell and others (1986).**

Recently the courts have had to consider the "inequality of bargaining power" of the respective parties. One relationship in which this arises is between banker and customer. For it has been held that the relationship between the parties is one of trust and confidence, and if the customer looks to the bank for advice (which many elderly people would do) and this is not given, then the contract (guarantee, mortgage, etc), between banker and customer can be voided at the option of the customer: **Lloyds Bank Ltd *v.* Bundy (1974).** The point about "inequality" was also considered in **Clifford Davis Management *v.* W.E.A. Records (1975)**, where a pop group was induced into giving an assignment of copyright for music that they would subsequently compose up to a certain future time. Because of the inequality of the bargaining power of the pop group, the contract was voidable at their option.

CONTENTS OF A CONTRACT

Even when a valid contract has been made, it will, on occasions be necessary to establish the extent of the obligations of the parties.

The first point to be decided upon is what terms have been expressly included in the contract. Clearly, it is better if all the terms of a contract have been expressed in a written form, but this may not always be so. As a consequence, the courts from time to time will have to look to custom, statute or the oral statements of the respective parties in order to give the agreement business efficacy or to include terms which the parties have overlooked by inadvertence from the written agreement.

1. EXPRESS TERMS

In general, there is no set form for a contract. Thus it can be wholly in writing, wholly by word, partly by word and partly in writing.

(a) ORAL CONTRACTS
When a contract has been made by word of mouth, if litigation results, it is necessary for the parties to state what they previously said, as a matter of evidence before the court. It is clear that major problems will arise if the evidence of the respective parties is conflicting and it is the task of the court to decide, from what had been said, what had been agreed.

(b) WRITTEN CONTRACTS
If a contract is wholly in writing, it is a simple matter to see what was agreed. Occasionally, the words of the contract may need interpreting, or it may be necessary to decide whether a stated term is a condition or warranty (see later). Again it is the task of the courts to do this.

PAROL EVIDENCE RULE

Generally, it can be said that parol (or extrinsic) evidence cannot be admitted to vary or contradict any written contract or deed. **Henderson v. Arthur (1907)**. But it may be used to establish a trade custom or usage, or where the court is of the opinion that the written agreement does not constitute the full contract: **Quickmaid Rental Services v. Reece (1970)**.

It can also be used to show that while, on the face of it, a document purports to act as a valid and immediately enforceable contract, there had been a previous agreement to only allow it to operate once a specified event had taken place, and this had not yet happened. **Pym v. Campbell (1856)**.

2. IMPLIED TERMS

There is a general presumption that the parties have expressed orally or in writing, every material term which they intend should govern their contracts. However, there may also be terms which have not been expressed by the parties, but are inferred by law. Both express and implied terms are binding to the same extent. There are three occasions when the court will infer a term:

(a) *To give an agreement business efficacy.*
(b) *To apply trade custom to an agreement.*
(c) *To apply statute to an agreement.*

TERMS IMPLIED TO GIVE THE AGREEMENT BUSINESS EFFICACY

A term may be implied by the court to give a contract business efficacy even though the contract is complete and enforceable as it stands. This is illustrated in:

The Moorcock (1889)
Although it was a third party who owned a river bed, the respondents made used of a wharf and jetty and they also owned a steamship called Moorcock. There was an agreement between the two parties that the ship could be discharged and loaded at the wharf. However at low tide one day, the ship rested on the river bed and was damaged. *Held.* Although the appellants had never been given a warranty that the ship would not be damaged by the sea bed, it was decided by the Court of Appeal that the warranty was implied. Thus, they were liable for damages.

The above case illustrates how the courts will, through necessity, give business efficacy to a transaction. In so doing, an attempt will be made to look at the position from the viewpoint of "the man in the street" and what he would presume the respective parties would have agreed. It has been seen, though, that some cases are very complex and, with some of these, terms have beem implied by law rather than by facts: **Liverpool City Council *v.* Irwin (1977)**. In this case, Denning had suggested that a term should be implied not only where it was necessary to do so, but also where it was just and reasonable to do so. This latter suggestion does not appear to have been approved either at that time or subsequent to it being made, as can be seen from the Court of Appeal's decision in **Mears *v.* Safecar Security (1982)**. Here, a decision had been made about whether or not wages should be paid to an employee during a period of sickness. Although it was considered reasonable to imply that such a provision would be included in a contract of service, it was not strictly necessary to do so and the action failed.

Implied terms, in a contract of service, were also considered in **Lister *v.* Romford Ice and Cold Storage Co. Ltd (1957)** (see the Chapter on Tort) and more recently, by the Court of Appeal in **Janata Bank *v.* Ahmed (1981)**. Here, an assistant bank manager allowed a relatively new customer to draw cheques which took his account balance to about £5,000 in overdraft. The customer provided the bank with an hotel address and, when the account became dormant, all efforts to trace the customer failed. The bank sued its assistant manager. *Held.* There was an implied term in an employee's contract of service that he would carry out his duties in a competent way. As this had not happened here, the action for damages succeeded.

TERMS IMPLIED BY CUSTOM

Although certain terms may not have been expressly mentioned, a contract may be subject to terms that are sanctioned by custom whether commercial or otherwise.

An example of an implied term sanctioned by custom occurs in **Hutton *v.* Warren (1836)**

A tenant was given notice to quit a farm, which he continued to cultivate until leaving. Upon leaving, he asked the landlord for a fair allowance for the seeds planted and his labour, and it proved necessary to bring an action for payment. *Held.* The outgoing tenant's action was successful, for there was a custom by which the tenant was bound to continue farming for the whole of his tenancy and upon quitting was entitled to a fair allowance for seeds and labour.

Note: Such customary terms can be expressly waived in the contract.

TERMS IMPLIED BY STATUTE

Certain statutes provide for the implication of terms in a contract, e.g. furnished accommodation, which is let, must be fit for human habitation: Defective Premises Act, 1972.

Over the past century, various statutes have been passed in an attempt to protect consumers and the pace has gathered momentum over the recent past by statutes such as Supply of Goods (Implied Terms) Act, 1973, Consumer Credit Act, 1974, and Sale of Goods Act, 1979, all becoming law. The provisions of an earlier statute (which today forms part of the Sale of Goods Act, 1979) were applied in:

Beale *v.* Taylor (1967), whereby it was held that goods should correspond to a description of them.

Godley *v.* Perry (1960), whereby if goods are sold by sample, the bulk should correspond with the sample.

Finally, by implication today, any goods sold in a shop must be of merchantable quality.

CONTRACTS – PARTLY IN WRITING, PARTLY ORAL

To exclude the oral element of a contract in such cases would clearly be unfair to one of the parties. But the basic problem for the courts to resolve is one of intention, and it is up to them to decide whether the parties have or have not restricted their agreement wholly to the terms expressed in writing. **Malpas *v.* London and South Western Railway Company (1866), Hutton *v.* Warren (1836).**

TERMS AND REPRESENTATIONS

While two people are negotiating a contract, they will both make a series of statements. Some of these statements will eventually become terms of the contract and will usually be expressly provided for in a written form although they may remain oral statements. As part of the contract, some of the terms will be considered to be conditions (see later) and a breach of them will entitle the injured party to treat the contract as discharged. In contrast some will be considered as warranties, and a breach of them will not allow the injured party to treat the contract as being discharged but will entitle him to claim for damages. There are other groups of statements that are made during the negotiating stage which may be described as representations. These are fully described below, but may be briefly described as inducements to get the other party to enter into the contract. Provided the representations are true, then it would be pointless for the other party to aim to seek legal redress, but where such statements are false, they are described as misrepresentations and in these circumstances, legal remedies may be available to the injured party. The three types of misrepresentation and the remedies available for each are described later in this chapter.

REPRESENTATIONS

A representation may be described as a statement made by the representer which has the effect of inducing one party (the representee) into entering a contract. If, as a consequence of the contract, the representee suffers damage, the court may consider the statement to have been not a representation but a misrepresentation. The statement itself must relate to some past event or present material fact and be made by a party to the contract or his agent with the effect that it induces the other party to enter into the contract. The statement may be made orally, in writing, by conduct and in special instances by silence. If the representee considers that the statement was a misrepresentation, he may pursue one of the remedies described later, but the action will not be successful if it be established that the statement was:

(a) One of Law – for everyone is deemed to know the law.
(b) One of opinion.
(c) One of future conduct or intention although there is an exception to this. For a statement of intention may contain within itself a representation of an existing fact. For example, a company may wish to raise money by an issue of debentures, and the directors may represent that the money so raised will be used for a particular purpose (e.g. extending the factory). If the real objective of raising the money is to pay off pressing creditors, then the directors will be held to have misrepresented this situation and be personally liable: **Edgington *v.* Fitzmaurice (1885).**
(d) A marketing term (otherwise known as a "trade puff"). When

interpreting words under this heading care should be exercised. For descriptions such as "best in the country", or "as good as" are not considered as representations. In contrast, a description such as "95% gold content" is, and if the latter is untrue, it is a misrepresentation.

(e) Not made by the representer or his duly appointed agent.

(f) Not relied upon by the representee.

(g) Never made, i.e. because the representer remained silent. Generally silence will not be held to be a misrepresentation (e.g. when a guarantee is being taken, for such contracts are not uberrimae fidei), but in some circumstances it will. A good example is where a contract of life assurance is being negotiated. For the proposer (the person asking for life assurance cover) misstates or does not disclose some material fact (e.g. he is suffering from a terminal cancer) at the time the contract is being negotiated, the contract can be avoided at the option of the injured party (i.e. the assurance company).

The way in which the courts apply some of the general rules (a) to (f) above can be seen by looking at the courts' decisions in each of the following legal cases and the reason why that decision was reached:

Bannerman *v.* White (1861)
When negotiating the purchase of hops, White made it clear that he would buy none if sulphur had been used to cultivate them. Bannerman said that sulphur had not been used and the sale proceeded on this basis. Later, White discovered that sulphur had been used and refused to pay the agreed rate for the hops which had been provided for in the contract. *Held.* The assurance about the sulphur was a good defence against the action by the plaintiff for the payment of the full contract price.

Routledge *v.* Mckay (1954)
The parties were both private persons who met on two occasions to discuss the sale of a motorbike. When they first met, the defendant innocently stated that the bike was a 1942 model. When they next met, a contract of sale was produced which did not refer to the bike's age (although it was later discovered that it was a 1930 model). *Held.* The earlier statement was a mere representation as the interval between the two dates was wide. Thus, the plaintiff's claim failed.

Oscar Chess Ltd *v.* Williams (1957)
When Williams bought a new car in 1955, he used his original car in part exchange. He described it as a 1948 model, and produced the registration book as proof. The garage allowed him £290 on the original car – an amount obtained from Glass's Guide. Some eight months later, the garage discovered that, in fact, it was a 1939 model, and had they known

this they would have offered only £175. Thus, they sued for the difference. *Held.* In equity, the claim may have succeeded, but for the eight month time lag. The plaintiff had to prove breach of warranty, but he was unable to do this and his action failed. It was suggested that because of their superior knowledge, the garage should have noted the engine and chassis numbers and written to the manufacturers asking them to quote the date of construction.

Porter *v.* General Guarantee Corporation and Another (1981)
Porter bought a car from a second-hand car dealer and indicated it would be used as a taxi-cab. The dealer indicated that one car, Porter was considering, was in excellent mechanical condition. As a consequence, Porter bought it, and the deal was financed by a hire purchase company. The car subsequently proved to be unreliable, so Porter repudiated the contract with the hire purchase company and they in turn sought indemnity against the dealer. *Held.* The statement about the car was a term of the contract and the term had been breached. Thus, the plaintiff's claim was successful and the hire purchase company could seek recovery from the dealer.

CLASSIFICATION OF MISREPRESENTATIONS AND AVAILABLE REMEDIES

Misrepresentations may be classified under three headings. Each of these is described below and a simple illustration is given to explain each type. Although there are a range of remedies available to the representee (and these are described in the next section), the only one referred to below is damages. But, this is only available at the discretion of the court.

INNOCENT

These are statements which, at the time they were made, were believed to be true. For example, if a car salesman says to a potential purchaser that the boot space in the particular model he is describing is four cubic feet (because all previous models had this amount of space), but the manufacturer recently reduced the space to 3·9 cubic feet and at that time had not notified the garage of the change, the representation would be considered as innocent. In these circumstances, if the person bought the car, a claim for damages may be made in accordance with s. 2(2) Misrepresentation Act, 1967 – although, in view of the small difference involved, this is very unlikely.

NEGLIGENT

These are statements which, at the time they were made by the representer, were believed to be true, but were given negligently. For example, if a car salesman said to a potential purchaser that the car he is describing will accelerate from 0 to 60 m.p.h. in six seconds, when in actual fact it would take seven seconds. If this error was made because he did not take the trouble to look the information up in the sales literature, the statement would be considered as negligent. In these circumstances, if the person bought the car, he may claim in accordance with s. 2(1) Misrepresentation Act, 1967. In assessing the level of damages, the courts will attempt to put the injured party back in the position he would have been if the misrepresentation had not been made. As a form of defence, the car salesman (in the above circumstances) would have to try and satisfy the court that at the time he made the statement, he had reasonable grounds for believing it to be true – and, if he can do this, a claim for damages will be unsuccessful.

FRAUDULENT

These are statements which are made dishonestly by the representer and which relate to some material fact. Furthermore, the representer knows that they are false, or believes them to be false: **Derry *v.* Peek (1889)**. For example, if a car salesman's sole objective is to sell a car to a potential purchaser and in achieving this objective makes a series of wild statements which he knows to be untrue, the statements would be considered to be fraudulent. If a purchaser buys the car because of the salesman's statements, the courts may allow the injured party to recover all his loss. The courts assessment of damages is rarely straightforward, as can be seen from the circumstances of:

Doyle *v.* Olby (Ironmongers) Ltd (1969)

Here, Doyle decided to buy a business from the Olby family. Based on certain statements which the family made, such as all the business was conducted over the shop counter, when in fact half the turnover was of a wholesale nature which required the employment of a travelling salesman which Doyle could ill afford to do. Doyle agreed to pay £4,500 for goodwill and fixtures and fittings and £5,000 for stock. When Doyle eventually took over the business, he discovered that some of the statements that had been made to him earlier were false and so he brought an action for damages for fraud. *Held.* The Court of Appeal calculated Doyle's loss on the deal amounted to £5,500 and damages of that figure were awarded.

GENERAL REMEDIES AVAILABLE FOR MISREPRESENTATION

Although it is possible for the representee to affirm a contract which was subject to misrepresentation, it is more likely that he will want to pursue one of the following remedies:

1. To have the contract rescinded. This is available for an action which relates to any type of misrepresentation. It is particularly appropriate to innocent misrepresentation, as the courts rarely award damages (which is discretionary in any case) in these circumstances.
2. To refuse to perform or complete his part of the agreement depending on whether the contract has or has not been started. In these circumstances, if an action is taken against the injured party for specific performance, the misrepresentation can be used in defence.
3. To sue for damages. This remedy is available for all types of misrepresentation and where it has been established that the statement was made fraudulently, then the action is based on the tort of deceit.

The Court of Appeal, in **Chesnau *v.* Interhome Ltd. (1983)** indicated that where an action is commenced, based on s. 2(1) Misrepresentation Act, 1967, damages would be assessed using the same parameters as would be used for assessing damages in tort.

Note: These remedies are fully described later on in this chapter where breach of contract is discussed.

EXAMPLES OF MISREPRESENTATION

IN A COMPANY PROSPECTUS

Subject to certain exceptions, directors and accountants are liable to pay compensation if statements they make in a company prospectus relating to the issue of shares, debentures or loan stock are false.

NO CONTRACTUAL RELATIONSHIP BETWEEN THE PARTIES TO THE ACTION

At one time, if there was no pre-contractual relationship between plaintiff and defendant, this would be a bar to an action for damages. However, at common law, an action may be available where a false statement has been made negligently and a special relationship exists between the two parties as shown in the following case:

Hedley Byrne & Co. Ltd *v.* Heller and Partners Ltd (1963)
The plaintiff (advertising agents) enquired through their bankers the National Provincial Bank as to the respectability, standing and trustworthiness in the way of business to the extent of £100,000 of Easipower

Ltd on whose behalf they were entering into advertising contracts. The following reply was sent by Heller – "For your private use and without responsibility on the part of the bank or its officials; respectably constituted company considered good for its ordinary business engagements. Your figures are larger than we are accustomed to see."

The plaintiff claimed that by relying on what they now regarded as a negligently prepared reply they had lost over £17,000 when Easipower went into liquidation. The court decided that Easipower's financial difficulties were known to Heller when they formulated their reply and this constituted negligence, the reply being insufficiently qualified. Nevertheless, Heller were under no duty imposed by law to exercise care in giving their replies, the duty being only to act **honestly** in so doing. The Court of Appeal and the House of Lords upheld the decision. However, the latter did so on a different basis: that the defendant banker **disclaimed all responsibility at the time they gave the reference.** The House of Lords made it quite clear that any future claim would be upheld if no disclaimer was made and if it could be proved that a reply had been given negligently.

PARTLY TRUE STATEMENTS

If, when a statement was made, it was only partly true and, as a consequence, the wrong overall impression had been created, there may be grounds for a legal action based on misrepresentation even if the contract contains an exclusion clause: **Curtis *v.* Chemical Cleaning & Dyeing Co. (1951)** (see later).

CHANGE OF CIRCUMSTANCES

When a contract is being negotiated, various statements will be made by the respective parties which should truly reflect current circumstances. If these circumstances change between this time and the date that the contract is finally entered into, the person who becomes aware of the changes should advise the other party. If this up to date information is not disclosed, then it is possible for the injured party to have the contract rescinded: **With *v.* O'Flanagan (1936)**. Here the purchase of a medical practice had been agreed on the basis that an income of £2,000 per annum would be created. However, by the time the formal contract had been entered into, the income had fallen to about £500 per annum because the vendor had been ill in the meantime. This information was not made available to the purchaser and by not disclosing the major reduction in income, the vendor had misrepresented the situation and the court held that the contract could be rescinded.

CONSTRUCTIVE FRAUD

This doctrine is somewhat similar to but wider ranging than undue influence (see earlier) and arises in circumstances where one party is in a position to induce another into a certain course of action.

Tate *v.* Williamson (1866)
An undergraduate, who owned a valuable piece of land, was being pressed to repay his debts and he sought the financial advice of Williamson. Williamson's advice was to sell the land – but he did not tell the undergraduate that the land contained mineral deposits and was thus more valuable than land which had no such deposits. He gave the undergraduate an indication of what the land was worth (if it had no mineral wealth) and offered to buy it at that price. The undergraduate agreed to sell at that figure and the title was conveyed on that basis. At a later date, the undergraduate's heir attempted to get the conveyance set aside. *Held.* Williamson had taken advantage of the confidence that was placed in him and was therefore guilty of constructive fraud. The conveyance could therefore be set aside.

BREACH OF CONTRACT

In certain circumstances today, the courts will award damages on the basis of breach of contract. **Davies & Co. (Wines) Ltd *v.* Alfa-Minerva (E.M.I.) Ltd (1974)** and:

Jarvis *v.* Swan Tours Ltd (1973)
Here Jarvis booked a holiday which turned out to be nothing like the description contained in the Tour Company's brochure. Upon return home, Jarvis sued for damages and in the County Court was awarded £31.72 – compared with the full cost of the holiday which amounted to £63.45. Upon appeal, Lord Denning awarded Jarvis £125, because, in Denning's opinion, there had been a breach of contract.

CONDITIONS/WARRANTIES

The law recognises that some terms in a contract are more important than others, and it therefore classifies them into conditions and warranties. A condition is a very important term and goes to the root of the contract. If it is broken, then the injured party may either refuse to continue what he had agreed to do in the contract whereby the contract is discharged, or claim damages but continue with the contract.

A warranty, although a term of the contract, is less important. If it is broken, then the injured party will have to continue with what he had agreed to do, but may be allowed to seek compensation by way of claiming for damages.

The problem which immediately comes to mind is how to decide what is a condition of a contract as opposed to a warranty and who decides this. For, although one party to the contract may consider the term to be a condition, the other may consider it to be a warranty – and it is for this reason that the courts have frequently got to be used to decide on the matter. In coming to their conclusion, the court will have to consider the contract as a whole and any statements that the parties have made. The following legal cases indicate how the courts decide upon this matter:

Bettini *v*. Gye (1876)
An opera singer had agreed to be in London six days before the first performance for rehearsal purposes. Due to an illness, she was delayed and arrived with only three days available for rehearsing. Because she was late, the opera director (the defendant) would not accept her services. *Held.* The period provided for rehearsing in the contract was a warranty and its breach could not discharge the contract. The plaintiff was entitled to damages – but was subject to a counter-claim for damages by the defendant because she had not attended six days of rehearsals.

Poussard *v*. Spiers and Pond (1876)
The plaintiff had agreed to perform in an opera for a given period. But just before the period started, she became ill. The defendants employed a substitute and they had to accept that the substitute would be employed for the complete engagement. When Poussard recovered, she wanted to take over, but the defendant's alternative arrangement meant that this was not possible. As a consequence, Poussard sued for breach of contract. *Held.* As the plaintiff could not perform on the first night, there had been a breach of condition. The contract had been discharged and so the defendants were not liable.

Harling *v*. Eddy (1951)
A heifer (a young cow) was put up for sale by auction. The catalogue listing this and other sale items contained a clause that "no warranties are given regarding animals purchased unless such warranties appeared on the purchaser's account", and was issued to all bidders. When the bidding started for the heifer, little interest was shown until, at the vendor's request, the auctioneer said that there was nothing wrong with the animal and he would be willing to take it back if this proved not to be so. The plaintiff bought the animal, but four months later it died. The plaintiff sued for damages, but the auctioneer looked to the exemption clause in the catalogue as a form of defence. *Held.* In normal circumstances

the action would have been unsuccessful because a statement about the soundness of an animal would be a warranty. But here, there had been a statement about taking the animal back and this meant the statement was a condition, not of the original contract, but of a collateral contract. Thus, the plaintiff's action was successful.

L. Schuler A.G. *v*. Wickham Machine Tool Sales (1973)
A contract had been entered into which gave the defendant the sole right to sell one of the plaintiff's products in the U.K. A clause in the agreement, described as a condition, indicated that a representative of the defendant had to visit six named businesses each week to generate new business. There were weeks when this condition was not satisfied and the plaintiff attempted to rescind the contract. *Held*. Even though the word "condition" had been used here, it would be unreasonable to apply the legal meaning of the word in these circumstances. So it was considered to be a warranty and as such the contract could not be rescinded.

Bunge Corporation *v*. Tradax S.A. (1981)
A term was incorporated into a contract which provided that a buyer of soya bean must give "at least fifteen consecutive days notice of probable readiness of a shipping vessel". On the occasion that led to this legal action, less than fifteen days notice was given and, as the price of soya bean had fallen by U.S. $60 per ton, the seller claimed that there had been a breach of contract and so he would not supply the beans. In the first instance, the matter was referred to arbitration and an award of U.S. $317,500 was made in favour of the seller. In the commercial court, the decision to make an award was reversed, as the "fifteen day" stipulation was considered to be an intermediate term, not a condition. However, both the House of Lords and the Court of Appeal considered the stipulation to be a condition and by failing to comply with it, a breach had occurred. The award of damages was restored, but at a lower figure.

COLLATERAL CONTRACTS

The courts can apply this principle when they consider that a statement is not a term of the main contract but a term of a subsidiary or collateral contract. The principle has been considered in relation to second hand car sales (**Andrews *v*. Hopkinson (1956), Webster *v*. Higgin (1948)**, etc.), and leasehold land (**De Lassalle *v*. Guildford (1901), City and Westminster Properties (1934) Ltd *v*. Mudd (1958)**, etc.) but a good example of how the courts apply the principle is in:

Shanklin Pier Ltd *v.* Detel Products Ltd (1951)
The plaintiff had contracted with a third party who was to paint the pier. However, the specification contained within this contract was changed after a director of the defendant had advised the plaintiff that one of their paint products, if applied to the pier, would last for between seven and ten years. In actual fact the paint only lasted for three months. *Held.* Although the original contract was between the plaintiff and the painting contractor, a collateral contract had been entered into between the plaintiff and the defendant. As the terms of this contract had been breached, the plaintiff's action was successful.

EXEMPTION (OR EXCLUSION) CLAUSES AND LIMITING CLAUSES

INTRODUCTION

For many years, the common law has been familiar with attempts by one party to introduce clauses in a contract which would either exclude (known as exemption or exclusion clauses) or restrict (known as limiting clauses) their liability upon the happening of certain contingencies. As may be expected, there has been much litigation on this area of contract law, and from it, certain general principles relating to such clauses (now, for convenience, referred to solely as exemption clauses) have evolved. These are described below.

(a) THE EXEMPTION CLAUSE MUST BE A PART OF THE CONTRACT

The court must satisfy itself that the document containing the exemption clause is an integral part of the contract. Where the exemption appears on a receipt, then it is not effective – because by then, the contract has been made and it would not be permissible for one party to be allowed to rely on a subsequent clause.

Chapelton *v.* Barry U.D.C. (1940)
Chapelton hired two deck chairs, and when he collected them, the only contractual notice displayed was that of the tariff. An attendant subsequently collected the fee, and issued him two tickets as a form of receipt. He placed them in his pocket, although if he had read the back, he would have read that "the council will not be liable for any accident or damage arising from hire of chairs". Chapelton later sat on one of the chairs, and it collapsed, injuring him. He sued the council for damages. *Held.* The only contractual conditions which could be applied were those on the display notice. There being no exemption clause on the display notice, then that on the receipt was ineffective, and so damages were awarded.

(b) DUE NOTICE OF THE EXEMPTION MUST BE SUITABLY GIVEN BEFORE OR AT THE TIME OF THE CONTRACT

If the exemption clause is to be regarded as part of the contract, the party against whom it is to operate should sign it as confirmation. If it is not signed, then the courts will have to decide if reasonable notice has been given.

Parker *v.* South Eastern Railway Co. (1877)
Parker left his bag (which he valued at £24/10/- together with contents) at a railway station for which he paid a 2d fee. He was issued with a ticket, which on the reverse stated that the railway would not be responsible for items valued in excess of £10. When he returned to collect the bag later in the day, it could not be found. *Held.* The plaintiff was not obliged to read or make himself aware of conditions on the ticket. Because of this, his action succeeded. [The case subsequently passed on to the Court of Appeal, where a retrial was ordered.]

It can be seen here that the time at which the notice is given is of great importance. For, protections afforded by exemption clauses are only effective if brought to the attention of the other contracting party before or at the time the contract is made. A subsequent notice is not binding.

Olley *v.* Marlborough Court Ltd (1949)
Olley paid for her hotel accommodation in advance. Upon arrival she was given her room key and upon entering her room saw a sign which said "The proprietors will not hold themselves responsible for articles lost or stolen unless handed to the manageress for safe custody." Later the room key was returned to the receptionist, and a third party took it and stole some of the plaintiff's furs. Olley sued for loss. *Held.* Olley's action was successful, for the contract was completed at the reception desk. Subsequent notices (here in the bedroom) were of no effect.

Note: If Olley had previously visited the hotel and had seen the notice, her claim would not have been successful: **Spurling *v.* Bradshaw (1956)**.

Thornton *v.* Shoe Lane Parking Ltd (1971)
Thornton sued the owners of a multi-storey car park for physical injuries sustained while on the proprietor's premises. At the entry barrier, the only notice on display was one which said "All cars parked at owner's risk". However, the ticket issued at the barrier made reference to further conditions which were to be found inside the premises – and which exempted liability for physical injury. The plaintiff did not read these, nor had he visited the car park before. *Held.* By the Court of Appeal, the defendants were liable as the only terms which formed part of the contract were those on the notice at the ticket barrier.

(c) HAS THE AGREEMENT BEEN SIGNED BY THE PARTIES?

In normal circumstances, it will be impossible for a party to deny knowledge or awareness of an exemption clause if he has signed an agreement containing such a clause. So, provided he was not induced into signing the agreement by fraud or misrepresentation, he will be bound by it whether he has read it or not.

L'Estrange *v*. Graucob (1934)
A shopkeeper bought a slot machine. When buying it, he signed a sales agreement which contained the following clause in small print "Any express or implied condition, statement or warranty, statutory or otherwise is excluded". As the machine did not work, he sued for damages. *Held.* Even though the shopkeeper did not read the clause, he was bound by it. There had been no misrepresentation and so his action failed.

But, misrepresentation did occur in **Curtis *v*. Chemical Cleaning & Dyeing Co. (1951)**. A lady took her dress, which had beads and sequins on it, to be cleaned. The cleaners made her sign a receipt, and when she asked about the conditions, she was told that certain types of damage, including that to beads and sequins was covered. In actual fact, liability for *any* type of damage was excluded. When the dress was collected, it was seen to have been stained in the cleaning process and, in view of what she had been told, sued the cleaner. *Held.* The cleaner had misrepresented the terms and, because of this, the exclusion clause could not be relied upon by them.

(d) AMBIGUOUS EXEMPTION CLAUSES ARE CONSTRUED AGAINST THE PARTIES INSERTING THEM

Where there is no doubt about the meaning and scope of an exemption clause, the ambiguity will be resolved against the party who inserted it. This is known as the Contra-Proferentem Rule and was applied in:

Hollier *v*. Rambler Motors Ltd (1972)
Mr Hollier had had his car repaired several times by the defendant garage and on each occasion he signed a form which stated "the company is not responsible for damage caused by fires to customers' cars on the premises". On this occasion, he signed no such form, but while in the garage, his car was damaged by a fire caused by the garage's negligence. Mr Hollier sued them for damages, but the garage contended that the exemption clause protected them even though Hollier had not on this occasion signed a formal contract. *Held.* By the Court of Appeal, Hollier's action was successful for it was necessary to have actual knowledge of an implied exclusion clause in a course of dealing. It was also pointed

out that the wording of the exclusion clause that had been used would be no defence against the garage's own negligence.

From this decision, it is clear that a party can only exempt himself from liability in negligence, if the exemption clause is expressed in very clear terms.

(e) BENEFIT OF EXEMPTION CLAUSES UNAVAILABLE TO THIRD PARTIES

Where an exemption clause has been included in a contract, the only persons who are bound by the clause are those who were parties to the original contract. For this reason, third parties are unable to use such clauses to eliminate or reduce their liability.

Scruttons Ltd *v.* Midland Silicones Ltd (1962)
Certain chemicals were shipped to the U.S.A. under a shipping contract which limited claims for damage to the chemicals to £179. When unloading the chemicals, Scruttons, a firm of stevedores employed by the shippers, did £593 of damage through their negligence. They attempted to limit the claim against them to £179. *Held.* As the stevedores were a third party as regards the shipping contract, they could not rely on the limitation clause, and were liable for the full £593.

(f) REPUGNANT EXEMPTION CLAUSES

Where a person contracts to deliver (or do) one thing and in actual fact delivers (or does) another, in law, he has failed to carry out his contractual duty. In circumstances like this, a person may attempt to use an all-embracing exemption clause to eliminate or reduce his liability. If he were allowed to rely on such a clause, clearly his action would be considered repugnant and thus the court would not allow it.

Karsales (Harrow) Ltd *v.* Wallis (1956)
After inspecting a car, Wallis contracted to buy it. The sale contract contained wide ranging exclusion clauses. Later, the same car but with the good tyres replaced by inferior ones and many parts taken from it, was delivered to Wallis' premises. In fact the car was just a shell incapable of self propulsion. Wallis refused to pay for it, and an action was taken against him for breach of contract. *Held.* The "thing" delivered was not the car he had contracted to buy. Thus, the exclusion clause contained in the contract and which he had agreed to be bound by, was ineffective and the action failed.

(g) CONSTRUCTIVE NOTICE OF AN EXEMPTION CLAUSE

Constructive notice of an exemption clause may be considered adequate provided it could be shown that a reasonable person, when reading the contract, would be aware of the existence of the terms and conditions.

Thompson *v.* L.M.S. Railway (1930)
An illiterate person asked her niece to buy her a train ticket. This was issued subject to conditions to be found elsewhere. One of the conditions was exclusion for liability due to injury however caused. Thompson was injured, and as a consequence sued the railway company. *Held.* As she had constructive knowledge, her action failed.

In consumer transactions, constructive notice will not apply where the plaintiff has not given a copy of the conditions of contract or indicated where they can be found, even if there have been previous dealings. See above **Hollier *v.* Rambler Motors Ltd (1972)**.

(h) ACTIONS BEYOND THE TERMS OF THE CONTRACT

Exemption clauses only protect a party if he is acting within the boundaries of the contract. As soon as he acts outside the boundaries, the clauses are ineffective: **Thomas National Transport (Melbourne) Pty Ltd and Pay *v.* May and Baker (Australia) Pty. Ltd. (1966).**

EXEMPTION CLAUSES AND THE DOCTRINE OF FUNDAMENTAL BREACH

When two parties are negotiating a contract, one of them may wish to exclude or limit his liability in the event that certain terms in the contract are either not complied with or not fully complied with. In common law, there was nothing to prevent one party from doing this – For, it would be presumed that both parties would negotiate all the terms of the contract and only when all matters had been decided upon to their mutual satisfaction would the parties enter into a formal contract. As between commercial enterprises, this would be the norm. For each party would normally have experience at negotiating a contractual agreement and, if one or several matters needed clarifying, their respective legal advisers could be consulted. In other circumstances, contracts were being entered into between commercial enterprises and private individuals and the latter invariably lacked negotiating expertise and could ill afford to pay for legal advice. Quite clearly, the latter group needed to be afforded legal protection and, to this end, the courts have adopted a strict approach to exemption or limiting terms. For, today, exemption or limiting clauses are strictly applied against the party who wishes to rely upon them and there is a rigid application where the clause is of an exemption nature. Furthermore, statute, notably the Unfair Contract Terms Act 1977 (the main provisions of which are described later), has been formulated to afford protection to private consumers in certain transactions.

Many reported cases in this area of the law have considered the relationship which exists between the two contracting parties where one has inserted an exemption clause and a fundamental breach has occurred and some of these are reviewed below.

It was in **Suisse Atlantique Société D'Armament Maritime S.A. *v.* N.V. Rotterdamsche Kolen Centrale (1966)** that the doctrine was defined. Here the House of Lords indicated that the principle is not one of law but a matter of construction and can only be decided upon by looking at the whole of the contract. The simple definition of a fundamental breach given by the House of Lords in the "Suisse" case was "a breach by one party entitling the other party to treat the contract as terminated". In this context, "breach" could either mean a fundamental breach of contract or a breach of a fundamental term of the contract. To help the courts decide on the matter and provide a remedy for the injured party the following general rules may be applied:

1. Where the injured party elects to repudiate the contract and thus bring it to an end, then the whole contract (including the exemption clause) is terminated.
2. The same conclusion would be arrived at where the breach brought about an automatic termination of the contract and so the innocent party would never be in a position to repudiate.

Harbutt's Plasticine Ltd *v.* Wayne Tank and Pump Co. Ltd (1970)
The defendant had contracted to install certain equipment in the plaintiff's factory. A clause in the contract provided that the cost of any damage caused by the defendant's employees would be limited to £2,330. In fact, due to the employees' negligence, the whole factory was destroyed. *Held.* The defendants were liable for the full loss because there had been a fundamental breach of contract and thus the limiting clause did not apply.

Note: In view of the decision in the Photo Production case (see later) and the provisions contained in s.9(I) Unfair Contract Terms Act 1977, the Harbutt's case (see above) would not be decided in the same way today. For, if a suitably worded limiting or exemption clause has been included in a contractual agreement and not only satisfies the test of reasonableness, but also covered the possibility of a fundamental breach, it can be relied upon by the party who is in breach.

3. When an exemption clause, if applied, would either lead to absurd-

ity or defeat the main object of the contract, the court has the power to reject it – "Suisse" case.

4. If the injured party is aware that the other party is in breach of contract, but still continues with the contract, any subsequent claim for damages will almost certainly be subject to the exemption clause – and it could be used as a form of defence.

Since the "Suisse" case, various other courts have considered whether or not fundamental breach has occurred. In **Kenyon Son & Craven Ltd *v.* Baxter Hoare Ltd (1971)**, it was held that a fundamental breach could only normally occur when the method of performance was totally different from that contemplated by the contract. Then, in **Wathes (Western) Ltd. *v.* Austins (Menswear) Ltd (1976)**, even though performance had not been totally different, the exemption clause was still struck out. In the same year, Denning indicated that the Court of Appeal would use a "policy" approach in cases like this. Therefore, it would never be possible for a party to rely on an exemption clause in an attempt to escape liability for a fundamental breach. The House of Lords disagreed with this "policy" approach as they propounded in **Photo Production Ltd *v.* Securicor Transport Ltd (1980)**. Here an employee of Securicor, who was on night patrol duty at the plaintiff's factory, dropped an ignited match which started a small fire. The fire spread quickly and soon got out of control and as a consequence £600,000 of damage was caused. The factory owners attempted to recover the loss from Securicor (rather than their insurers) on the basis that they were liable for their employee's actions. But Securicor referred them to an exemption clause in the contract that had been entered into between themselves and the plaintiff whereby they would not be liable for "injurious acts or defaults of any employee". Although the Court of Appeal held that there had been a fundamental breach, and as a matter of policy, the exemption clause had to be struck out, the House of Lords reversed the decision. It was held that where both parties are businesses, then each should read the small print most carefully in an attempt to establish if there are any exclusion clauses, and, if so, the nature of them. Moreover, businesses should insure themselves against business liabilities.

It seems that although the courts will lean heavily against exemption clauses, where such clauses are clear and unambiguous, they will be applied rigidly (as in the 'Photo Production' case). Furthermore, where a clause has been constructed with the objective of limiting liability rather than excluding it altogether, the clause is more likely to prevail, provided the clause passes the test of reasonableness. The two cases described below, indicate how the test of reasonableness has been applied.

George Mitchell (Chesterhall) Ltd. *v*. Finney Lock Seeds Ltd. (1983) Here, the plaintiff ordered a quantity of a specific type of cabbage seed. The defendant sold some seed to it which cost just over two hundred pounds. Because the supplied seed was not that which had been contracted for, the crop was a failure and the plaintiff estimated that he had lost just over £61,000 as a result of being sold the wrong seed. He attempted to recover the amount he had lost even though the remedy provided for in the contractual agreement entitled him to either have defective seed replaced or have his purchase money returned. *Held*. The House of Lords, Court of Appeal and High Court all found for the plaintiff. For, the limiting clause, as constructed;

(1) Did not cover Finney's negligent breach; and,
(2) Was unreasonable in the sense that:
  (a) Finney was solely to blame for not recognising that the wrong seed had been supplied; and,
  (b) The limiting clause was inserted without negotiation between the parties; and,
  (c) Although Mitchell could not insure itself against the type of event that happened, Finney, the supplier, could have done.

An award of almost £100,000 was made by the judge. This was to cover not only the actual loss that had occurred, but also interest. The decision here should be compared with that made by the House of Lords in **Ailsa Craig Fishing Co. Ltd. *v*. Malvern Fishing Co. Ltd. and another (1983).**

A ship sank in Aberdeen harbour on a rising tide and also fouled a neighbouring vessel which also sank. The sunken ships were supposed to have been protected by a Securicor representative in accordance with the provisions of a contract entered into between Securicor and Aberdeen's fishing boat owners association. At the time the ships sank, the patrolman had left his post to join in some New Year festivities. In the hearing, Securicor was a joint defendant. Securicor accepted that it, through its employee, had been negligent. The security company also made it clear that it was not trying to exclude itself from total liability, only to limit it in accordance with the terms of the contract. *Held*. This was a very complex case but, when the natural and plain meaning of the words which constituted the limiting clause was applied, the clause was held to be effective. Hence, recovery was limited to the amount specified in the contract (i.e. £1,000 maximum per vessel), rather than the full loss.

STATUTE AND EXEMPTION CLAUSES

Over the years, many statutes have been written which have sought to prevent the stronger party introducing exemption clauses into a contract which would act to the detriment of the weaker party. Especially over the past 20 years when consumer protection has gathered momentum, these statutory protections have increased – typical examples of statutes where protection has been provided for are:

Misrepresentation Act, 1967
Fair Trading Act, 1973
Supply of Goods (Implied Terms) Act, 1973
Consumer Credit Act, 1974
Unfair Contract Terms Act, 1977

The Unfair Contract Terms Act 1977 concerns itself with the effectiveness of exemption or limiting clauses as related to business liabilities within the provisions of contractual agreements. The main impact of the Act is to afford protection, subject to certain criteria being satisfied, to consumers who enter into a business transaction. For this reason, the majority of the provisions relate to transactions between business customers and consumers rather than between two businesses or two consumers.

The Act provides that, in certain circumstances, any attempt by a business to exclude or limit liability by incorporating appropriate notices or terms in a contract is wholly ineffective. Examples of **notices or terms** which are considered ineffective are where:

(1) death or personal injury results from negligence: s.2(1).
(2) loss or damage arises from defective goods supplied for consumer use caused by either negligence in the manufacture of the goods or distribution and where the limiting/excluding clause forms part of a guarantee.

Examples of **terms** which are considered ineffective are where:

(1) there has been a breach of obligations under s.2 Supply of Goods and Services Act 1982: s.7(3)(a).
(2) there has been a transfer of possession or ownership of goods, other than by sale or hire, as against a consumer, but only in respect of certain implied terms: s.6(2) and s.7(2).
(3) there has been a sale or hire purchase contract, where implied terms with regards to title cannot be excluded, irrespective of whether the parties are consumers or non-consumers or both: s. 6(1) and s.6(2).

The Act also provides that certain exemption clauses are effective provided they are found to be reasonable. In litigation, the burden of proof of reasonableness is the responsibility of the person who is seeking to rely on the clause: s.11(5). Thus, in the following circumstances, notices or terms will be considered effective, subject to them passing the test of reasonableness.

(1) where, although negligence has occurred, neither death nor personal injury has resulted: s.2(2).
(2) where provision has been made to exclude liability for breach of contract generally. This may be considered under two headings:
    (a) where a contract has been entered into by a consumer; or,
    (b) where a contract has been entered into with a consumer or non-consumer on written standard terms: s.3(1) and s.3(2)(a).
(3) where a contracting consumer is required to indemnify the other party as regards his possible negligence or breach of contract: s.(4).
(4) where, in a non-consumer transaction, there are terms implied by statute, such as those that relate to the merchantable quality of goods: s.6(3) and s.7(3).

Quite clearly, what is or what is not reasonable in a particular set of circumstances is up to the court to decide should litigation have to be resorted to. The court, though, does have guidelines to help it and where this relates to the supply of goods, these are contained within s.11(2) and schedule 2.

MISTAKE

In law, the validity of a contract cannot be questioned simply because, had all the true facts been known, one or both parties would not have entered the contract. So, if someone sells a "penny red" postage stamp for 10p thinking it to be a relatively common issue, but in fact, it is a rare variety having an auction value of £30,000, the contract of sale is still valid. Here, the buyer is fortunate (some would say very fortunate) and the vendor is not. On occasions the opposite may occur – say where both parties believe they are dealing in a Rembrandt painting and a price of one million pounds is agreed. If, at a later date, an expert examines the painting and points out that the painting is not a genuine Rembrandt, then provided the situation was not misrepresented at the time the contract was being negotiated, there are no legal remedies available to the buyer against the vendor. Here, the maxim "*caveat emptor*" (let the buyer beware) would be applied. From these examples, it is seen that even though one party has made a mistake, the contract is still binding.

However, there are certain circumstances where a mistake will affect the validity of a contract and such mistakes are described as operative mistakes. They must be mistakes of fact and not of law and where this can be established, the contract will be held to be void ab initio (from the outset).

CLASSIFICATION OF MISTAKE

Mistakes, as related to factual situations, may be classified under three headings.

1. BILATERAL MISTAKE

(a) *Common Mistake*
This occurs when both parties make the same mistake. For, although they both understand the other's intentions, both are mistaken about an underlying or fundamental fact, e.g. neither are aware that the subject matter has been stolen.

(b) *Mutual Mistake*
This occurs when both parties make a mistake but each makes a different mistake.

2. UNILATERAL MISTAKE

This occurs when one of the parties is mistaken, and the other is aware or must be aware of the mistake.

3. DOCUMENT MISTAKENLY SIGNED (NON EST FACTUM - NOT MY DEED)

This occurs when one party signs an agreement which has a totally different nature to what the party had contemplated.

From this general classification, it can be argued that only two legal categories exist:

(a) *Where there is a dispute regarding the existence of a contract*
Thus, despite the outward appearances of a contract, there is a contention that the contract is void for lack of offer and acceptance. This is known as an "Agreement Mistake" and it covers both mutual and unilateral mistakes.

(b) *Where there is no dispute regarding the existence of a contract*
Here there has been an argument, but a common mistake has been made which relates to a fundamental fact, and thus the agreement has been robbed of its efficacy. This is known as a "Possibility Mistake", and it covers all types of common mistakes.

AGREEMENT MISTAKE

Even though the agreement has an outward appearance of a contract, one party may allege that he has been mistaken about a fundamental fact and the other party knew or ought to have known of the mistake, when the contract was being negotiated. If this can be established, the contract will not be binding – see for instance **Legal and General Assurance Society Ltd *v*. General Metal Agencies (1969)**. Here, the assurance company was attempting to terminate a tenancy with the Metal Agencies because they were slow payers. In error, the assurance company sent out a demand for the quarterly rent and on this occasion the payment was promptly made. The assurance company continued in their efforts to terminate the tenancy but in their defence the Metal Agencies pleaded that a new tenancy had been agreed by implication. *Held*. There had been an agreement mistake and so the tenancy could be terminated and the plaintiff given possession. In contrast, if it can be shown that the "other party" was unaware of the mistake, the contract will be binding.

W. Higgins Ltd *v*. Northampton Corporation (1927)
Higgins had agreed to build a number of houses for sale for a set price. However, in arriving at this figure, the company made a mathematical error. The contract between the parties was sealed before the company realised its mistake. It then attempted to get the contract rescinded. *Held*. As the contract had not been induced by fraud, misrepresentation or unlawful concealment, it was binding.

Agreement mistakes can be classified under various headings, viz.

(a) MISTAKE AS TO THE PERSON
In circumstances where the identity of one of the parties is important, if a mistake is made with regards to this party, then it may render the contract void. Here, the mistake would be described as unilateral.

Cundy *v*. Lindsay (1878)
A fraudulent person named Blenkarn ordered some handkerchiefs from Lindsay. The order appeared to come from someone called Blenkiron, whom Lindsay knew. Upon receipt of the goods, Blenkarn sold them to Cundy. Blenkarn was later convicted for fraud, and Lindsay attempted to recover the goods from Cundy on the basis that the original contract was void – because of mistake as to the person. *Held*. By the Court of Appeal – as there had been a mistake as to the person, Lindsay's action was successful.

In contrast, there is:

Kings Norton Metal Co. Ltd *v.* Edridge, Merrett & Co. Ltd (1897)
The plaintiff received an order for some metal wire supposedly from "Hallam & Co.". In actual fact, the order was fraudulently placed by someone called Wallis who was operating from Hallam & Co.'s factory and who had acquired some of their letter headed paper. The wire was not paid for. In the meantime, Wallis sold the wire to the defendant who took it bona fide and for value. Rather than sue Wallis for fraud, the plaintiff took an action in conversion against the defendant and thus tried to prove that the contract with Hallam & Co. was void for mistake. *Held.* The claim failed, for although the contract with Hallan & Co. was voidable because of fraud, it was not void for mistake. For the plaintiff actually wanted to deal with Hallam & Co. – with whom business had been done in the past.

With any situation involving an agreement mistake, there will be a presumption in the first instance that a contract has been concluded between the parties. If the presumption is to be rebutted, the responsibility falls on the party who pleads the mistake. To be successful, the following must be proved:

1. The intention was to deal with someone other than the person whom he dealt with. It is this point that distinguishes the "Cundy" decision from the "Kings Norton" decision.
2. The person actually dealt with was aware of the above.
3. When the agreement was being negotiated, the identity of the other party was regarded to be of crucial importance to him.
4. Reasonable steps were taken to identify the other party.

The courts applied the same principles in:

Ingram and others *v.* Little (1961)
Three ladies, who were joint owners of a car, sold it to a fraudulent person. A payment by cheque was offered, but was only accepted after the "drawer's" details had been confirmed as accurate by one of the plaintiffs who inspected a telephone directory. The rogue took the car away and sold it to the defendant, but in the meantime, the cheque the rogue had issued was dishonoured. The plaintiffs sued for return of the car (or its value) on the basis that the contract between them and the rogue was void for mistake. *Held.* At both the trial and in the Court of Appeal, the contract was held to be void and so the car was recoverable. At Appeal, Devlin J. dissented saying that the mistake was of quality of

the person contracted with and this does not void a contract. Furthermore, he suggested that legislation should be introduced to provide for the apportionment of loss in circumstances like this.

Lewis *v.* Averay (1972)
Lewis sold his car to a rogue person who stated that he was Richard Green, a famous actor. After identifying himself using a pass for gaining entry to a leading film studio, Lewis accepted "Green's" cheque then handed over the log book and allowed him to drive the car away. Upon presentation, the paying banker returned "Green's" cheque unpaid, but in the meantime the rogue had sold the car to Averay. *Held.* Lewis had contracted to sell the car to the rogue, and thus could not recover the car or any damages from Averay. The contract between Lewis and the rogue was voidable for fraud, but not void for unilateral mistake. This Court of Appeal decision followed the precedent set in **Phillips *v.* Brooks Ltd (1919)** rather than **Ingram and others *v.* Little (1961)** which has been described above.
The dividing line between the above decisions is a fine one and it is generally thought that the "Ingram" decision was an exception to the general rule and thus would rarely, if ever, be followed in future.

(b) MISTAKE AS TO THE SUBJECT MATTER
If this is contended, it is the task of the court to decide "what a reasonable man would conclude had been agreed from the circumstances", as the following cases illustrate:

Raffles *v.* Wichelhaus (1864)
The defendant agreed to buy cotton "to arrive on the S.S. Peerless sailing from Bombay". The Peerless referred to by Wichelhaus was one which was leaving Bombay in October, while Raffles was referring to one which was leaving Bombay in December. *Held.* There was no binding contract because both parties made a different mistake. For they were both referring to different ships.

Scriven Bros & Co. *v.* Hindley & Co. (1913)
As printed, an auction list contained certain ambiguities. Several of the lots on the list related to hemp, while others related to tow (a cheaper commodity). During the auction, Hindley (and others), because of the ambiguities, bid as though the lots consisted of hemp. In fact, he found out later that he had actually purchased tow. Consequently, he refused to take delivery and was sued by the plaintiff for breach of contract. *Held.* Because of the high price that had been bid, the auctioneer must

have been aware that the bidders were mistaken about the subject matter. Thus, the contract was void for uncertainty and it could not be enforced against Hindley.

(c) MISTAKE AS TO THE TERMS OF THE CONTRACT

This type of plea is rarely made but it is possible to see how it may be applied by considering the facts of **Wood v. Scarth (1858)**. Scarth arranged to lease a public house through an agent who had been given instructions that a premium of £500 would have to be paid by the person who was to take up the lease. Unfortunately the agent did not tell Wood of this. Later Wood agreed to take up the lease "on the terms already agreed on". From his viewpoint, there was no premium involved, but from Scarth's viewpoint, there was. Although an earlier action for specific performance had failed in equity. Wood now sued for damages for breach of contract on the basis that Scarth had promised to grant a lease of the property but later refused to execute an assignment. *Held.* As there had been a mutual mistake, the court considered the conclusion a reasonable man would arrive at from the circumstances. This was that no premium would be payable. So, Wood's action for damages was successful.

Where there has been a mistake about the value or quality of the subject matter, then it is impossible to plead "Agreement Mistake" – for this is clearly a situation of caveat emptor: **Smith v. Hughes (1871).**

POSSIBILITY MISTAKE

Here, there is a complete and undeniable agreement between the parties but one of them contends that there was a common mistake – and thus the agreement cannot be allowed to stand because certain fundamental assumptions upon which the agreement was based, were false. Because of its nature, such mistakes can only refer back to the time when the contract was made – rather than to something which occurred subsequently.

(a) *Mistake as to existence of the subject matter* (*Res extincta*)

Where the subject matter is non-existent (even if the parties are unaware of it), then the contract is rendered void.

Strickland v. Turner (1852)

A person bought an annuity on the life of X from another person. At the time of sale, neither party knew that X had already died. *Held.* The contract was void for "mistake as to existence".

A similar decision was arrived at in **Couturier v. Hastie (1856)** which related to a contract for the supply of corn. At a time before the contract was signed the corn had become overheated and unknown to the parties was landed at an intermediary port and sold. So, at the time the contract was signed, the corn was unavailable for sale.

(b) *Mistake as to Ownership* (*Res sua*)
This occurs where say A agrees to buy something from B and both parties believe that B is the legal owner. If, in fact, A is already the title holder of the subject matter, then the contract of sale is void as B has nothing to sell: **Cochrane *v.* Willis (1865)**.

QUALITY OF THE SUBJECT MATTER

It has been established that mistake as to the quality of the subject matter does not invalidate a contract. For, it is the subject matter which is being sold, not the quality of it. Thus, the general rule "caveat emptor" (let the buyer beware) is always applied, provided there has been no misrepresentation.

Bell *v.* Lever Bros (1932)
Bell had a service contract with Lever Bros (a U.K. based company), although he was the chairman of a subsidiary company incorporated in Nigeria. He was later made redundant and was paid £30,000 by Lever Bros for his loss of office with the Niger subsidiary. Lever Bros later found that he had breached his service contract while in their employment and if they had known this earlier, Bell could have been dismissed without the payment of any money. Thus, they attempted to set aside the £30,000, on the basis of mistake. *Held.* Bell had an obligation to disclose if he had made any secret profits to his employee – the Niger subsidiary. There was no equivalent obligation to disclose such details to Lever Bros, who made the redundancy payment. As a consequence, Bell could keep the money for Lever's mistake was one of quality (here, quality of the director) and this could not void the redundancy payment.

The decision above should be compared with that more recently made in **Horcal *v.* Gatland (1983)**. Here, a company refused to pay a golden handshake to one of its directors who had allegedly misappropriated some of his employer's profits for his personal use. *Held.* As the director was obliged to disclose, under the terms of his contract of employment, any past or present breaches of duty to the company that employed him and, here, he had not done so, he was unable to claim a golden handshake from the company.

The background to the following case also referred to the principle of mistake, but here it was applied to a painting.

Leaf *v.* International Galleries (1950)
A gallery sold a painting which was described as a "Constable". Some five years later, the plaintiff attempted to sell it as a "Constable", only to be told it had not been painted by the famous artist with that name. As a result of this discovery, Leaf unsuccessfully attempted to have the contract of purchase rescinded. For, here, the Court pointed out that the mistake was one of quality, which could not void the contract. Furthermore, the Court of Appeal decided that the Galleries' statement, that the painting was a "Constable", was a representation. As the representation was given innocently, the right to rescind was unavailable because of the length of time that had lapsed since the date of purchase.

Note: If a similar case was being heard today, no doubt a plaintiff would try to have the contract rescinded on the basis of the defendant's misrepresentation, using the appropriate provisions of the Misrepresentation Act 1967. Such actions, though, can only be successful if they have not become statute barred. This means that the plaintiff must commence a legal action within a defined period of becoming aware of the cause of the action. With contracts executed under hand, this would be within six years of discovering that a painting is a forgery or copy – rather than six years from the date of purchase, as the following case shows:

Peco Arts Inc. *v.* Hazlitt Gallery Ltd. (1983).
Here, a painting had been bought for $18,000 in 1970. Neither in 1970 at the time of purchase, nor in 1976 when the painting was revalued, was its authenticity questioned. However, when it was valued again in 1981, the expert, at that time, pointed out that the painting was a reproduction. As a consequence, the purchaser (the plaintiff, here) sought to have the contract rescinded and his consideration monies (plus interest) paid back. After various technical matters had been resolved, the sole defence that was used was that the action was statute barred. *Held.* The defence failed, for the action was not statute barred. It had, in fact, been commenced within six years of the cause of action (i.e. realising that the painting was a forgery).

EQUITY

All the above are common law remedies. In certain circumstances, a common law remedy would be unavailable and so a plaintiff may seek to have a contract set aside in equity.

The general forms of equitable relief are:

1. *By the court setting aside agreements on terms which initially are*

considered to be neither fair nor just.* **Solle *v.* Butcher (1950)** – see below.

2. *By rectification.*
3. *By the court refusing to grant an order of specific performance.*
4. *By rescission.*

Note: The meaning of specific performance and rescission are described in the section of this chapter relating to remedies for breach.

UNFAIR/UNJUST AGREEMENTS

Solle *v.* Butcher (1950)
Solle was the lessee of one of Butcher's flats paying an annual rental of £250. At that time, there was a statutory maximum annual rent on certain types of property amounting to £140, but both parties believed it did not apply to the leased flat. When Solle found out it did, he attempted to recover the difference. *Held.* There had been a common mistake – which was fundamental to the lease. Although at common law, the contract was valid because the mistake was one of quality, the contract could be rescinded on the grounds of equity. Solle was offered two alternatives – (a) to surrender the lease or (b) to remain in occupation as a licencee until a new lease, with new terms, could be agreed.

A similar decision was made in **Grist *v.* Bailey (1966)** which related to the sale of a house which was believed to be subject to an existing tenancy agreement.

So it can be seen that the courts have the power to set aside contracts when there has been a mistake of material fact. However, the court will not set any contract aside where:

(a) There has been affirmation, or
(b) The status quo cannot be restored, or
(c) Third party rights exist – this is known as rescission of terms.

RECTIFICATION

Common Mistakes

There are occasions where equity will rectify a written agreement upon which there has been a common mistake, thus bringing it into line with the contemplated agreement. For this equitable remedy to be available, the following conditions must be proved:

1. The writing does not correctly express what had been agreed between the parties: **Frederick Rose (London) Ltd. *v.* William H. Pim Jnr & Co. Ltd. (1953)**

2. After the parties have agreed to terms there should be no disputes prior to the written contract being executed. If there had been any disputes during this period, the court would consider the written form of the agreement to have been prepared after the disputes had been resolved.

3. There was complete agreement in the contractual sense.

Craddock Bros *v.* Hunt (1923)
There had been an oral agreement to sell a house, but not the adjoining yard. However, when the conveyance was prepared, by mistake it included the yard and was sealed in that form. When the vendor discovered the error, he sought the remedy of rectification. *Held.* As the mistake was common to both parties, the court could rectify the conveyance.

Unilateral Mistakes
It was held in **W. Higgins Ltd *v.* Northampton Corporation (1927)** (see back) that where a unilateral mistake had been made the equitable remedy of rectification is only available where a fraud had been committed, misrepresentation had occurred or unlawful concealment could be established.

DOCUMENTS MISTAKENLY SIGNED – NON EST FACTUM (NOT MY DEED)

This is a further category of operative mistake.

On occasions, a person may be induced into signing a written document containing a contract which is fundamentally different in character from the one he contemplated. In early legal cases, defences of non est factum were successfully used to avoid liability on the contract signed, but in view of the House of Lord's decision in the Saunder's case (see below), such pleas, in future, will only be successful where the party seeking it as a defence can show that he has not been negligent. In general today, a person is bound by what he has signed irrespective of whether he has read it or understands it.

The way in which the law has evolved under this heading can be seen by considering the following cases:

Foster *v.* Mackinnon (1869)
Mackinnon, an elderly person, who had poor sight, endorsed a bill of exchange although he believed he was signing a guarantee. *Held.* As he was not negligent in signing the bill, he successfully pleaded "non est factum" and was not liable on the bill.

Lewis *v.* Clay (1897)
Clay was asked by a third party to act as a witness for signatures contained within various documents. As Clay had been told that the contracts were of a confidential nature, he was never given the opportunity to read and see what he was signing. In fact, they were a series of promissory notes which were used by a third party to obtain advances from Lewis. In due course, the promissory notes were dishonoured, and the plaintiff sued on them. *Held.* Clay was not liable on the promissory notes because the documents had mistakenly been signed.

Carlisle and Cumberland Banking Co. *v.* Bragg (1911)
Bragg was induced into signing a bank guarantee having previously been told he was witnessing the signature of an insurance document. *Held.* The defence of non est factum succeeded, even though Bragg was shown to have been careless.

Saunders *v.* Anglia Building Society (1970) (Also known as **Gallie *v.* Lee.)**
An old lady of 84 who had lost her glasses believed she was signing a deed of gift of a lease to her nephew when in fact she was completing an assignment to another party. She later tried to avoid liability on the lease pleading non est factum. *Held.* This plea cannot succeed where the party claiming has been careless or negligent – as here. Because of this House of Lord's decision it will be extremely difficult in future to successfully claim non est factum.

Note: This House of Lord's decision effectively overrules the decision in the Bragg case above.

Finally where a person signs a document knowing its nature but without reading it, liability has always remained.

Today, the primary rule is that for the plea to succeed, the court must be satisfied that the instrument signed is "different" from the one which was intended to be signed and that the mistake was not due to a person's own carelessness. The "degree of difference" has been subject to discussion by the House of Lords and is interpreted as something radically, fundamentally, basically, totally or essentially different in character or substance from the contract intended – Saunder's case.

DISCHARGE OF A CONTRACT

When a contract is discharged, in general, the parties to it are freed from their agreement. The extent of this freedom, however, must be related to the method of discharge. Discharge may be by any of the following methods:

1. Performance.
2. Express agreement to vary by both parties.
3. Breach.
4. Subsequent impossibility or frustration.
5. Lapse of time.
6. Operation of law.

PERFORMANCE

When both parties perform their part of the contract as agreed, then the contract is completely discharged. When only one of the parties performs his agreement, he is discharged, while the other party still remains liable and will be in breach until he completes his agreement. It is in this area that the majority of litigation results.

In general, to be discharged, each party must completely and precisely perform what they have agreed to do. As a consequence of this, a party who has performed only part of his agreement is usually unable to recover anything for that part he did perform.

Cutter *v.* Powell (1795)
Powell agreed to pay Cutter thirty guineas for acting as second mate on a vessel sailing from Jamaica to Liverpool. However, shortly before arrival in Liverpool, Cutter died, and his widow claimed an amount from Powell which related to a proportion of the contracted payment. *Held.* The claim failed, as Cutter had not fully performed his part of the contract.

> *Note:* Similar actions would be successful today, for such payments have been provided for by Merchant Shipping Act, 1970. However, to this general rule of precise performance, the common law had provided exceptions. Thus there are a limited number of situations where a party who has not fully performed his part of the agreement is afforded protection. These are:

(a) Severable (Divisible) Contracts
Contracts may be entire, as in **Cutter *v.* Powell** above, or severable. In the latter case, a contract may provide for the delivery and payment of a given quantity of goods per week over ten weeks. Here, payment would have to be made on a week by week basis for goods actually delivered – rather than waiting for the ten week period to expire.

(b) Prevention of Performance
On occasions, one party will be prevented from performing his part of the contract because of acts or omissions of the other party. When this happens, the party prevented from performing may either sue for dam-

ages or take an action for quantum meruit – reasonable remuneration for what he has done: **De Barnady *v*. Harding (1853)**. In **Planché *v*. Colburn (1831)**, Planché agreed to write an article for publication for a fee. Before completion, the periodical in which it was to appear ceased to be published. Planché sued for work done. *Held*. Although the contract had been discharged, Planché was entitled to recover for the work he had done by quantum meruit.

(c) Acceptance of Partial Performance
Even though a contract has only been partly performed, it may be possible, from the circumstances, to infer that a fresh agreement had been made in which payment would be made for goods already supplied or services already rendered. Where this exists, it is possible to take an action for quantum meruit – which will only succeed if the defendant expressly promised to make payment. Inference of payment will not be an acceptable proof unless the beneficiary was given the option to accept or reject the benefit of the work.

Sumpter *v*. Hedges (1898)
Sumpter agreed to build a house on Hedges' land for a specified sum, but before he had completed the house, he ran out of money. He was unable to complete it and sued Hedges for the value of materials and his labour costs under quantum meruit. *Held*. The action for quantum meruit failed as the contract stated that payment would be made by a lump sum on completion. However, the court allowed him to recover the cost of materials.

(d) Substantial Performance
This is a doctrine which allows someone to recover for work done under a contract even though he had not performed the full agreement – because the part he had not performed was minor. However, he will still remain liable to pay damages for partial non-performance. Various legal cases illustrate how this doctrine is applied. **Boone *v*. Eyre (1779), H. Dakin & Co. Ltd *v*. Lee (1916), Bolton *v*. Mahadeva (1972)** and **Hoenig *v*. Isaacs (1952)**. Hoenig was employed to provide certain furniture for Isaacs. The total cost was £750, payable in stages and the balance on completion. At the time of completion £300 had been paid, so Hoenig asked for the balance. Isaacs would only pay £100 because of alleged bad workmanship and after accepting this sum, Hoenig sued for the difference. *Held*. An official referee indicated substantial performance, and calculated that the cost of rectifying the defects amounted to £55 18s 2d. Thus, the plaintiff was awarded £294 1s 10d. (i.e. the £350 owed minus the cost of rectifying).

It is a matter for the court to decide if substantial performance has occurred. As was said by the Court of Appeal in the "Dakin" case, in deciding this matter, it is necessary to take into account both the nature of the defects and the relation between the cost of rectifying the faults and the contract price. Furthermore, it is necessary for the courts to decide whether the legal action for substantial performance relates to a condition or a warranty. For "conditions" must be wholly performed whereas "warranties" need only be substantially performed.

TENDER OF PERFORMANCE

When a party is unable to complete performance without the concurrence of the other party, the tender (or offer) of performance is considered to be equivalent to performance provided it complies with the terms of the contract.

Tenders may apply to goods or money.

Tender of Goods

If the seller tenders goods and the buyer refuses to accept them, then the seller is freed from liability provided the goods comply with the terms of the contract.

Tender of Money

If it is a tender of money which is refused, then the tenderer is not discharged. But, if the tender of money is paid into a court, the tenderer will have a good defence for any possible action brought against him. When tendering money the amount offered must exactly equal the sum owed, because where an excess is offered with a request for change, this does not constitute a legal tender. In England, notes are legal tender up to any amount but coins are only legal tender up to certain amounts (e.g. 50ps up to £5) and those constraints must be complied with. If a negotiable instrument is offered as a medium of payment because it is not legal tender, the creditor is not obliged to accept it. If the instrument is accepted, the debt is discharged when the instrument is paid, not when it is received.

TIME OF PERFORMANCE

When the parties to a contract fix a definite date by which the contract must be completely performed, the court must decide whether the specified time goes to the essence of the contract. *In general*, the answer in Common Law is yes, while in Equity, the answer is no.

Various statutes contain clauses which indicate whether time of performance is or is not of essence to a contract. For example, the Sale of Goods Act, 1979, provides that stipulations as to time of payment do not go to the essence of a contract for sale of goods unless a different intention appears from the terms of the contract.

VICARIOUS PERFORMANCE

In general, one party (say A) may delegate the performance of his duties under a contract to a third party (say B) – and this remains so even where the other party to the contract (say C) objects. Subsequently, if B does not perform what has been asked of him or does it improperly, then C has the right to sue A as he is vicariously liable.

EXPRESS AGREEMENT TO VARY

When there has been an agreement between parties to do something, then the same parties can agree to cancel it. This cancellation will be binding on the parties provided it is supported by consideration or made under seal. The agreement to discharge may form part of the original contract and may be a condition precedent (or warranty) or condition subsequent. An example of the former is an agreement to purchase a plot of land subject to planning permission being obtained – if permission is refused, then the prior agreement will contain a provision for the contract to be rescinded. An example of the latter is where the promoters of a company enter into pre-incorporation contracts. By s. 36(4) Companies Act 1985, the promoters in these circumstances incur personal liability: **Phonogram Ltd. *v.* Lane (1981)**. In order to avoid personal liability in these circumstances the promoters should draw up contracts in such a way that if incorporation does not follow, or if incorporation does follow but the company does not accept the promoters' contract by novation, the promoters will be discharged.

The following comments apply to discharge by express agreement:

(a) *Formality*

In general, discharge (or variation) can be effected in any form the parties wish it to take.

For certain contracts (e.g. guarantees or those for the disposition of land or any interest therein), an oral form of variation is sufficient.

For an oral discharge to be valid, it must be a total discharge **Moore *v.* Marrable (1866)**. Where the discharge is to be partial, it must be evidenced in writing. **Goss *v.* Lord Nugent (1833)**.

(b) *Consideration*

Consideration must be given where a contract is not discharged under seal. Two situations must be distinguished.

1. Where the contract is executory (and neither party has started to perform their obligations) the discharge is described as bilateral. For,

here, both parties surrender something of value and the consideration is the mutual release.

2. In contrast, the contract may have been performed in whole or in part by only one of the parties. If such a contract is to be discharged, it will only be effective if made under seal or if the other party gives consideration. When the latter method is chosen, the discharge has to be given by what is called *Accord and Satisfaction*. The *Accord* is the agreement to discharge, while the *Satisfaction* is the new consideration which makes the agreement operative.

APPLICATION TO VARY

Where the variation takes place for the benefit of both parties, then the arrangement contains its own consideration. But where it is for the benefit of one party only, then consideration might not be present. In this situation, the court will have to consider whether the change is a variation or a waiver – even though most lawyers say there is no substance to the distinction. In common law, the court would give effect to a change that was a waiver, but not to one which was a variation. In contrast, equity considered that a party who granted a change was bound by it – under the doctrine of equitable estoppel.

BREACH

A breach does not automatically discharge a contract, but it may in some circumstances allow the innocent party to treat it as discharged. These circumstances are where there has been:

1. *Repudiation.*
2. *Fundamental breach.*
3. *An action by one party which makes performance impossible.*
4. *Failure by one party to perform his part of the agreement.*

1. REPUDIATION

This occurs when one of the parties indicates by words or by conduct that he does not intend to honour his future obligations: **Hochster *v.* De La Tour (1853)**. De La Tour agreed to give Hochster a job as a courier, but before the starting date had arrived, De La Tour wrote to say that Hochster's services would no longer be required. Instead of awaiting the due date and at that time bringing a legal action, Hochster commenced an action immediately. *Held.* Although the defence counsel pleaded that no action was available until the due date had been reached, the court held that, by his action of cancelling the job, De La Tour had breached the contract. This enabled Hochster to pursue an immediate action.

From the introductory statement, it can be seen that repudiation may be express or by implication. After repudiation, the innocent party can immediately begin an action for breach if he wants to – or he can wait for the due date of performance, and if performance has not been completed by that day, treat the contract as discharged and at that time take an action against the other party. Where the breach takes place before the due date of performance, it is known as anticipatory breach.

Frost *v*. Knight (1872)
Here Knight promised, upon his father's death, to marry Frost. While Knight's father was still alive, he broke off the engagement, and later (again before his father's death) Frost claimed damages for breach of promise of marriage. *Held*. As there had been a breach of contract, her claim was successful.

> *Note:* A breach of promise, in circumstances like this, is no longer actionable.

Where the innocent party decides to wait for the due date of performance before taking a legal action, certain events may occur in the meantime which prevent a successful action for breach. This is ideally illustrated in:

Avery *v*. Bowden (1855)
The defendant chartered the plaintiff's ship and agreed to load it with a cargo within forty-five days. Before the forty-five day period expired, the defendant told the ship's captain that he would not be providing a cargo and he might as well leave immediately. However, the captain decided to stay. Just before the end of the forty-five day period the Crimean War broke out which would have resulted in any contract being illegal. Even so, the plaintiff sued for breach of contract. *Held*. The plaintiff could have treated the defendant's action as an anticipatory breach of contract, but because the captain (his agent) had remained, this right had been waived. The contract had been discharged by the war (something which was outside the control of both parties) and the action failed.

It is usual for someone who has become subject to an anticipatory breach not to take an immediate legal action but to wait and see, and thereby keep the contract alive. Sometimes though, he may continue with his contractual duties even though he does not have the other party's co-operation, and still retain his legal rights against the other party.

White and Carter (Councils) Ltd *v*. McGregor (1962)
The sales manager of McGregor (M) without authority entered into a contract with the White and Carter (Councils) Ltd (W and C). Payment

under the contract was to be made by instalment and failure to pay one instalment or any other breach would result in the whole amount falling due. Before W and C started to perform under the contract, M wrote to repudiate the contract. W and C did not comply with the request and subsequently carried out their part of the agreement. M refused to pay and so W and C brought an action for the sum due. *Held.* The action succeeded, for, although M repudiated the contract, W and C were not obliged to accept it.

2. FUNDAMENTAL BREACH

When one party commits a fundamental breach (without repudiating his obligations), the other party can treat himself as discharged from further liability. To establish whether a breach is fundamental, the courts will have to analyse the words used in the contract. For the court must decide whether the violated promise was of major importance. Where it goes to the root of the contract, a violation of it is a fundamental breach.

3. ACTION MAKING PERFORMANCE IMPOSSIBLE

A typical example of how this may arise is shown by the principles in:

Omnium D'Enterprises and others *v.* Sutherland (1919)
A vessel called Robert Bruce, while under construction, was chartered by Sutherland to Omnium for a period of three years from the date the ship would be fit to sail. There was a provision in the charter concerning requisition of the ship by the admiralty either while it was under construction, or, it had been completed, during the three year term of the charter. The provision was that for the first set of circumstances, the charter term of three years would begin to run immediately from the date that the requisition was terminated, while for the latter set of circumstances, the uncompleted part of the three year charter term would begin to run from the date that the requisition was terminated. In fact, the ship was requisitioned by the admiralty at the time it was completed. But while still in the possession of the admiralty, Sutherland sold the ship free from the charter agreement. Upon discovering what had happened, Omnium sued for breach of contract. *Held.* By his action, Sutherland had repudiated the contract, and, as a consequence was liable for damages.

4. FAILURE TO PERFORM

This is the most usual form of breach and typical examples occur when:

(a) a seller does not deliver the duly contracted goods by the due date, or

(b) when a seller delivers the goods, but the buyer either does not take them up or pay for them because they are not wanted or of the required quality or of insufficient quantity.

SUBSEQUENT IMPOSSIBILITY OR FRUSTRATION

After the making of a contract, certain events may happen which prevent the objective of the contract being fulfilled.

The law relating to contracts which are affected in this way has evolved over the years and is certainly less rigorously applied now compared with many years ago. In **Paradine *v.* June (1647)** it was held that a person could not escape liability for rent payments by proving that performance was subsequently impossible or futile due to future unforseen events (because soldiers threw him out of his house). At that time, the courts held the view that if a person wanted to avoid liability in these circumstances, there should be a term to expressly provide for this in the contract. However, the hardship suffered by the application of this strict rule has slowly been eroded away. Today, the court will apply the following principle where possible. "Where a contract is brought to an abrupt stop by some irresistible and extraneous cause for which neither party is responsible, the contract shall terminate forthwith and the parties be discharged."

Taylor *v.* Caldwell (1863)
Caldwell gave Taylor permission to use his hall for a certain period, but before the contracted period had been reached, it was destroyed by fire. Taylor sued for damages for breach. *Held*. The contract had been frustrated. So the agreement was discharged and both parties excused.

When one party to a contract incurs expenses which relate to a frustrated contract, he may be allowed by the court to recover such money: Law Reform (Frustrated Contracts) Act, 1943.

TYPES OF FRUSTRATION

(a) SUPERVENING ILLEGALITY
Where the illegality affects the whole of the contract or some major part of it, then the contract is described as frustrated.

Denny, Mott & Dickson Ltd *v.* James B. Fraser & Co. Ltd (1944)
The principal agreement between the parties was to sell timber, although there was also an option to purchase a timber yard. Subsequently, various government orders were passed which prevented the import of timber. The appellants attempted to enforce the option to purchase the yard. *Held*. The whole contract had been discharged because its main purpose was frustrated by supervening illegality. So the option could not be enforced.

This decision may be compared with situations where the main purpose is not frustrated. In these circumstances, the parties must perform the legal parts of their agreement or pay damages. An example can be seen in **Eyre *v.* Johnson (1949)**, where a tenant was held liable for not repairing a house (when his covenant obliged him to repair damage) even though later regulations made such repairs illegal.

(b) PHYSICAL IMPOSSIBILITY

This may be considered under various headings.

1. Destruction of the Subject Matter

Frustration occurs when the subject matter or a major part of it is destroyed with the result that the major purpose of the contract is defeated. This is supported by the decision in **Taylor *v.* Caldwell (1865)** described above.

2. Non-Availability of the Subject Matter

Frustration occurs when the person or thing ceases to be available for the purpose of the contract. The conclusion is the same when there is a temporary unavailability if it makes the contract greatly different from the one originally agreed.

Jackson *v.* Union Marine Insurance Co. Ltd (1874)

A ship owned by Jackson was chartered to carry iron rails from Newport, Wales to San Francisco. However, on the way to collect the rails from Newport, it ran aground. It was some time before it could be refloated and repaired. In the meantime, the charterer hired another vessel. Jackson claimed on the insurance company with whom he had taken out a policy which covered failure to carry out the charter. *Held*. The charterer's action in hiring another ship was good as the original contract had been frustrated. Even though the charter had lost no money (for the new vessel enabled him to deliver the rails to America), Jackson had. But, because Jackson had taken out insurance to cover himself against not completing the contract, his claim under the insurance policy was good.

3. Non-Availability of the Party

If a person contracts to perform a personal service but dies or becomes incapacitated before he can do so, the contract becomes frustrated. Where there is a temporary non-availability (say through illness of one of the parties), then the court will have to consider how this affects the overall situation. In the main, it will not discharge the contract: **Mount *v.* Oldham Corporation (1973)**. However, where it was for a personal service, illness will frustrate the contract if this substantially affects the performance.

Robinson *v.* Davison (1871)
Davison was taken ill before he could perform a piano concert which he had contracted to give. *Held.* As the pianist was unable to perform through no fault of his own, frustration had occurred and the contract was discharged. The same decision was made more recently in **Condor *v.* The Barron Knights Ltd (1966)** where a drummer was contracted to play seven nights a week when the Barron Knights band had engagements. He became ill and his doctor indicated that he could only play on four nights. *Held.* His illness prevented him satisfying his contract and thus it was terminated. Where illness occurs when someone is in general employment, frustration will not be found. But, if the illness is of a chronic or serious nature, then a contract may be discharged.

4. *Frustration by the Happening of an Unforeseen Event*
Where an expected event does not occur, a contract is regarded as discharged.

Krell *v.* Henry (1903)
Henry agreed to hire Krell's flat in Pall Mall to watch the procession of King Edward VII. However, the king was taken ill and the procession was cancelled. *Held.* As the contract was discharged by frustration, no rent was payable. This decision should be compared with that of:

Herne Bay Steamboat Co. *v.* Hutton (1903)
Hutton hired a vessel for two days. On one day, it was the intention to watch Edward VII review the fleet and on the other day to go for a general cruise. Edward VII had to cancel his engagement, but the fleet was available for general review. As Hutton did not take up the boat, the plaintiff (the owners of the boat) used it in their ordinary business. They then sued Hutton for £200 (the agreed hire charge). *Held.* The contract had not been discharged because the hire did not solely relate to watching Edward VII. Even though Edward VII did not review the fleet, this did not go to the root of the contract. The plaintiff's claim was successful, but not for the full amount – for he was given £200 (the agreed hire charge) minus the profits made in the ordinary course of business during the two days in question.

Davis Contractors Ltd *v.* Fareham U.D.C. (1956)
The plaintiff contracted to build seventy-eight houses for £92,435 within eight months. Because of problems with the supply of materials and labour, it took twenty-two months to complete and, in this period, the plaintiff incurred £17,651 of additional expenses. They claimed the contract had been frustrated and attempted to recover the extra cost on

quantum meruit. *Held.* Although the contract was more onerous to the plaintiff, it was not frustrated. The plaintiff could only recover £92,435. Furthermore, an award of quantum meruit was not available as frustration could not be established.

LIMITATIONS TO THE DOCTRINE OF FRUSTRATION

(a) *Self-Induced Frustration*

Maritime National Fish Ltd *v.* Ocean Trawlers Ltd (1935)
A vessel was chartered for fishing use, but a special licence was needed. Five licences were applied for and only three were granted, all of which were used for other vessels. The appellant claimed the contract had been frustrated and thus he was not liable to pay the hire charges. *Held.* Frustration was self-induced and thus the contract was not discharged.

(b) *Lease*

In the courts, it had been held that leases fell outside the doctrine of frustration and this could be ideally illustrated by the circumstances of:

Cricklewood Property and Investment Trust Ltd *v.* Leighton's Investment Trust Ltd (1945)
In 1936, a building lease had been entered into for a term of 99 years. While the site was undeveloped no ground rent was payable. But, there was an agreement that twelve months after notice had been given that construction of certain parts of the site may proceed, the tenants would be liable for payment of ground rents. Although, in due course, notices covering the whole site were given, no construction ever started. From the builder's viewpoint, the problem was made worse because of the second world war and the government restrictions which applied to building construction and the supply of building materials. As the buildings were never completed, the tenants paid no rent and in 1945 the lessors sought recovery of unpaid rents. *Held.* Although the defence pleaded that the contract had been frustrated, the court held that this defence was not available for actions relating to real property – such as leasehold land. Thus, the claim for unpaid rents was successful.

However, the House of Lords has recently indicated that the doctrine of frustration is capable of being applied to leases of land, albeit on very rare occasions. An example which can be cited is the judgement in

National Carriers Ltd. *v.* Panalpina (Northern) Ltd (1981)
National Carriers leased a warehouse to Panalpina for a period of ten years. During the term of the lease, the local authority closed off the only access road for a period of twenty months and Panalpina refused to pay

the rent during this period. *Held*. Rent had to be paid. Leases could be frustrated, but when considering twenty months unavailability within a ten year period, this was held to be an insufficient period of time for the lease to have been frustrated.

(c) *Express provision*
The contract may provide for what should be done if certain events happen. Thus, these provisions apply rather than allow the contract to be frustrated.

EFFECTS OF FRUSTRATION

Frustration naturally occurs at the date of frustration. Thus a contract would be discharged as regards the uncompleted part(s) of it and not void ab initio (from the beginning). The common law application of this ruling was sometimes harsh. For, before 1943, the courts applied the principle "the loss lies where it falls". Thus, money not due at that time could not be claimed, money due but not paid could be claimed and finally money paid under the contract before it became impossible could not be recovered. The harshness of the latter principle is seen in:

Chandler *v*. Webster (1904)
Webster agreed to let his room for £141.75 so that Chandler could watch the Coronation procession of Edward VII. The contract provided for payment in full immediately, but Chandler paid £100 on account. Due to the king's illness the procession did not take place and so Chandler refused to pay the balance. Moreover, Chandler attempted to recover his earlier payment of £100, but Webster counter-claimed for the balance of £41.75. *Held*. By the Court of Appeal, the Plaintiff's action failed, but Webster's counter-claim was successful. For here, frustration occurred after the date of obligation to pay.

In contrast with the above decision, if there had been a total failure of consideration, money already paid could be recovered.

The Fibrosa Clause (1942)
An English company agreed to sell machinery to a Polish company, which paid a £1,000 deposit with its order. War broke out before delivery and the Polish company attempted to recover their £1,000. *Held*. By the Court of Appeal, the contract was frustrated, so the action failed. But the House of Lords overruled this, saying that here, there was a quasi-contract upon which there had been a total failure of consideration and thus the £1,000 already paid was recoverable.

This rather grey area of the law was later codified in the Law Reform (Frustrated Contracts) Act, 1943, which provided that:

1. All amounts paid before frustration are recoverable.

2. Any amounts due for payment before frustration are no longer payable.

3. If expenses have been incurred before frustration, a reasonable amount may be retained by the party who has already received the money, or if no money has been received, he may be allowed by the court to claim reasonable expenses.

4. Where a benefit (other than in monetary terms) has been conferred on one party before frustration, the court may permit recovery of a reasonable sum for such benefit. This is an application of quantum meruit.

This Act is not all embracing and thus will not always apply, e.g. It does not apply to a contract of carriage of goods by sea or contracts of insurance.

LAPSE OF TIME

If a contract is entered into for a stated period, then upon expiry of that period, the contract is discharged. For contracts entered into for an unspecified period, the Limitation Act, 1980, may render certain contracts unenforceable in a court of law unless the aggrieved party commences an action within a specified time period. The main provision of this Statute as it affects contracts are:

1. Simple contracts are barred six years from the date on which the plaintiff could have brought an action, e.g. a bank which is attempting to recover a debt from a customer has six years from the date it makes formal demand for repayment to recover the money, unless the customer in the meantime makes a repayment or acknowledges the existence of the debt (see below).

2. Specialty contracts (e.g. deeds) are barred twelve years from the date on which the plaintiff could have brought an action.

Where contracts have been entered into for a specified period, the statute barred periods mentioned in points (1) and (2) above begin to run from the expiry date of the contract. However, the time period can be revived by either:

(a) A subsequent payment of money or interest being made by the debtor. Or,

(b) A written acknowledgement being made by the debtor or his agent of the existence of the debt.

It should be remembered here that the time begins to run from the date of cause of action, not the date of the contract and that the time will be revived by the happening of either (a) or (b).

OPERATION OF LAW

1. MERGER

This occurs when a simple contract is later embodied in a specialty contract which includes all the terms of the former.

2. MATERIAL ALTERATION

This occurs when one party alters significant details of the contract such as dates, names, amounts of money, etc. without the consent of the other. The rule does not apply when a correction is made, e.g. something originally mis-described is corrected.

3. BANKRUPTCY

When a person is adjudicated bankrupt, someone called a Trustee acts on behalf of both the bankrupt and his creditors in dealing with the bankrupt's affairs. The Trustee has wide ranging powers which include the ability to disclaim contracts containing onerous clauses, thereby discharging the "bankrupt" from his obligations under the contract. More importantly, he can pursue actions for breach of contract which were available to the "bankrupt" and, if successful, it will increase the dividend payable to the creditors. However, the right to sue in actions for injury to the debtor's character or reputation do not pass to the Trustee.

4. DEATH

Where personal services are involved, the death of one party immediately discharges the contract.

Any other type of contract is not discharged and the contractual rights and duties survive for the benefit of (or against) the estate of the deceased.

REMEDIES FOR BREACH

An injured party has the following remedies available:

1. *To refuse further performance.*
2. *To take an action for damages.*
3. *To take an action on a quantum meruit.*
4. *To take an action for specific performance.*
5. *To take an action for an injunction.*
6. *Rescission.*

1. TO REFUSE FURTHER PERFORMANCE

Upon breach, an injured party may treat the contract as terminated and refuse to perform any further parts of it. Because of this action by the injured party, the person who has breached the contract may sue for the enforcement of it. Then, the injured party will use the breach as a means of defence and counterclaim for any loss sustained.

2. TO TAKE AN ACTION FOR DAMAGES

This is a common law remedy whereby the court attempts to put the injured party in the same financial position he would have been in if the contract had been completed as originally planned: **B. Sunley Co. Ltd *v.* Cunard White Star Ltd (1940)**. It is up to the courts to assess the level of damages, in money terms, and although this sometimes may be very difficult, it does not prevent a successful claim being made. Where such difficulties arise, the court will award nominal damages, as it did in **Chaplin *v.* Hicks (1911)** and **Entertainments Ltd *v.* Great Yarmouth Borough Council (1983)**.

On occasions, claims for damages will not be successful because the actual damage is too remote. The principles which should be used to establish this point were laid down in **Hadley *v.* Baxendale (1854)** and later expanded on in **The Heron II (1967)**:

Hadley *v.* Baxendale (1854)

Here, a miller engaged a carrier to take a broken part of his mill to an engineer so that he could make a new one. At that time, although the miller said the matter was not urgent, he did not say that until the replacement was received, the mill would be idle. The carrier delayed taking the part to the engineer and, as a consequence, the mill was idle for longer than necessary. The miller sued the carrier. *Held.* As the full circumstances were not explained, the damage was too remote and the action failed.

The rules laid down by Baron Alderson for the assessment of damages, where there has been a breach of contract, were as follows: "Where two parties have made a contract which one of them has broken, the damages which the other party ought to receive in respect of such breach of contract should be such as may fairly and reasonably be considered either arising naturally (i.e. according to the usual course of things), from such breach of contract itself, or such as may reasonably be supposed to have been in the contemplation of both parties, at the time they made the contract as the probable result of the breach of it".

Note: This principle has now been expressly provided for in s. 50(2) Sale of Goods Act, 1979.

This decision should be compared with the one in:

Victoria Laundry (Windsor) Ltd *v*. Newman Industries Ltd (1949)
The defandant promised to deliver a boiler by a certain date. It was not delivered until some months later and the plaintiff sued for:

1. Loss of normal business profits during the period of the delay; and
2. Profits on dyeing contracts offered during the period of delay.

Held. Damages for (1) were claimable but for (2), they were not – as they could not have been contemplated at the date of the contract.

Although, at one time, it was not possible for a plaintiff to be awarded damages for an action relating to inconvenience or injured feelings (**Hobbs *v*. London & South Western Railway Co. (1875)**) the House of Lords, in **Addis *v*. Gramophone Co. Ltd. (1909)** held that damages could be awarded in respect of injured feelings. More recently, damages have been awarded in respect of distress and upset when:

(1) a solicitor failed to enforce an injunction against a man who subsequently caused additional molestation against a female: **Heywood *v*. Wellers (1976)**; and,
(2) a surveyor failed to draw attention to defects in a property over which, one of his clients, was negotiating a purchase: **Perry *v*. Sidney Phillips & Son (1982)**.

CLASSIFICATION OF DAMAGES

There are various terms which may be used to describe damages and each one may be applied to an action in tort or contract. These are:

1. ORDINARY (GENERAL OR COMPENSATORY) DAMAGES

In contract, these are damages which the court will assess based on a loss which has arisen naturally from breach, whereas, in tort, the court will have to consider the nature of the plaintiff's injury. For here, losses cannot be positively proved or ascertained, e.g. damage to a person's character caused by a libellous statement.

2. SPECIAL DAMAGES

In contract, these go beyond naturally arising damages and will only be awarded when they are within the contemplation of the parties. They apply to special losses which can be positively proved or ascertained, e.g. damage to a vintage car, to which a garage owner had agreed to repair the steering, but which he had negligently damaged beyond repair while the vehicle was in his possession.

3. EXEMPLARY (PUNITIVE) DAMAGES

Although the main objective of awarding damages is to compensate, occasionally they are used to punish (i.e. an extra amount of damages is awarded) in an attempt to deter the defendant and others from doing the same thing in the future. Today though, the awarding of such exemplary damages will only be made in exceptional circumstances: **Rookes *v*. Barnard (1964); Cassell & Co. Ltd *v*. Broome (1972)**.

4. AGGRAVATED DAMAGES

These mainly apply in tort and can be awarded where the plaintiff has established that the tort committed against him was more unpleasant than the normal – Thus, he requires higher damages to compensate him.

5. NOMINAL DAMAGES

These apply when a plaintiff has, say, established a breach of contract, but has suffered no actual loss. Damages of this type are awarded to personal bank customers if the bank returns the customer's cheques in error and no special damage can be proved. In **Gibbon *v*. Westminster Bank Ltd (1939)** damages of £2 per cheque were awarded.

6. SUBSTANTIAL DAMAGES

These are awarded where it has been established that the plaintiff has suffered some loss and their purpose is to compensate for that loss. Such damages may be ordinary or special.

7. CONTEMPTUOUS DAMAGES

These are awarded when the plaintiff's claim has been successful, but the court disapproves of the plaintiff's conduct in bringing the action – thereby awarding a trivial amount, such as a halfpenny, as in **Dering *v*. Uris (1964)**. Here, Uris had written a book entitled "Exodus" which referred to certain attrocities carried out by the Germans in concentration camps. The book clearly libelled Dering, a doctor, but because the jury felt little sympathy for the cause of the action, only contemptuous damages were awarded.

8. LIQUIDATED DAMAGES

In contract, this term applies when a breach has been proved and the parties to the action agree upon the level of damages, e.g. because it had been provided for in the contract. In tort, damages are never liquidated.

9. UNLIQUIDATED DAMAGES

In contract, where the level of damages are not fixed by the contract itself, the plaintiff must establish that he has suffered a loss, then the court will decide how much damages are to be awarded. In tort, the latter procedure is the standard.

It has recently been established that damages need not be awarded in sterling. For, they can be awarded in any foreign currency specified in the contract or if the contract does not contain such a clause, in any currency which "most truly expressed the plaintiff's loss". This was the House of Lords' decision in **The Despina R (1979)** and **Services Europe Atlantique Sud (Seas) v. Stockholms Rederiaktiebolag Svea of Stockholm (1978)**.

Another decision the Court of Appeal has been faced with relates to how changes in the sterling exchange rate affect the level of damages awarded (or the payment of a debt). **H. Parsons Ltd v. Uttley Ingham Co. Ltd (1977)**. It was held that the defendant must pay at the exchange rate ruling on the date that the damages were awarded (or the debts fell due). If the rate changes after the date on which the damages have been assessed or debt became due, the change can be ignored. If the rate changes before or on the date on which damages were assessed or the debt became due, again the change can be ignored unless it was expressly provided for in the contract or had been contemplated by the parties. Thus, it would only be under this final set of conditions that the court would use an up to date exchange rate to establish how much the injured party should receive in his own currency. **Aruna Mills v. Dhanrajmal Gobindram (1958)** and **The Teh Hu (1969)**.

3. QUANTUM MERUIT

Upon breach, the injured party may not want to make a claim for damages, but instead, treat the contract as discharged and make a claim for payment for what has already been done under the contract. To do the latter, he must sue on a "Quantum Meruit" – as much as he has earned. Under this heading different types of claim may be distinguished.

(a) Where one party refuses to perform or abandon the contract. **Planché v. Colburn (1831)**, see earlier.

(b) Where work has taken place under a void contract. It should be noted here that the court will not award damages on a void contract but will be prepared to hear a quantum meruit claim.

Craven-Ellis v. Canons Ltd (1936)

The plaintiff was the managing director of Canons Ltd. A deed provided for the level of his remuneration. The Articles of Association of the company stated that any director must acquire a specified number of qualification shares (which the plaintiff never acquired) within a stipulated time. As he did not satisfy the requirement contained in the articles, the deed appointing him was void and he had no automatic right to be remunerated. However, he sued on a quantum meruit for reasonable remuneration. *Held*. His claim was successful.

(c) Where a contract has been frustrated, a claim under quantum meruit is available provided frustration can be established – see **Davis Contractors Ltd *v.* Fareham U.D.C. (1956)**.

In general, a claim for quantum meruit will not succeed when one of the terms of the contract requires complete performance before payment is to be made – see **Sumpter *v.* Hedges (1898)** and **Cutter *v.* Powell (1795)** earlier.

4. SPECIFIC PERFORMANCE

This is a discretionary equitable remedy. As its name suggests, it is an order by the court for the other party to carry out or perform in accordance with the terms of the contract. Specific performance may be granted over contracts relating to land, the taking of debentures, the payment of money (see the **Beswick** case below) and occasionally the sale of goods (i.e. where it is difficult to assess the value of the goods).

The remedy is available at the court's discretion, and in making its decision, the court will have the following points in mind.

(a) If damages are an adequate remedy, specific performance will not be granted.

Beswick *v.* Beswick (1967)

A coal merchant sold his business to his nephew under an agreement which provided for a weekly payment to the uncle of £6 10s during his lifetime, and upon his death, a weekly payment of £5 to his widow during her lifetime. Following his death, the widow was only given one payment of £5. She brought an action for the arrears and for specific performance as regards future payments of £5, both in her personal capacity and that of administratrix. *Held.* In the lower court, both actions were unsuccessful. Following an appeal, the Court of Appeal, amongst other things, decided that:

(1) Specific performance could, in certain circumstances (as here), be ordered on a contract to pay money.
(2) As the widow's claim did not relate to property as defined in s. 56(I) Law of Property Act 1925 (i.e. it was not realty – see Chapter 6), even though she was a third party to the agreement, a claim in her personal capacity was still considered good.
(3) In her capacity as administrator, both her claims were good.

Following an appeal to the House of Lords, it was agreed that the widow's claims, as administratrix, were good, because she was suing on behalf of her deceased husband who had been a party to the original agreement.

It was noted though, that the Court of Appeal had been incorrect in their judgement in point (2) above, thus a personal action in these circumstances was unenforceable.

(b) The remedy is not available for contracts which are uncertain, or unfair, or unjust.

Grist *v*. Bailey (1966)

Mrs Bailey had agreed to sell her house for £850. This was approximately £1,500 below its vacant possession value. She believed she had to do this because it was thought that there was a tenant in occupation. When she discovered her error, she indicated that she was no longer prepared to sell at the artificially low figure and Grist took an action against her for specific performance. *Held*. It would have been unjust to allow the sale to take place at such a low price, particularly with the agreement being subject to a common mistake. As a consequence the action failed.

(c) The remedy is not available where the court would not be in a position to supervise the performance or execution, e.g. the completion of a half-built house or seeing that a porter employed to look after a block of flats, adequately carries out his duties. **Ryan *v*. Mutual Tontine Westminster Chambers Association (1893)**.

(d) The remedy is not available when one party is a minor.

(e) The remedy is not available for contracts of a personal nature, e.g. if a person contracts to work for a particular company but never joins them, an order for specific performance could not be made to operate against him. Instead, a claim for damages would be more appropriate. Neither will agreements between partners be enforced in this way: **Rigby *v*. Connol (1880)**.

5. INJUNCTION

An injunction is an equitable remedy. It involves the court granting an order restraining a person from doing a particular act and is commonly used when damages would not be an adequate remedy, e.g. where an agent agrees to work for one principal only, the agent can have an injunction enforced against him, preventing him from working for any other principal. This example relates to the provision of a personal service. In general, injunctions for service contracts will only be granted against express negative covenants.

Lumley *v*. Wagner (1853)

Wagner agreed to sing a series of concerts at Lumley's theatre and not sing elsewhere during the agreed period (this is an example of an express negative covenant). She later contracted to sing elsewhere and refused to sing in Lumley's concerts. *Held*. An injunction was granted preventing her from singing elsewhere, although an order for specific performance compelling her to sing only for Lumley was not granted.

The same decision was made in **Warner Bros *v*. Nelson (1937)** where Nelson (Bette Davis), even though she was solely contracted to Warner Brothers for a period of twelve months contracted to act for another during this period because they offered more favourable terms.

In the absence of a negative stipulation, injunctions will not be granted where the defendant will be working for the plaintiff and no other, or would be without a job. **Whitwood Chemical Co. *v*. Hardman (1891)**. This ruling was codified in the Trade Union and Labour Relations Act, 1974.

There are various types of injunction and a simple classification, with brief description is given below:

Interlocutory: This is granted before a case is heard in court. However, the plaintiff must give an undertaking to pay the defendant damages if the legal action is unsuccessful.
Perpetual: This is granted when the legal action has been heard and the decision made.
Prohibitory: This orders that a certain act shall not be done.
Mandatory: This orders that a certain act shall be done.

6. RESCISSION

An alternative way of expressing this term is "to set aside". It is a discretionary equitable remedy which is available for either breach of contract or misrepresentation – as described earlier.

It is not a universal remedy and will certainly not be available in the following circumstances:

1. Where the parties are not capable of putting themselves back into their original positions – restituto in integrum: **Clarke *v*. Dickson (1858)**.
2. Where the party who was misled knew of the misrepresentation, but even with this knowledge has either taken benefit under the contract or affirmed the contract.
3. Where third parties have acquired rights under the contract: **Lewis *v*. Averay (1972)**. See earlier.
4. Where there has been undue delay in commencing a legal action to rescind the contract. For delay will be interpreted by the courts as an affirmation. **Leaf *v*. International Galleries (1950)**. See earlier.

If the misrepresentation is shown to be fraudulent, then rescission is still available provided the delay in taking legal action is not defeated by the provisions contained within the Statute of Limitations.

If a party is claiming under rescission, he cannot at the same time claim for damages: **Horsler *v.* Zorro (1975)**, unless the failure to perform by the other party was a breach of contract: **Buckland *v.* Farmer and Moody (1978)**.

Finally, if the action for rescission is successful, all part payments must be returned.

PRIVITY OF CONTRACT

A contract is a private contractual agreement between the respective parties and under the contract the parties acquire rights against each other which are enforceable at law. Thus, there is a general rule that only parties to the contract can sue on it. For, to allow third parties to acquire rights under contracts that did not involve them would clearly be inequitable as illustrated in:

Dunlop *v.* Selfridge (1915)
Dunlop sold some of their tyres to Dew & Co. who were wholesalers and under the contract it was agreed that the tyres would not be sold at less than Dunlop's list price. Selfridges ordered two of Dunlop's tyres from Dew & Co., and although Selfridges agreed not to sell at less than list price, they sold one below the figure, and said they would sell the second at list price. Dunlop's then tried to get an injunction preventing further sales at below list price and damages against Selfridges. *Held.* There was no contract between the parties to the action and so the action failed. (*Note:* Because of the provisions of s. 26 Resale Prices Act, 1976, then this would be decided differently today. For Dunlop can insist that a tyre fitter, irrespective of whether he had obtained the tyres directly from Dunlop or from a wholesaler, would have to sell the tyres at not less than a stipulated minimum price.)

Several other cases, notably **Tweddle *v.* Atkinson (1861)** and **Scruttons Ltd. *v.* Midland Silicones (1962)**, which have already been described in the text, have referred to privity of contract and it is recommended that you read these again now to see how the doctrine was applied.

The doctrine does not apply universally, and the main exceptions to the general rule are:

1. For a trust, where it is proven that a person is a beneficiary, he has the right to sue under the trust – but not on the contract.

2. Certain types of insurance (e.g. car insurance) compel the insured to be covered against third party risks. So, if a third party (e.g. a passenger) is injured in a car accident which is the result of negligence of the person driving him or that of the person driving another car, then the third party will have rights against the negligent driver and the insurance company with whom that the driver had taken out a policy: Road Traffic Act, 1972.

3. Negotiable instruments. On a fully negotiable instrument, a holder in due course can sue all prior parties on a bill (see Chapter 11), even though he was not a party to the original contract.

4. In the Law of Agency. A principal is able to sue on a contract entered into by his agent.

5. In certain circumstances, price maintenance agreements under the Restrictive Trade Practices Act, 1956 and 1976. This enables actions to be taken by any party in the sale chain against any prior party.

6. Under s. 56(1) Law of Property Act, 1925. This provides that "a person may take an immediate or other interest in land or other property or the benefit of any condition, right of entry, covenant or agreement over or respecting land or other property although he may not be named as party to the conveyance or other instrument". The subsection was applied by the House of Lords when the appeal in **Beswick *v.* Beswick (1967)** (see back) was considered.

7. A legal assignee of a debt or chose in action may sue prior assignors.

8. Certain life assurance policies are issued under s. 11 Married Womens Property Act, 1882. These are taken out on the life of one spouse for the benefit of the other and/or children. A trust is created over the policy monies in favour of the latter group and although they are not parties to the contract, they can sue on it.

9. Although it is accepted that a person can only sue in his own name on a contract to which he is a party, it is now possible for a party to sue on behalf of others at the same time as illustrated in:

Jackson *v.* Horizon Holidays Ltd (1975)

Mr Jackson booked a holiday "of the highest standard" in his own name. He took his family with him and all were disappointed by the facilities that were available for they nowhere near complied with the description contained within the advertising brochure. Upon his return, he sued the holiday company for damages, not only for himself but also his family. *Held*. The holiday company were liable, and it was permissible, in the circumstances, to recover damages for everyone who was booked on the holiday in his name.

10. If one party, X, acts in such a way to induce Y to breach his contractual duty with another party, Z, then even though X is not a party to the contract, if Z suffers a loss, he may sue X in tort.

EXAMINATION QUESTIONS

Question 1

"A contract is an agreement which will be enforced by the law." (Charlesworth)

(a) Do you agree? Give your reasons.
(b) State the five characteristics which the agreement or parties to it must have to be a valid contract.

(Chartered Institute of Bankers)

Question 2

(a) Why is it necessary to distinguish an offer from an invitation to treat?

(b) At an auction sale Tom made the highest bid for an old chest. Before the auctioneer struck his hammer on the table a friend told Tom that the chest was riddled with dry rot so Tom called out "Bid withdrawn." "Too late," said the auctioneer, who then banged his hammer on the table for the third time. Explain to Tom the contractual rules relating to auction sales and advise him in these circumstances.
(A.E.B. A-Level)

Question 3

Geoff, a plumber, advertises for the supply to him of copper piping and copper goods over a period of 12 months and not exceeding a total length of 10,000 metres. Stock submits a written tender on which he has written, "If this tender is accepted, orders for piping must be notified in writing to the tenderer." Stock's tender is accepted by Geoff. One week later, Geoff posts a letter to Stock ordering 100 metres of copper piping but this letter never reaches Stock. Being dissatisfied at hearing nothing from Stock, Geoff telephones him, repeats the order and explains that a letter has already been sent. Stock then replies that the whole deal is off as he can sell his copper piping at a far higher figure elsewhere. Advise Geoff.
(J.M.B. A-Level)

Question 4

"In the formation of a contract a key feature is 'communication' whether of offer or acceptance." Discuss.
(A.E.B. A-Level)

Question 5

Arthur offers by letter to sell his car to Bertram for £1,000. State the circumstances:

(a) when that offer lapses;
(b) when that offer may be revoked by Arthur.

(Chartered Institute of Bankers)

Question 6

(a) When does an offer lapse?

(b) A offers to sell his car to B for £1,500. B writes back that he will only pay £1,400. A refuses to sell for that reduced sum, whereupon B informs A that he will now pay him the original price of £1,500. Have they made a valid contract?

(Chartered Institute of Bankers)*

Question 7

(a) "An offer may lapse before acceptance." Explain and discuss.

(b) TE, a transport enthusiast, offered to sell his collection of timetables to A for £100. A replied that he was definitely interested but that he would have to see if any of his friends were prepared to lend him the money. Six months later A telephoned TE to say that he was able to accept TE's offer unconditionally but TE replied that the timetables had already been sold. Advise TE.

(C.I.T.(I))

Question 8

(a) Explain the ways, other than by revocation, in which an offer may be brought to an end.

(b) Alan offered to sell his house to Bob and said, "I will give you five days to make up your mind." Before the five were over Bob heard from Alan's daughter in the course of casual conversation that Alan had sold the house to Clive. Advise Bob.

(A.E.B. A-Level)

Question 9

(a) Mrs L loses her handbag. She puts an advertisement in a shop window offering £10 for its return. M finds it and returns it to her. Later on M sees the advertisement. Is M entitled to the £10 reward?

(b) On Monday Frank offers to sell his motor scooter to Gregory for £40, the offer to remain open until noon on Thursday. On Wednesday Frank sells it to Henry for £45. On Thursday morning at 10 a.m. Gregory posts a letter to Frank accepting his offer but the letter does not reach him until Friday. Indicate the legal position.

(Chartered Institute of Bankers)

Question 10

Consider whether there is a contract in the following situations:

(a) Amy offers to sing at a concert organised by Pear Promotions. Amy dies, but Pear Promotions, not knowing of her death, write accepting her offer.

(b) Roger offers to buy coal from Eastern Fuels Limited. Roger dies, but Eastern Fuels, not knowing of his death, deliver the coal.

(A.E.B. O-Level)

Question 11

On Monday, 2nd April 1973, at 4 p.m., George posted a letter to Harold with an offer to sell him a motor car for £1,000. Harold received it on Tuesday, 3rd April 1973, at 4 p.m. and posted a letter accepting this offer at 5 p.m. Is there a contract between these two persons? Give reasons for your answer.

Would your answers differ if:

(a) Harold died at noon on Tuesday, 3rd April? and,
(b) George died at noon on Tuesday, 3rd April?
or
(c) Harold died at 6 p.m. on Tuesday, 3rd April? and,
(d) George died at 7 p.m. on Tuesday, 3rd April?

(Chartered Institute of Bankers)

Question 12

On 1st April Fred offered to sell his car to George for £1,000 and told him that he would keep the offer open until 5th April. On 3rd April Fred sold and delivered the car to Harold for £950 and Fred wrote George a letter informing him of that sale. George did not receive the letter until 5th April. On 4th April George wrote to Fred agreeing to buy the car for £1,000. He posted his letter the same day and it reached Fred on 6th April.

Can George sue Fred for breach of contract?

(Chartered Institute of Bankers)

Question 13

(a) A and B have been corresponding with each other regarding the proposed sale of A's house to B. A wanted £25,000 for it, but B was willing to pay £24,000 only. Last week A wrote and offered to sell it to him for £21,450. B knew that A had made a mistake and meant to state £24,150, but nevertheless he accepted the offer. What is the legal position?

(b) X offered to sell his farm for £60,000 to Y, who wrote in reply that he would pay £50,000. A few hours later Y posted another letter to say he would pay £60,000. Discuss the legal position.

(Chartered Institute of Bankers)

Question 14

Abel, an auctioneer, advertised in various newspapers and international trade journals that a sale of paintings and jewellery would be held at 10 Gambit Mansions on 11th October at 11 a.m. Bertram and many others travelled to attend the auction but it was not held. Bertram wishes to sue Abel for his loss of time and expenses. Advise Bertram.
(Chartered Institute of Bankers)

Question 15

Richard, a famous actor, agreed with Stanley, for a fee of £1,000, to act as Master of Ceremonies at a beauty competition organised by Stanley. The competition was to last one day commencing at noon and ending at midnight. Richard attended and did all the duties assigned to him but collapsed and died at 23.59 p.m. that day. Is the widow entitled to the agreed fee which Stanley refuses to pay?
(Chartered Institute of Bankers)

Question 16

Consider whether Mark has a legal remedy in the following situations:

(a) Harold has invited Mark to his Golf Club for lunch but Harold never arrives.

(b) Mark sees a jacket in a shop window labelled £5. When he tries to buy it he is told that the correct price is £25.

(c) Mark lends £10 to his nephew Steven, aged 16, to buy a guitar. Steven never repays the money.
(A.E.B. O-Level)

Question 17

"An agreement is not always a contract, but a contract must be an agreement." Explain this statement.
(Chartered Institute of Bankers)

Question 18

Alison, aged 17, intended to pursue a career as a journalist. She ordered some "A" level text books from Zoe's Book Shop and whilst there ordered a typewriter which cost £1,300. Richard lent her £1,500 specifically to buy the typewriter and some clothes but Alison bought a diamond ring for £1,200. Alison now tells Zoe that she requires neither the books nor the typewriter since she has decided to become a teacher. Zoe and Richard now seek your advice as to whether they have any case in law against Alison. What would your advice be?
(A.E.B. A-Level)

Question 19

What does English law mean by a minor and how does the legal capacity of a minor differ from that of an adult?
(A.E.B. O-Level)

Question 20

"In some cases a minor's contract is voidable: that is it binds both parties but the minor can escape liability in certain circumstances." Assess the truth of this statement, explaining to which situations it applies and when and how the minor "escapes".
(A.E.B. A-Level)

Question 21

(a) What contracts are binding upon a minor?

(b) M, a minor, by fraudulently representing himself to be of age persuaded A, an adult to lend him £3,000. M has repaid £1,500 but failed through impecuniosity to repay the balance, arguing that he is not legally bound so to do even if he were able. Consider the legal position. Would it make any difference to your answer if M were to be left £10,000 in a rich uncle's will?
(C.I.T.)

Question 22

(a) X, aged 17, hired a car from Y. Owing to his bad driving he damaged the engine and gears. Is X liable to Y for this damage?

(b) A, aged 17, hired a car from B for a week. At the end of the week he had not returned it to B, although he had been requested to do so. A had in fact lent the car to C, who has disappeared without trace of him or the car. Is A liable to B?
(Chartered Institute of Bankers)

Question 23

Bill, who is 17 years of age, borrowed £200 from Tony by pretending to be 19. He spent £150 on a suit because his old one was worn out, bought books costing £25 and put £25 in his money box for a new radio. Tony wants Bill to repay the loan and seeks your advice. What would that advice be?
(A.E.B. A-Level)

Question 24

Define and explain what is meant by "consideration" in the law of contract. Why is it important? Illustrate your answer with examples.
(A.E.B. O-Level)

Question 25

"Save the Old Folks" is a registered charity. As it urgently needed money to build a convalescent home, Sir Julian Stonebroke agreed to donate £500,000 to assist with the project. He now refuses to do so. Can the charity compel him to do so?
(Chartered Institute of Bankers)

Question 26

Can the following promises be enforced by law:

(a) a promise by Alfred to Brian that, if Charles paints Alfred's house, Alfred will pay Brian £100;

(b) a promise by Peter to Quentin, a policeman, that if Quentin recovers some goods which have been stolen from Peter, then Peter will pay Quentin £100;

(c) a promise by George to William that, if Edward will accept 50p in the £ in full settlement of a debt which William owes Edward, George will similarly accept 50p in the £ in full settlement of a debt which William owes George?
(Chartered Institute of Bankers)

Question 27

Explain to Linda the factors which the courts would consider in deciding whether she must carry out her promises in the following situations:

(a) David, who was going to London, was asked by Linda to buy her a scarf for which she gave him the money. When he returned Linda told David that she would give him some money for his fare. She decided subsequently that she could not afford to give him the fare money.

(b) Jane was an air hostess on Linda's holiday flight. Linda told Jane that she would give Jane a bottle of expensive perfume if Jane looked after her especially well.

(c) Linda promised her boyfriend, Andrew, that he could have her car for £5 although it was worth £5,000.
(A.E.B. A-Level)

Question 28

(a) Sam and Tom were neighbours. One day Sam told Tom that he wanted to buy a lawn mower. Tom told Sam that he had one for sale, showed it to him and said he wanted £70 for it. Sam said he would think it over. That night Sam wrote a letter to Tom in which he said that he wanted the mower and enclosed £70. When Tom received the letter he had already sold the mower to Ursula. Advise Sam as to his legal position.

(b) Ken announced to his guests at a party that he would give £30 to any of them who swam the Swanee River before dawn. Len did not hear the announcement, though he was at the party, and later went for a swim in the river and crossed it. On his return he was told of Ken's statement and tried, unsuccessfully, to obtain the £30. Explain to Len his chances of success if he were to take action in the courts against Ken.
(A.E.B. A-Level)

Question 29

Advise Albert in the following cases:

(a) Albert bought a second-hand car from Bertram. On discovering, after delivery, that the engine was unusually noisy, he asked Bertram whether the car was roadworthy. Bertram assured him that it was, but the car has now broken down completely.

(b) Albert agreed to pay Cuthbert £800 for a car. Being pressed for money, Albert asked Cuthbert if he would accept £400 immediately and the balance on 1st June 1978. Cuthbert agreed to this arrangement but is now threatening to sue for the balance without waiting until 1st June 1978.
(Chartered Institute of Bankers)

Question 30

James owes Kenneth £100 and the debt is now due. Last night Kenneth told James that if he paid £50 by noon today he need not pay the balance. James paid the £50 this morning. Can Kenneth compel James to pay the balance? Would your answer differ if Kenneth, instead of asking for £50, had agreed to accept James's watch in settlement of the debt?
(Institute of Bankers)*

Question 31

Dan, a builder, constructed a garage for Stan and sent him a bill for £2,000 being the cost of the work. Stan then told Dan that he could only pay him £1,555. Dan agreed to accept £1,555 so Stan sent him a cheque for that amount. Some months later Dan told him that he now wanted the balance of the original sum and was therefore going to sue him for £445. Advise Stan.
(A.E.B. A-Level)

Question 32

A took his motor car to B's garage for repair. Nothing was said about payment. When the repair work was done, A was so pleased with the quality of the work that he told B he would pay him £200. What claim has B against A, who has failed to pay anything?
(Chartered Institute of Bankers)

Question 33

(a) Some contacts are said to be contrary to public policy. Why is this so?

(b) A tells B that if B gives £5,000 to the X charity then B will receive a public honour. The money has been paid but B has not received any honour. B wishes to recover the money he has paid. Can he do so?
(Chartered Institute of Bankers)

Question 34

(a) Distinguish between contracts of indemnity and contracts of guarantee.

(b) A trader is willing to supply goods on credit to a minor if the minor's father will make himself responsible for the price. What type of contract should the trader require the father to enter into?
(Chartered Institute of Bankers)

Question 35

(a) Agatha orally agrees to guarantee payment of a debt of £100 owed by her friend Bertha to Clarissa. Is this guarantee enforceable?

(b) Robert orally agrees to sell his house to Simon for £20,000 and allows Simon to carry out some structural alterations to the property. Subsequently, Robert changes his mind and says that he no longer wishes to sell the house. Does Simon have a remedy open to him?
(Chartered Institute of Bankers)

Question 36

Albert wishes to sell his car and house. The sale price of the car is £1,000 and that of the house £10,000. Charles has spoken to Albert and agreed to buy the car and house for those prices.

Have they made a valid contract? State your reasons for your answer.
(Chartered Institute of Bankers)

Question 37

State with examples what is meant by a contract **uberrimae fidei**.
(Chartered Institute of Bankers)

Question 38

David has entered into a guarantee of the bank account of his friend Edward with the Metropolitan Bank. The bank officers knew that Edward's wife, Mary, could draw on that account, also that she was an inveterate gambler with previous convictions for crimes of dishonesty. The bank did not inform David of these facts and have now requested David to honour his guarantee. The unsatisfactory state of the account

is due to several cheques for large amounts drawn by Mary and cashed at the bank counter by her. These monies she spent on gambling. Is David liable under his guarantee?
(Chartered Institute of Bankers)

Question 39

(a) Distinguish between duress and undue influence.

(b) (i) Blake, a policeman, wanted Milton to supply him with goods but Milton refused. Blake told Milton that, if he did not supply the goods, Blake would initiate a prosecution with respect to some other activities of Milton about which Blake had information. To avoid harmful publicity and scandal Milton agreed to enter a contract with Blake for the supply of the desired goods. Advise Milton as to the effect of this contract.

(ii) John was a client of Ivor, a stockbroker, who advised John to sell some shares which he offered to buy himself. John agreed to sell the shares to Ivor but now regrets it. Advise John as to whether he can refuse to perform the contract.

(A.E.B. A-Level)

Question 40

In what circumstances is the court prepared to recognise that terms are implied in a contract?
(A.E.B. A-Level)

Question 41

(a) The terms of a contract are of two types. State them and give an example of each.

(b) Peter advertises the sale of a portrait of his ancestor which he honestly believes was painted by the famous English painter, Turner. Quentin inspects the painting and is also advised by an experienced art critic. Both are satisfied that it was painted by Turner. Quentin pays Peter £200,000 for this picture but recently it has been discovered that it was painted by an obscure amateur artist. Quentin wishes to return the picture to Peter and obtain a refund of his money. Peter has refused. Will Quentin succeed if he sues Peter?
(Chartered Institute of Bankers)

Question 42

Julia was told by Barry that a car had travelled only 10,000 miles. In fact, the car had travelled over 70,000 miles. Julia bought the car, believing it to be excellent value, but has now discovered the true mileage. Advise Julia as to her contractual rights on the basis that Barry's statement is

not a term of the contract. She is not sure if Barry himself was aware of the facts.
(A.E.B. A-Level)

Question 43
Jerry Builders Ltd entered into a contract with X to install new machinery at his (X's) factory, and to complete the work not later than 1st June 1987. The contract stated that the company would pay X £50 per week compensation for any delay in completing the work beyond this date.

There was a delay of ten weeks, which caused X a trading loss of £5,000. Can X recover the amount of this loss from the company?
(Chartered Institute of Bankers)

Question 44
Better Builders contracts to reconstruct a laundry and to complete the work within eight weeks. The work in fact takes ten weeks and the laundry is now claiming damages for the loss of normal profits during the two additional weeks and also for the loss of a particularly valuable contract which it could not accept because its plant was out of action.

(a) Advise Better Builders.

(b) To what extent would your advice differ if the contract had contained a clause under which Better Builders agreed to pay £200 by way of penalty for each week late in completing the work?
(I.C.M.A.)

Question 45
A builder agrees to erect a factory within one year. Discuss the validity of the following defences if he has failed to complete the work on time and is being sued for breach of contract.

(a) The Government imposed building regulations which prevented him from continuing with the work.

(b) The cost of building materials increased, obliging him to buy in smaller quantities because of a shortage of working capital.

(c) An influenza epidemic led to the illness of a number of his specialist workers.

(d) Some building materials on the site were damaged by a fire.
(I.C.M.A.)

Question 46
(a) Under what circumstances may a person who alleges that he has been induced to enter into a contract by reason of a misrepresentation have a remedy? What remedies are available?

(b) At the start of negotiations for the sale of a retail shop the seller makes a true statement regarding annual turnover and profits. Whilst the negotiations are proceeding a supermarket opens a branch nearby and the trade of the shop declines considerably. After the sale is completed the purchaser discovers this. Advise the purchaser.
(I.C.M.A.)

Question 47

(a) Examine the main requirements of actionable misrepresentation and consider the remedies available therefor.

(b) In negotiating the sale of a garage last January, B a businessman correctly told X, who was proposing to buy the business, that the annual turnover was in the region of £200,000 with an annual profit of about £25,000. In March, B's health deteriorated and he decided to go on a world cruise, leaving his foreman in charge of the business. At the end of April internal accounts showed that the turnover was down to an annual rate of about £100,000 with the possibility of a loss of about £10,000 by the end of the year. Only after the contract for the sale of the business was signed at the beginning of May did X become aware of the new financial position. Advise X.
(C.I.T.)

Question 48

Harold, a chemist when negotiating for the sale of his business, stated in his offer to sell to Ian that his customers included all the nursing homes within five miles of his shop. Since he made that offer the largest nursing home within that area informed Harold that they had formed their own dispensary and regretted that they would cease to deal with him. Ian bought the business, but became aware of this development only after completing the purchase. He wishes to sue Harold for damages, for Harold had not informed him of the change in the terms of the offer. What legal advice would you give Ian?
(Chartered Institute of Bankers)*

Question 49

Frank has sold his retail milk business to George for £22,000; a term of the sale was that Frank should promise not to be involved in any way in any retail milk business within 50 miles of Marble Arch, London. Is this promise valid in law?
(Chartered Institute of Bankers)

Question 50

Albert, in England, contracts with Badov to sell and deliver to him one

hundred steel ingots for use by Badov in his factory in Ruritania. After their manufacture and preparation for shipment to Ruritania there was an earthquake which destroyed Badov's factory. Badov had paid Albert a deposit of £10,000. Badov now refuses to accept the goods. What is the effect on the contract of this refusal?
(Chartered Institute of Bankers)

Question 51
S Cleaners Limited offered "to clean two garments for the price of one". A notice was displayed in the shop to this effect but with the addition, in smaller print, of a statement that the customer must agree to accept full responsibility if anything should happen to the garments. A similar statement was printed on the back of the tickets which were handed to customers when they deposited the garments.

Albert brought two jackets for cleaning. Because of poor eyesight he was unable to read the small print on the notice, and he put the ticket in his pocket without reading it.

Some days later when Albert collected the jackets he saw that one had now been badly torn. After wearing the other jacket he contracted a skin disease which was caused by a chemical which the cleaner had used. Advise Albert.
(I.C.M.A.)

Question 52
Describe the different types of mistake in the law of contract and the effect of each type of mistake.
(A.E.B. O-Level)

Question 53
(a) "At common law a contract is not void merely because the parties have made the same mistake, however fundamental." Discuss.

(b) Peter received an order from Wendy for "Sennet Nuts". Peter inquired from Hook, his wholesaler, whether he could supply Peter. Hook told Peter that he could supply "Smee Nuts" which were exactly the same as Sennet Nuts. Peter then ordered 75 kilos of Smee Nuts to meet Wendy's order. Hook delivered the Smee Nuts to Peter but when Peter sent them to Wendy she told him that Smee Nuts were not Sennet Nuts as she required. Advise Peter whether the law affords him any redress against Hook.
(A.E.B. A-Level)

Question 54
Sarah was the managing director of a large company. One day, while she

was talking to another director, Sarah was given a pile of letters to sign by Tina, her secretary. Sarah, relying on Tina, only glanced at the letters before signing them. One of the letters was an undertaking to the Ultracautious Finance Company (U.F.C.) in which Sarah agreed to act as guarantor in respect of a loan to Tina by U.F.C. Sarah discovered the true nature of the letter only when Tina defaulted on her payments to U.F.C. Advise Sarah as to her liability, if any, to U.F.C.
(A.E.B. A-Level)

Question 55

Kathy went into a jeweller's shop and asked to see some rings. As she was examining the rings her conversation with Don, the shop owner, led him to believe that she was the daughter of Lord Barset, a well-known millionaire. She chose three rings worth a total of £7,000 and gave Don a cheque for that amount saying that she would collect the rings the next day. As she was leaving the shop she saw a gold watch worth £800. She asked if she could take it with her and Don agreed. Kathy gave Don another cheque, left the shop and pawned the watch with Freda. When Kathy's cheques proved to be worthless Don sought to recover the watch from Freda. Advise Freda as to her legal position.
(A.E.B. A-Level)

Question 56

"When two parties have come to a contract – or rather what appears, on the face of it, to be a contract – the fact that one party is mistaken as to the identity of another does not mean that there is no contract, or that the contract is a nullity and void from the beginning." per Lord Denning M.R. in **Lewis *v.* Averay (1973)**.

How far is the above statement a true reflection of the law?
(J.M.B. (B))

Question 57

Dullard an elderly man with weak sight has two cars for sale. Smart agrees to buy one and, by pretending to be a well-known local business man, is allowed to drive it away in return for a cheque. The cheque is dishonoured. Alec asks if he may hire the second car for a week and persuades Dullard to allow him to draw up a hire agreement which Dullard signs. The agreement in fact transfers the ownership of the car to Alec. Both Smart and Alec have now sold the cars and disappeared. Advise Dullard as to his rights to recover the cars from the subsequent purchasers.
(I.C.M.A.)

Question 58
Explain the forms which equitable relief for mistake can take.
(A.E.B. A-Level)

Question 59
Leslie showed Kenneth an antique which he described as a "gold snuff box", and said he was willing to sell it. Kenneth examined it and offered £800. Leslie knew from the amount offered that Kenneth thought the box was solid gold. Leslie knew it was only gold plated. He nevertheless accepted that offer without comment or explanation. Two months later Kenneth discovered the true quality of the box, and now wishes to recover the £800 he paid Leslie. Will he succeed?
(Chartered Institute of Bankers)

Question 60
Describe the different ways in which contracts can be discharged.
(A.E.B. O-Level)

Question 61
"As a general rule parties must perform precisely all the terms of the contract." Illustrate this general rule and consider the extent to which exceptions have been recognised by the courts.
(A.E.B. A-Level)

Question 62
George is a retained professional soccer player with Grantchester Rovers. In breach of his contract of employment he has left and is playing for another soccer club, Penalltee United. If Rovers sue United, will the court order him to play for Rovers and fulfil his contract?
(Chartered Institute of Bankers)

Question 63
Cecil, a road haulier, contracted with Frank to transport 1,000 tons of steel ingots from London to Liverpool. Owing to delays caused by Cecil, the steel did not reach Liverpool on the agreed date. Frank had intended to sell the steel on its arrival in Liverpool but during the period of delay the market price of steel fell sharply and Frank has sold at a considerable loss. Is Cecil liable to him for that loss?
(Chartered Institute of Bankers)

Question 64
(a) Explain what is meant by the doctrine of frustration and consider its application in the law of contract.

(b) E, an exporter, contracted to deliver goods from London to Lisbon within three weeks for £3,000. E normally sends goods by sea and the

price is calculated on that basis. However a dock strike now prevents shipments by sea though delivery by air at £6,000 is still possible. Consider the legal position.
(C.I.T.)

Question 65

(a) Explain the following classification of damages:
(i) *normal*; (ii) *general*; (iii) *aggravated.*

(b) Explain what is meant by *exemplary* damages and the basis on which such damages are awarded by the courts.
(A.E.B. A-Level)

Question 66

Turner agreed to appear in a small part in a play at Una's theatre but he was only able to attend the last three rehearsals. Una does not think that Turner should be allowed to appear and seeks your advice as to whether she is legally entitled to refuse to pay him. Advise her. What would your advice be if the theatre was destroyed by fire before the first night?
(A.E.B. A-Level)

Question 67

Explain the meaning of:
(a) quantum meruit;
(b) injunction; and
(c) specific performance,
and the circumstances when each might be appropriate in the event of a breach of contract.
(I.C.M.A.)

Question 68

P, a painter, agreed to paint a portrait of Miss X, the Managing Director of a small but prosperous airline. However, after hearing what he considered to be scandalous reports about Miss X's private life, P told her that he had changed his mind about painting her portrait. Advise Miss X.
(C.I.T.)

Question 69

(a) A contract may be changed by accord and satisfaction. What does this mean?

(b) Albert owes Bertram £200 and the latter agrees to accept £150 in satisfaction of the debt. Albert has paid him £150 but Bertram is now asking for the balance. Must he pay him? Would your answer differ if

Bertram agreed to accept a motor cycle in lieu of payment but after obtaining it still claims the original debt?
(Chartered Institute of Bankers)

Question 70

(a) What is the measure of damages awardable for breach of contract?

(b) What remedies other than an action for damages are available for a broken contract?

(c) B agrees to build a garage for £3,000 and to complete the work not later than 31st December 1987. In fact, B completes the work over the following Easter. What damages (if any) are awardable to A for this breach?
(Chartered Institute of Bankers)

Question 71

Tony hired a hall with a seating capacity of 2,000 from the Seaside Corporation at a charge of £1,000 for one week. He also hired an internationally-known pop group to appear in concert at the hall for a fee of £3,000. All 14,000 concert tickets at £2 each were sold in advance of the concert week.

Two days before the first concert, Seaside Corporation informed Tony that his letting had been cancelled in favour of another client who was prepared to pay more for the hire of the hall.

(a) Advise Tony, who wishes to hold the Corporation to the agreement.

(b) What, if any, would be the difference to your answer if Tony could not persuade the Corporation to allow him the use of the hall and as a result he has been obliged to pay the group its fee for the week and return the £28,000 ticket money to the ticket holders.
(J.M.B. (B))

Question 72

(a) What do you understand by "privity of contract"?

(b) John wishes to give a Christmas gift to his wife Jane. He takes out an annual subscription for the monthly magazine "Ladies Choice" in her name. The publishers fail to send her the monthly issues and she wishes to sue them for breach of contract. Can she do so successfully?
(Chartered Institute of Bankers)*

CHAPTER 5

UNINCORPORATED ASSOCIATIONS AND CORPORATIONS

UNINCORPORATED ASSOCIATIONS

There are certain groups of people, who as far as the law is concerned, have no separate legal identity from the persons who constitute the group. These are known as unincorporated associations and they can be set up for many reasons. Some will be for the mutual benefit of the individuals (e.g. Philatelic Societies, Tennis Clubs, etc.), others will be set up for religious reasons, others as trade unions, and finally, there are those which are set up for profit making purposes. This latter group are defined as partnerships and are more fully covered later in this chapter.

LAW RELATING TO UNINCORPORATED ASSOCIATIONS

Because the law does not differentiate an unincorporated association from its members, the members bear individual responsibility for the association's actions. This and other important characteristics are summarised below.

(a) LAND OWNERSHIP

All land must have private individuals (or corporations) as title holders, and the law provides that at least one and no more than four people can be defined as a title holder. This presents a problem for unincorporated associations, because if they own land, it cannot be registered in their association's name. In practice, this problem is overcome by the association agreeing that any land should be registered in the name of up to four of their key members, who are really considered to be holding the land in trust for the association. Once registered in their name, they may sue or be sued as a group in respect of the property.

(b) ENTRY INTO CONTRACTS

It is not possible for an unincorporated association to enter into a contract. Where a contract is made, it will be regarded as a contract entered into by the individual members who made it or authorised it.

(c) TORTS
Torts that are committed in relation to the association's activities are considered to be torts of the members responsible.

Brown *v.* Lewis (1896)
A football stand, for use by the public, was repaired following approval by the committee. The repair work was badly carried out, and subsequently the stand collapsed and injured a member of the public. *Held*. The committee, because it had authorised the work, was liable.

(d) DEBTS
Where a debt is created by a contract entered into by an authorised agent (e.g. a committee member as provided for by the rules) the members as a whole are liable.

(e) COMMITTEE
Powers may be conferred on the committee to control membership, and in particular, it may be given the power of expulsion. When acting in the latter role, a committee decision may be overruled by the court where it is considered that the committee's decision is contrary to public policy.

PARTNERSHIPS

DEFINITION

By s. 1(1) Partnership Act, 1890, a partnership is "the relationship which subsists between persons carrying on business in common with a view to profit". Section 2 of the statute then examines and interprets the definition, but there are three points of general nature which will establish whether a given relationship is a partnership or not.

NUMBERS. A partnership must consist of at least two persons and in normal circumstances is not permitted to exceed twenty persons.

ACTIONS IN COMMON. The people who make up the partnership should act together rather than pursue individual objectives of their own.

PROFIT. It is essential that the partners have a profit making motive, for if they are acting together merely for their mutual common good or for educational purposes, then they will not constitute a partnership.

It is important to know whether a group of people are, in law, a partnership or not. If they are, their relative rights, responsibilities and duties are provided for in the Partnership Act 1890 unless they have expressly excluded certain of the provisions contained therein and/or included others. Exclusion or inclusion could be by oral statement, or by the more formal method of having Articles or Deeds of Partnership prepared which have varied certain of the statutory provisions.

Note. In the popular press, partnerships are frequently referred to as firms.

FORMATION

Partnerships may be formed by:

(a) *Implication; or*
(b) *Oral agreement; or*
(c) *Simple agreement in writing; or*
(d) *Deed.*

The first two methods are self explanatory, while the third and fourth require some explanation. Where the agreement is a simple one in writing and signed (i.e. under hand) by the partners, then the written document is known as "Articles of Partnership". In contrast, where the arrangement has been completed by way of deed (i.e. sealed), the document is known as "Deed of Partnership". All the partners are bound by the Articles (or Deed) where they exist, and if particular points have not been covered therein, then the Partnership Act, 1890, applies. As indicated previously, the Articles (or Deed) may vary the terms of the Partnership Act.

Although legally the two types of agreement should be discussed and described separately, in practice, both types of document are invariably described as Articles – Mainly because the content of each can be exactly the same, it only being the method of completion, i.e. signature or seal, that distinguishes one from the other. The typical content of any Articles (or Deed) will be:

1. The business name for trading purposes.
2. The general nature of the business and how the nature may be changed.
3. The capital and/or property contribution.
4. The ratio for sharing profits (or losses!).
5. The powers of each partner.
6. The powers of admission and expulsion.
7. Particular or general grounds for dissolution.
8. The method of determining the value of goodwill on retirement or death.
9. The method of calculating the amount payable to outgoing partners or estates of deceased partners.

TYPES OF PARTNER AND THEIR LIABILITY

(a) GENERAL PARTNER

A general (or active) partner is one who usually provides capital and takes an active part in the management of the firm.

(b) SLEEPING PARTNER

A sleeping (or dormant) partner is one who takes no active part in the management of the firm, but he does contribute to the capital.

(c) PARTNER BY ESTOPPEL

Such a partner is often known as a quasi (or nominal) partner being one who by his conduct leads others to believe that he is a partner even though he is not one. Under the doctrine of "holding out" s. 14. P.A. 1890, such a person is estopped from denying that he is a partner. Thus a person who in writing, or orally, or by conduct, leads others to believe that he is a partner, resulting in credit being given by them to the firm, is liable to these "others" as though he were a partner.

(d) LIMITED PARTNER

A limited partner is one whose liability is limited to the amount of capital he has agreed to contribute. This type of partner is rarely seen, and is provided for by the Limited Partnership Act, 1907. Such a partner cannot take any part in the management of the business.

Note: Every partner of type (a) to (c) above shares in any losses of the partnership to the full extent of their private resources, but only in (a), (b) and (d) do the partners share the profits.

THE PARTNERSHIP'S TRADING NAME

Many partnerships trade under a name which uses the surnames of the individual partners, e.g. Evans, Evans, Jones and Griffiths (a partnership of Welsh solicitor's!). Occasionally partners initials are also seen in the title. Registration of such trading names has never been necessary. In contrast, some businesses do not trade under a name which uses the true surnames of the individual partners, e.g. Chop Suey and Chow Mein who own a take away restaurant trading under the name Cantonese Cuisine. Between 1916 and mid 1981, all such businesses had to register their trading name in accordance with the Registration of Business Names Act, 1916. Provided the appropriate papers were submitted, the registrar would issue a Certificate of Registration. Due to Government cutbacks announced by the Tories who came to office in 1979 the registry has now been abolished.

In future, the ownership of a business is to be disclosed solely by:

(a) signs at the business premises, and
(b) names on documents, including letters, order forms, invoices and receipts.

BASIC RIGHTS OF PARTNERS BETWEEN THEMSELVES

Unless specifically provided for in the Articles or Deed of Partnership, then the rights of partners are defined in the Partnership Act, 1890. The more important rights that are provided for are as follows:

SHARE OF PROFITS/LOSSES EQUALLY: s. 24 (1). All partners share equally in profits and losses.

INDEMNITY: s. 24(2). A partner is entitled to indemnity by the firm when acting properly in the ordinary course of the firm's business.

INTEREST ON LOANS: s. 24(3). A partner is entitled to 5% interest per annum on advances other than capital which have been introduced in accordance with a partnership agreement.

MANAGEMENT: s. 24(5). A partner may take part in the management of the partnership business.

INTRODUCTION OF NEW PARTNER: s. 24(7). No person may be introduced as a partner without the consent of all.

NATURE OF BUSINESS: s. 24(8). The nature of the partnership business cannot be changed without the unanimous consent of all partners, though ordinary matters may be decided by majority.

INSPECTION OF BOOKS: s. 24(9). Each partner or his agent may inspect the partnership books.

EXPULSION OF PARTNER: s. 25. A partner cannot be expelled by a majority of co-partners unless power to do this has been conferred by express agreement between all partners.

UBERRIMAE FIDEI: s. 29. Between themselves partners are entitled to the utmost fairness and good faith from co-partners in all partnership matters. Each partner must account for any benefit derived without consent of the other partners, in regard to the use of partnership property or business connection.

CONFLICT OF INTEREST: s. 30. No partner may, without authority of all partners, carry on business which competes with that of the firm.

POWERS OF PARTNERS AS AGENT TO BIND THE FIRM

Section 5 Partnership Act, 1890, provides that every general partner is deemed to be an agent for the firm and for the other partners. Also the acts of any partner within the ordinary course of business of the firm bind the firm and the other partners, unless the third party dealing, knew of any lack of authority or did not know or believe that the other party was a partner.

Clearly a third party will usually be unaware of such lack of authority, and consequently the common law presumes that certain implied powers rest with a partner which will bind his firm. Greater implied powers are presumed for a partner in a trading partnership as opposed to a partner in a non-trading partnership, viz:

1. IMPLIED POWERS OF A PARTNER TO BIND A TRADING OR NON-TRADING PARTNERSHIP

In any partnership, a general partner has the following implied powers:

(a) To sell and buy goods for the partnership business.
(b) To give receipts to debtors.
(c) To engage and dismiss employees.
(d) To draw cheques, unless this is not in the usual course of the firm's business: **Backhouse v. Charlton (1878)**.

2. ADDITIONAL IMPLIED POWERS OF A PARTNER TO BIND A TRADING PARTNERSHIP

In a trading partnership (one which is principally engaged in buying and selling **Higgins v. Beauchamp (1914)**), a partner may impliedly bind the firm by:

(a) Contracting and paying debts on the firm's account.
(b) Drawing, accepting, discounting, etc., bills of exchange or other negotiable instruments.
(c) Borrowing money.
(d) Pledging partnership goods or chattels as security for the firm's business.

Note: For a non-trading partnership (e.g. doctors, solicitors, accountants, etc.), the above powers can be expressly provided for in Articles or Deed of Partnership.

3. SITUATIONS WHERE A PARTNER MUST HAVE EXPRESS POWERS BEFORE HIS FIRM WILL BE BOUND

There are certain acts which partners in either a trading or non-trading partnership do not have implied authority to carry out. These include:

(a) The execution of deeds (an agent cannot bind his principal by deed unless he himself has been appointed by deed).

(b) The giving of a guarantee in the firm's name (unless there is a trade custom or the giving of guarantees forms part of the firm's usual business).

(c) The acceptance of property instead of money in satisfaction of a debt due to the partnership.

(d) Authorising a third party to use the firm's name in legal or other proceedings.

(e) Submitting disputes to arbitration.

4. PARTNER'S APPARENT OR OSTENSIBLE AUTHORITY

To bind a firm under the doctrine of apparent or ostensible authority, an act must be carried out in relation to the partnership business. If a partner exceeds this authority, then he is personally liable.

The firm will be liable if the act of the partner would appear to be within his expected authority so long as the third party was unaware of any restriction.

NATURE OF LIABILITY TO THIRD PARTIES

Section 9 Partnership Act, 1890, provides that "every partner in a firm is liable jointly with the other partners, and in Scotland severally also, for the debts and obligations of the firm incurred while he is a partner".

Note that each partner is liable "jointly" with the others and not by himself. The extent of liability includes all the private resources of each partner.

Partners can agree though, to be jointly and severally liable rather than jointly liable, and the distinction, even in the light of the passing of the Civil Liability (Contribution) Act, 1978, is still of great importance.

1. JOINT LIABILITY

Prior to the Civil Liability (Contribution) Act, 1978, where joint liability was concerned, a plaintiff who only sued one of the partners lost his right to sue the others. **Kendall *v.* Hamilton (1879)**. This proved a minor problem in practice because a plaintiff would sue the firm and thus be deemed to be suing each partner. Since the passing of the 1978 Act, if only one partner (or some of several) is sued then a judgement obtained against one (or several) is no bar to an action against the others. Thus **Kendall *v.* Hamilton** is defunct.

2. JOINT AND SEVERAL LIABILITY

Where this has been admitted by the partnership, then various courses of action are available to a plaintiff. The partners may be sued together or separately, and if one action is unsuccessful then successive actions can be taken against the other partners.

3. LIABILITY FOR TORTS

A firm and each of its partners are jointly and severally liable for the wrongful acts and omissions (torts) which are committed by any partner in the ordinary course of the business of the firm or with the authority of his co-partners. However, if a tort is committed outside a partner's ostensible authority, the firm will not be liable. **Arbuckle *v.* Taylor (1815)**.

INCOMING PARTNER: SECTION 17(1)

When a new partner joins a firm, he will not be liable for debts created before he joined it. However, he can become liable by "novation". This requires an agreement between the firm's creditors and the newly constituted firm (i.e. including the new partner). Such agreement can be express or implied from the conduct of the parties.

OUTGOING PARTNER: SECTION 17(2)–(3)

1. LIABILITY FOR EXISTING PARTNERSHIP DEBTS

By s. 17(2) a partner who retires from a firm, does not cease to be liable for partnership debts or obligations **incurred before retirement**. However by s. 17(3) he may be discharged by an agreement between himself, the new firm, and the existing creditors, and this agreement may be express (e.g. novation – see above) or implied as a matter of fact from the future conduct of the new firm and the creditors. From an outgoing partners viewpoint an "express" release would be the best proof of an agreed release.

2. LIABILITY FOR FUTURE PARTNERSHIP DEBTS

Upon retirement, an outgoing partner should carry out both of the following actions in order to avoid liability for **debts created after his retirement**:

(a) Give notice in the Gazette. This action is considered sufficient to prevent the outgoing partner from liability to any party who had not previously dealt with the firm.

(b) Give written notice to all parties who had had previous dealings with the firm. Clearly this would enable the outgoing partner to avoid any liability on future contracts with these parties.

If he does not carry out (a), he will be liable to new contracting parties while if he does not carry out (b) he will be liable to prior contracting parties – by the doctrine of "holding out". Sections 14(1) and 36.

DISSOLUTION

The means of dissolving partnerships are outlined in the Partnership Act, 1890. Some occur automatically, whilst others require reference to the Court.

DISSOLUTION WITHOUT REFERENCE TO THE COURT: SECTIONS 32-34

Subject to any contrary agreement between the partners, dissolution will occur:

(a) When the partnership has been entered into:
- (i) For a fixed term – at its expiration;
- (ii) For a single venture or undertaking – when completed;
- (iii) For an undefined time (i.e. a partnership at will) – by one partner giving notice to the others: s. 32.

(b) On the death or bankruptcy of one partner: s. 33(1).

Note: Where there is an agreement that the partnership will continue, the remaining partners must account to the representatives or trustee, for the partner's share.

(c) When a partner's share of partnership property is charged by court order for a private debt – here dissolution is optional, and depends upon what the remaining partners wish to do: s. 33(2).

Note: A voluntary charge or assignment is excluded.

(d) When the partnership becomes bankrupt: s. 34.

(e) When the partnership becomes illegal. An example of this is where war breaks out between the U.K. and an overseas country, and prior to that date a partnership existed between a U.K. citizen and a citizen of the overseas country: s. 34.

(f) When all the partners agree (i.e. mutual consent).

Note: There are several other circumstances not provided for by statute, which result in dissolution without reference to the court, viz:

(a) Where fraud has made the original contract of the partnership voidable at the option of the deceived party.

(b) Where there is express provision in the Articles or Deed, if they exist. Such provisions may relate to mental disorder, incompatability of temperament or criminal conduct. An example of case law which applies to the final item is **Carmichael *v.* Evans (1904)**. There was a provision in the Articles that "If a partner was addicted to scandalous conduct detrimental to the partnership or guilty of any flagrant breach of the duties of a partner", he could be expelled. In this case, a partner was convicted of dishonesty because he had defrauded a railway company by travelling on the railway although he had not purchased a ticket. It was held that the partner could be expelled and the partnership had to be dissolved – as originally there were only two partners.

DISSOLUTION BY ORDER OF THE COURT: SECTION 35

Sometimes, an application to the court is needed to bring about the dissolution, e.g. where it has not been automatically provided for by ss. 32–34 P.A. 1890 or by the partnership agreement. A partner, by s. 35, may apply to the Court for dissolution when:

(a) One partner becomes mentally incapacitated. Although today this does not lead to automatic dissolution, unless the partners have agreed otherwise, although it forms grounds for dissolution. (Reference must also be made to the Mental Health Act, 1983.)

(b) A partner, other than the party applying becomes permanently incapable of performing his part of the partnership contract.

(c) A partner, other than the party applying, has been guilty of conduct prejudicial to the firm's business. See **Carmichael *v.* Evans (1904)** case above.

(d) A partner, other than the partner applying, wilfully or persistently breaks the partnership agreement so that it is not reasonably practicable for the other members to continue in partnership with him.

(e) The business can only be carried on at a loss.

(f) The court considers it to be just and equitable.

When the Court considers applications under (c) above, clearly the circumstances will have to be related to the type of business conducted – a question of fact. Thus, if a partner is convicted of a motoring offence, the offence would not usually be considered as "prejudicial" unless the partnership was say that of a taxi-firm or funeral undertakers. If say in the **Carmichael *v.* Evans (1904)** case described above, there had been no provision in the Articles for the dissolution on the grounds of dishonesty, then an application to the Court could have been made under this heading. The Court would have considered the case on its own merit and would have made its decision accordingly. Finally, heading (f) gives the Court a very wide discretion. Taking the **Carmichael *v.* Evans (1904)** case one stage further, it could have been decided that dishonesty was not "conduct prejudicial to the firm's business" and dissolution on those grounds was not possible. However an application could have been made under heading (f), and if the Court considered dissolution to be just and equitable, then it would decree so.

ARTIFICIAL PERSONALITIES

In law, legal personality is not restricted to human beings, for it extends to any entity which is able to exercise legal rights and duties. It is possible for groups of individuals to combine together to form a separate single entity. This entity has its own name and personality which is sometimes described as artificial, fictitious or juristic, and is known as a corporation. A simple definition of a corporation is "a legal entity or artificial person, with a distinctive name, perpetual succession and a common seal".

TYPES OF CORPORATION

A corporation may either be

(a) *A corporation sole; or*
(b) *A corporation aggregate.*

(a) CORPORATION SOLE

This type consists of a single person who not only has his own personality as a human being but also has a separate and distinct legal personality and it is in this latter respect, that he is known as a corporation. Typical examples of such corporations are the Monarch, the Treasury Solicitor, a Clergyman in the Church of England, a Bishop, etc. With regard to the latter, upon his appointment as Bishop, certain church property will be vested in him in his position as a Bishop. Upon death, the church property does not form part of his personal estate but automatically vests in the name of the next appointed Bishop.

(b) CORPORATION AGGREGATE

In contrast to the corporation sole which consists of one member, a corporation aggregate consists of a number of people. The most important category of this type is a company registered under one of the Companies Acts. It also includes corporations which are incorporated by Royal Charter or by special statute.

TYPES OF CORPORATION AGGREGATE

To become incorporated, certain formalities must be carried out. These will vary depending upon the type of corporation being created, as described below.

FORMATION BY ROYAL CHARTER

The Crown, because it has been given common law rights to do so, may agree to the creation of a corporation. Thus, it is possible for a group of people to submit a petition to the Monarch for approval, and if given, a new corporation will have been created. Corporations (such as the Bank of England), certain state undertakings (such as the B.B.C.), some professional bodies (such as the Chartered Institute of Bankers and the Institute of Chartered Accountants), most universities and a small number of trading companies (Hudson's Bay Company) have been created this way. Today, this method of incorporation is infrequently seen although it tends to be used by educational bodies (e.g. new universities) or certain charitable or scientific organisations.

FORMATION BY SPECIAL STATUTE

Such corporations are created by special Act of Parliament and today the method only really applies to public utilities, and certain nationalised industries and county councils.

Typical examples are:

NAME OF CORPORATION	STATUTE
British Coal (formerly National Coal Board	Coal Industry Nationalisation Act, 1946
British Railways Board	Transport Act, 1962
County Councils	Local Government Act, 1972
Independent Broadcasting Association	Television Act, 1954

FORMATION UNDER THE COMPANIES ACTS

Prior to 1844, the majority of businesses were either partnerships or unincorporated associations. Since then, various Companies Acts have been passed which have provided for limited liability. The most recent was the Companies Act 1985. This Act consolidated all previous Companies Acts, notably those of 1948, 1967, 1976, 1980 and 1981. So, all companies incorporated after 1st July 1985, became subject to the provisions of the most recent Act. In the remainder of this chapter until the section on Winding up is reached, references such as s. 5 mean section 5 Companies Act 1985. All other references will state the relative statute to which they relate.

It should be noted that prior to the passing of the 1980 Act, it was not possible to differentiate between a public and a private company from their titles – although, it was possible for each to be distinguished in other ways. Since the 1980 Act came on the statute book, all public companies have been obliged to use the words public limited company, or the abbreviation (PLC or plc) or the Welsh equivalents after their name. So, today, the status of a company can immediately be identified by its title. Having made the distinction between public and private companies, there are three types of company which can be incorporated under this heading – companies limited by shares, companies limited by guarantees and unlimited companies.

COMPANIES LIMITED BY SHARES

This is by far the most common type of registered company, whereby the liability of the company's members (i.e. its shareholders) is limited by the amount, if any, which is unpaid on their shares. As an example, if a member has bought a one pound share (issued to him at par i.e. nominal value) and only paid 40p, he is liable for further calls amounting to 60p. If the company goes into liquidation without having made a request for the balance (a call) then 60p is the maximum amount the liquidator can claim. Hence, there is a limit to any extra amount the member will have to pay whether the company continues to trade or is wound up. Companies of this type may be either public or private.

COMPANIES LIMITED BY GUARANTEE

These are not a commonly created type of company where there is a profit making motive, but where they exist, a member's liability is limited to the amount he has undertaken (guaranteed) to contribute in the event of the company being wound up. Thus if a member has given a guarantee for £200,000 in the event of liquidation, he can be called upon to pay up to this amount, but no more. Companies formed for charitable or educational purposes are often incorporated in this way. Today, such companies may no longer be formed with a share capital: s. 1(4). Guarantee companies incorporated before this recent act may have a share capital, and if so, may be public or private.

UNLIMITED COMPANIES

These are companies whose members have no limit to their personal liability. Most people consider this to be a serious disadvantage and consequently few have been formed in this way. However, they do benefit from perpetual succession, and more importantly secrecy of financial affairs, for annual returns do not have to be submitted to the Companies Registry. Today, only private companies can now be formed in this way: s. 1(2) (c).

Reference has previously been made above to public companies.

Before the passing of the Companies Act, 1980, there were many differences between the two types. Today there are few distinctions but those which exist are described below.

PUBLIC COMPANIES

This type of company can ask for a stock exchange quotation, but this will only be granted subject to certain conditions, e.g. that the Articles indicate that there are no restrictions on the transfer of its shares, etc.

Its membership must not fall below two, while the maximum can clearly be no greater than the number of issued shares. Furthermore, there must be at least two directors: s. 282(1).

The Memorandum of Association (see later for description) must now state that the company is to be a public company and its name must end . . . Public Limited Company (or abbreviation PLC or plc) or Welsh equivalents. Ss. 1(3) and 25, Companies Act, 1985. In addition, the share capital stated in the Memorandum of Association must not be less than the authorised minimum, i.e. £50,000 or such other sum as the Secretary of State may determine: s. 118(1). Furthermore, whatever the level of authorised capital, at least £50,000 must be issued at all times.

Public companies, if they so desire, may register as private companies, but this transformation is rarely seen in practice.

Before being allowed to issue shares, the promoter of the company will have to prepare a prospectus. The prospectus will provide many details including, inter alia, past history of the business, the objectives of the business and details of the directors and their interests. It will also contain an offer to the general public to enable them to purchase shares. If a prospectus is not issued, then it is necessary for a "statement in lieu of prospectus" to be prepared in its place. This provides similar information to a prospectus and must be filed with the Registrar of Companies at least three days before any shares or debentures are allotted. The foregoing only applies to public companies.

Most public companies have their shares listed on the Stock Exchange. This means they must comply with stringent rules regarding disclosure of information to the public, etc. The Stock Exchange also operates the Unlisted Securities Market (U.S.M.) and a third tier market for those smaller or new public companies.

PRIVATE COMPANIES

Prior to the 1980 Companies Act, the transfer of shares in this type of company was severely restricted. However, since the passing of the Act, these restrictions have been abolished and if a private company so wishes, it can now, under the terms of its Articles of Association (see later for description), make its shares freely transferable.

Note: This does not mean that a public offer of shares can be made.

For companies incorporated before the 1980 Act became law, this freedom of transfer can only be achieved by amending the Articles, while new companies can, if they so wish, restrict the transfer by including a suitable clause in their Articles.

As before, the minimum number of members remains at two. The maximum number of members is no longer fifty but can be no greater than the number of issued shares. There need only be one director but he may not also be the secretary.

For a private company to register as a public company, a special resolution must be passed which authorises the company to conform with the capital and other requirements described in the previous section.

It can be seen from the above, that today, there is very little difference on paper between a public and private company, but difficulties will still arise with the sale and marketability of private company shares. Such a difficulty does not arise for any public company which has its shares quoted on the Stock Exchange. Nevertheless the changes provided by the 1980 Act do permit greater opportunity for growth, as regards access to capital and loans.

COMPANY AS A SEPARATE ENTITY

From the above comparison it is seen that a company has its own legal entity which is quite distinct from its directors (who manage it) and its members (the shareholders who own it).

This distinction was established in the classic legal decision by the House of Lords in **Salomon *v.* Salomon & Co. Ltd (1897)**. Salomon incorporated his business as a limited company in which he held 20,000 shares and his family 6. Salomon lent money to the company which issued a debenture in his favour as security. The company later went into liquidation and Salomon claimed his money back as a secured creditor in priority to the unsecured creditors. *Held.* Salomon was a distinct person from Salomon & Co. Ltd. Therefore his contract with the company was good and he was entitled to claim in priority to all unsecured creditors of the company.

COMPARISONS OF COMPANIES AND PARTNERSHIPS

COMPANIES	PARTNERSHIPS
FORMATION	
Usually by registration in accordance with the Companies Acts. Costly procedure.	By agreement, express or implied. Inexpensive procedure.
SEPARATE ENTITY	
A distinct and separate entity from its members (shareholders) and directors (managers) **Salomon *v.* Salomon & Co. Ltd (1897)**	Not a separate entity. It is made up of the persons of whom it is comprised.
SUCCESSION	
Perpetual succession unless or until wound up.	No perpetual succession – although clauses in articles/deed can prevent termination upon the occurrence of certain events.
LIABILITY	
Limited to the amount of shareholding (or guarantee).	Liability of each partner unlimited and so applies to full extent of private resources. (Except for limited partners.)
POWERS	
Defined for the company in the memorandum and for the directors in the articles. Amended in accordance with the procedures and limitations imposed by the Companies Acts, and subject to special internal procedures.	Usually determined by simple agreement of the partners. Usually amended by simple agreement.
TRANSFER OF INTERESTS	
Freely transferable – although there may be restrictions for some private companies.	Needs the consent of all other partners.
FINANCIAL DETAILS – ACCOUNTS	
Company must file these at companies registry (capable of being inspected by anyone) – unless company is unlimited.	Private – only available to the partners.
MEMBERS	
Minimum 2, maximum up to number of shareholders.	Minimum 2, maximum usually 20.

METHOD OF CREATION OF A COMPANY TO BE INCORPORATED UNDER THE COMPANIES ACTS

To create a company certain formalities must be followed, the company only coming into existence as a separate entity at the date of incorporation. The formalities necessary (which are usually attended to by a solicitor) relate to the submission of documents to the Companies Registry. The documents must include:

1. A copy of the Memorandum of Association, signed by the original members; and
2. A copy of the Articles of Association, signed by the original members; and
3. A signed statement by the original members, confirming that the formalities necessary to conform with registration under the respective Companies Act have been complied with.

If the Registrar at the Companies Registry is satisfied with these documents, he will issue the company with a Certificate of Incorporation (this can be described as the company's "birth certificate"). After its issue, a private company can immediately commence trading. However a public limited company cannot commence trading until the Registrar has issued a "certificate to do business": s. 117.

MEMORANDUM OF ASSOCIATION

The Memorandum is a deed agreed by the promoters which states and defines the constitution and powers (objects) of the company. To conform with s. 2, a Memorandum must contain five clauses. In brief, these are:

(a) NAME OF COMPANY

Where the company is a private one, its name should end with the word limited, or if it is public, with the words Public Limited Company (or abbreviation PLC or plc), or Welsh equivalents. On occasions, a name submitted for registration will not be accepted because the Department of Trade and Industry considers it to be undesirable. (e.g. Where it is similar to an existing name, contains the word bank or Royal, etc.) This power to reject names which are considered as unacceptable is provided for by s. 26.

(b) WHETHER THE REGISTERED OFFICE IS SITUATED IN ENGLAND, WALES OR SCOTLAND

The reason for this is that a company is governed by the law of the country in which it is incorporated – and English Law and the Law of Scotland differ to some extent. Three further points should be noted:

(1) England and Wales are considered as one!
(2) The address of the registered office is not stated in the Memorandum, but filed separately.
(3) It is not permitted to change the registered *address* from England to Scotland or vice versa, although within a country, a change of registered address is permitted.

(c) THE OBJECTS OF THE COMPANY

These describe the type of business which the company wishes legally to be empowered to carry out. In a modern Memorandum, object clauses tend to be as far reaching as possible and therefore subject to a certain amount of interpretation. If it proves impossible to positively identify the purposes of a business from the clauses contained therein, then legal advice should be sought. The reason for this is that technically, any act carried out by the company over and above the objects as set down in the Memorandum is defined as being "ultra vires" (beyond the power of) and therefore void. Not only that, but these actions cannot be ratified by the members at a later date.

Two legal cases amply illustrate these points:

Ashbury Railway Carriage and Iron Co. *v*. Riche (1875)
The company's objects allowed it to build railway carriages. However, it later bought a concession to build a railway line in Belgium. *Held*. (House of Lord's decision.) The Belgian concession was ultra vires the company and therefore void. Even if all the members agreed to it, the action could not be ratified at a later date.

Re Introductions Ltd (1969)
This company had originally been formed to provide facilities for visitors to the Festival of Britain in 1951. In 1960, the company changed hands and began a pig breeding scheme contrary to its objects. The National Provincial Bank lent it £29,000 (secured by debenture) for the pig scheme (which ultimately failed). The bank were relying on an "independent objects clause" viz, "to borrow . . . in such a manner as the company shall think fit". The venture failed and the company became subject to a winding up order. The liquidator's claim that the borrowing was "ultra vires" was upheld by the Court of Appeal which stated that "borrowing" was a "power" which could not be exercised independently of an "object". Thus, the bank advance was void and the amount had to be written off.

The way in which the Courts view ultra vires acts was modified by

s. 9 European Communities Act 1972 and has now been expressly provided for in sections 35 and 36 Companies Act 1985. It is section 35 which is more relevant and it makes provision as follows:

(1) In favour of a person dealing with a company in good faith, any transaction decided on by the directors is deemed to be one which is within the capacity of the company to enter into and the power of the directors to bind the company is deemed to be free of any limitation under the memorandum or articles.
(2) A party to a transaction so decided upon is not bound to enquire as to the capacity of the company to enter into it or as to any such limitations on the powers of the directors and is presumed to have acted in good faith unless the contrary is proved.

Thus, today, if an injured party can show that he satisfies both (1) and (2), the directors' actions will have bound the company. Some third parties (for example, banks) would prefer not to have to rely on this statutory provision. As a consequence, they would continue to ask for corporate customers to lodge copies of their Memorandum and Articles of Association (assuming they were not requested when the account was opened or have not subsequently been obtained) at the time contracts, etc. are being negotiated, thereby, ensuring that, as far as possible, any acts are intra vires.

Note. Early in 1987, indications had been given to the effect that in the current parliamentary session, the "ultra vires" rule is to be abolished. Thus, it is important for the legal/financial press to be looked at to establish the date from which such changes take effect and the nature of them.

(d) That the liability of the members is limited. This relates to companies limited by shares or guarantee. For the latter, the liability undertaken by each member must be stated.

(e) The share capital, showing the amount and division thereof. This relates to companies having a share capital (e.g. "the share capital of the company is £500 divided into 1,000 ordinary shares of 50p each"), but not to those which are unlimited.

The copy of the Memorandum which is submitted to the Companies Registry must be signed by at least two persons for either a public company or for a private company. Each signatory must take and pay in cash for at least one share and, by his signature, indicate the number of shares he has taken up. All signatures must be duly witnessed: s. 2(6).

Note: A Memorandum may contain many more clauses (e.g. power to issue debentures, ability and extent to which it can borrow, power to give guarantees, etc.) and it would certainly be of help if you could obtain a copy to look at its contents.

Any of the clauses already contained in the Memorandum can be added to, amended, and in some cases deleted, or new clauses can be inserted. All changes, though, are subject to the company approving them and passing an appropriate special resolution at a duly convened meeting.

Some of the changes, although approved by the company, require the confirmation of an outside third party, before they become legally effective. A typical example is that changes of company name require Department of Trade and Industry approval.

ARTICLES OF ASSOCIATION

The Articles are a set of internal rules which define the rights of the members of the company between themselves (including the powers of the directors) and also describe the manner in which the business of the company is to be conducted. Included in the Articles will be details of the directors' borrowing powers, method of transfering shares and the voting rights of members.

The Articles must be printed, divided into paragraphs, numbered consecutively, signed by each original member and witnessed: s. 7(3). As with the Memorandum, the original Articles of the company must be registered at the Companies Registry.

If a company does not want to prepare its own Articles, or fails to deposit a copy of them when they have been prepared, then the company is deemed to have adopted a model set of Articles, known as Table A. The model set of Articles is today provided for by Statutory Instrument No. 805, 1985 and will apply to any company incorporated after 1st July 1985 which does not adopt its own set of Articles.

In practice, most companies adopt part of Table A, and modify and/or exclude the remainder. By looking at the first page of any company's Articles, the adopted parts, if any, can quickly be established because they are listed in the preamble to the Articles proper.

The ultra vires doctrine applies not only to the Memorandum but also to the Articles. Although actions in the former category are incapable of ratification (confirmation), for the latter, they can be.

The clauses in the Articles can be amended subject to an appropriate special resolution being passed at a duly convened meeting of the company.

TYPES OF CAPITAL OF A COMPANY

This is made up of funds subscribed by the members (shareholders). It is a word which needs qualification. For there is:

(a) AUTHORISED CAPITAL (or nominal capital). This is the maximum amount of capital that a company is allowed to issue. The figure will be quoted in the last clause of the Memorandum and is usually quoted in a company's balance sheet.

(b) ISSUED CAPITAL (or subscribed capital). This is that part of the authorised capital which has been issued by the company.

(c) UNCALLED CAPITAL. Although rarely seen today, this relates to the unpaid portion of partly-paid shares. Thus, if a company had issued a million one pound shares at par, and the subscribers had paid only 40p for each share, there would be an unpaid portion of 60p per share. This would mean that the uncalled capital of the company amounts to £600,000. The uncalled amount may be called up by the company as and when it is needed, either in full, in stages known as "calls", or upon liquidation.

When shares are issued, they can be sold at par or premium (see comments below about discount), and these terms mean:

PAR. This means that a one pound share is issued for one pound, a fifty pence share is issued for fifty pence, etc. Thus the share is being issued at its nominal value.

PREMIUM. This means that a share is issued at a higher price than its nominal value, e.g. a £1 share offered for £3.50. Clearly the level of the premium will reflect the attractiveness of the share as an investment.

DISCOUNT. This means that a share is issued at a lower price than its nominal value. However, by s. 100, no further issues at a discount will be permitted.

As will be seen below, the holders of shares are entitled to dividend payments. These are usually paid at regular intervals (e.g. every six months) by public companies, although not all private companies pay them. However, the important point is that when they are paid, they must be paid out of profits.

TYPES OF SHARE

1. ORDINARY

These are recognised as the true risk capital of a company and, as such, usually rank after preference shares (see below) for dividend purposes and usually also in the event of winding up. The holders are entitled to dividends, which will vary with the level of profitability and usually they will have voting rights. Sometimes the shares are divided into "A" holders and "B" holders, with the former (usually family members) having voting rights and therefore having a higher value than the latter, who have no voting rights.

Subject to either a public or private company complying with the provisions s. 159, it is now possible for a company to issue redeemable ordinary shares.

2. PREFERENCE

These form part of the capital and by the Articles usually entitle the holder to preferential rights relating to dividends and/or return of capital in the event of winding up. The rate of dividend will be fixed upon issue. Like ordinary shares, the holder may or may not have voting rights. Also there are various types of share, viz.

Cumulative

If the profits in any one year are insufficient to pay the fixed dividend then the shortfall must be made good in future years.

Non-Cumulative

If there is a shortfall in one year, it cannot be made good in future years. If it is of this type, the share certificate must specifically say so.

Participating

If the company in any one year makes exceptional profits and the preference and ordinary holders have already received their full entitlement, any surplus can be paid to such holders.

Redeemable

Permission to issue these must be expressly authorised by the Articles. The shares must be fully paid and redeemed out of profits or a new issue of shares specifically made for the redemption.

Note: Unless the terms of the issue are expressed to be otherwise, all preference share issues are regarded as cumulative.

3. DEFERRED

These are also known as founder or management shares and are nowadays rarely seen. On the few occasions that they are issued, they are usually taken by the founders or promoters of a company and entitle the holders to a proportion of the profits if the ordinary dividend exceeds a specified amount. Thus, they act as an incentive to the holders to maximise profits. They have voting rights which are weighted in such holders favour – e.g. a 20p deferred share may attract the same voting rights as a one pound ordinary share.

COMPANY DIRECTORS

These collectively act for the company when they are known as a board. They are headed by a chairman, while the day to day business is attended to by the managing director. The directors act as both trustees (issuing shares, approving transfers) and agents (dealing with third parties) of the company.

The directors, under the terms of the Articles, may have to hold qualification shares in the company. If this condition is not met within a period of two months of appointment or such shorter period as otherwise specified in the Articles (s. 291(1)) or if he subsequently gives a legal charge to a third party over shares required for qualification, he ceases to be a director.

Every company must have a secretary (s. 283(1)) and now by s. 286, the secretary of a public company must have "the requisite knowledge and experience and usually a specified qualification". Furthermore, it is not permissible for someone who is a sole director to be appointed as secretary (s. 283(2)).

SHAREHOLDERS

LEGAL RIGHTS OF A SHAREHOLDER

The principal rights of a shareholder are:

1. To receive dividends declared by the company.
2. To vote at shareholders meetings provided the shares are of the voting type.
3. To have his capital repaid to him in the event of winding up. Whether this is repayment in full depends upon whether the company is then solvent or insolvent.

LEGAL DUTIES OF A SHAREHOLDER

The principal duties of a shareholder are:

1. To meet call payments as and when they fall due.
2. Where the shares are not fully paid, if the company winds up, then the shareholder must pay over to the liquidator of the company a further contribution, but this cannot exceed the par value of the share.

PRE-FORMATION CONTRACTS

Pre-formation contracts do not bind a company because a non-existent person cannot contract. Furthermore, the contract cannot be ratified once the company has been formed.

It is unusual for the persons who sign the contracts to be held personally liable **Kelner *v.* Baxter (1866)**. If there had been indications that the signatories had limited authority, then no one may be liable: **Newborne *v.* Sensolid (Great Britain) Ltd (1954)**. However, s. 36(4) has overruled this decision in that now anyone who purports to act for a unformed company assumes personal liability.

This was confirmed by the decision in **Phonogram Ltd *v.* Lane (1981)**. The plaintiff agreed to provide £6,000 to a pop group which was to be run by a company. At a time before the company's incorporation, Lane entered into a contract 'For and on behalf of . . . . Ltd." In fact, the company was never formed and when a condition of the contract failed, the plaintiff sued Lane under the provisions of s. 9 European Communities Act 1972. (now s 36(4) C.A. 1985) *Held*. By the Court of Appeal. Lane was personally liable as he had entered into a contract on behalf of an unformed company. It was irrelevant whether he signed in his own name or "For and on behalf of", for he would still have been personally liable.

In practice, however, as soon as "incorporated", the company would create a new agreement which incorporates the terms of the pre-incorporation contract.

DEBENTURES

Companies usually raise cash by the sale of shares, or borrowing from banks or other financial organisations. However, they can also issue debentures, provided the Memorandum allows them to do so. A debenture is an acknowledgement that a debt is owed by a company. The company will issue a certificate to all those who have advanced money to it, and usually the debenture certificate is executed under the company's seal.

More often than not, the issue of debentures is termed debenture stock and usually is issued in amounts of £100. Sometimes, the issue is not secured on the company's assets, and hence it is known as a "naked debenture" or "unsecured loan stock". Usually it will be secured, either by at least a floating charge (see below) and sometimes also by a fixed charge (see below).

The interests of the debenture holders are represented by a trustee whose powers are provided for in a Trust Deed. If say there is a breach of covenant by the company then a Receiver can be appointed and various remedies exercised.

Debentures may be issued to bearer or be registered. They may be redeemable or irredeemable. As with shares, they may be sold in the market and can be transferred.

Debentures may be compared with ordinary shares in the following ways:

DEBENTURES	SHARES
(1) Loans to a company. Therefore holder is a creditor.	(1) Forms part of the capital. Therefore holder is a member.
(2) Pays loan interest at a fixed rate, which is due irrespective or whether profits are made or not.	(2) Pays (or may pay) a dividend which will usually vary with the level of profits.
(3) In the event of winding up, paid according to status. Viz. secured or unsecured.	(3) In the event of winding up, paid last of all.
(4) Repayable or redeemable at a future date (unless irredeemable).	(4) Not repayable at a future date.
(5) Usually will have no voting rights.	(5) Have voting rights attached to them.

SECURED DEBENTURES

When a debenture is secured, it usually means that a company's fixed and floating assets are charged. Occasionally, only floating assets are charged and there could be several reasons for this.

Note: Fixed assets are those assets which a company uses permanently in its business (e.g. factory premises, machinery, motors, etc.). Floating assets are those assets which are circulating and change on a day-to-day basis (e.g. stock, debtors, work-in-progress, etc.).

(a) The company has no fixed assets, or their fixed assets are charged against other loans which the company has taken, or

(b) Although the company does have some fixed assets, they are of little or no value, or

(c) The debenture holders do not want a charge over the fixed assets, for they feel that the floating assets are sufficient for their needs.

It is essential to understand the difference between a fixed charge and a floating charge. This is particularly important in the event of the company winding up as the description below indicates.

CHARGE OVER FIXED ASSETS

This clause ensures that specific assets are legally charged and therefore a company cannot deal with or dispose of them without the express permission of the holder. Usually the debenture holder will be given a first fixed charge over freehold and/or leasehold property and over plant and machinery. Other less common assets, which may be subject to a fixed charge are goodwill and uncalled capital. Today it is possible to take a fixed charge over book debts and the effectiveness of such a charge has been supported in **Siebe Gorman and Co. Ltd *v.* Barclays Bank (1979)**. Note particularly that the holder of a fixed charge has absolute priority over all other creditors in the event of a winding up.

CHARGE OVER FLOATING ASSETS

This clause ensures that a debenture holder is given a charge over company assets, usually the circulating ones (i.e. current assets), but it allows the company to deal with them in the ordinary course of business. Thus it relates to assets such as stock in trade, work in progress, debtors (but see above), etc. For these assets, express permission is not needed from the debenture holders to deal with (or dispose of) the assets charged.

THE CHARACTERISTICS OF A FLOATING CHARGE WERE DEFINED IN: RE **YORKSHIRE WOOLCOMBERS' ASSOCIATION (1903)** AS:

1. A charge on both present and future assets.
2. The assets are constantly changing from time to time in the ordinary course of business.
3. Until the holder takes some steps to enforce the security, the company can carry on its business in the usual way.

A FLOATING CHARGE WILL CONTINUE UNTIL EITHER:

1. The holder appoints an administrative receiver, or
2. The company enters liquidation, or
3. The company ceases business.

Upon the happening of these events, the charge is said to have crystallised – i.e. "settled" on the assets remaining at that time.

Note: A floating charge can never turn into a fixed charge. When it has crystallised, a floating charge is always subject to the prior claims of the preferential creditors (see later) at that date.

WINDING UP

As mentioned earlier in this chapter, all companies benefit from perpetual succession. Hence they will continue to exist until something is done to terminate their existence. Termination may be at the instigation of the court, creditors or the members themselves. The act of terminating a company is known as winding up and is now fully provided for in the Insolvency Act 1986. All statutory references in the remainder of the chapter refer to this Act unless otherwise indicated. In brief, the Act divides winding up into two types – compulsory and voluntary.

SUMMARY OF TYPES OF WINDING UP

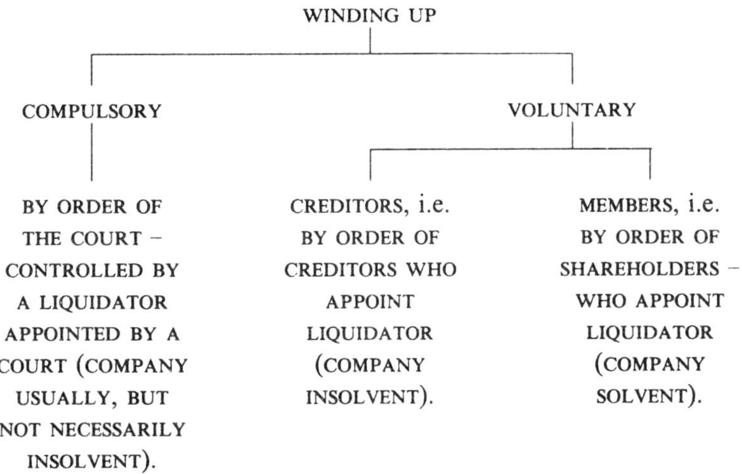

Note: The term solvency means the ability to settle debts as and when they fall due.

COMPULSORY WINDING UP – BY ORDER OF THE COURT

GROUNDS FOR WINDING UP

By s. 122, a company may be ordered by the court to wind up when:

1. The company has so resolved by special resolution.
2. The company does not commence business within a year of incorporation or suspends business for a year.
3. The number of members is reduced below two.
4. The court considers it just and equitable that the company should be wound up (e.g. deadlock among the directors).
5. The company is unable to pay its debts.
6. A company registered as a public company on its original incorpor-

ation has not been issued with a certificate under s. 117 C.A. 1985, and more than a year has expired since it was so registered, or if the company was an "old company" and had not become either a public or private company during the "transitional" period.

Item (5) is the most common reason for winding up. Section 123 more fully describes the occasions when a company is deemed to be unable to pay its debts and these are where:

1. A creditor, who is owed at least £750, leaves a demand for the sum at the company's registered office and the company does not settle, secure or compound the debt within three weeks.
2. An execution or other process (e.g. judgement) is issued against the company but it is returned unsatisfied in whole or in part.
3. It is proved that the company is unable to pay its debts.

VOLUNTARY WINDING UP

By s. 84 a company will voluntarily wind up:

1. When the period if any, fixed for the duration of the company by the Articles expires, or the event, if any, happens on the occurrence of which the Articles provide that the company is to be dissolved, and the company passes a resolution to wind up voluntarily.
2. If the company resolves by special resolution that the company be wound up voluntarily.
3. If the company resolves by extraordinary resolution that it cannot by reason of its liabilities continue its business, and that it is advisable to wind up.

By s. 85(1), it is necessary to advertise the resolution in the Gazette within fourteen days of it being passed. As mentioned before, voluntary winding up commences on the date of the resolution being passed: s. 86. The effect is that the company thereupon ceases to carry on business except for the purpose of beneficial winding up: s. 87(1).

As mentioned earlier there are two types of voluntary winding up – a members voluntary winding up and a creditors voluntary winding up.

1. MEMBERS VOLUNTARY WINDING UP

This occurs if the directors of the company (or majority of them) file a "statutory declaration of solvency". Under the terms of s. 89 this has to be within five weeks before the passing of the resolution to wind up. The declaration will indicate that the company can repay all its debts in full within twelve months and will include a statement of assets and liabilities at the lastest practicable date. Because the company has indicated that all its debts can be fully repaid, the members are permitted to appoint a liquidator, and upon his appointment, the directors' powers cease (unless the liquidator or the company – by general meeting – sanctions otherwise): s. 91(2).

Clearly, any unsecured creditor will prefer this type of winding up as opposed to a creditors voluntary winding up (see (2)) below because of the indications that full repayment will be made within twelve months.

2. CREDITORS VOLUNTARY WINDING UP

All voluntary winding ups are deemed to be creditors unless a declaration of solvency is filed in accordance with s. 89 (see above). This means that the creditors' claims will not be paid in full, and therefore they will appoint a liquidator (s. 100(1)) and control the winding up.

PRIORITY OF CREDITORS' CLAIMS

1. WITHOUT SECURED CREDITORS

The order of priority for the distribution of assets of an insolvent company where no security is held is:

(a) The cost of liquidation including the liquidators expenses.

(b) Preferential creditors (s. 386 and schedule 6). This group of creditors rank equally, but will be subject to claims for specific amounts and/or periods as defined in the relevant statute). The most common preferential creditors are:

   (1) Twelve months' deductions of PAYE prior to the relevant date.
   (2) VAT claims up to six months before the relevant date.
   (3) Assessment of Class 1 or Class 2 social security contributions for twelve months prior to the relevant date.
   (4) One year's assessment of Class 4 social security contributions before 5th April prior to the relevant date.
   (5) State and occupational pension scheme contributions due by the company but not paid.
   (6) Employee's arrears of wages or salary for four months prior to the relevant date subject to a financial limit to be set by delegated legislation (but, currently £800 per employee).
   (7) Accrued holiday remuneration.
   (8) Advances by any person (e.g. bank or director) to enable (5) and/or (6) to be paid.

In the above, the "relevant date", which is to be used, depends upon the type of winding up which the company is following or being subjected to. The rules used to determine such a date are contained within schedule 4 and 6 of the Act. These, though, are very complex and go well beyond your present level of studies.

If after realisation, preferential claims cannot be met in full they abate proportionately.

(c) If the above two categories have been paid in full, then the unsecured creditors are next in priority and rank equally. If claims cannot be met in full, the realised proceeds are applied rateably.

(d) Any surplus is then available for distribution to the members (shareholders), who rank equally or as indicated in the Articles.

2. WITH SECURED CREDITORS

Let us now consider how the previous list changes if there are secured creditors. Assuming that there are fixed charges and a floating charge, the order of priority is:

1. Fixed chargor to the extent of his security. It should be noted, though that the chargor has four alternatives:

   (a) Rely on the security and not prove at all.
   (b) Value the security and prove as an unsecured creditor for the deficit, if any.
   (c) Realise the security and prove as an unsecured creditor for the deficit, if any.
   (d) Release the security and prove for the whole debt as an unsecured creditor (an unlikely event!).

   Any surplus which has been derived from the direct security must be handed over to the liquidator.

2. Costs of liquidation. See previous section.
3. Preferential claims. See previous section.
4. Floating charge holder. The old rules governing the validity of a floating charge have been somewhat amended by the provisions now contained in s. 245 of the 1986 Act. Now a floating charge is valid whenever created to the extent that consideration is received by the company. A floating charge may be invalidated if it was created within a "relevant" time period of the company being liquidated and the extent of the period depends upon the identity of the chargee. Thus, for a "non-connected" person (such as a bank or finance company), the relevant period is one year from the onset of

insolvency. This only applies if, at the time the floating charge was created, the company was unable to pay its debts or, if, as a result of the transaction under which the charge was created, it became unable to pay its debts. However, even if a floating charge is invalidated on either of the above grounds, then so long as the chargee advances monies, either at the time of the charge or later and in consideration for the charge, the floating charge, as security, remains enforceable. **Re. Thomas Mortimer Ltd (1925)** and **Re. Yeovil Glove Co. Ltd (1965)**. Any amount which is not secured by the floating charge will have to be proved for on an unsecured basis.

5. Unsecured creditors. See previous section.
6. Shareholders. See previous section.

EXAMINATION QUESTIONS

Question 1

(a) Explain the meaning of a "partnership", illustrating your answer with examples.

(b) What are the legal liabilities of partners?

(A.E.B. O-Level)

Question 2

A, B and C are a trio in the entertainment business. Their act includes acrobatics and the singing of "pop" songs.

(a) Is the trio a partnership in the legal sense?

(b) Can the trio become a corporation? If so, by what means and with what legal consequences?

(Chartered Institute of Bankers)*

Question 3

(a) How may a company be created?

(b) What are the advantages to be gained by a partnership if it registers as a limited company?

(A.E.B. O-Level)

Question 4

(i) State and describe briefly the three chief methods by which a corporation can be created.

(ii) There are two main types of corporations – corporations "sole" and corporations "aggregate". Are the following persons corporations, and, if so, in which category:

(a) H.M. the Queen;

(b) the Bishop of London;

(c) the Lord Chief Justice;
(d) British Coal (formerly the National Coal Board)?
(Chartered Institute of Bankers)

Question 5
Compare and contrast companies and partnerships as methods of carrying on a business.
(A.E.B. A-Level)

Question 6
What is meant by "legal personality"? How does the legal personality of a company registered under the Companies Acts differ from that of an ordinary private person?
(A.E.B. O-Level)

Question 7
Bat and Ball are the partners in a firm whose business is dealing in securities. Rough and Smooth are the directors and members of Rough Holdings Co. Ltd, a private company which has contracted to buy certain investments from the firm for £1,000.

(a) Who can the company sue if the firm does not transfer the investments?
(b) Who can the firm sue if the company does not pay the £1,000?
(c) Would your answers differ if, according to its memorandum of association, the sole object of the company was the acquisition and disposal of land?
(Chartered Institute of Bankers)

Question 8
Explain and contrast the memorandum and articles of association of a limited company.
(Chartered Institute of Bankers)

Question 9
Motorail Co. Ltd is a company formed under the Companies Act, 1948, to manufacture, supply and deal in railway carriages, wagons and all types of railway rolling stock. This company contracted with the government of Ruritania to construct a mountain railway there and to build and supply special carriages and wagons suitable for use on that railway. The company had failed to fulfil this contract. Advise the Ruritanian government whether it has a remedy against this company or against its shareholders (whose shares are only partly paid up).
(Chartered Institute of Bankers)

Question 10

MD, the Managing Director and Chief Engineer of a transport maintenance business, tells you that he is shortly required to take the chair at his company's Annual General Meeting because the legally qualified Chairman has had a heart attack. MD understands that S, whom he regards as a particularly cantankerous shareholder, is planning to raise various issues at the AGM and he asks you to write a note – "in purely general terms" – on:

(a) the possibility of a company changing its name;
(b) the powers of a public limited liability company to make contracts;
(c) the significance of the concept of limited liability – with special reference to a likely claim by S that the business may soon make a loss thus causing some shareholders to incur personal liability for the company's debts.

Draft such a note.
(C.I.T.)

Question 11

Outline the legal rights and duties of a shareholder of a limited company.
(Chartered Institute of Bankers)

Question 12

Define:
(a) debenture; and
(b) floating charge.
(Chartered Institute of Bankers)

Question 13

Jones is a wholesale butcher. He has been advised to form a private limited company to purchase his business as a going concern. The company has been formed with a share capital of £500 divided into £1 shares, of which 499 are allotted to Jones and one to his wife. The balance of the purchase price of £15,000 has been paid by the issue of a single debenture of £14,500 to Jones, secured by a first charge on its assets.

If the company goes into liquidation and becomes insolvent, state how the assets of the company will be applied to repay:

(i) the share capital of £500;
(ii) the debenture of £14,500;
(iii) the creditors.

(Chartered Institute of Bankers)

CHAPTER 6

PROPERTY, OWNERSHIP AND POSSESSION

PROPERTY

The legal meaning of this word differs from its meaning in every day usage. For, in law, it is used to denote the relationship between a person and a thing and implies an appropriation of some part of the world's resources to a person.

In law, property is not restricted to objects, for it also relates to rights of ownership and possession over material objects (e.g. land), and non-material objects (e.g. copyright). But, before the term "property" is described, it is essential to have an understanding of the separate meanings of ownership and possession and how one differs from the other. A simple illustration which indicates the difference between the two is – I lend my car to a neighbour so that he can visit a sick relative in hospital. During this visit, he is in possession of my car, but I remain the legal owner.

OWNERSHIP

This may be described as the power of use and disposal of property allowed by law. The range of available rights are:

1. Enjoyment
2. Destruction
3. Disposition

} subject to the rights of others.

So, with my car, I can drive it sensibly, drive it over the side of a cliff (hopefully, without me inside!), or sell it to another. But there are certain limits to these rights. I am not permitted by law to drive my car negligently, or while under the influence of too much alcohol. Nor am I permitted to destroy the car in such a way that I physically injure other people, or in an attempt to defraud my insurers. By doing one of these things, I would be committing a crime, and certainly, if I physically injured others by my negligence, I would also face an action in the civil courts. Examples of ownership may arise by:

1. *Creation* – e.g. by painting a picture.

2. *Occupation* – e.g. where abandoned property is occupied.

3. *Progeny* – e.g. where a farmer becomes the owner of animals born of his current stock.

4. *Purchase, gift, or acquisition by law.*

5. *Succession* – e.g. under the terms of a will or as a result of the laws of intestacy – see Chapter 8.

Today, the rights of owners are becoming more and more restricted, particularly with regard to land and its use; e.g. by reason of the Town and Country Planning Acts.

POSSESSION

There are two elements to possession, both of which are derived from Roman Law. These are:

Corpus Possessionis
This means the continuous control over a thing by a person. Control may be direct, or indirect through another person such as an agent or servant.

Animus Possidendi
This means the intent to have exclusive control over the thing, thereby excluding others from using it.

Although these elements provide some assistance as regards the understanding of the term possession and, thus, where possession lies, they do not provide a full answer. For, English law has never worked out a completely logical and exhaustive definition.

To develop the topic further, it can be seen that possession may arise legally or illegally. An example of the former has been given in the introduction, e.g. where one person lends a thing to another. But, through a theft, it may arise illegally, e.g. A thief steals a car and then sells it to someone. Although the buyer is in possession of the car, he is not the legal owner, and therefore acquires no legal rights over the car. This does not mean to say that such a possessor has no legal rights, for he does. Thus, he can seek recompense against the thief – if he can be found!

Finally, it should be noted that possession often evidences ownership, although in some situations it may be difficult or costly to verify ownership. For example, when buying a piece of unregistered land, it would be preferable to employ a solicitor who would borrow the title deeds (previously in the owners' possession), so that he could prepare a report on title. This report will confirm who, in the solicitor's opinion, the true owner is, and whether the solicitor's client (the purchaser) will acquire a good title if the purchase is completed. i.e. Whether possession of the title deeds, after conveyance, will result in the purchaser being considered as the legal owner.

CLASSIFICATION OF PROPERTY

In English law, property is classified in accordance with the table below.

REAL PROPERTY

This consists of freehold land and buildings and rights over such land. The word "real" is used because if an owner is dispossessed of it, the owner can use the court system to repossess the thing (res).

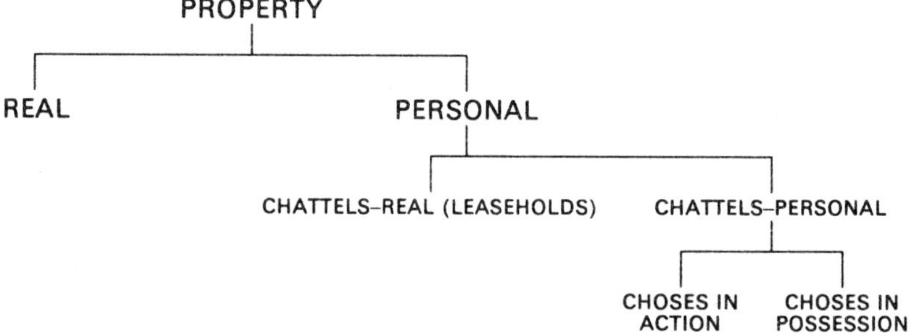

When ownership of real property is transferred, disputes occasionally arise concerning attachments to such property. For sometimes the question arises as to whether or not such attachments make up part of the property which has been transferred. Clearly, these disputes will not arise if the attachments are expressly provided for in the document evidencing transfer. However, if they are not, a dispute may arise and the legal problem to be decided is whether the attachments are fixtures or chattels.

A fixture is legally defined as anything which is permanently attached to the land (e.g. a building), or anything else which is itself fixed to the attachment (e.g. a fixture to a wall). Where there is a fixed attachment, it could be presumed that this has ceased to be a chattel and has become part of the real property. However, this presumption could be rebutted if it could be proved that the disputed attachments are wholly unconnected with the realty and have only been affixed to it for its better enjoyment. This was confirmed in **Leigh *v.* Taylor (1902)**, where it was held that a valuable tapestry which had been affixed to a wall was not a fixture but a chattel, and, as a consequence, did not form part of the property being transferred. By a similar argument, attachments such as a painting, ornaments or kitchen utensils affixed to walls by screws or other methods would not be considered as fixtures.

PERSONAL PROPERTY

This consists of all other property which is not real and so if the owner is dispossessed of it, it may not always be possible for him to recover it. Legal actions which may result from such wrongs are personal ones against the wrong-doer, either for recovery of the property or a payment of its value.

Personal property from the diagram may be divided into:

(a) *Chattels–Real.* Leasehold land is included under this heading.
(b) *Chattels–Personal.* This is subdivided into:
  (1) *Choses in Action.* These are sometimes described as incorporeal chattels. They are intangible and because of this, it is impossible to take physical possession of them. Examples of such items are mortgages, goodwill, debts, patents and trade designs, trade marks, trade names, and finally, the topic which makes up Chapter 11, negotiable instruments. All of these items give rights which are enforceable by law.
  (2) *Choses in Possession.* These are sometimes described as corporeal chattels. They are chattels that can be possessed and passed on by physical delivery. Examples of such items are cars, caravans, televisions, horses, jewellery, etc.

Finally, personal property includes rights over both choses in action and choses in possession.

The remainder of this chapter is devoted to land – or to use the terms described above "Real Property" and "Chattels–Real (Leaseholds)". It seems simpler to use the term land!

LAND

The legal description of land goes much further than its usual grammatical meaning. For it it includes:

(a) The soil.
(b) Certain mines and minerals below the surface.
(c) Trees, crops and anything else growing on the land.
(d) Buildings and other structures erected thereon.

(e) Rights relating to the air above the piece of land.

For freeholds, this ownership is absolute – but there are certain limitations imposed upon the owner by law which include:

Civil Aviation Act, 1949
Aircraft must be allowed to fly over the owner's land;

Town and Country Planning Acts
With exceptions, most types of alteration relating to structure or use of the land can only be carried out after obtaining specific permission from the local planning officers.

Coal Nationalisation Act, 1947
The majority of minerals lying under the owner's land belong to the state, to which the state has access.

ORIGINS OF LAND LAW

The origins date back to the conquering of England by William I in the eleventh century after which he became the sole land owner. After this, the king made grants of land to groups of people, including his followers and certain English barons. These land owners became known as tenants in chief. For services rendered to them, they made sub-grants to a group who were called the Mesne Lords and the same happened between this group and lesser knights. The tenants in chief, Mesne Lords and lesser knights acquired what was called a free tenure (later to be known as freehold) of the land. The third group, the lesser knights, were able to sub-grant to people called villeins. These acquired what was called unfree tenure or copyhold. Where the sub-grant related to a freehold estate passed on to two or more parties, the process was known as subinfeudation. This process was abolished in 1290 by the Statute of Quia Emptores.

TENURE

As described above, grants of land were given to tenants based on the type of service they offered. This resulted in specific types of tenure being granted and a simple classification would be free tenure and unfree tenure.

FREE TENURE

The various types of free tenure were:

1. *Military Tenure* (*Knights Service*). This related to the supply of a given number of men to fight for the king for a given number of days in each year. In fact, this type of tenure was converted into freehold socage (see below) by the Statute of Tenures 1660.

2. *Spiritual Tenure (Frankalmoign)*. This related to land held by the church in return for spiritual services.

3. *Socage Tenure*. In the main, this related to the supply of men to work on the farms.

4. *Serjeanty*. This related to personal services given to the king or a lord.

UNFREE TENURE

1. *Villein Tenure*. This was land held by the serfs or villeins (a class of labourers or servants) who were attached to the land and who were sold with it when the Lord of the Manor transferred it. Originally, serfs and villeins had no security of tenure, but, by Tudor times, they could not be ejected if they satisfactorily performed their services. Furthermore, they were entitled to a copy of a document which evidenced their holding, and thus, the tenure became known as copyhold land. This type of tenure remained until the Law of Property Act, 1925, turned it into freehold.

ESTATES IN LAND

This denotes the duration of an interest in land and answers the question "For how long is the land held?" It contrasts with tenure described above which denotes the nature of quality of land ownership and answers the question "From whom is the land held?"

LEGAL ESTATES IN LAND

These are provided for in section 1 of the Law of Property Act, 1925, and are freehold and leasehold.

FREEHOLD

Legally, this is called "fee simple absolute in possession". The person holding the freehold estate has absolute ownership capable of lasting indefinitely and he can deal with the land as he chooses. The land descends to his heirs for ever, unless the land is sold or devised (i.e. left by will) to someone else. However, there are certain restrictions imposed upon the owner by law, e.g. by Town and Country Planning Acts.

TRANSFER

Transfer of title is effected by means of a conveyance, irrespective of whether the land has a registered title or unregistered title.

LEASEHOLD

Legally, this is called "a term of years absolute". The person holding the leasehold estate will have been granted it for a limited period by the freeholder. From this simple statement, it is seen that there are two parties to any lease:

The person granting the lease: the lessor who is also known as the freeholder or landlord; and

The person to whom the lease is granted: the lessee, who is also known as the leaseholder or tenant.

The lessor grants a term of years absolute to the leaseholder and, upon expiry of this term, the full title to the land reverts back to the lessor. During the term of the lease, the leaseholder is entitled to exclusive possession of the land, provided he complies with the terms of the lease (e.g. keeping the property in a good state of repair, paying the ground rent, etc.). If there is any contravention of these or other terms, the lease can be voided and the tenant expelled. Furthermore, during the term of the lease, it will often be a provision that the lessor has the power to inspect the land (and the inside of any building erected thereon) at any time he wishes. Where the lease is of a long term (e.g. 999 years), the land is considered to be the equivalent of freehold – but clearly, it is subject to terms of the lease.

TRANSFER

Transfer of the full term of a leasehold estate by the lessor is effected by means of an assignment. Where the lessor only wishes to transfer part of the unexpired term of the lease, say, the next five years of a ten year lease, then this is done by way of a sub-lease (or underlease). Often by the terms of a lease, the freeholder must either give his agreement before an assignment or sub-lease is created and invariably he must be given notice of the transfer.

CONVERTING A LEASEHOLD ESTATE TO A FREEHOLD ESTATE

The simplest way of achieving this is for the lessee to ask if he can buy the freehold of the land from the lessor, and, if the lessor agrees, then this can be conveyed.

If the lessor does not agree, then prior to the Leasehold Reform Act, 1967, there was nothing (with the exception of further requests at a later date) that the lessee could do. But, by a provision in this statute. certain powers are given to lessees whereby they can either buy the freehold or have the term of years extended by fifty years. These powers only apply to land which has a low rateable value, and where the tenant has held the lease for a minimum period of five years and where the original lease was for a term in excess of twenty one years. These provisions were subsequently amended by the Leasehold Reform Act, 1982. For example, the qualifying period for holding the lease has now been reduced to twelve months. It also provides that if the lessee has applied to extend the lease once, this does not debar him from applying for a further extension or purchasing the freehold – a right which was denied a lessee in the past.

EQUITABLE ESTATES IN LAND

The following equitable estates can exist in land:

FREEHOLD

1. *Estate in Fee Tail*

This type of estate only descends to a particular class of heirs, e.g. all males. However, since 1925, an owner in fee tail can "bar the entail" – i.e. cancel the restriction. The estate then becomes "fee simple absolute in possession".

2. *Estate for Life*

This type of estate remains for the duration of a tenant's life or a third party's life. The latter is known as an "estate pour autre vie" – i.e. an estate during the life of another.

LEASEHOLD

This type of estate relates to any leasehold estate which is not for a term of years absolute.

CREATION OF LEGAL AND EQUITABLE ESTATES

Grants of land by deed may take many forms. Some of these will give a legal estate while others will given an equitable estate. The type given can be established from the title or interest granted to the transferee as the following examples illustrate.

LEGAL ESTATES

These may be created in any of the following ways:

1. *To A*. By virtue of s. 60 Law of Property Act, 1925, the necessity for words of limitation to create a fee simple estate was abolished for conveyances executed after 1925. Thus, if X is a fee simple owner who conveys his land to B, B acquires the fee simple estate unless words to the contrary appear. There is a similar interpretation relating to gifts inter vivos forming part of a will – but this dates back to the Wills Act, 1837.

2. *To A in Fee Simple*. Here, a fee simple absolute in possession is

created. If no date for the creation is stated, it is deemed to take immediate effect.

3. *To A and His Heirs*. Again, a fee simple absolute in possession is created in A – the words "and his heirs" have no immediate effect.

EQUITABLE ESTATES

1. *To A In Tail* (*or to A and the Heirs of His Body*). This is an estate less than a fee simple. However, the tenant has full rights of possession and enjoyment and these pass on to his heirs upon his death. The heirs would be deemed to be of his body or his descendants but could be restricted to a tail male (descending through males only) or to tail female (descending through females only).

2. *To A For Life*. This is an estate which is granted to A during his lifetime and thus, upon his death, the estate terminates.

3. *To A as Long as B Shall Survive*. This is sometimes described as an "estate pour autre vie" and the estate continues during the life of another. It is very similar to 2. above.

INTERESTS IN LAND

These may be divided into legal or equitable interests.

LEGAL INTERESTS

These are rights over land not amounting to possession and they must be created by Deed. They are enforceable in any court against any person. By section 1(1) Law of Property Act, 1925, there are five legal interests (which bind a purchaser for value even if he has no notice of them):

(a) Easements – e.g. rights of way.
(b) Profits a prendre – rights to hunt and shoot etc.
(c) Rent charge and (land taxes) – the right of a person with no possessory right to receive a yearly sum out of the profits of the land.
(d) Rights of entry respecting legal leases or legal rent charges.
(e) Charge by way of legal mortgage.

EQUITABLE INTERESTS

All other interests (or charges), except those described above are equitable and must therefore exist behind a trust. Thus, life interests are equitable and so are entails, reversions and remainders.

CO-OWNERSHIP

All land in England and Wales will be owned by someone, and these people are known as the title holders. Certain titles will be registered in the name of one person, but there is also provision for a maximum of four people to be registered as the title holders of the same piece of land. When more than one person buys a piece of land, the "tenancy" will be in the form of either joint tenancy or tenancy in common. The type which exists depends upon the wording of the conveyance which transferred the title to them. For, where the conveyance was to X and Y, a joint tenancy would be created, but where it was to X and Y equally, it would be a tenancy in common.

JOINT TENANTS

When joint tenancy has been established, then it can be said that each tenant is an owner of the whole. The right of survivorship (jus accrescendi) is such that when one tenant dies, his share of the land passes to the survivor(s) and this continues until only one tenant is left, and then he becomes the sole owner. This type of tenancy has the disadvantage that upon death, a tenant cannot dispose of his tenancy by will, because title automatically passes to the surviving tenant(s). It is only when the last tenant dies that land may be dealt with in accordance with the provisions of a will or the rules of intestacy.

TENANTS IN COMMON

Where a tenancy in common has been established, then it can be said that each tenant owns his own share of the property, even though the share cannot strictly be applied to a specific part of the whole. The right of survivorship is such that the tenant may dispose of his share of ownership by will. So, upon death, his share of the land automatically forms part of his estate for distribution in accordance with a will or the rules of intestacy.

SOLE REGISTERED TITLE HOLDER NOT THE SOLE OWNER

Over the recent past, there have been a series of legal cases some of which have passed right up to the House of Lords and two have involved Williams and Glyn's Bank. The two cases in question are **Williams and Glyn's Bank Ltd *v.* Boland (1981)** and **Williams and Glyn's Bank Ltd *v.* Brown (1981)**. The facts of the cases (which were almost identical), were that a house was bought by a husband and wife for their occupation, but the title was registered solely in the name of the husband, even though the wife had contributed part of the consideration monies. Subsequently, the husband borrowed from the bank which took security in the form of a legal mortgage over the house. As the bank satisfied itself that the husband was the only title holder, then he alone was asked to execute (sign) the bank mortgage form. Later, the husband defaulted and the bank commenced proceedings to realise its security, but they were quickly halted by the wife who was attempting to protect her position. *Held*. Persons who had contributed towards the purchase monies of land and who had not become registered title holders at the time of conveyance had an overriding interest in that land which ranked before any legal or equitable mortgage. The only ways in which the bank could have proceeded with a vacant possession sale were:

(a) If the wife had joined in the execution of the bank's mortgage, or,
(b) If she had signed a separate document which postponed her interest behind the bank's.

In either instance, from the bank's standpoint, it is better if the wife (or any other person who is not a title holder), receives independent advice as to what their legal position is, prior to going ahead and executing the mortgage or document. The action would avoid any successful claim of undue influence should such a claim be made by the non-registered title holder at a later date.

In these cases, as neither (a) nor (b) had been carried out, the bank's security was of no value, even over the husband's title.

This decision has now been accepted by those institutions that advance money against the security of land and, as such, they have amended their procedures for taking land as security. It should be noted that although the above cases related to husband/wife relationships, the ratio will apply to boyfriend/girlfriend, fiancees and also occasionally to parties in occupation where the latter have improved the value of the land.

Even though mortgagors have amended their procedures, the changes introduced certainly did not help a building society in **City of London Building Society *v*. Flegg (1986)**. Here, Mr and Mrs Flegg sold their house and put the proceeds towards a house which they bought and occupied with their daughter and son-in-law (the Maxwell-Browns). The Maxwell-Browns took out a mortgage of £20,000 as their share of the purchase monies and the property was registered solely in their joint names. They also took out second and third mortgages at later dates. Subsequently, they defaulted on the first mortgage, but the plaintiff building society refinanced the three mortgages. The Maxwell-Browns defaulted again and it was only when the plaintiff sought a possession order that the Flegg's existence became known. The plaintiff argued that the decisions in the Boland and Brown cases did not apply here as the property had originally been bought in joint names, i.e. the Maxwell-Browns. *Held*. The plaintiff's action was unsuccessful. The Boland principles did apply here and thus the Flegg's had an overriding interest which ranked in priority to the plaintiff's.

UNREGISTERED AND REGISTERED TITLES

In England and Wales, all land has either an unregistered or registered title and the meaning of these terms is described below.

UNREGISTERED TITLE

Title to unregistered land is evidenced by a bundle of deeds and documents collectively known as title deeds. Each time a transfer of ownership occurs then, additional documents such as, discharged mortgages, assents, conveyances, are added to the original ones, and so the pile of papers increases. It is essential for all these documents to be retained together to establish the chain of title. The process is clearly cumbersome!

Many years ago it became recognised that the procedures and paperwork should be streamlined by establishing a system of land registration and this is briefly described below.

As the title deeds are not negotiable very formal procedures are necessary when transferring title on a sale. The transfer is effected by means of a conveyance.

REGISTERED TITLE

Registration is now governed by the Land Registration Act, 1925, and subsequent amendments. Title to registered land is evidenced by a Land Certificate – which takes the place of the bundle of deeds which evidences title for unregistered land. The Land Register provides a state guarantee of title subject to entries on the certificate and on the District Register where the land is registered, and subject also to what are called overriding interests. The Land Certificate is issued under the seal of the Land Registry. As entries against the property are recorded on the District Register, then when the Land Certificate is next handed in (some entries not being permissible without its production), it is up-dated and old entries deleted.

Similarly, as for unregistered title deeds, the Land Certificate is not negotiable and formal (but simpler) procedures are necessary to effect a transfer of title. This involves amendments being made to the register of entries maintained by the District Land Registrar.

ADVANTAGES OF A REGISTERED LAND SYSTEM

(a) The method of transferring title to registered land is superior because it is quicker and the legal costs are lower.

(b) A potential mortgagee is able to establish if the mortgagor has power to deal with the land or if the land is subject to incumbrances by inspecting the land register. This is carried out by obtaining an office copy, costing £1.00, or simply inspecting the land certificate if it is to hand.

(c) If a proprietor's name is inadvertently omitted or removed from the register, the proprietor is usually entitled to claim indemnity from a fund established by the state.

(d) Investigations of title are much easier and quicker.

The main register is kept at Lincoln's Inn Fields, London, but the country as a whole is divided up into areas and each has its own District Registry to which all enquiries, notices and charges should be sent. A typical example is: WM 12487, This means title 12487 in the West Midlands area whose District Registry is at Gloucester.

In most areas of the country registration of land is compulsory. However, even in compulsory registration areas not all the land is yet registered, as registration only becomes obligatory: (a) on a sale of freehold, or (b) on grant or assignment of a lease with 40 years or more to run, or (c) on grant of a lease for 21 years or more where the freehold has been registered with absolute title. (Leases under 21 years cannot be registered.)

Sometimes a land certificate may evidence title even though it relates to an area which is not subject to compulsory registration. This is because a system of voluntary registration is available. Today, its use is severely restricted and tends to be used in cases of lost deeds or large house building projects, etc.

MORTGAGES

The word "*mortgage*" is of French origin and it stems from:

"*mort*" meaning dead, and
"*gage*" meaning pledge.

The names of the persons who become a party to a mortgage are:

(a) The *mortgagor* – this is the person who is giving the mortgage and for a legal mortgage it is executed under seal. The reason for giving a mortgage is that usually it is in the form of security to cover a person's own liabilities, e.g. for a loan of money given by another party (see (b)).

(b) The *mortgagee* – this is the person in whose favour the mortgage has been given and effectively it is security for him.

As they appear, the combination of the two words "dead pledge" means nothing. But their effect is as follows. Let us assume that A (a mortgagor) has borrowed £3,000 from B (a mortgagee), and a legal mortgage (see below) of A's land has been given as security. If A honours his promise of repayment, then A has the legal right to go to B and ask for the mortgage to be cancelled (discharged). Thus A would have full possession of his land again. By doing this, A is exercising what is called "*the equity of redemption*". However, what happens if A does not repay? The answer is that B would treat the mortgage as a dead pledge (because the promised repayments had not been met) and so B could retain possession of the documents of title and thus be considered as the legal owner of the land. This is a simplified explanation of what a legal mortgagee's powers were according to the law which existed many years ago. The powers available to mortgagees today are much wider than these and are fully covered within this chapter.

It should be remembered that mortgages can be executed over freeholds or leaseholds whether the title is registered or unregistered, and the mortgage created can be either legal or equitable.

TYPES OF MORTGAGE OVER LAND

LEGAL MORTGAGE

By s. 85 of the Law of Property Act, 1925, a legal mortgage can only be created in one of two ways:

(a) For freehold land, by granting a long lease of land for a term of years, e.g. 3,000 years, subject to the promise that the lease will terminate upon repayment of the debt.

For leasehold land, there must be a sub-lease for a term which is at least one day less than the unexpired term of the original lease, or;

(b) A charge by deed expressed to be by way of a legal mortgage. This method can be used for both freeholds and leaseholds.

For both methods, the legal estate remains with the mortgagor, but a legal interest is created in favour of the mortgagee. The legal interest remains until the mortgage is paid off, and, at that time, the mortgagor will usually want to exercise his "equity of redemption". The most common method of creating a legal mortgage is method (b).

EQUITABLE MORTGAGE

This may be created by any one of the following methods:

(a) By depositing the title deeds (unregistered land) or land certificate (registered land) with the necessary intent.

(b) By depositing the title deeds (unregistered land) or land certificate (registered land) and putting the intent beyond doubt by the mortgagor(s) completing a memorandum which evidences that the title documents have been deposited as security. *NB:* The memorandum is usually signed under hand. But, if executed under seal, it will contain special clauses (see later) which give the mortgagee the equivalent rights of a legal mortgagee.

> *Note:* As a further safeguard with registered land, a mortgagee may register his equitable charge at the appropriate District Land Registry, and this is very much favoured as the registration becomes "notice to the world".

COMPARISON OF EQUITABLE MORTGAGES WITH LEGAL MORTGAGES

The methods of taking equitable or legal mortgages are very much the same. However, there are several disadvantages of equitable mortgages. The main one is that the remedies available in the event of a mortgagor defaulting are inferior to those of a legal mortgagee, unless it has been taken under seal – which, in fact, is rarely done.

REMEDIES OF A LEGAL MORTGAGEE

Subject to any provisions in the mortgage form there are five remedies available to a legal mortgagee.

These can be remembered by the mnemonic *SAFES*

S ue for the debt on the mortgagor's personal covenant to repay.
A ppoint a Receiver.
F oreclose.
E nter into possession.
S ell the property.

Of these alternatives, a mortgagor will usually either sell the property (after obtaining vacant possession), or appoint a Receiver (to collect rents). Foreclosure will rarely be granted by a court, whilst entering into possession is considered too onerous. All of these are described in more detail below.

When attempting to exercise these powers, a mortgagee must now comply with the provisions of the Consumer Credit Act 1974. Thus, where a mortgage is security for a "regulated agreement", the power to enter into possession or sell the property can only be exercised by court order: s 126 C.C.A. 1974.

1. SUE ON THE COVENANT TO REPAY

This remedy is available also to unsecured creditors and is used when the mortgagor is unwilling rather than unable to settle a debt. It saves realising the security, but is a process rarely taken because the mortgagor's unwillingness to pay is invariably due to him having insufficient funds. Today, some mortgage forms omit the availability of this remedy – but it is available as a right, anyway.

2. APPOINT A RECEIVER

This remedy is most appropriate to a property which is let to tenants. The Receiver, who must be appointed in writing, collects rents from the mortgaged property and applies them in the following order:

(a) in payment of outstanding amounts to any prior mortgagee;
(b) in payment of rates, taxes and other outgoings;
(c) in payment of his own commission;
(d) in payment of insurance;
(e) in reduction of the principal amount due, when directed by the mortgagee.

The Receiver is deemed to be an agent of the mortgagor, and therefore the mortgagee is not liable for any of his actions, nor is he liable for the costs of Receivership.

3. FORECLOSE

A foreclosure order deprives the mortgagor of his equity of redemption (see *Note* below), and thus the property becomes vested forever in the name of the mortgagee.

Consent of the court is needed for this action, and is rarely granted these days as a sale is usually ordered. If approved, an order "nisi" is usually granted, and then, if repayment has not been effected within (usually) six months, the order then becomes "absolute".

On the granting of an "absolute" order, the rights of subsequent mortgagees become extinguished – this is one reason why such orders are not readily granted.

Note: "Equity of Redemption" is a mortgagor's right to redeem his property by paying off the principal sum plus interest, irrespective of whether a contractual date for redemption is stated in the mortgage form and that date has passed. There can be no clog to the equity of redemption, although there are a few exceptions. Attempts to postpone the contractual rights to redeem will be considered by the Courts after due consideration of the facts.

Knightsbridge Estates Trust Ltd *v.* Byrne (1939)
The company mortgaged one of their properties as security for a loan agreed to be for a period of forty years. Shortly after the mortgage had been executed, the company wanted to repay the loan early and get the mortgage discharged. *Held.* By the House of Lords. A provision of the Companies Act 1929, which now forms part of Section 193, Companies Act, 1985, applied here. So, the mortgage given by the company was a debenture, and, as these could be perpetual, the rule preventing the clogging of equity did not apply. Thus, the company was prevented from exercising its equity of redemption until the forty-year period had expired.

4. ENTER INTO POSSESSION

This remedy is rarely pursued because the same effect is achieved more economically and without onerous responsibilities by appointing a Receiver.

However, in theory, this right is available. When it is used, the mortgagee becomes accountable not only for the profits which he received, but also for those which might have been received, had he, as mortgagee, not been negligent.

White *v.* City of London Brewery Co. (1889)
Here, the defendants took possession of the plaintiff's public house which had been mortgaged to them. They then leased it to a tenant who was restricted to buying beer solely from them. This arrangement meant that the rent charged was lower than that which could be obtained if the public house was free to buy beer from any supplier. The plaintiff sued for the difference. *Held.* By the Court of Appeal. The defendant was accountable for the difference in rental incomes.

5. SELL THE PROPERTY

This remedy is the one most often carried out. Legally under the Law of Property Act, 1925, by sections 103, (power to sell) and 109 (power to appoint a Receiver), these rights can only be exercised after one of the following has occurred:

(a) Repayment having been demanded, the mortgagor has defaulted in whole or in part, for a period of three months, or;

(b) Some interest under the mortgage is two months in arrears, or;

(c) There has been some breach of the mortgage deed other than the covenant to repay.

A mortgagee legally can – and usually does, delete these requirements and provides for repayment "on demand", thus giving him either an immediate power of sale or the ability to appoint a Receiver on the mortgagor's default.

(i) MORTGAGEE'S DUTIES WHEN SELLING

Court consent may or may not be necessary for this action (see introductory comments to this section). Usually a mortgagee will wish to obtain the "full market value with vacant possession". If the mortgagor will not vacate voluntarily, then a court order for possession is always necessary. Problems may arise due to the protection afforded to spouses by the Matrimonial Homes Act, 1983, and through rights of occupation.

A mortgagee of land must, when selling, act honestly and equitably. He cannot sell to himself, and he must act in good faith, effecting a sale which realises the true market price at the time he chooses to sell. All known material and relevant details likely to affect the price should be disclosed, e.g. planning permission, permitted change of use etc., **Cuckmere Brick Co. Ltd *v*. Mutual Finance Ltd (1971)**. It has also been established that a mortgagee need not delay a sale in expectation of a rising market: **Bank of Cyprus (London) Ltd *v*. Gill (1979)**. The law on this matter has recently been extended by the decision made in **Standard Chartered Bank Ltd *v*. Walker and Walker (1982)**. Here, Lord Denning indicated that a mortgagee (or a Receiver) should not sell property (which, in this instance, was machinery), at an unfavourable time. The assets of the company were being sold by way of auction by a Receiver. But a series of problems resulted. Firstly, the auction took place at very short notice and also, the Receiver did not circulate any of the customers who were on the company's normal mailing list. Secondly, the auction was arranged in the early part of February when it was very cold. Initially, a series of heaters kept the auction room warm, but, because the noise of the heaters made it difficult for the bidders to hear what the auctioneer was saying, a request was made to turn them off. This request was complied with, but as a consequence, the room quickly became very cold and the bidders began to leave. The assets only realised half of what was anticipated. *Held*. In these circumstances the sale took place at an unfavourable time.

Note: The ratio of this precedent was wider than stated above, but in this book, only general principles are being considered.

In practice, a mortgagee of land will always take the advice of an estate agent and, where appropriate, will endeavour to sell by public auction – as there can then be no possible argument regarding price.

More recently, an interesting decision was made by the Privy Council in **Tsi Kwong Lam v. Wong Chit Sen (1983)**. Here, a mortgagee exercised his power of sale and, in so doing, the property was purchased by a company in which he had an interest. *Held*. As the sale had been made in good faith and all reasonable steps had been taken to ensure that the best possible price had been obtained at the time, the sale was good.

(ii) APPLICATION OF SALE PROCEEDS

After sale, the proceeds should be applied in the following order:

(a) The costs of the sale (which should be kept to a minimum).
(b) Repayment of mortgage debt plus interest.
(c) To subsequent mortgagees, if any.
(d) To the mortgagor, if any proceeds remain.
A full account of the sale and expenses paid should be given to the mortgagor.

REMEDIES OF AN EQUITABLE MORTGAGEE

The remedies depend upon whether the mortgage was given under hand or seal.

(i) UNDER SEAL

When an equitable mortgage has been executed under seal, a mortgagee will have the same powers as a legal mortgagee. Thus, it will always have the power to convey the legal title to a purchaser without reference to the Court, i.e. to deal with the legal estate: **Re White Rose Cottage Ltd (1965)**.

This power is conferred by the insertion of one or both of the following clauses:

(a) *A Power of Attorney*

Here, the mortgagor irrevocably appoints a third party as his agent to either sell, grant leases or execute a legal mortgage on the property. The "third party" is usually a senior employee of the mortgagee.

(b) *A Declaration of Trust*

Here, the mortgagor acknowledges that he is only holding the property as Trustee. The mortgagee will be given the power to change the Trustee when he sees fit. Thus the mortgagor can be removed by the mortgagee, and a different person appointed in this capacity.

(ii) UNDER HAND

Because an equitable mortgagee does not have a legal interest in the property, he cannot convey any interest to a purchaser without reference to the Court, i.e. he cannot sell. Nor can he appoint a Receiver or enter into possession, unless expressly authorised to do so under the terms of the equitable mortgage.

However, when the mortgagor signs a form of equitable mortgage, he will usually have given an undertaking to complete a legal mortgage if requested to do so. If he satisfies the request, then the mortgagee may register its legal mortgage and thus have the full range of remedies available. If he fails to satisfy the request, then reference must be made to the Court.

Notes: (a) An equitable mortgagee can sue the mortgagor for repayment of the loan plus interest without getting court approval to do so.

(b) Certain restrictions on realising land as security are outlined in the Consumer Credit Act 1974 – these are beyond the scope of this book.

SECOND MORTGAGES

It is possible for a number of legal mortgages to be taken over the same piece of land. From a practical viewpoint, "second legal mortgages" are regularly taken by banks and finance companies as security, and, nearly always, the first mortgage has been given in favour of a Building Society. Further (or subsequent) mortgages – e.g. third, fourth etc., are possible, but rare.

EXAMPLE OF A SECOND MORTGAGE

A. Scouser is the legal owner of "Anfield". When he bought it for £30,000 in 1975, it was with the help of a Building Society mortgage of £10,000. Today, he wants to build an extension on the house and a finance company has agreed to the request of a £5,000 loan in principle but it is subject to Scouser giving a mortgage over his house. Thus, when the finance company takes its security over "Anfield", it will be taking a second mortgage as the one the Building Society took in 1975 was a first mortgage.

CREATION OF A SECOND LEGAL MORTGAGE

This may be created in one of two ways:

(a) A charge by deed expressed to be by way of a legal mortgage.
(b) A lease for a term longer by one day than the term vested in the first mortgagee.

SUB-MORTGAGES

This is simply a "mortgage of a mortgage" and arises where a mortgagee himself wishes to borrow money from, say, a bank or finance company against the security of the mortgage he holds.

Example: A has borrowed £5,000 from B and, as security, has mortgaged his property to B. B now wishes to borrow £1,000 himself and as he does not wish to call in his loan, he asks a bank or finance company to lend him the money using, as security, the mortgage he is holding in his favour, – i.e. he creates a sub-mortgage.

More than an outline of sub-mortgages is beyond the scope of this book – but briefly, the sub-mortgagee obtains the rights of the sub-mortgagor in respect of:

(a) the recovery of the debt under the original mortgage (called the "head mortgage"); and
(b) enforcing the "head mortgage" should the original mortgagor fail.

SUNDRY POINTS CONCERNING LAND

CONSOLIDATION

This is the right of a mortgagee, to whom a mortgagor has given several mortgages on different properties, to refuse to redeem (cancel or discharge) one mortgage while others remain in existence until all are redeemed. Thus, it prevents a mortgagor from redeeming a valuable mortgaged property, whilst leaving as security, unsatisfactory ones. However, this right has to be acquired by express provision and mortgagees do this by inserting an appropriate clause in their mortgage forms. Without such a clause, s. 93 Law of Property Act, 1925, would apply whereby a mortgagor seeking to redeem one mortgage is entitled to do so without paying any money due under any separate mortgage made by him.

Customer A has two loans:

Loan 1	Debit balance	£30,000	
	Security value	£22,000	This is a house and its value has fallen because it has become dilapidated.
Loan 2	Debit balance	£7,000	
	Security value	£15,000	This is a different house whose value has been steadily rising.

In normal circumstances, the customer could clear Loan 2 and ask for the mortgaged security (valued at £15,000) to be discharged. This would leave Loan 1 still outstanding and inadequately secured. A consolidation clause prevents the mortgagor from compelling the mortgagee to release the security valued at £15,000 and so, even if A clears the debt on Loan 2, the mortgagee has the right to retain the security valued at £15,000.

TACKING

This is the right of a prior mortgagee to advance further monies which will rank in priority over the claims of subsequent mortgagees (e.g. second, third, fourth etc.). It is clearly important for a subsequent mortgagee to clarify this matter. For, when tacking is permitted, the subsequent mortgagee's security position is weakened.

Example:

Mortgagor's land (charged as security) is valued at	£40,000	
Debt owed to 1st mortgagee is	£20,000	
A further advance, which is to be tacked, of	£15,000	has been agreed in the original mortgage deed to be available on demand.

Say, a potential second mortgagee is considering a request for an advance of £10,000.

Without the tacking, there would be sufficient equity (value of security minus amount of outstanding claims, i.e. £40,000–£20,000 = £20,000) for the proposed second mortgage, but, with it, there is insufficient equity (40,000–(£20,000+£15,000)=£5,000). In such situations, the potential second mortgagee would either decline to offer the advance or ask if there is any alternative security which would fully cover the requested advance.

Tacking is one of the three occasions provided for in s. 94(1) Law of Property Act, 1925, whereby a prior mortgagee has a right to make further advances which rank in priority to subsequent mortgagees.

EXAMINATION QUESTIONS

Question 1

(a) Define "ownership" and "possession".

(b) Geoffrey has contracted to sell his house to Henry and he proposes to vacate the house on 1st June 1989. Before doing this he intends to remove certain pictures which are fixed to the walls of the library room by plugs and screws. Can he lawfully do so?

(c) Last week Albert stole a fountain pen from Bernard. Yesterday Claude damaged the pen intentionally. Can Albert sue Claude for this damage?

(Chartered Institute of Bankers)

Question 2

(a) How does English law classify "property"?

(b) What proprietary classification would you give to:

(i) a house, (ii) a caravan, (iii) a horse, (iv) a debt, (v) a cheque?

(Chartered Institute of Bankers)*

Question 3

Explain and distinguish with examples:

Chose in possession and chose in action.

(Chartered Institute of Bankers)

Question 4

"Property is any object which men may own or possess." (James)

(a) Giving examples, describe the difference between real and personal property.

(b) State four important types of chose in action.

(Chartered Institute of Bankers)

Question 5

Distinguish between ownership and possession and explain how ownership may be acquired.

(A.E.B. A-Level)

Question 6

Which of the following grants of land by deed create a legal estate?

(a) To X.

(b) To Y in fee simple after A's death.

(c) To Z for life.
(d) To T for seven years.

State the legal estate (if any) created by each grant and if a grant does not create a legal estate, state what interest is created.
(Chartered Institute of Bankers)

Question 7

(a) Define a mortgage.

(b) Bernard borrowed £10,000 from Charles on the security of a legal mortgage of Bernard's freehold shop. In the mortgage deed Bernard covenanted to repay the principal sum by yearly instalments of £1000, and to purchase all supplies for his shop from Charles, if Charles was willing to supply them. Are these provisions valid?
(Chartered Institute of Bankers)

Question 8

John, the fee-simple owner of Blackacre farm, is insolvent and borrows £10,000 from his friend Kenneth on the security of his farm at an interest rate of 15% per annum. John signed a written note to acknowledge these terms and handed the title deeds to Kenneth. Is Kenneth a legal or an equitable mortgagee and what are his remedies (if any) if John defaults in paying the interest due?
(Chartered Institute of Bankers)

Question 9

George wishes to borrow £5,000 from his friend Herbert, who is willing to lend him this sum if George will provide "real" security. George owns his freehold house worth £10,000 and offers this property as security. Herbert agrees to this. How will the transaction be carried out and what will be the rights of both?
(Chartered Institute of Bankers)

Question 10

X borrowed £500 for a term of two years from his bank and deposited the title deeds of his house as security.

(a) Does this transaction constitute:
  (1) a sale of the house by him to the bank;
  (2) a contract to sell the house;
  (3) a mortgage of the house?

(b) What is the legal position of the bank if X fails to repay the loan after it becomes due?

(Chartered Institute of Bankers)

Question 11

Tom is the yearly tenant of a shop let to him by Lionel. He has failed to pay his rent and to perform his covenant to keep the premises in repair. What legal remedies are available to Lionel?
(Chartered Institute of Bankers)

Question 12

Explain the expression "equity of redemption" in respect of a mortgage.
(Chartered Institute of Bankers)

Question 13

Compare the remedies of a legal mortgagee of land with those of an equitable mortgagee.
(Chartered Institute of Bankers)*

Question 14

Two persons may own land simultaneously. Albert and Bernard are the joint owners of freehold property "Blackacre".

In law, what is their precise ownership in this property?

The document vesting the property in them stated "to Albert and Bernard". Are they joint tenants or tenants in common of this property?
(Chartered Institute of Bankers)

CHAPTER 7

TRUSTS

A trust has been defined by many eminent lawyers but perhaps the most widely accepted definition is that given by the late Sir A. Underhill as "An equitable obligation binding a person (who is called a trustee) to deal with property (which is called 'trust property') over which he has control for the benefit of persons (who are called beneficiaries or cestui que trust) of whom he may himself be one; and any one of whom may enforce the obligation." The words in brackets do not form part of the definition and have been inserted by way of explanation. Even so, the definition is still somewhat difficult to understand and a simple illustration may eliminate the difficulty.

Let us say that my grandfather wants to give me some of his T.S.B. shares. But, because he knows that I am a spendthrift, he does not immediately want to transfer ownership to me as he knows I would instantly sell the shares and quickly spend the sale proceeds. Instead, he sets up a trust. In accordance with its terms, the shares are transferred into the names of trustees (say, my parents), who, during the existence of the trust, will be paid the dividend income as they at this time appear to be the legal owners, In turn, they may have to pay the income over to me at regular intervals (say, every six months). The way in which my parents must act as trustees is governed by a document called a trust deed. The trust will remain in force until some event brings it to an end: say, by me attaining eighteen years of age.

From this description, if it is seen that the shares (and any other property held in trust), are "owned" by two people. The trustees – who are the legal or nominal owners of the shares, and the beneficiary – who is recognised as the owner in equity. The person who is giving over the property is legally described as the donor or settlor.

In general, all kinds of property may be held in trust, although in practice, most property subject to a trust relates to land or stocks and shares.

There are many reasons why trusts are set up. The more common types of trust are as follows:

1. For the benefit of children (or grandchildren as in the above example), or,

2. To administer property (e.g. settlements under the terms of a will) or,
3. For charitable purposes.

In law, trusts are classified into either private trusts or charitable trusts. The distinctive feature between the two is that the former are enforceable by the trustees, whereas the latter are generally only enforceable at the suit of the Attorney General acting on behalf of the Crown. Other classifications have been proposed, but this simple classification is believed to be the best.

PRIVATE TRUSTS

These are created when the beneficiary is an individual or corporate body. Such trusts may be subdivided into either an express trust or an implied trust.

(a) EXPRESS TRUSTS

This type of trust is one which is created by a settlor and it must be for the benefit of one person or a group of people (not for the public in general). It can be created either in writing, by deed, by will or orally.

For every express trust there must be three certainties. **Knight *v.* Knight (1840)**. These are:

(1) CERTAINTY OF WORDS

This means that there must be a clear intention to create a trust which is binding in law. For, if words described as precatory are used, which merely request or hope that someone will act, then the Courts will hold that a valid trust has not been created.

(2) CERTAINTY OF SUBJECT MATTER

This means that the property to which the trust relates must be clearly defined. For documents containing descriptions such as "some portion of my property" or "a decent sum" would fail as valid trusts, for lack of certainty.

(3) CERTAINTY OF OBJECTS

The "objects" referred to here are the beneficiaries. For, the property referred to will revert to the donor if he dies without specifically naming the beneficiaries. However, the trust will not fail if all the beneficiaries are not named in person. **Wishaw *v.* Stephens (1970)**.

(b) IMPLIED TRUSTS

These may be classified into resulting trusts or constructive trusts. The former arise through presumed intention, whereas the latter arise from the rules of law or equity.

(1) RESULTING TRUSTS

These arise from the conduct of the settlor. By way of explanation, assume A buys some property but has it conveyed into the name of B. Here, there will be a presumption that B is holding the property as A's trustee – although the presumption can be rebutted by evidence to the contrary.

(2) CONSTRUCTIVE TRUSTS

These are imposed by law (or equity) and are independent of anyone's express or presumed intention. For example, if a trustee conveys trust property to C, and, when in taking it, C knows that the conveyance is a breach of trust, then C will be held to be a constructive trustee. Thus, C will be holding the property in trust for the actual beneficiaries.

CHARITABLE TRUSTS (PUBLIC TRUSTS)

There is no comprehensive definition of such trusts, but they can be described as those for the benefit of the public in general or a section of the public. They were classified in the leading case **Income Tax Special Commissioners *v.* Pemsel (1891)**, into those for:

1. *The relief of poverty; or*
2. *The advancement of religion; or*
3. *The advancement of education; or*
4. *Other purposes beneficial to the community.*

To satisfy the Courts that the trust is a charitable one, it must be shown that it is for the benefit of the public as a whole, or at least a section of it, irrespective of whether the beneficiaries are rich or poor. **Goodman *v.* Mayor of Saltash (1882)**. Furthermore, trusts which are for the relief of poverty or relatives or employees of the donor have been held to be valid, and so have trusts in favour of Womens Institutes. In contrast, trusts set up for the education of a child or "lawful descendants of three named persons" will not be charitable trusts. **Re Compton (1945).**

With regard to Charitable Trusts, certain special rules apply, most of which are provided for in the Charities Act, 1960: The most important features of such trusts are:

1. **They must be registered**
Most charities have to be registered with the Charity Commissioners (a department of the Home Office). The Commissioners have a wide range of powers which includes authorising deals which relate to the property held by the charity.

2. **Legal proceedings**
At one time, only legal proceedings taken by the Attorney General were possible. However, the Charities Act, 1960, has made it permissible for trustees and certain other parties to take level proceedings subject to them having been given authority to do so by the Charity Commissioners.

3. **Taxation**
Provided the income of the trust is used for charitable purposes, then, in general, it will be exempt for taxation.

4. **Uncertainty of objects**
In contrast with private trusts, if a charitable trust indicates a general charitable intention, the trust will not fail for uncertainty of objects. In situations like this, the trustees may apply the income to any charity (or charities) of their choice, but, on occasions, they may need the prior approval of the Charity Commissioners.

5. **Cy-Près doctrine**
When the trustees try to act under the terms of the trust, they will occasionally be prevented from doing so because, for example, the beneficiary no longer exists or never existed. In this and similar situations, the Court will apply the Cy-près (i.e. as near as can be) doctrine, viz. the gift will be applied to a charity which is as similar as possible to the one the settlor intended to benefit. The same doctrine applies when the original objects of the trust become highly undesirable, **Re Dominion Students' Hall Trust (1947)**.

6. **The perpetuity rule does not operate against them**
For centuries, there have been conflicting interests concerning property. On the one hand, the owners, upon their death, wanted to pass it on to their family, while on the other hand, the state wanted it to pass to the nation so that everyone could benefit. In an attempt to retain ownership within the family, a person could consider setting up a trust in the family's favour for an indefinite period. However, the common law would not allow this, for the Courts formulated a rule which dictated the time period for which property could be tied up. This was known as the Rule of Perpetuity. It stated that "trust property must vest in the recipient within

the period of a life or lives in being at the time when the gift is made, and twentyone years thereafter". **Cadell v. Palmer (1833)**.

However, this strict rule, and particularly the words "must vest", caused many trusts to be void. To make the system more flexible, certain provisions were made in the Perpetuities and Accumulations Act, 1964. By s. 1(1), provision was made for an alternative period "not exceeding eighty years" from the date the trust was created. Furthermore, by s. 3(3), a "wait and see" principle was established. This overcame the problem of the words "must vest", for now the perpetuity rule is not offended until it can be shown that the gift *would* vest outside either the common law or statutory period.

TRUSTEES

The law relating to trusts evolved, in the main, from decisions taken in the Court of Chancery. However, the law was codified by the Trustee Act, 1925, and this Act, with slight amendments, still applies today.

APPOINTMENT OF TRUSTEES

GENERAL

Anyone of full age, sound mind and full legal capacity may be appointed and may act under an express trust. Furthermore, a company can act as a trustee and in this context, it is known as a trust corporation.

Generally, there is no limit to the number of trustees, but there is usually more than one. When the trust relates to land, then the maximum permissible number is four, because there can be no more than four people who are registered title holders to land. When land is sold, at least two trustees must sign the receipt for the consideration monies. In the latter case, where a trust corporation is the sole trustee, then it alone can give a valid receipt for the consideration monies.

METHOD OF APPOINTMENT

Generally, the method of appointment is provided for within the instrument that creates the trust. Otherwise, such appointments may be made by:

1. The creator of the trust (the settlor or testator); or
2. The Court; or,
3. Under the provisions of s. 36 Trustee Act, 1925.

TERMINATION OF APPOINTMENT

The five ways in which a trusteeship may be terminated are:

1. DISCLAIMER

A trustee is not legally bound to accept a trusteeship. But where he wishes to disclaim, he must do so within a reasonable time of his "appointment", otherwise he will be deemed to have accepted the office. The disclaimer has to cover the whole of the office, and is best evidenced by deed rather than by implication. If all trustees disclaim, then their duties devolve upon the settlor or his personal representatives.

2. REMOVAL

This may be achieved through:

1. An express power contained within a will or deed; or,
2. The statutory power contained within sections 36 or 41 Trustee Act, 1925; or,
3. A Court action – say, where the Trustee has been found guilty of fraud concerning the Trust.

3. RETIREMENT

Although the trust deed may provide for retirement without replacement, such express provision is not really necessary as:

(a) Provision has been made within s. 39 Trustee Act, 1925, which allows a Trustee to retire without replacement, subject to:
   (1) A Trust Corporation or at least two individual trustees being left to carry on the trust; and,
   (2) The consent of co-trustees, or any person empowered to appoint trustees being obtained.

Further methods available are:

(b) By application to the Court, although this method is very rarely used.

(c) By obtaining the consent of all beneficiaries who are competent to approve this type of request.

4. REPLACEMENT

Replacement of an existing trustee by a new trustee is permissible and the method of achieving this will be provided for in the Trust instrument. The duly authorised persons, who may attend to obtaining a replacement, may be named in the instrument, but if none are specifically named, then all the remaining trustees are empowered to appoint someone: s. 36 Trustee Act, 1925.

5. DEATH

When a trustee dies, the trusteeship devolves in the survivors, s. 18(1) Trustee Act, 1925. If the deceased was the last surviving or sole trustee, the trust estate devolves in his personal representatives s. 18(2) Trustee Act, 1925.

DUTIES OF TRUSTEES

The duties of trustees may be wide and complex, and will depend upon the provisions in the trust deed. Their main duties will be:

To administer the trust property prudently; and,

To comply strictly with the terms of the trust.

1. ADMINISTRATION

All trustees must exercise the same care over trust property that a prudent man would exercise over his own. Thus, if a trustee acts negligently, then he may be personally liable for any losses which result.

Trustees must collect all debts owing to the trust. They must also exercise due care over all trust property, and if it is found that such property has come into the possession of someone who was not entitled, then actions (legal ones if necessary), must be taken to reclaim it.

Where surplus trust funds are available, these may only be applied to authorised investments. The types of authorised investment may be provided for by statute or by the trust instrument. Where there is no provision in the trust instrument, then the trustees are bound by statute. Historically, the Trustee Act, 1925, only permitted investments in safe securities such as Gilts, Local Authorities, etc. However, after the passing of the Trustee Investments Act, 1961, the area for investment was widened so that up to half of the trust funds could be put into "wider range investments", i.e. equities. The remaining 50% could be put into "narrower range investments requiring advice" (such as Gilts, first mortgages of freeholds), and "narrower range investments not requiring advice" (such as National Savings Certificates). Thus, today, the Trustees are able to widen the portfolio in an attempt to achieve higher capital gains and/or dividends in an effort to overcome the effects of inflation on the capital value of the trust.

2. NOT TO MAKE A PROFIT OUT OF THEIR POSITION

Trustees are not permitted to make either a direct or indirect profit out of their trusteeship: **Bray *v.* Ford (1896)**. Where a profit arises, then they are compelled to pay the amount over to the beneficiaries. **Keech *v.* Sandford (1726)**.

3. DELEGATION

Trustees cannot generally delegate their duties but their are exceptions contained in s. 23 Trustee Act, 1925, whereby provision has been made to enable other parties (agents) to be employed where they are needed for the due performance of contracts, e.g. stockbrokers who must be used to buy and sell investments. Such agents may have their commission paid out of trust monies.

4. ACCOUNTS

These must be adequately maintained and available for inspection by any of the beneficiaries. There is a provision in the Trustee Act, 1925, for the accounts to be audited not less than once in every three years and the fee for this service may be paid from either the trust income or capital.

5. VARIATION OF TRUSTS

Generally, the trustees have no power to vary the provisions contained in the trust instrument but there are a limited number of exceptions to this, and they are:

1. Where all the beneficiaries are of full age and capacity, and they are collectively entitled to all the benefits of the trust, they may instruct the trustees to deal with the trust property in any way.
2. Under the Variation of Trusts Act, 1958, the Courts are empowered to vary (revoke or enlarge) the administrative powers of the trustees provided it improves the position of the beneficiaries. This may arise for example, where a beneficiary becomes mentally incapacitated.

6. REMUNERATION

A trustee can only make a charge for his service when he has been given authority to do so. The authority may be:

1. Contained within the trust instrument. This will usually be provided for where the trustee is either a trust corporation, banker or solicitor; or,
2. Given by all the beneficiaries, provided they are of full age and capacity; or,
3. Given by the Court.

Furthermore, a trustee can recover, from trust monies, any expenses he incurs when performing his duties as trustee.

7. LIABILITIES FOR BREACHES

A trustee is liable for losses which are suffered by the trust estate and which are caused by his negligence or omission. In general, this would be classified as "Acting in excess of powers conferred by the trust instrument" or "Acting in a way which is not provided for in the trust instrument". In the event of such a breach, the beneficiaries have the following remedies available:

1. Damages or an order from the Court to make good the loss to the trust fund.
2. Requesting a Court injunction.
3. In certain instances, by taking out a criminal prosecution order under s. 1(1) Theft Act, 1968.
4. By following the trust property, e.g. by tracing order.

Each of these points is more fully described immediately below:

1. DAMAGE/LOSS

A typical example of when such an action is taken is where a trustee invests in an unauthorised security. Where a loss results, it must be made good by the trustee or trustees who caused the loss. Trustees are only liable for their own acts or defaults. There is an exception to this and it occurs where a liability arises for actions of co-trustees or agents where he has contributed to the loss due to his own, wilful default. **Townley *v.* Sherborne (1633).**

If all trustees have an action taken against them, and one trustee settles the claim in full, then he is entitled to claim against his co-trustees in an attempt to get the loss shared equally.

2. INJUNCTION

Here, the Court will issue an order in which it directs that the trustee either:

(a) Refrains from doing some particular act or thing – when it is known as prohibitory injunction, or,

(b) Performs some positive act – where it is known as a mandatory injunction.

3. CRIMINAL PROSECUTION

A typical example is where a trustee acts dishonestly by misappropriating part of the trust property. When this occurs, an offence under the Theft Act 1968 has been committed and it is usual for the Police to take criminal proceedings against the trustee (although occasionally, this may be taken by a beneficiary), after obtaining the sanction of the Attorney General.

4. FOLLOWING THE PROPERTY

This right of action is possible when the trust property has been misappropriated, and the future possessor and the property can be traced. Thus, if a trustee has given a valuable clock to a third party, when the beneficiaries discover this fact if they can trace who is currently holding the clock, they can repossess it. (However, if the third party had accepted the clock in good faith and for value, and without notice that it was trust property, then it cannot be reclaimed. The beneficiaries here could only claim the consideration monies paid to the trustee.)

Occasionally, breaches occur even though the intention was not deliberate. Under s. 61, Trustee Act, 1925, provision has been made for the Court to grant relief to a trustee provided he has acted honestly and reasonably and ought fairly to be excused for breach of trust, or for omitting to obtain the directions of the Court in a matter where the trustee was required to do so.

TRUST CORPORATIONS

By s. 68 Trustee Act, 1925, provision was made for a corporate body to act as a trustee. This body is commonly described as a trust corporation, and typical examples are the trustee departments of commercial banks, insurance companies and the Public Trustee. There are numerous advantages of using a trust corporation as opposed to an individual or individuals. The principal advantages are:

A company does not die, and,
A company will not retire or become ill, and,
Professionals would carry out the work as part of their normal job, and,
Losses or defaults will be made good by the company.

SECRET TRUSTS

Lawyers argue about whether such trusts are express or constructive, but in this book they are considered under the heading of "express trusts".

EXAMPLES OF SECRET TRUSTS

The most common way in which such a trust arises is where a testator makes provision for a particular person in his will (a beneficiary), but does it indirectly through the medium of a trustee, and in this way he keeps the name of the actual beneficiary a secret. (*Note:* If he did specify the beneficiary in his will, the whole world would be able to identify this person and thus there would be no secret.) Although it is possible for the disposition of the property to be "inter-vivos" (i.e. between a live donor and donee), the disposition will usually be provided for by the testator making a will in the favour of one person, on the basis that upon that person's death, he will dispose of the property to the actual beneficiary. For example, A wants to give property to C, but does not want C to know of this. So, A makes a provision in his will that upon his death, this property will go to B. In turn, B makes a provision in his will, that, upon his death, the same property will pass on to C.

In essence, a secret trust, which must be communicated to the trustee to be admissible, imposes an equitable obligation on the specified trustee. It relies on the existence of a valid will in which the title to the property passes on to the trustee upon the testator's death. Furthermore, the trustee must accept the binding nature of the obligations that go with the trust and the acceptance must be given during the testator's lifetime. **Re Young (1950)**.

Secret trusts may be classified under two headings:

1. Fully secret trusts.
2. Half secret trusts.

1. FULLY SECRET TRUSTS

This type of trust is one which is fully concealed by the testator and for it to be created, the following requirements are necessary. **Ottoway *v.* Norman (1972).**

1. The testator must create the intention that the trustee is to carry out an obligation in favour of the beneficiary.
2. The trustee must accept this obligation, either expressly or impliedly.
3. The intention must be communicated to the trustee during the testator's lifetime.

Furthermore, the trustee must:

4. Take the property absolutely and beneficially through the testator's will.
5. Hold the property on specified trusts.

From these and other legal points, certain general principles have been established. These are:

1. The testator during his life time must communicate the existence of the trust to a trustee who must accept it. Where communication takes place after the testator's death, the trust fails and thus, the trustee would take the property absolutely for himself.
2. Although communication of the trust can take place before or after the date of the will, it must take place before the testator's death. Communication need not be carried out by the testator, for it can be made through an agent. **Moss *v.* Cooper (1861)**.
3. Even when a secret trust has been accepted, it will fail if the objects of the trust are not communicated during the testator's lifetime. Without

communication of the objects, the property has to be held for a residuary legatee or devisee, or distributed in accordance with the rules of intestacy. (See Chapter 8 for an explanation of these terms.)

4. The communication to and acceptance by the trustee may be constructive: **Re Boyes (1884)**. A solicitor prepared a will in which he was appointed as sole executor and legatee of Mr Boyes. The property which was to comprise Boyes' estate was to be disposed of in accordance with later written instructions. Thus, as regards the disposition of property, the solicitor would be acting as a trustee. The promised instructions were not received by the solicitor in Boyes' lifetime. However, following the death of Boyes, two letters, containing the same directions, were found which indicated that the whole of the deceased's estate, except for a small amount of money, was to pass to a lady friend. A relative of the deceased contested the validity of these letters. *Held.* As the testator had not communicated, during his lifetime, the object of the trust to the solicitor, no valid trust in favour of the lady friend had been created. Accordingly, the solicitor, by constructive notice, held the property in trust for the next of kin who became entitled under the laws of intestacy.

5. The property, which is the subject of the trust, must be certain.

2. HALF SECRET TRUSTS

This type of trust is one which occurs when a trustee accepts his position as communicated to him in the testator's will, but the exact terms of the trust are not specified in the will. For example, where "property is to be given to Mr B for purposes which I have advised him of". Here, there is an indication of a trust, but no more. In a fully secret trust, the equivalent clause would read "property is to be given to Mr B".

The general principles which govern such types of trust are:

1. The terms of the will of the testator will take priority. Thus, where the will indicates a future communication (but see later), then nothing communicated before the will was executed, or contemporaneous with its execution, is effective. Furthermore, where the will indicates a past or contemporaneous communication, anything dated after execution of the will is inadmissible.

2. Where the trust is communicated before or at the same time that the will is executed, evidence can be produced to indicate the terms of the trust and the trustee is bound by the interpretation. **Blackwell *v.* Blackwell (1929)**.

3. Where the trust is communicated after the date of the will but before the testator's death, the situation is somewhat uncertain, although it has been held that if communication does take place during this time period, then a half-secret trust can be created.

4. The party(s) named as trustee(s) cannot be beneficiaries. **Re Rees (1950)**.

5. Where a testator wants to increase or amend the property which is to be held in trust, such increases or amendments, for them to be effective, must be communicated to the trustees. **Re Colin Cooper (1939)**.

EXAMINATION QUESTIONS

Question 1

(a) What is a trust?

(b) S created a trust in favour of A, B and C and the trustees appointed were P, Q and R who have committed several breaches of trust. What remedies are available to the beneficiaries?

(Chartered Institute of Bankers)

Question 2

(a) What are the "three certainties" required to create a valid trust?

(b) Timothy, in his will, directed that his executor hold "some portion of my estate in the London area in trust for my nephew Arthur". Timothy died recently. Advise Arthur of his legal position under this will.

(Chartered Institute of Bankers)*

Question 3

Tom and Jerry are trustees of a trust for A's infant children. Tom allowed Jerry to invest a part of the trust fund in shares of a private company which are now worthless; also to pay another part of the fund into Jerry's private bank account. Jerry has drawn a cheque on that account to buy for himself a second-hand car, which he still possesses.

What is the legal position of the beneficiaries?

(Chartered Institute of Bankers)

Question 4

(a) What is a "secret trust"?

(b) Explain how the law would operate in the following cases:

(1) X, by his will, gives property to A "as trustee" but does not declare any trusts in the will. He later tells A that he wishes the property to be held in trust for B: A agrees, X died recently.

(2) X, by his will, gives property to A and B as joint tenants. Before the will is executed. A agrees with X to hold the property in trust for Y. No intimation of the trust is given to B. X has died recently.

(Chartered Institute of Bankers)

CHAPTER 8

SUCCESSION

INTRODUCTION

When a person dies, he can no longer own property nor exercise rights over property. In recognition of this, it is necessary for another person to distribute the deceased's property, if he has any, and the method of carrying this out is subject to certain rules and regulations. If the deceased had made a valid will, then the estate will be distributed according to its terms. In contrast, if no will had been made, or the will was found to be invalid, then the estate will be distributed according to the laws of intestacy (see later). There is a third situation which may occur, and this is when there is a valid will but it does not cover the whole of the deceased's estate. Here the property covered by the will is dealt with in accordance with its terms while the balance has to be dealt with in accordance with the rules of intestacy.

A person who makes a will is known as a testator (if male) or testatrix (if female). In a will, normally the testator or testatrix specifically appoints another person (or persons) to administer their estate upon death, and this person is known as an executor (if male) or executrix (if female).

Persons who have not made wills or made invalid wills are said to have died intestate. Here, no-one has been specifically appointed to distribute the estate, and it is then necessary for someone (usually a party who will benefit from the estate, e.g. a near relative) to apply for Court permission to do so. Such a person, if approved by the probate registry of the Court, is known as an administrator.

Executors and administrators are known as personal representatives, and, in brief, their duties are to collect in the assets of the deceased, pay his debts and then distribute that which remains.

Note: Throughout this chapter, the terms testator, executor and administrator are used to cover both male and female persons.

PERSONS WHO MAY MAKE A VALID WILL

Generally speaking, anyone with the exception of minors and mentally incapacitated persons may make valid wills. This statement must be qualified to the extent that any minor over the age of fourteen, who is on military service or a sailor at sea, may make a valid will.

At one time, it was not possible for a married woman to make a valid will. Today, she can, because of changes imposed by the Married Womens Property Act, 1882, and the Law Reform (Married Women and Tortfeasors) Act, 1935.

Persons who make wills must do so with the "full and free intention of making a will" (animus testandi). It is for this reason that a mentally incapacitated person cannot make a valid will. For it will be presumed that such a person is incapable of appreciating the action he is carrying out.

The same argument applies to people suffering from an excess of alcohol.

Finally, a will executed under duress or undue influence will be invalid for want of "free intention".

FORMALITIES NECESSARY FOR MAKING A VALID WILL

The majority of the necessary formalities are provided for in s. 9 Wills Act, 1837. This statute has been amended over the years, most recently by Part IV Administration of Justice Act, 1982.

For a will to be valid, it must be:

1. IN WRITING

A will must be in the form of a written document and may be styled in the form of a letter. Handwriting, print and typescript or a combination come within the meaning of "writing". When the will is in the handwriting of the testator, it is known as a holograph will. The writing may be in pencil (**In Re Hall (1871)**) or in ink and can be expressed in a foreign language **Kell *v.* Charmer (1858)**. Furthermore, it is not necessary for the writing to be that of the testator.

(There are a limited number of exceptions to this general rule – for soldiers on active military service, seamen at sea, etc., can make valid oral wills.)

2. SIGNED

A valid will must be signed by the testator, or alternatively by a deputy provided it is in the presence of and directed by the testator. The deputy may sign in his own name (**In the goods of Clark (1839)**) or that of the testator. (**In the goods of Bailey (1838)**). Signature may be by way of initials, (**In the goods of Savory (1851)**) or a partial signature (**Re Chalcraft Deceased (1948)**) or a mark or thumb print in ink (**In the Estate of James Finn Deceased (1935)**), or a sealed stamp which bears the testator's initials. Whatever method is used, it must contain the unmistakeable mark of the testator. Finally, if a will has been attested by two witnesses but not signed by the testator then placed in an envelope and sealed, and the outside of the envelope signed by the testator, the will may be considered valid: **In the goods of Mann (1942)** where a testator merely prints his name on the cover and envelope in similar circumstances, it has been held that a valid will has not been executed: **In the estate of Bean (1944)**.

3. ATTESTATION

The signature on a will must be attested by two or more witnesses in the testator's presence. It is usual for attestation to take place at the time the testators signs the will. However, it is permissible for the testator to sign the will then at a later date and in the presence of both witnesses to confirm that the document bears his signature and for the witnesses to add their signatures by way of attestation. The witnesses cannot add their signatures until the testator has signed the will or acknowledged his signature in their presence. **White *v.* Jones (1932)**. It should be remembered that the witnesses are just confirming the testator's signature and as such need not know that the document is a will. (**In the Estate of Benjamin (1934)**.)

It is essential that both witnesses be present and together when the will is signed or the signature acknowledged by the testator **Re Colling Dec'd: Lawson *v.* Van Winkler (1972)**. Provided this occurs, they may later add their signatures as long as they sign in the presence of the testator. Furthermore, by s. 17 Administration of Justice Act, 1982, provision has been made for a witness to acknowledge his signature in the testator's presence rather than sign it in the testator's presence. Usually, after their signature, witnesses add their address and occupation. This makes the person readily identifiable and easier to trace, if at a later date, a dispute arises and they are needed for evidence purposes.

"Signature of the witness" has been interpreted as either full name, or initials (**In the goods of Christian (1849)**) or marks (**In the goods of Ashmore (1843)**). Furthermore, minors can witness wills provided they are sufficiently mature, but a blind person may not. For it was held in the case **In the Estate of Gibson (1949)** that as a blind person could not see a testator's signature he could not attest the signature on the will.

It is permissible for an executor to attest the will in which he has been appointed (s. 17 Wills Act, 1837), and by doing so, he does not bar himself from appointment. However, by s. 15 Wills Act, 1837, a person who acts as a witness to a will, is not entitled to benefit under the will. This ruling also applies to parties who are spouses of witnesses at the time of signature. But, if a beneficiary and witness marry after attestation, the bequest is valid. **Aplin *v.* Stone (1904)**. Section 15 was modified to some extent by the Wills Act, 1968, in the sense that a bequest will not be made invalid if a will has been duly executed, e.g. without taking into account the beneficiary's attestation. Thus, provided there are at least two independent witnesses, attestation by benefiting witnesses can be disregarded. Furthermore, where a testator makes a will in which a bequest is made to a specified person, this person may act as a witness in the signing of a codicil, without prejudicing the bequest contained in the main body of the will.

There is no special form for an attestation clause, but the one usually inserted is " . . . signed by the above named testator as his last will and testament in the presence of us present at the same time who in his presence and in the presence of each other have hereunto subscribed our names as witnesses".

POSITIONING OF THE TESTATOR'S SIGNATURE

By s. 9 Wills Act, 1837, this had to appear "at the foot or end" of the will. For anything above the signature was considered as a testamentory disposition while anything below it, was not considered to be part of the will and was therefore invalid. This ruling was amended by s. 1 Wills Amendment Act, 1852, which enabled the signature to be placed beside the end of the writing or after a blank space separating it from the end of the will or even on another page not containing any part of the will provided that the signature purports to give effect to the writing so signed. However, by s. 17 the Administration of Justice Act, 1982, it is now no longer essential for the signature to be "at the foot of the will". The provision now is that the signature may be anywhere provided it appears that the testator intended by his signature to give effect to the will.

METHODS OF ADDING TO OR ALTERING WILLS

ADDITIONS TO A WILL

It is permissible for a testator to write additional entries below his signature on the original will. However, "at the foot or end of" the additional entries, the testator must add his signature and have it attested in exactly the same way as described above. A more formal way of adding further provisions is by codicil, and this document must be signed and witnessed also.

CODICIL

This is an additional clause or clauses attached to or referring to a will and which either adds to and/or cancels and/or alters the provisions contained in the original will. To be valid, it must be signed by the testator and two witnesses who need not be the same as those who witnessed the original document.

ALTERATIONS TO A WILL

It is permissible to make changes to the content of an original will. But this is only valid if the alteration is initialled (or signed) as confirmation by the testator and two witnesses.

Any alterations made without the presence of witnesses should be recited in a special alteration clause, once the parties are gathered together. Furthermore the clause should be initialled or signed by the testator and witnesses.

WILLS OF SOLDIERS, SAILORS AND AIRMEN

Special provisions relate to this group of people, and they date back as far as Roman times. For it was recognised that the strict rules of the regular law could not apply to soliders where battles, and possible death, were imminent. Thus oral declarations and other informal dispositions were acceptable. Such rules subsequently became part of English common law and were later codified in s. 9 Wills Act, 1837, and extended by the Wills (Soldiers and Sailors) Act, 1918. The rules apply to any person on actual military service and to seamen who are at sea under any conditions. Furthermore, the rules extend to minors, provided they are over fourteen. The wills of this type of minor could either be in the form of an oral declaration or in writing.

Actual military service exists when either a serviceman is:

(a) Called up for service; or
(b) Engaged in hostilities; or
(c) About to proceed in hostile engagement; or
(d) On embarkation leave from a foreign station in connection with operations of war.

The meaning of the words also extends to men or women acting as nurses, typists or in any other occupation provided it falls under the control of the military or naval authorities.

Where a will is made orally, then the declaration needs to be witnessed and the witness may benefit under it. However, where it is made in writing, then it is not essential to have it witnessed. The essential requirement is that the testator must have wanted the will to be binding. Finally, the will remains valid when the testator leaves active service or ceases to be a seaman.

CONTINGENT WILLS

This is a type of will which becomes valid only if a specified event happens (and if it does not happen, the document remains an invalid will). So, if someone enters hospital for a serious operation and makes a will which states that "The will is to be effective if I die as a result of the operation", then if death occurs, the document becomes a valid will. If the patient recovers, but is subsequently knocked down and killed in a road accident, the document cannot be used to obtain probate. Wills made in contemplation of marriage may also be considered as contingent, and these are described later.

TESTAMENTARY DISPOSITIONS

After paying the deceased's debts, the personal representatives will have to distribute the surplus of the estate in accordance with the terms of the will and/or to laws of intestacy – whichever situation applies.

Where a valid will has been made, the dispositions contained therein may be of two types:

A DEVISE

These are dispositions which relate to freehold land. Here, the person who receives the disposition is known as a devisee. Such dispositions may be specific (e.g. My freehold house . . .) or residuary (e.g. The rest of my realty to my son James Edward).

A LEGACY

These are dispositions which relate to any other type of property, including leasehold land. As such, they are known as legacies or bequests. Here the person who receives the disposition is known as a legatee.

The second group of dispositions may be divided under many headings, but the three key ones are:

1. GENERAL LEGACY

This relates to a gift which cannot be distinguished from any other of the same type. Thus, gifts such as a car, a table, £500 of 3½% War Loan Stock, a clock, or five thousand pounds (this is also known as a pecuniary legacy) all fit into this category. If at the time of death, the testator owned several cars, tables, etc., then the legatee may choose any one of them. If there are none at the time of death, the executors must buy one.

2. SPECIFIC LEGACY

This relates to a gift which is specifically described. Thus gifts such as "My Rover Car", "My Chippendale Table", "My gold watch", "My holding of £500 of 3½% War Loan Stock", all fit into this category. If the testator disposes of the legacy prior to his death, the legatee receives nothing because the legacy is said to have adeemed.

3. DEMONSTRATIVE LEGACY

This is, in its nature, a general legacy but which indicates which particular fund is to be used to satisfy it. Thus, gifts such as "£500 from my 3½% War Loan Stock", "£2,000 from my Abbey National Building Society Share Account Number 1248762", "One of my black stallions", all fit into this category. If the fund has been realised prior to death, then the legacy is still payable but under the heading of a general legacy.

That which remains after all the outside debts have been paid and devises and legacies distributed, is known as the residuary estate. It is better to indicate in the will how the residue should be disposed of, for if silent on the matter, it will have to be disposed of in accordance with the Laws of Intestacy. Clearly, the testator will never be able to predict what the exact values of his estate will be at the date of his death, and therefore he cannot precisely define what the residue will be. Therefore, as mentioned above, it is better to bequeath "the residue to . . ." but to refer to no specific property.

RIGHT TO BENEFIT

In the past, when it was shown that a beneficiary had committed the murder or manslaughter of the testator, it was not possible for this party to take any benefit from the deceased's estate. **In the Estate of Crippen (1911) and Re Giles (dec'd): Giles *v.* Giles (1971)**. Furthermore, prior to the passing of the Suicide Act, 1967, if someone committed suicide while sane, it was not possible for their estate to benefit from any life policy monies. **Beresford *v.* Royal Insurance Co. Ltd (1938)**. To allow such benefits in either of these circumstances was always considered to be contrary to "public policy".

Following the passing of the Forfeiture Act, 1982, the court has now been given the power to amend the "public policy" ruling in certain circumstances. This may arise where a beneficiary unlawfully kills, aids, abets, counsels or procures the death of a testator but where the surrounding circumstances may be such that the criminal act is condoned. By s. 2, this power is available even if the beneficiary is convicted of manslaughter, infanticide or death by reckless driving, but not murder s. 5. Any claim made by a beneficiary must be commenced within three months of conviction s. 2(3).

One of the first reported cases which considered the provisions of the Forfeiture Act was **Re. K dec'd (1985)**. Here, a housewife was subject to extreme violence by her husband since their marriage in 1974. In September 1982, she killed her husband with a shotgun and was subsequently convicted of manslaughter. The deceased had made a will which provided that his estate should pass to his wife on trust for her life, then be held for four named beneficiaries. It was noted that the Forfeiture Act became effective on 13/10/82 (which was two weeks after the killing took place), but provision had been made for the Act to take retrospective effect in certain circumstances. *Held.* The forfeiture rule could be modified here so that the wife could take all under the deceased's estate. In the circumstances which prevailed in their marriage, she had been a loyal wife, even though subject to violence, and the deceased had no moral duty to provide for others.

LAPSING

If a person who is a non-descendant of the testator, has been given a bequest or legacy and predeceases the testator, then the bequest or legacy is said to lapse (or fail). As a result, the person who was to take the residue of the deceased's estate will receive the benefit.

But where the devisee or legatee is a descendant of the testator and predeceases him, different rules apply. For here, if the deceased devisee or legatee leaves issue, the gift is considered to have been received before his death. As a result, it will be distributed in accordance with the terms of the devisee's or legatee's will, if he made one, or the rules of intestacy, if he had not made one. This has been provided for in s. 37 Wills Act, 1837.

ADEMPTION

On occasions, a legacy provided for in the will either no longer exists or no longer belongs to the testator at the time of his death. When this happens the rule of ademption applies (See Legacy section). It only relates to specific legacies, and when it applies the legatee receives nothing. Examples of the application of the rule of ademption are:

1. A specific legacy of the testator's stamp collection – and this is stolen prior to his death.
2. A specific legacy of the testator's painting by L. S. Lowry – and this is destroyed by fire prior to his death.
3. A specific legacy of the testator's Rover car – and this is sold prior to his death.

ABATEMENT

After the death of the testator, one of the personal representative's first duties is to settle the testator's debts which exist at the date of his death – and also pay the funeral expenses. When these have been settled, then the remainder of his estate is available for distribution to the beneficiaries. However, in some cases, the amount remaining will be insufficient to meet all the bequests provided for in the will. Sometimes the bequests will have to be reduced to a proportion of the stated legacy. While in other cases they will not be met at all. The legal description of the process used to decide a legatee's entitlement is abatement, and the law indicates the order in which this must take place:

1. Residuary gifts abate first, then;
2. General legacies abate second, then;
3. Specific legacies.

Demonstrative legacies only abate when the fund out of which they are paid is unable to meet bequests in full. When this happens, they are considered as general legacies and abate with them.

A simple illustration is a testator who leaves a house together with a nest estate of £1,500, of which £500 is held in a Halifax Building Society Account. If the legacies in his will were:

To A, I leave my house	(*A is a specific legatee*)
To B, I leave £1,000 for my Halifax, Building Society	(*B is a demonstrative legatee*)
To C, I leave £1,500	(*C is a general legatee*)
To D, I leave £500	(*D is a general legatee*)
To E, I leave the residue	(*E is a residuary legatee*)

Here A, will receive the house and B the balance of five hundred pounds which remains in the Building Society Account. As there is insufficient to settle the general legatees entitlement and the balance to the demonstrative legatee, then abatement must be considered. The residuary legatee, E, abates first and receives nothing. The general legatees (C and D) abate next – and they will be joined by B, for the balance of his entitlemen. By a simple calculation, there is one thousand pounds available for two thousand five hundred pounds of claims. Thus each legatee receives 40% ((1,000/2,500) × 100) of their entitlement. So, B will receive a further two hundred pounds, C receives six hundred pounds and D receives two hundred pounds.

METHODS OF TRANSFERRING DECEASED'S PROPERTY

With most types of property, no special form of transfer needs to be completed by the personal representatives. It is simply a matter of the personal representatives assenting to the transfer to allow ownership to pass on. However, for stocks and shares and land, additional formalities are needed.

(a) *Stocks and Shares*. To transfer ownership from the testator to the beneficiary (or to effect a sale), then the personal representatives need to sign a Stock Transfer Form for each holding. The registrar of the shares will not only want the share certificate plus duly completed stock transfer form but will also want to see the testator's death certificate and the authority to allow representatives to act (i.e. Grant of Probate or Letters of Administration).

(b) *Land*. To transfer ownership of land, then the assent of transfer must conform with s. 36(4) of the Administration of Estates Act, 1925. The additional documents referred to in the statute, must also be produced to convey title.

REVOCATION

All wills are described as ambulatory because the testator may revoke the will at any time before death. Revocation may be express, or implied by the conduct of the testator.

EXPRESS REVOCATION

This must be carried out by way of a properly executed document, signed by the testator and duly witnessed. In fact when a testator executes a new will, if it has been properly prepared, it will always expressly indicate that all previous wills are revoked.

IMPLIED REVOCATION

1. EXECUTION OF A SUBSEQUENT WILL (OR CODICIL)

When a new will is made, it will usually contain a clause stating that all previous wills and testamentary documents are revoked. When such a clause is not included, the provisions in the earlier dated will remain valid except where there is inconsistency. Two examples may be used to illustrate this point:

(a) In the first will "My Chippendale Table is left to A", but then a later will contains a provision that "My Chippendale Table is left to B". Here, the table will go to B upon the testator's death.

(b) In the first will "£2,000 is left to C", and in a later will "£2,000 is left to D". Here, both will receive legacies of two thousand pounds provided the later will contains no revocation clause and the rule of abatement does not have to be applied.

2. BY MARRIAGE

By s. 18 Wills Act, 1837, a will is revoked by the marriage or remarriage of the testator which takes place at a date after that of the will irrespective of whether the testator is male or female. This provision was modified by s. 177 Law of Property Act, 1925, which applies to any will made after 1925 and which is made in express contemplation of marriage. If the contemplated marriage subsequently takes place the will is not revoked. In contrast, if the will was made in general contemplation of marriage, or marriage takes place to a person other than the person contemplated then it will be revoked upon the testator's marriage: **Sallis *v.* Jones (1936)**. This strict ruling has been modified by s. 18 Administration of Justice Act, 1982. The testator's intentions in the will must now be looked at. For expressions may be contained within the will that indicate that it should survive in whole after marriage, or in part, or the whole should be revoked.

3. BY DESTRUCTION

Destruction may be by way of burning, tearing, etc., and must be carried out by the testator (or someone directed by him in his presence) with the express intention of revoking the will: s. 20 Wills Act, 1837. To establish that revocation took place, it is essential that the following points be proved.

(a) The destruction was a physical act. There are no strict rules relating to the degree of destruction needed, but the appearance of a line or series of lines across the will, will not be accepted as proof of revocation, see below.

(b) It was the intention (animus revocandi) to revoke by destruction.

Where destruction takes place by accident (e.g. in a house fire), then the will is not revoked, and a copy may be used for probate purposes.

(c) The destruction was carried out by the testator, or someone directed by him and in his presence.

Thus, a destruction cannot be delegated to a third party (or agent) even if this party is the testator's solicitor unless he conforms with point (c). **Gill *v.* Gill (1909)**. Destruction may be partial provided there was clear intention to revoke, e.g. by ripping off or erasing the testator's signature and the attestation clause. **Hobbs *v.* Knight (1838)**.

Where the testator draws lines across the will and/or puts the words "This will is revoked" across its face, then this is insufficient. **Cheese *v.* Lovejoy (1877)**.

(d) Where the testator, while drunk or under stress, deliberately destroys his will, the action will not be held as proper destruction for want of animus revocandi.

4. DIVORCE

Until 1982, the law did not provide for what should happen in these circumstances. However, the Law Reform Committee, had for some time been considering the situation, and by a majority devision, the Administration of Justice Act, 1982, provided for a new section 18A to be inserted in the Wills Act, 1837. From October 1982 onwards, whenever a marriage is dissolved, annulled or declared void, if the other spouse had been appointed as executor, or executor and trustee or had been nominated as a beneficiary in the will, then the appointments are automatically cancelled and the devises or bequests lapse unless a contrary provision has been made in the will. Whichever situation applies, it does not prejudice these former spouse's rights under the Inheritance (Provision for Family and Dependants) Act, 1975.

REVIVAL OF A REVOKED WILL

If a will has previously been revoked, it may be revived by either:

1. Re-execution as a will; or
2. Proper execution of a codicil provided there is a clear intention that the original will shall be revived. s. 22 Wills Act, 1837.

However, it should be remembered that where an original will has been superceded by a later will, the original will cannot be revived by destruction of the later will. For, if the testator destroys the later will then in such circumstances, upon his death, he will die intestate.

With regard to point 2, a codicil cannot revive a will that has been revoked by destruction. It can only revive a will if it still exists and the intention to revive the earlier will is stated in the codicil. **In bonis Steele (1868)** and **In the Estate of Taylor: Goldie *v*. Adam (1938)**.

DEPENDANT RELATIVE REVOCATION

There will be occasions when a testator revokes his will with the intention of making a new one, but before he can make the new one, something prevents him from doing so, e.g. he becomes mentally incapacitated. In such circumstances, the original will, even though on the face of it, it has been revoked, remains valid. It should be remembered that the ruling only applies when the original will has been revoked with the intention of making a new one. If a will has been revoked absolutely, then this doctrine of "dependant relative revocation" will not apply.

RECTIFICATION OF WILLS

Prior to the new provisions contained in s. 20 Administration of Justice Act, 1982, it was only possible to rectify a will if it could be proved that the problem had arisen because of fraud. But now, if a court is satisfied that the testator's intentions had not been adequately expressed due to either a clerical error or failure on behalf of the preparer to understand what the testator intended, it is possible to have the will rectified. A request for rectification should be made within six months of the grant of representation although requests after this period has expired may be made, but this is subject to leave of court.

When trying to decide what the testator's true intentions were or where clauses are meaningless or ambiguous, it is permissible to use outside evidence in order to rectify the will. s. 21 Administration of Justice Act, 1982.

FAMILY PROVISION

Prior to 1938, a testator was free to dispose of his property in any way that he wanted to, and he could therefore, completely exclude his wife and/or children. However, this situation was changed by the Inheritance (Family Provision) Act, 1938 – as amended by the Intestates' Estates Act, 1952. For, after the passing of the 1938 Act, the court was given the power to vary a will for insufficient provision, subject to an application by the widow (or widower), an unmarried daughter, a son who is a minor or who although no longer a minor had not attained the age of 21, or a son or daughter incapacitated by mental or physical disability.

The courts recognised that wills or the laws of intestacy did not always reasonably provide for certain dependants. Thus, upon the dependant's application, the court would consider their request, and if approved, would provide adequate maintenance from the net estate. Any application needs to be made within six months of grant of representation, although the courts have been given power under the Family Provisions Act, 1966, to extend this term if it is considered right to do so.

The two Acts mentioned above, were superceded by the Inheritance (Provision for Family and Dependants) Act, 1975. This act applies to any person domiciled in England or Wales, who died after 1st April 1976 and provides a list of those persons who have a statutory right to claim provision from the deceased's estate. These include:

1. The surviving spouse.
2. A former spouse who has not remarried.
3. A child of the deceased. This category would include for example, illegitimate or adopted children of the deceased's wife by a former marriage.
4. Any person who immediately before the deceased's death was being maintained wholly or partly by the deceased.

Claims by any of the above must be made within the six months time limit previously mentioned. The Chancery Division will have to consider all relevant facts in deciding what is "reasonable financial provision" for each claimant. These include the existing resources of the claimant and also the conduct of the claimant with regard to the deceased. Two cases illustrate how the courts have applied the above statutes.

Re Cook Deceased. Cook *v*. Cook (1956)
Here, an unmarried daughter spent a considerable amount of time looking after her mother who towards the end of her life was very ill and needed a lot of attention. When she died, she left a net estate of approximately £2,500. Besides the unmarried daughter, there were three surviving sons and another daughter. Because of the time she had devoted to her mother, the unmarried daughter made an application under the Inheritance (Family Provision) Act, 1938, but then was opposed by the other daughter (who in fact had not seen her mother since 1919) and two of the sons (neither of whom had seen their mother since 1932). *Held*. If the strict rules of intestacy had been applied, she would only have received £500. But because her claim was successful she received £1,000 in total.

Re Andrews Deceased. Andrews *v*. Smofitt and Another (1955)
A daughter left home to live with a married man in 1911. Upon her father's death, she discovered that no provision was made for her in his

will and she therefore made a claim on the estate. The court rejected her claim because she had left the parental home to live on a permanent basis with a married man, and that this man took on the responsibility of satisfying her financial needs.

The method and frequency of payment to the dependant relatives will be decided by the court. Sometimes this will be by way of a lump sum from the estate, otherwise it will be by way of periodic payments from income. Upon the death or re-marriage of the surviving spouse such payments will immediately cease.

INTESTACY

As we saw earlier, intestacy relates to a situation whereby a person dies without having made a will or without having made a valid will. The law detailing the ranking of beneficiaries in these circumstances has changed over the years, particularly after 1926.

For, prior to 1926, any freehold land (real property), passed to the intestate's heir at law (e.g. his eldest son), while the remaining assets (personal property passed to his next of kin (e.g. his wife). However, this method of distribution was abolished by the Administration of Estates Act, 1925, and the Intestates Act, 1952. (Various other amendments were contained in the Family Provision Act, 1966. The Family Provision (Intestate Succession) Order, 1972, and The Family Law Reform Act, 1969). Now, after paying the funeral and other necessary expenses and settling the deceased's debts, the balance of the estate has to be distributed in accordance with the above statutes. The statutes show that consideration must be given to five separate groups. They can be interpreted as defining what the deceased would have said if he had made a will. Thus, the surviving spouse is considered first in priority, and so on through the list appearing below:

1. The surviving spouse.
2. Surviving children.
3. Surviving parents.
4. Surviving brothers and sisters of whole blood.
5. Surviving relations of a lesser degree,

The full set of rules and regulations relating to intestacy are very complicated because of all the possible permutations of family trees. However, two simple illustrations will show how the basic rules apply:

1. Where there is a surviving spouse

The whole of the estate passes to the surviving spouse where there is no issue (i.e. children).

Where there is issue, the surviving spouse, is entitled to take:

(a) All personal chattels (car, furniture, etc.) but not business chattels.

(b) £40,000 free of taxation and costs together with interest at the rate of 7% p.a. from the date of death until payment. These costs and interest are payable from the residue, if any, of the estate,

(c) A life interest on half the residue, if there is any. (The residue is invested which then provides an income for the survivor.)

The remaining property goes to the issue by a method called a statutory trust.

The law relating to statutory trusts is set out in s. 47 Administration of Estates Act 1925. The provision is that the deceased's property will be held equally for all children of the estate who are alive or, as yet, unborn, at the date of the intestate's death. Children who satisfy this requirement have a contingent interest until they attain the age of eighteen or marry under that age. If a child dies before attaining majority and is unmarried, the property is divided equally among the surviving children, if any – just as though the deceased child had never existed.

2. Where there is no surviving spouse

Where there is issue, then it is held on statutory trust for them.

Where there is no issue, but one or both parents are alive, the property passes to them absolutely.
Where only relatives survive, then the order is:

(a) Brothers and sisters of whole blood – or their issue.
(b) Brothers and sisters of half blood – or their issue.
(c) Grandparents – if neither (a) nor (b) apply.
(d) Uncles and aunts of whole blood – or their issue.
(e) Uncles and aunts of half blood – or their issue.

Finally, where a person dies intestate and leaves no surviving relatives, the estate passes to the crown. However, the crown may provide for persons who might have expected to benefit from the deceased's estate had he made a will.

PERSONAL REPRESENTATIVES

Where a person has made a will, he usually appoints one person or several to act as his executor(s). These persons have been given the power to execute the will (i.e. carry out its terms) upon his death. Examples of persons often named as executors are the other spouse, a relative, a friend, a solicitor or a bank, or a combination of them. Executors are collectively known as personal representatives because they represent the deceased. In common law, after they have obtained probate, they can sell or transfer ownership of the deceased's property (e.g. land, stocks and shares, etc.).

Generally, it can be said that the deceased's rights and liabilities are transferred to them, and so as soon as they are officially appointed they can continue any legal action brought about by the deceased while alive, and have actions enforced against them as though they were the deceased.

Executors

These may be appointed expressly (e.g. where they are appointed in writing in a will or codicil to act as executor for the testator) or by implication (e.g. where the testator, while alive, nominated a person to attend to such matters as paying debts, etc. upon his death). In this latter context, the person so acting is known as "an executor according to the tenor".

Administrators

This term is usually related to the personal representatives of someone who has died intestate. However, the term can also be applied to situations where a will has been made but because no named executor has been provided for, or a named executor is unable (because he predeceased the testator) or unwilling (because of illness or other commitments) to act in his capacity, then an administrator must be appointed.

Valid acts before Probate or Letters of Administration have been obtained

Prior to obtaining probate, the executors' actions are limited but certainly not non-existent. For, provided Probate is obtained within the twelve month period following the date of death, certain actions that they take immediately after death are valid if they are considered necessary to preserve the estate. Thus, funeral expenses can be met, the deceased's business may be sold as a going concern, etc. However, withdrawals from bank accounts are not permitted nor are sales or transfers of property. They can, however, gather together the assets of the deceased, receive payments from debtors, and carry on any business.

EXECUTOR DE SON TORT

This term relates to anyone who interferes with the deceased's property without having been given the legal authority to do so, i.e. without having been given express or implied permission to act as executor, or without having obtained Letters of Administration.

By interfering in this way, he assumes the role of executor and if he carries out a wrong, he may have the following actions taken against him. He may:

1. be sued by the true executor or administrator after appointment;
2. be liable for the due payment of inheritance tax;
3. be sued (as if he were the true executor) by creditors or beneficiaries of the estate.

His liability is generally limited to the extent of the assets that have come into his hands and, no doubt, he would pass these on to the legally appointed personal representatives when they have assumed office. Actions against him will not suceed if it is established that he has either carried out lawful acts or acted for the good of the deceased's estate, say, where he incurs costs in attending to the:

1. burial of the deceased. **Harrison *v.* Rowley (1798)**.
2. feeding of the deceased's cattle. **Long *v.* Symes (1832)**.

Such an executor, even if he is subsequently appointed in accordance with the law, still remains personally liable for acts carried out prior to his appointment.

PROBATE

When a testator dies, certain formalities must be attended to before the personal representatives acquire the legal right to deal with the deceased's estate. Where a will has been made with named executors, then they need to acquire this legal right to act on behalf of the deceased by obtaining a Grant of Probate. The Grant cannot normally be obtained until seven days have expired after death.

Grant is obtained by the executor (or his solicitor) personally taking the following documents to either the Principal Probate Registry (in London) or more likely a (local) District Registry:

1. The testator's will (This is retained by the Registry and a copy given to the executor in replacement).
2. The death certificate.
3. Particulars of the testator's assets and a figure for Inheritance Tax liability, where a liability arises. The legal term for these documents is an Inland Revenue Affidavit and Estate Account.

4. A statement of the deceased's debts which should include funeral expenses.

5. An executor's oath in which the executor(s) swears that he will deal with the estate according to the law and will produce accounts when called upon to do so, following court confirmation of his appointment.

In most cases, this will be a straightforward matter and upon payment of the tax liability, the Grant of Probate will be issued. This is known as a "Probate in Common Form". Certain testators will have complicated estates due to their wide and varied range of investments and business interests and therefore accurate figures for items falling into the third and fourth categories will take time to prepare. This, in itself, presents no problems, for the Probate office will accept estimates of these figures at that stage.

Sometimes complications arise, particularly where the validity of a will is challenged. When this happens, "Probate in solemn form" has to be obtained, and this usually involves a hearing before a judge of the Chancery Division of the High Court or in a County Court.

Although typical examples have earlier been given of who may be appointed executor, it does not follow that they will automatically be given Grant of Probate upon application. For, probate will not be granted to executors who are either:

1. Mentally incapacitated, or
2. Infants during minority (by s. 165 Judicature Act, 1925), or
3. A person who has become bankrupt after his appointment as executor in the will but prior to the testator's death. This is normally so, for the Chancery Division will usually restrain the person from acting in this capacity.

Also Grant of Probate will only be given to a maximum of four people (**Re Holland (1936)**) irrespective of the number of executors provided for within the will.

LETTERS OF ADMINISTRATION

When a person dies without having made a will, the distribution of his estate will be governed by the rules of intestacy. To enable the personal representatives to act on behalf of the deceased, one or more of the persons entitled, e.g. next of kin, have to apply to the Family Division of the High Court for a grant of Letters of Administration. Where persons die wholly intestate, the Court will follow the guidelines contained in Proviso (a) Section 162 of the Judicature Act, 1925, and the order of priority to the Grant contained in the Non-Contentious Probate Rules, 1954.

The procedures necessary to gain appointment are broadly similar to those for probate. After their appointment they become known as administrators. However, the appointment is usually subject to the administrators giving a bond. This is an undertaking by the administrators to pay the Principal Registrar twice the value of the deceased's estate if the administration is not carried out according to the law, and is usually backed up by two sureties. This procedure is considered necessary because an administrator is never appointed by the deceased (compare this with the appointment of an executor in a will).

As seen earlier, there are occasions when the deceased had made a will whilst alive, but did not nominate an executor, or having named an executor, that person was unable or unwilling to act after the death of the testator. When this happens, it is usual for the person who will benefit the most from the estate, to take out Letters of Administration. If the main beneficiary does not want to become the administrator, then other beneficiaries may apply (or a bank or solicitor with the beneficiaries permission) and again there is an order of priority contained in the Non-Contentious Probate Rules, 1954. In these circumstances, when the grant is made, it will be with the will annexed, and is known as a grant "cum testamento annexo".

Sometimes, an executor will die without having completed his task. Here, a further grant "with the will annexed" will have to be obtained and this will relate to that part of the estate which had not been administered. This type of grant is called a grant "de bonis non administratis" – a grant concerning property not yet dealt with.

Minors cannot, by law, be appointed as a personal representative, s. 165 Judicature Act, 1925. Furthermore, if they have been nominated as executor they cannot act in this capacity whilst in minority. It is essential, in the latter situation for an administrator "durante minore actate" to be appointed. Occasionally, the validity of a will is contested, and this prevents the executor from acting in his usual capacity. To enable the deceased's estate to be dealt with while a legal decision is awaited, then someone is appointed "administrator pendente lite" s. 163 Judicature Act, 1925. This person may continue with the administration, but he may not distribute the property.

POWERS AND LIABILITIES OF PERSONAL REPRESENTATIVES

As soon as Grant of Probate or Grant of Letters of Administration have been obtained, the personal representatives have absolute power to dispose of the deceased's property in accordance with the terms of the will or according to the rules of intestacy.

Some of the deceased's property may have to be sold, and the power of personal representatives to do this is provided for in s. 39 Administration of Estates Act, 1925.

The personal representatives should take no more than one year to complete the winding up of the estate, but where necessary, this period can be extended.

When acting in this capacity, the representatives are considered as equivalent to trustees. They are responsible for their own acts, and if for example they delay payments to creditors, then they may have a personal action taken against them. If the representative is found to have acted honestly, reasonably and ought fairly to be excused, then the courts have power to find in his favour.

DUTIES OF PERSONAL REPRESENTATIVES

The general duties of the representatives are to collect the debts owed to the deceased and settle the two principle classes of claims, e.g. the creditors and the beneficiaries.

More specifically, the five main duties are:

1. To collect all debts owing to the estate,
2. To obtain possession or control of all the assets that make up the estate.
3. To pay all debts and satisfy all liabilities of the deceased including the costs of administration and Inland Revenue debts.
4. To convert unauthorised investments into authorised ones.
5. To distribute the estate in accordance with the terms of the will or the laws of intestacy.

INSOLVENT ESTATES

In most cases, the deceased's estate will be sufficient to pay all debts and other liabilities, and provide for the beneficiaries. In contrast, there will be some estates where even the debts and other liabilities cannot be settled in full. These are known as insolvent estates, and rules have been laid down in s. 34 Administration of Estates Act, 1925, indicating which group of creditors have priority over others in these circumstances. The list, in order or priority, is:

1. Funeral, testamentary expenses and the costs of administration. Then,

2. Preferential creditors, e.g. Arrears of taxes, but subject to defined time periods. See Chapter 5. Then,

3. Unsecured creditors, e.g. Debts owing to third parties, which do not fit into categories 2 or 4. Then,

4. Deferred Creditors, e.g. Claims by the surviving spouse on the deceased's estate for money lent for business purposes.

When administering the estate, the representative at one time had two special rights.

(a) *The right of preference.* This confered the right to pay one creditor in a particular class in full to the exclusion of all other creditors.

(b) *The right of retainer.* This conferred the right to retain in full any debt owed to the representative to the exclusion of other creditors of the same rank.

These were both abolished by the Administration of Estates Act, 1971.

It should be noted that if the deceased had given any security to cover his debts and/or other liabilities, then the secured creditor would not normally have to prove on the insolvent's estate. However, if the security taken did not fully cover the debt, then a claim would have to be made for the difference.

The law relating to bankruptcy is now contained within the Insolvency Act 1986 and the Statutory Instruments made thereunder. Quite clearly, the procedures which must be followed are defined in the above Act and these will have to be followed when winding up the estate.

EXAMINATION QUESTIONS

Question 1

What are the essential requirements of a valid will?
(A.E.B. O-Level).

Question 2

(a) Where must the testator sign his will?

(b) Amos dictated his will to his friend Benas who wrote it down verbatim on a single piece of paper, which Amos signed in the top right corner, and put in an envelope which he sealed and signed in the presence of two witnesses. Is the will validly executed?
(Chartered Institute of Bankers)

Question 3

Silas, a wealthy widow, is seriously ill. He is engaged to marry a widow.

Rosie O'Grady, who advises that he should marry her as a matter of urgency and then make a will in her favour. His children disagree and advise him to make his will and then marry her. Whose advice should he accept and why?
(Chartered Institute of Bankers)

Question 4

(a) A will is ambulatory. What does this mean?

(b) Jerome, an artist, using his paint brush, wrote his will on a wall in his studio. His wife Kate wrote her will in pencil on the back of a painting hanging in the studio. Assuming that these wills satisfy all other legal requirements, are they valid?

(c) Lionel's signature on his will was witnessed by his brother who is totally blind. Is the will validly executed?
(Chartered Institute of Bankers)

Question 5

Mr A wrote his will in pencil, and added his signature at the end of the will. The signatures of Mr B and Mr C appear as witnesses. Is this will valid if Mr A:

(a) omitted to appoint an executor;
(b) appointed the two witnesses as the executors;
(c) signed the will before the two witnesses entered his room to sign as witnesses;
(d) did not inform the witnesses that the document was his will;
(e) told the witnesses that the document was a hire purchase agreement;
(f) did not show his signature to the witnesses?

(Chartered Institute of Bankers)

Question 6

Consider the validity of the following wills:

(a) Harry wrote and signed his will in the presence of Peter (who is blind) and Fred (aged 17) and they both signed as witnesses.

(b) In her will Agnes leaves her property to her daughters, Gladys and Doris. Agnes's will is witnessed by Gladys and Doris and their respective husbands.
(A.E.B. O-Level)

Question 7

Conrad has made his will. His wife, Ada, and his friend, Donald, are the executors named in it. He has (inter alia) given a legacy of £1,000 to Ethel, who is the wife of George and the mother of Frank. Consider in each case whether the will is valid if it was witnessed by:

(a) Ethel and her sister, Margaret, who is 19.

(b) George and Frank, who is blind.

(c) Donald and his wife, Sally.

(d) Robin and John, who are the brothers of Conrad and did not sign it in the presence of each other.

(e) Jill and Polly, who are the sisters of Conrad and did not sign in the presence of Conrad.

(Chartered Institute of Bankers)

Question 8

State, giving full reasons, whether the deceased died intestate or testate in each of these instances:

(a) Last year B made his will. A month ago he drew a line through it with his fountain pen and wrote upon it "This will is revoked". He threw it in the waste paper basket but, unknown to him, it was retrieved by his housekeeper, who has kept it safely. B died yesterday.

(b) Last month Charles died. Two days before his death his housekeeper found his will torn up into four pieces in the waste paper basket. She has kept these pieces safely.

(Chartered Institute of Bankers)

Question 9

(a) State the various ways in which a will may be revoked.

(b) John, who is engaged to marry Mary, makes his will and in it he stated "I give all my estate to my fiancee Mary". Later he married her but was killed recently in a car accident. Is that will effective at his death?

(Chartered Institute of Bankers)

Question 10

Albert has made his will but is now dissatisfied with it as drawn. Betram, his friend, tells him it suffices if he tears it up and makes a new will. Is this advice correct?

(Chartered Institute of Bankers)

Question 11

Gordon in his will left all his property to his sister Henrietta. At a recent meeting with you he produced this will saying he was going to cancel it because he understood that if he died intestate his sister would still inherit his estate. Accordingly in your presence he wrote in pencil on the will "Cancelled" and cut it neatly in two parts. Gordon died yesterday.

Was this will valid at his death?

(Chartered Institute of Bankers)

Question 12

(a) Gifts in a will are described as devises or legacies. What is the difference (if any) between a devise and a legacy?

(b) A gift in a will may be general, specific, demonstrative or residuary. In his will Harry made these gifts:

(a) £100 to my brother Charles;
(b) a horse to my brother David;
(c) my Rolls-Royce Silver Cloud car to my brother Edward;
(d) £5,000 out of my 3½% War Loan to my brother Frank.

What type of gift has been given in this will to:
(a) Charles;
(b) David;
(c) Edward;
(d) Frank?

(Chartered Institute of Bankers)*

Question 13

In his will, Alfonso gave his friend Blythe a legacy of £1,000 and appointed him the sole executor. They were both killed in an air crash. Christopher is the sole executor of Blythe's will.

Is this legacy now payable to Christopher? Give reasons for your answer.

(Chartered Institute of Bankers)

Question 14

(a) Explain and Distinguish between:
(1) a specific legacy in a will;
(2) a general legacy in a will.

(b) If Kenneth by his will bequeaths "£1,000 3% War Stock" to Henry but has no War Stock when he dies, to what, if anything, is Henry entitled? Would your answer be different if the gift has been "any £1,000 3% War Stock" and again at his death Kenneth had no War Stock?

(Chartered Institute of Bankers)

Question 15

What is meant by the ademption and abatement of a legacy?

(Chartered Institute of Bankers)

Question 16

(a) Explain what is meant when a person dies:
(a) Testate;
(2) Intestate.

(b) How is a person's property distributed when he or she dies intestate?
(A.E.B. O-Level)

Question 17

Bert died without leaving a will. Who can apply to administer his estate? How will the estate be distributed?
(A.E.B. O-Level)

Question 18

David, a widower, has died intestate survived by his children Elsie and Frank. A third child, George predeceased his father but he left a widow and two children, Harold and Ivor. Who is entitled to the estate of David and in what shares?
(Chartered Institute of Bankers)

Question 19

Silas, a widower, died intestate, survived only by his two sons Richard and Thomas. His eldest son Uriah had predeceased him, but was survived by his two sons Quintin and Vernon. Who is entitled to the estate of Silas?
(Chartered Institute of Bankers)

Question 20

Charles had three sons: Tom, Dick and Harry. When he retired he asked them to carry on his garage business for him for a nominal salary but promised that, if they would do so, he would leave it to them in his will. They agreed and carried on the business for many years. Charles has died leaving the entire business to Harry. What is the legal position of Tom and Dick?
(Chartered Institute of Bankers)

Question 21

What are the effects and main provisions of the Inheritance (Provision for Family and Dependants) Act, 1975?
(A.E.B. O-Level)

Question 22

Eric, a wealthy business man, died last week. Last month he made a will appointing his best friend Ernest to be the sole executor and beneficiary. His widow, Fanny, his daughter and his mother are understandably disappointed at this testamentary disposition. State and discuss what claim (if any) they may have against Ernest.
(Chartered Institute of Bankers)

CHAPTER 9

TORT

Many eminent lawyers have defined a tort, and the one most often quoted is that propounded by Professor P. H. Winfield as "A tortious liability arises from the breach of a duty primarily fixed by the law; such duty is towards persons generally and its breach is redressible by an action for unliquidated damages."

To obtain a better understanding of the definition, it is preferential to compare a tort with other wrongs.

TORT AND CRIME

The distinction between a tort (which is a civil wrong) and a crime (which is a criminal wrong) is the nature of the remedy provided by the law. For criminal wrongs primarily have punishment as their aim. In contrast, the objective of proceedings in tort are compensation and reparation. It should be remembered that in some instances an action may be both a civil and a criminal wrong, e.g. assault, theft, libel, etc.

Although a tort is a civil wrong, not all civil wrongs are torts. The essential feature of a tort is that its remedy is primarily an action for unliquidated damages – although there may be, and often are, alternative remedies available.

TORT AND CONTRACT

The distinction between tort and contract is that the duties of the parties in the former are primarily fixed by the law, whereas in the latter, they are fixed by the parties themselves. Furthermore, in tort, the duty is towards persons generally, whereas in contract, it is towards a specific person or persons.

TYPES OF TORT

There are a range of Torts which may be committed and the range includes negligence, defamation, nuisance, trespass of the person and land. Of these, the tort of negligence is described in this chapter while defamation is described in Chapter 10.

FUNCTION AND PURPOSE OF THE LAW OF TORT

The law of tort is concerned with those situations where the conduct of one party causes or threatens harm to the interests of other parties. The aim of this law is to compensate for the harm suffered by those whose interests have been invaded by the conduct of others. The law divides harm up under the following headings:

(a) *Damnum Sine Injuria* (even though a loss has been suffered, there is no cause of legal action). There are many forms of harm for which the law does not provide a remedy. For example, the opening up of a supermarket in a particular area may harm the trade of existing local shopkeepers, but the shopkeepers cannot take a tortious action against the supermarket. Thus, any damage or harm which results from the action of setting up in competition is called Damnum Sine Injuria.

(b) *Injuria Sine Damno* (legal action available even though no harm or loss has occurred). There are occasions where a person's behaviour causes no damage or loss at all but it is still actionable in tort. Some of this class of torts, e.g. trespass or libel are actionable per se (in themselves), and thus no loss or damage needs to be alleged or proved. Other torts in this class are not actionable per se. An example is slander, where a plaintiff will only succeed in his action if he can prove that he has suffered damage.

THE FACTOR OF MALICE

In law, "malice" has two different meanings, viz.

1. The intentional doing of a wrongful act without just cause or excuse, or,
2. The doing of an act with some improper motive.

As regards the law of tort, it can generally be said that the defendant's motives or intentions are irrelevant – For a good motive will not excuse a tortious act and a bad one will not make tortious an otherwise innocent act – as illustrated by the following:

The Mayor of Bradford *v*. Pickles (1895)
Pickles in an attempt to make Bradford Corporation pay a higher price for his land, dug a well which interfered with the supply of water into certain of the city's springs. *Held*. Because it was lawful to drill such a well (a point established in **Chasemore *v*. Richards (1859)**), the bad

(malicious) motive was irrelevant. For the action could not make something illegal which in the absence of a bad motive would have been perfectly legal.

Wilkinson *v*. Downton (1897)
Downton, as a practical joke, visited Mrs Wilkinson and told her that her husband had been in an accident and broken both his legs. As a result, the lady suffered a nervous shock and then became seriously ill. She brought an action against Downton for false and malicious representation. *Held*. The fact that the act which was committed was a joke was irrelevant. A tort had been committed and the defendant was liable to pay damages.

Malice (in the sense of improper motive) is an essential requirement to tortious liability.

CAPACITY IN RESPECT OF TORT

As a general rule, all persons of full age may sue or be sued in tort. There are exceptions to this general rule, and these are described below:

1. THE CROWN

Since the passing of the Crown Proceedings Act, 1947, actions in tort can be brought against the Crown. This power is contained within section 2(1) of the Act, but there is no provision for taking an action against the monarch in his (her) private capacity.

2. JUDGES

They have judicial immunity for acts within their judicial capacity. Such immunity also applies to counsel and witnesses as regards matters relating to the case they are concerned with, and has also been applied to Justices of the Peace. **Law *v*. Llewellyn (1906)**.

3. CORPORATIONS (i.e. Companies, etc. – see Chapter 5)

They can sue in their registered name for torts committed against them. Furthermore, they can be sued in their registered name.

As a company only acts through its agents or servants, it can be considered that all wrongful acts are committed by this group of people. Where they are acting within the scope of their authority, the company is vicariously liable (i.e. liable on their behalf) for any committed tort. Actions which are carried out beyond the authority of the directors and/or the company are defined as being "ultra-vires" and, in the past, it has meant that any underlying agreement has been unenforceable. As mentioned in Chapter 5, the implications of the doctrine of ultra-vires has been changed since the early 1970s.

4. MINORS

Minority in itself is no defence, though extreme youth may be relevant in cases where some special mental element is needed.

Where a minor commits an act which is both a tort and a breach of contract he cannot be sued in tort where this is an indirect way of enforcing a contract against him on which he is not liable.

Jennings *v.* Rundall (1799)
A minor hired a mare and injured her by overriding. *Held.* Since the act was substantially no more than a breach of contract, the owner could not sue the minor in tort for the damage caused by the breach.

The decision here went in favour of the minor because the tort arose directly out of the contract. In contrast, if the committed act is not one contemplated by the contract, then the minor can be sued in tort, viz:

Burnard *v.* Haggis (1863)
The defendant, a minor, hired a mare for riding. But in breach of an express term in his agreement, he used the mare for jumping and so injured the animal. *Held.* The minor was liable in tort, despite the fact that the act was also a breach of contract.

A parent of a child is not usually liable for their child's tort. However this does not debar actions against parents for the torts of their children. For, where the parent has authorised, or commissioned or ordered a tort, he will be vicariously liable. Also, where the minor has been given the opportunity of doing harm because of the parent's negligence, liability may arise. **Bebee *v.* Sales (1916).** In contrast, where a parent takes suitable precautions and cannot reasonably predict that his child will be disobedient, there will be no liability. **Donaldson *v.* McNiven (1952).**

5. HUSBAND AND WIFE

The Law Reform (Husband and Wife) Act, 1962, allows spouses to sue each other, but the court is given discretion as to whether it should allow such an action to proceed. Since the Law Reform (Married Women and Tortfeasors) Act, 1935, a wife has been fully liable for her own torts. However, a husband will be vicariously liable for his wife's torts in the principal/agent or employer/employee relationship.

6. MENTALLY INCAPACITATED PERSONS

Generally such a person will be liable for his torts, but he will not be liable when either:

(a) His actions are considered involuntary; or,
(b) He is incapable of forming the necessary intent or malice, and where this is an essential requirement in establishing that a tortuitous act has been commited.

Morriss *v.* Marsden (1952)
Marsden took a room in a hotel, and whilst staying there, attacked the manager. *Held.* He was liable in tort for assault and battery. For even though he did not know that what he was doing was wrong, he did know the nature and quality of his act.

7. JOINT TORTFEASORS

A tort may be committed by two or more persons acting together. Collectively, these persons are known as joint tortfeasors and their liability is joint and several. Thus, a plaintiff may sue all of them together or each separately and successively until his claim has been fully satisfied.

Formerly, if one tortfeasor was sued and he paid all the damages, he could not claim a contribution from the other wrongdoers. This situation was changed by the Law Reform (Married Women and Tortfeasors) Act, 1935, which gave the right of one tortfeasor to recover from the others an amount "as may be found by the court to be just and equitable having regard to the extent of the joint tortfeasors responsibility for the damage".

ACTIO PERSONALIS MORITUR CUM PERSONA

This maxim is literally translated as "a personal action dies with the person". Thus, it was that tortious actions could not be pursued by either a plaintiff or continued against a defendant if either died before the legal action had been decided upon.

However, this ruling was changed by the Law Reform (Miscellaneous Provisions) Act, 1934, which permitted tortious actions, subsisting at the date of death of a party, to be continued on behalf of or against the deceased's estate.

But, there are certain exceptions to this general rule. For;

1. Actions relating to defamation do not survive; and
2. Damages of an "exemplary" nature cannot be awarded in favour of the estate of a deceased plaintiff.

CLASSIFICATION OF TORTIOUS LIABILITY

A simple classification may be made under the following headings:

1. *Personal*
This indicates that the person being sued is the one who committed the tort.

2. *Strict*
Here the liability of the defendant is calculated irrespective of any fault, negligence or wrongful intent by him. This situation is commonly referred to as one of "liability without fault" and is ideally illustrated by **Rylands *v.* Fletcher (1868)**. Such a liability could also arise through statute, and is typically illustrated by infringements of the Factories Act 1961.

3. *Vicarious*
In the main, the person(s) who commits a tortious action is solely liable. But, in certain circumstances, another party will be liable even though he was not a party to the tort nor did he commit it. In such situations, the other party is described as being vicariously liable for the tortious act and he may be sued on that basis. However, for a plaintiff to proceed with such an action, it is essential to show that:

(a) The person who committed the tort was acting as the servant (see below) of his master, and,
(b) The servant was acting within the normal course of employment at the time the tortious action was committed.

MASTER AND SERVANT RELATIONSHIP

The relationship of master (employer) and servant (employee) is created when one person employs another to do a particular job and fully controls the manner in which it is to be done. For these reasons, servants (now referred to as employees) will include chauffeurs, apprentices, clerks, etc. But, skilled people such as electricians, central heating engineers or the like who are involved in installation or repair work at the request of another are not employees but independent contractors (see the next section). The reason they are not held to be employees is because the methods they use to do their work are not under the "employers" control. The meaning of the word employees has expanded over the years and has been seen to include nurses (where the respective hospital authority is held liable), company executives (where the company is held liable), etc.

TORTS COMMITTED IN THE COURSE OF EMPLOYMENT

To establish if the wrong was committed in the course of employment is very much a question of fact as the following illustrates:

Say an employer asks his employee to drive a lorry from the company's factory in Liverpool to Bristol to collect some machinery. If the lorry driver commits a tort while on his journey, the employer will be liable provided the tort is committed while on the authorised route or upon a slight or unavoidable deviation from the authorised route. However, if the tort is committed in London (clearly well off the authorised route) the employer will not be liable.

One further point to note is that even if an employer expressly forbids his employee from committing an action which is tortious but subsequently the action is committed by the employee, the employer remains liable.

Limpus *v.* London General Omnibus Co. (1862)

Although a bus driver had been expressly instructed not to obstruct the buses of rival companies, he subsequently did so when involved in a race to pick up passengers at a stop. This caused the rival bus to overturn. *Held.* The plaintiff's action for vicarious liability was successful for the bus driver was found to be acting within the course of his employment at the time of the act. The fact that this action had been forbidden by the employer was irrelevant.

Storey *v.* Ashton (1869)

A driver employed by the defendant, agreed to do a favour for a fellow employee which took him off his normal route. But in so doing, he was involved in an accident with Storey. *Held.* Ashton (the employer) was not liable as the driver, at the time of the accident, was not considered to be in the course of employment.

Beard *v.* London General Omnibus Co. (1900)

A bus conductor (clearly someone not authorised to drive a bus) drove a bus and through his negligence caused a collision. *Held.* As the employee was not acting in the course of employment, the employer (the defendant here) was not liable.

Century Insurance Co. *v.* Northern Ireland Road Transport Board (1942)

While a petrol tanker driver was discharging petrol at a garage, he threw away an ignited match which caused an explosion and serious damage to the garage. *Held.* The driver was negligent and as this occurred during the course of his employment, his employer was vicariously liable. As the employer (the respondent in this case) had insured themselves against such risks, their insurance company had to settle the claim.

When legal actions are taken under this heading, it should be remembered that the liability which attaches is joint and several (against the employer and employee). However, in the courts, the action is usually only taken against the employer on the basis that he is more likely to be in a position to pay, while the employee is considered to be "a man of straw". Where the action against the employer is successful, he can recover some or all of the loss (e.g. if an indemnity had been taken) from the employee.

Lister *v.* Romford Ice and Cold Storage Co. Ltd (1957)
A lorry driver employed by the defendant negligently reversed a lorry and in so doing injured another employee. The injured employee received damages which were settled by the defendant's insurers as such risks were covered by their insurance policy. In turn, the insurers sued the lorry driver in the employer's name (under the doctrine of subrogation). *Held.* The lorry driver, because he was negligent in performing his duties, caused his employers to be vicariously liable. By his actions, he had breached his contract of employment, and thus the employer (or as here, the employer's insurers) could successfully recover the whole of the monies paid out to the injured plaintiff.

> *Note:* This case had very wide legal implications and subsequently resulted in the British Insurance Association publishing a report upon how their members should act in similar circumstances in the future. It was agreed that the B.I.A. members (and certain non-members) would only enforce their rights of subrogation in future when it could be shown that there was evidence of collusion or wilful misconduct by the employee.

Harrison *v.* Michelin Tyre Company (1985). The plaintiff was standing on a duckboard by the side of a machine that he operated. At a time when he was talking to another employee, a third employee was passing by pushing a truck. As a joke, he pushed the truck in such a way that part of it went under the duckboard, which tipped and, as a result, the plaintiff was injured. He took an action against the employer on the basis of vicarious liability. A defence was set up to say that the third employee had caused the accident by carrying out an act for which he was not authorised. *Held.* If an act is carried out during the course of employment, even though it may have been unauthorised or prohibited, and injury results, the employer will be liable. The only exception to this would arise where the act diverges widely from what is considered to be part and parcel of a worker's employment. As the Court did not consider that the latter applied here, the employer was held liable.

INDEPENDENT CONTRACTOR

This is a person, who is employed by another, to carry out a particular job. As the contractor's actions are not under the direct control of the employer, in general, the contractor alone will be liable for his own tortious actions. However, there are certain exceptions to this, which result in the employer also being liable.

Examples of such exceptions are:

1. When the employer authorises or ratifies the tort of the contractor. **Ellis *v.* Sheffield Gas Consumers Co. (1853)**.
2. When the employer himself is negligent.
3. When the liability in tort is strict and because of this, the responsibility cannot be delegated. **Rylands *v.* Fletcher (1868)**.
4. When the contractor is asked to undertake work which is of a potentially hazardous nature. For example:
   (a) At one time, pavements were illuminated by street lamps, some of which were attached to terraced properties and the lamps, thus, overhung the pavements. If such lamps fell into disrepair, responsibility rested on the shoulders of the property owner (or, his lessee) to make good the lamp by, say, replacing brackets, etc. If a contractor is employed to do this work and he acts negligently, liability still remains with the owner (or lessee) for damage that may be caused. viz: if a lamp falls on to someone who was walking by and that person was injured through the negligent act of the contractor in not satisfactorily repairing the lamp, liability still remains with the owner (or lessee): **Tarry *v.* Ashton (1876)**.
   This decision needs to be compared with work which is carried out by contractors which is well away from the pavement or road, For, if a person, who is walking along a pavement, is, say, injured by a tree which has been felled by a contractor in a front garden, the contractor is liable – not the owner (or lessee) of the land: **Salsbury *v.* Woodland (1969)**.
   (b) Although of a historical nature, taking photographs indoors and using magnesium powdered flashlights for illumination purposes. **Honeywill & Stein *v.* Larkin Bros Ltd (1934)**.

It should be noted that an employer's liability only arises where the wrongs are committed in the normal course of the contractor's employment and not collateral to it (say, where the contractor stole from a third party while carrying out the due task): **Padbury *v.* Holliday (1912)**.

GENERAL DEFENCES TO ACTIONS IN TORT

Although there are special defences available for specific torts, the majority of actions will be defended by one of the general methods described below, if a defendant neither denies the facts nor sets up a defence based on a point of law.

The general defences are:

1. VOLENTI NON FIT INJURIA (CONSENT)

A literal translation of this term is "no injury is done to one who consents." Thus a person who voluntarily consents to the harm done to him may not sue on it. It is convenient to divide this defence up under two headings.

(a) Consent to intentional harm.
(b) Assumptions of risks to negligent harm.

(a) CONSENT TO INTENTIONAL HARM

No act is actionable as a tort at the suit of any person who has expressly or impliedly assented to it. For no man can enforce a right which he has voluntarily waived or abandoned, e.g. Consent to physical harm which would otherwise be an assault. Typical examples here occur in sports such as rugby, boxing, etc. In **Simms *v.* Leigh Rugby Football Club (1969)**, Simms (a visiting player) broke a leg as he was tackled and thrown towards a concrete wall. His action in tort against the Rugby Club failed because Simms had "consented" and the concrete wall had been erected in accordance with the league's guidelines.

With there now being a great deal of violence taking place on a sports field (as well as off it), a number of legal actions have passed through the courts where one player has sought damages against another for injuries caused. In **Condon *v.* Basi (1985)**, the Court of Appeal upheld the County Court judge's decision to award the plaintiff £4,900 in damages. The legal action resulted because the plaintiff sustained a broken leg that was caused by the defendant's late and reckless tackle. For, it was established that participants in any competitive sport owe a duty of care to their fellow sportsmen. If a participant breaches his duty of care (as regards sporting activities, each situation will have to be judged on its own merits) or injury is caused in circumstances to which the other participant would not have been expected to consent, liability in negligence arises.

(b) ASSUMPTIONS OF RISKS TO NEGLIGENT HARM

The maxim also applies to consent to run the risk of accidental harm which would otherwise be actionable "as due to the negligence of he who caused it". There is much case law which can be used to explain the meaning of this statement, and two cases are described below.

Hall *v*. Brooklands Auto-Racing Club (1933)

Following a collision, a racing car ploughed through the protective railings killing two spectators and injuring others. It was the first time such an accident had occurred at this track and the court found that the precautions were adequate. *Held*. Hall, a spectator, must have consented to the risk of accidental injury, and so his action failed.

Wooldridge *v*. Sumner (1962)

A horserider at a show injured a cameraman who had entered the arena and remained there even after stewards had asked him to move outside. Although the decision of the lower court was that the horserider had been negligent, upon appeal the earlier decision was reversed. Diplock L.J. indicated in the Appeal Court that such actions by plaintiffs will not succeed "unless the participant's conduct is such as to evince a reckless disregard of the spectator's safety".

The essential question to be asked in all such cases is "Did the plaintiff give real consent to the assumption of physical and legal risk without compensation?" Consent here may be interpreted as express (either orally or in writing) or implied from the facts established in the case. This must be distinguished from knowledge (sciens) of a risk, for knowledge of an impending wrongful act or of the existence of a wrongfully caused danger, do not in themselves amount to consent. The distinction between volenti and sciens is occasionally difficult to determine, but is illustrated by the legal cases described below. The first two relate to the master/servant relationship, while the following three relate to rescue situations.

Smith *v*. Baker and Sons (1891)

The plaintiff had a job drilling holes in rock by a railway cutting. When drilling, a crane often swung heavy stones over Smith's head, and both he and his employers knew that there was a risk that the stones might fall. One day, some stones fell because of faulty loading. This injured Smith and, as a consequence, he claimed for damages. *Held*. Smith had not voluntarily undertaken the risk of his employer's negligence. Thus, even though he had knowledge of the risk, this did not prevent his action from being successful. This was a House of Lord's decision.

Bowater *v*. Rowley Regis Corporation (1944)
The defendant made Bowater, who drove a horse-drawn cart, take out a horse which was known to be vicious and capable of bolting. Although Bowater had protested about using the horse, he continued to use it until one day it again bolted and injured him. *Held*. Even though Bowater had consented to the risk, it was not freely given, and the Corporation's defence of volenti was not successful. For Lord Chief Justice Goddard said "it must be shown that he agreed that what risk there was, *should lie on him*".

RESCUE SITUATIONS

Haynes *v*. Harwood and Son (1935)
The defendant's servant had left his van and horses unattended in a crowded street. The horses bolted after a young boy had thrown a stone at them. Because of the possible risk of injury to the people in the street, Haynes (a policeman) at great personal risk to himself, siezed one of the horses and eventually managed to stop them all. In so doing, he sustained serious injuries to himself. *Held*. Haynes was not guilty of contributory negligence, nor was the negligence too remote. Furthermore, although he was aware of the risk, this was not a bar to his claim. Thus, he was entitled to damages and the defence of volenti was unsuccessful.

Baker *v*. T. E. Hopkins and Son Ltd (1959)
Two of the defendant's servants went down a well to clean it out and were overcome by carbon monoxide fumes which were exhaust gases from a petrol-driven pump. Baker, a local doctor, on hearing what had happened, went to the well to see what he could do. He was then lowered down the well by rope to the injured workers and after deciding he could not help, signalled that he wanted to be lifted up. However, the rope carrying him became caught and the doctor was overcome by fumes and died. The doctor's executors claimed damages. *Held*. By using a petrol driven engine, the defendants were guilty of negligence towards their servants. Baker in these circumstances acted as any brave man and doctor would have done, and though he may have had knowledge of the risk he was running, his actions were not considered as freely and voluntarily undertaken. Thus, the defence of volenti was unsuccessful.

Cutler *v*. United Dairies (London) Ltd (1933)
While a dairyman was delivering his milk, his horse was startled and bolted off down the road and into a meadow. The dairyman chased after it and Cutler watching what was going on went to assist. In the process

of controlling the horse, he was injured. *Held*. The plaintiff here had voluntarily and freely assumed the risk. For he knew the risk, had time to consider it and must have agreed to incur it. As the horse was in a meadow, there was no urgency to prevent a major accident as there was in **Haynes *v*. Harwood and Son (1935)**. Thus, the defence of volenti was successful.

Videan *v*. British Transport Commission (1963)
A minor wandered onto a railway line and was injured by a trolley. The child's father, who happened to be the stationmaster, injured himself in his attempt to rescue the child. *Held*. By the Court of Appeal. The circumstances were subject to the test of forseeability. In what can only be described as a strange decision – as regards the child, the Court held that there was no liability as it could not be foreseen that a child would wander onto a railway line. However, with regards to the father, it was held that it was forseeable that he would injure himself attempting to rescue someone in such circumstances and damages were awarded against B.T.C.

More recently, the courts have had to consider whether or not a person who has been rescued owes a duty of care to his rescuer as illustrated in:

Harrison *v*. British Railways Board (1981)
A railway employee tried to board a moving train, but as he slipped in the process of jumping on, he could only hang on to one of the carriage doors. The guard (the plaintiff) saw what happened and jumped off the train in order to help his fellow employee. In so doing, he was injured, and commenced an action for damages. *Held*. The employee who tried to board the moving train was solely liable in damages.

2. MISTAKE

Generally it can be said that mistake is no defence in tort. It does not matter whether the mistake was one of fact or law.

As regards mistake of fact, there are certain exceptions to this rule. For, where a policeman arrests someone on reasonable suspicion of crime but it is later proven that he is innocent, then the policeman is not liable in tort. This defence does not apply to individuals who in similar circumstances make wrongful citizen's arrests. **Beckwith *v*. Philby (1827)**

As regards mistake of law, the hearing of legal actions would be quickly ground to a halt if defendants pleaded not guilty because of a mistake of law. However where attempted, the maxim "ignorantia non excusat" is applied – ignorance of the law is no excuse.

3. INEVITABLE ACCIDENT

Even though damage is sometimes caused by accident, this cannot be used by itself as a defence if there was a duty to take necessary precautions. In contrast, some accidents occur which could not be avoided by any precautions which a reasonable man would be expected to take. These are known as inevitable accidents and are illustrated in the cases below.

Stanley *v.* Powell (1891)
Stanley was employed by a shooting party and was injured by a shot which glanced off a tree and into his eye. *Held*. The defendant's action was neither intentional nor negligent and so the plaintiff's claim failed.

National Coal Board *v.* J. E. Evans and Co. (Cardiff) and Maberley Parker Ltd (1951)
Evans and Co. had been employed by a County Council to dig a trench on their land. This job was sub-contracted and, while digging, the sub-contractor damaged an electricity cable. Water then seeped into the cable causing an explosion and the electricity supply to one of the plaintiff's collieries was cut off. The plaintiff then sued for trespass and negligence. *Held*. In the lower court, the defendants were not liable in negligence but were liable in trespass. However the Court of Appeal's decision was that the defendants were neither liable in negligence nor in trespass.

4. ACT OF GOD

To be successful in this defence, there are two essential elements which must be proven.

(a) The event happened through natural causes, i.e. without human intervention.
(b) The act was so unpredictable that even a reasonable man would not be expected to foresee and guard against it.

The two legal cases described below indicate how this defence is used in practice.

Nichols *v.* Marsland (1876)
The defendant had a series of artificial lakes on her land which had been created some years earlier by damming a natural stream. An extremely heavy rainfall occurred which swelled the lakes and caused the artificial banks to burst. The tide of water carried away four bridges belonging to the County Council and as a result the County Surveyor sued Marsland. *Held*. Marsland was not liable because the escape of water here was

considered as an Act of God – for, although it is necessary to provide against the ordinary operations of nature, it is not necessary to provide against miracles.

Slater *v*. Worthington's Cash Stores (1930) Ltd (1941)
After a heavy snowfall, which then froze, a passer-by slipped and was injured when walking past a shop. An action was taken against the shop which set up a defence of "Act of God". *Held*. The accident was not caused by an Act of God but by the shops negligence in not clearing the snow before it froze. Hence, the owners of the shop were liable.

5. SELF DEFENCE

A person may use reasonable force to defend himself or members of his family or anybody else against unlawful force. The word reasonable means that the action of defence must be proportionate to the harm threatened. However, no defence is available under this heading when one person hits another because he has been provoked by words. **Lane *v*. Holloway (1967)**.

Consider the following case also:
Cresswell *v*. Sirl (1948)
Cresswell's dogs had been annoying some in-lamb ewes on a farm, and the farmer's son went out to investigate. When he shone a light on the dogs, they turned on him, and when they were some forty yards away, he shot and killed one of the dogs. The owner then sued the farmer's son for damages. *Held*. In the County Court, the action was successful because it was only considered justifiable to kill a dog while it was actually attacking sheep. However, the Court of Appeal overruled this decision. It considered that the action was justifiable in the sense that it was necessary to avert immediate damage to property, here a further attack on the ewes (such actions are now permitted by section 9 Animals Act, 1971).

Finally, reasonable force may be used to protect one's property. Thus someone may put barbed-wire fencing around their property – but they may not mine the surroundings nor attempt to injure trespassers by setting traps.

6. NECESSITY

The general principle seems to be one of reasonableness, taking into consideration all the circumstances of the case – which includes the nature of the jeopardy, the defendant's dilemma and the urgency of the action.

Leigh *v*. Gladstone (1909)

A suffragette, who went on hunger strike while in prison, was forcibly fed by the wardens. She later sued them for assault and battery. *Held*. The defence of necessity was good, for if she had not been fed she would have died.

Cope *v*. Sharpe (1912)

A tenant had shooting rights over part of the plaintiff's land. When a fire broke out on another part of the land, the defendant (the head gamekeeper of the tenant) entered the plaintiff's land to build a fire break and thus prevent the fire from spreading – particularly to his master's land where the pheasants were sitting. However, the fire was extinguished before it reached the fire break, and the owner sued the gamekeeper for damages for trespass. *Held*. The defence of necessity was good for the gamekeeper's action seemed reasonable in the circumstances.

7. ACT OF STATE

Here reference is being made to an act committed by a servant of the Crown which comes within his duties and upon which he is being sued.

Buron *v*. Denman (1848)

The Captain of a British warship set fire to a depot holding slaves in West Africa, and thereby enabled the slaves to escape. The Spanish slave trader sued him for trespass. *Held*. The Captain's general instructions were to suppress the slave trade. The action he took was within his duties, and was later approved by the Crown, and therefore there was no liability for trespass.

8. STATUTORY AUTHORITY

Certain actions in tort may be defended by showing that there was a statutory authority permitting the alleged wrong. Such authority may be classified under two headings:

Absolute (*imperative*) – Which authorises acts even though they may cause harm to others. Here, there is a duty for the act to be carried out and no liability arises provided the person acts reasonably and there is no other way of carrying it out. See the "Vaughan" case below.

Conditional (*permissive*) – Only allows the act provided it does not cause harm to others. Here, the act is not bound to be carried out. See the "Penny" case below.

Vaughan *v.* Taff Vale Railway (1860)
Sparks, from a railway engine, set fire to the plaintiff's woodland. *Held.* As the railway company had been authorised by statute to run a railway through the plaintiff's land, and had taken all known care in the construction of the engine to prevent spark emission, it was not liable.

Penny *v.* Wimbledon Urban Council (1899)
The Council, under a Statutory Act, employed someone to make up a road. In the course of his duties, he piled up quantities of soil on the road. One evening when it was dark the plaintiff injured herself as a consequence of falling over one of the piles. She then sued the Council. *Held.* Although the Council had statutory powers to carry out this work, it was essential to see that the public were not endangered. As the piles were not illuminated, then the Council was negligent and the plaintiff's action succeeded.

9. ILLEGALITY

In **Ashton *v.* Turner (1980)**, three men committed a burglary and drove off in a car owned by one of them. All three had been drinking that evening and the car in which they were travelling crashed and caused injury to one of them. The injured party claimed damages against the owner and driver. *Held.* The claim was dismissed as a matter of public policy. (Irrespective of this, a defence of "volenti" would have been successful in the circumstances of such an accident – although, here, it was not necessary to use it).

10. CONTRIBUTORY FAULT

On occasions, it will be established that damage has been caused not only by the tortious conduct of the defendant, but also as a result of the plaintiff's own actions. In these circumstances, the Law Reform (Contributory Negligence) Act 1945 provides that damages recoverable "shall be reduced to such an extent as the Court thinks just and equitable having regard to the claimant's share in the responsibility for the damage".

Thus, this form of defence does not totally eliminate the claim that has been made, but, where successful, it reduces the amount of damages that has to be paid.

Although most claims of contributory fault will be based on the plaintiff's negligence or carelessness, it may also, for example, be based on a breach of the plaintiff's statutory duty.

When pleading contributory negligence, the defendant must show that:

(1) the plaintiff had been negligent; and,

(2) the plaintiff contributed to the loss he had sustained.

Each case will have to be judged on its own merits, but the following case provides an illustration:

Jones *v*. Boyce (1816)
Jones was travelling as a passenger on top of Boyce's horse-drawn coach. During the journey, a rein broke and Jones, believing that the coach would overturn and injure him, jumped off. Unfortunately, he broke his leg as a result of leaping off and, to make matters worse, the coach was stopped without it overturning. Jones claimed damages against the coach owner. *Held*. In the circumstances, Jones had acted reasonably and the defence of contributory negligence failed. So, Jones was awarded damages in full.

NEGLIGENCE

Although negligence may make up one of several factors in certain torts, in this section of the book, it is being considered as a specific tort in its own right. The specific tort has three elements to it and, for a legal action to be successful, a plaintiff must satisfy the three points listed below and which are more fully described thereafter:

(a) The defendant was under a **duty of care** not to damage or injure the property or person of the plaintiff. In the leading case **Donoghue *v*. Stevenson (1932)**, Lord Atkin stated that "There is a duty not to injure your neighbour. Who then is my neighbour? The answer seems to be persons who are so closely and directly affected by my act that I ought reasonably to have them in contemplation as being affected when I am directing my mind to the acts or omissions which are called in question," and,

(b) There was a **breach of that duty of care**. The plaintiff has to prove that the defendant either:
   a. Did something that a reasonable man would not do; or
   b. Did not do something that a reasonable man would do, and,

(c) That **damage was caused** by the defendant's negligence and **was not too remote**.

1. DUTY OF CARE

To decide whether, in any particular situation, a duty of care exists is a question of fact for the judge. The leading precedent in this matter is:

Donoghue (or McAlister) *v.* Stevenson (1932)
This is a classic case in English law and because of the fundamental legal principles involved, it went as far as the House of Lords. The background was that the appellant's friend purchased a bottle of ginger beer which contained a decomposed snail. When the bottle was full, the snail could not be seen because the bottle was made of dark glass and it was only when the final dregs of the bottle were poured out that the "foreign body" was noted. By that time, the bulk of the contents of the bottle had been drunk, and subsequently, the appellant became ill and served a writ on the gingerbeer manufacturers (the respondents), claiming damages. *Held*. The manufacturers had been negligent for they owed a duty of care to the consumer even though the consumer was not the purchaser. In the Donoghue case, Lord Atkin propounded the now famous neighbour test which was described in the introduction, and which has since been applied in many cases concerning a manufacturer's negligence.

The principles of the above case were applied to subsequent cases relating to negligent deeds or injury to persons or property. It was not until much later that the tort of negligence was applied to a situation where careless words were published and where, as a result, an economic loss resulted. The classic case on this matter is **Hedley Byrne & Co. Ltd *v.* Heller and Partners Ltd (1963)**, the background to which is described in the Contract chapter. Although the decision in this case had wide ranging implications, it did not provide an explanation of the legal position which subsists when a careless act causes economic loss. This situation was more recently discussed and the principles established in **Anns and Others *v.* Merton London Borough Council (1977)**. Here, when a block of maisonettes was being built, inadequate foundations were laid. Statute obliged the local authority to inspect and approve foundations. The local authority carried out these duties negligently, a point unknown at the time. In due course, the building was completed and some of the maisonettes were purchased. Later on, walls cracked and other faults developed. Anns (one of the purchasers) and other residents joined in an action against the local authority alleging carelessness and negligence. The authority denied that it owed a duty of care to any of the purchasers. *Held*. The authority did owe a duty of care to the purchasers of the maisonettes and, having been negligent in carrying out its duties, was held to be liable.

In his judgement, Lord Wilberforce made the following statement concerning duty of care: "the position has now been reached that in order to establish that a duty of care arises in a particular situation, it is not necessary to bring the facts of that situation within those of previous situations in which a duty of care has been held to exist. Rather the question has to be approached in two stages. First one has to ask whether, as between the alleged wrongdoer and the person who has suffered damage there is a sufficient relationship of proximity or neighbourhood such that, in the reasonable contemplation of the former, carelessness on his part may be likely to cause damage to the latter, in which case a prima facie duty of care arises. Secondly, if the first question is answered affirmatively, it is necessary to consider whether there are any considerations which ought to negative, or to reduce or limit the scope of the duty or the class of person to whom it is owed or the damages to which a breach of it may give rise." The duty of care principle was again looked at in **Junior Books Ltd *v*. Veitchi Company Ltd (1982)**. Here, the defendant (V) laid a floor in the plaintiff's (J.B.'s) premises. There was no contractual relationship between V and J.B. because V had had the work sub-contracted to it by J.B.'s main builder. Because V was careless, the floor was laid in a defective way and J.B. was placed in a position where it had to pay for the cost of a replacement. Furthermore, while the work was being carried out, a loss of profits arose. Even though there had been no threat of injury to person or property, J.B. claimed damages for the additional costs incurred and the lost profits it had sustained. *Held*. In the circumstances, V owed J.B. a duty of care and so the claim for damages was successful.

Finally, under this heading, it is necessary to establish if a successful action can be taken against a public body where one or several of its employees have breached statutory provisions in the course of their duties. In fact, the position has already been determined if reference is made to the background and decision in the "Anns" case. Here, the action was successful, just as it was in:

Dorset Yacht Co. Ltd *v*. Home Office (1970)
After escaping from a borstal, some boys set adrift and damaged a yacht. The owners of the yacht sued the Home Office (this is the Government department responsible for borstals). *Held*. The Home Office was liable for the damage, for it was shown that the boys had escaped from the borstal officers' custody because of their negligence and that the officers owed a duty of care to the yacht owner.

2. BREACH OF DUTY OF CARE

The standard of care required is that of a reasonable man. As highlighted in the introduction, a breach of duty can be committed by an omission to do something which a reasonable man would do if placed in the same circumstances or the doing of something which a reasonable man would not do.

The care, which a reasonable man would show, varies with the circumstances but the test is the same in every case.

Relevant factors may be:

(a) What was the magnitude of the foreseeable risk?
A defendant is required to guard against a risk of injury or damage which is reasonably foreseeable but not one which is remotely possible.

Fardon *v*. Harcourt-Rivington (1932)
The defendant left a dog in a parked car. The dog bit one of the windows causing a splinter of glass to enter the plaintiff's eye. *Held*. The defendant was not liable since he was only bound to guard against reasonable probabilities not extreme possibilities.

(b) What were the known characteristics of the party exposed to the risk?
A reasonable man will adapt his conduct and activities to safeguard his companions and if his companions are particularly susceptible to certain risks, then the reasonable man will use special care.

Paris *v*. Stepney Borough Council (1950)
A one-eyed fitter in the employment of the defendant lost the sight of his good eye while working under a car without goggles. *Held*. A reasonable man would supply goggles to such a person.

Note: Children require more care than adults.

(c) Was the defendant faced with an emergency?
A person may be justified in taking further risks in an emergency – for even a reasonable man takes such risks in an emergency.

Watt *v*. Hertfordshire County Council (1954)
A woman had been trapped in the wreckage of an accident. On the way to the scene of the accident, a fireman was injured by a heavy jack which slipped while being taken to the scene in a lorry not equipped to carry such a jack. *Held*. By the Court of Appeal. At the time notice of the accident was received by the fire service, they had no suitable vehicle to carry the special jack that was needed. So, in the emergency situation, the fire service was justified in using a vehicle which, although not perfect for the job was considered to be the most suitable of those available. Furthermore, employers could ask employees to take exceptional risks in emergency situations and if personal injury resulted, the employer need not be liable. So stated Lord Denning and, as a consequence, Watt's action failed.

(d) Did a special relationship exist? e.g. Such as that between a spectator at a sports event and a participant. For here, mere errors of judgement or lapses of skill by the participant will not render him liable. (See **Hall *v*. Brooklands Auto-Racing Club (1933)**.)

Wilks *v*. Cheltenham Home Guard Motor Cycle and Light Car Club. The Times 25.3.1971
A father and daughter, who were attending a motor cycle scramble, were injured when a competitor left the course and passed through a series of ropes before striking them. *Held*. By the Court of Appeal, the competitor was not negligent. For it was shown that he had exhibited reasonable care when riding his cycle. It is expected that competitors should do all that they can to win events that they enter for and will not be liable unless they are foolhardy.

(e) Was Economic Practicability relevant?

Latimer *v*. A.E.C. Ltd (1953)
A heavy rainfall caused flooding in one of the defendant's workshops. This resulted in oil, previously contained in open channels, spreading over the workshop floor. The company attempted to soak up the oil by spreading sawdust over the floor, but there was insufficient to cover everywhere. Later, the plaintiff slipped and injured himself on one of the untreated areas. *Held*. The defendant was not liable, as the company had done all that could be reasonably expected of it. The alternative was for the company to close the workshop which would have resulted in great economic loss to the workers and the company.

(f) Is the action being taken against a professional person or someone possessing special skills, such as a tradesman.

From doctors, surgeons, accountants, architects, solicitors, barristers, etc., a high degree of professionalism is expected. Hence, it may be held that such a person is negligent even though, at the time of the cause of the action, the professional person was shown to have done his best.

Doctors/Surgeons

With regards to the medical profession, the number of legal actions taken against them is increasing rapidly. In this matter, though, it has been established that an error of clinical judgement will not, in itself, amount to negligence:

Whitehouse *v*. Jordan (1981)
The defendant was a hospital registrar, who, in a difficult child birth, used forceps to deliver a baby. The baby was born with severe brain damage and Jordan was alleged to have caused this condition by pulling

the baby too hard and for too long using forceps. *Held*. By the House of Lords. It could not be proved that the use of forceps had caused the baby's medical condition. At best, it could be said that, with hindsight, the use of forceps was an error of clinical judgement. Thus, the action failed.

Architects

It has now been established that an architect must not simply design a building which is structurally sound but design one which is fit for the purpose to which it is to be put.

Greaves & Co. (Contractors) *v*. Baynham Meikle & Partners (1974)
The defendant was a firm of consultant structural engineers who had been asked to design a warehouse for the plaintiff builder. It was known that heavy loaded lorries would be calling at the warehouse which would, therefore, be subject to their vibrational effects. The architects designed a structurally competent building. However, it was unsuitable for accommodating the vibrational effect of the loaded lorries. The plaintiff alleged, amongst other things, that there had been a breach of duty of care in designing the warehouse. *Held*. The building should have been designed for the purpose of its proposed use. As the designers had been presented with all the relevant factors and had not taken into account all of them while designing, they were liable.

3. DAMAGE CAUSED WHICH WAS NOT TOO REMOTE

The defendant's conduct must be an effective cause of the plaintiff's injury and the damage must not be too remote. Looking at each of these points in turn:

(a) *Causation*

Negligence is a tort that is only actionable upon proof of damage and the damage must result from the breach.

Barnett *v*. Chelsea and Kensington Hospital Management Committee (1968)
A night watchman took a drink of tea, which unknown to him contained arsenic. After vomiting for some three hours, he went to the casualty department of a hospital, but the doctor did not examine him. Instead, he was told to visit his own doctor. Some five hours later he died, and his widow sued the hospital for damages. *Held*. The action for negligence failed. Although the casualty officer breached the duty of care, this negligence in itself did not cause death. The man died of arsenic poisoning, and even if the casualty officer had identified the reason for vomiting, the man would have died in any case.

(b) *Remoteness*

This is a very complex area, as will be seen by the cases described below. In the first instance, the plaintiff must establish that the defendant's wrong caused his loss. But having established this point, he may be unable to recover damages because it is held that the loss is not sufficiently connected with the defendant's wrong to make him liable. Thus, the loss is *too remote*. Formerly, the principles which needed to be proved were:

(a) A reasonable man would have foreseen that his act would have caused the plaintiff some harm.

(b) Liability arises from all the direct consequences of the act, even though such consequences could not possibly have been foreseen.

Smith *v.* London and South Western Railway (1870)

The defendant's employees left clippings, from hedge and grass cuttings, by the side of a railway track. Sparks from a passing engine ignited them, and a fire spread along the side of the track across a road and then damaged the plaintiff's cottage. *Held.* The railway company was liable. A reasonable man would have foreseen the possibility of fire, and the damage caused was a direct consequence of the employee's act – even though it was a freak.

Re Polemis and Furness Withy and Co. (1921)

A group of stevedores were employed by charterers of a ship to unload its cargo of drums of petrol. Because certain drums leaked, inflammable vapours built up in the ships hold. One of the stevedores negligently knocked a plank into the hold, and this caused a spark which ignited the vapours and the resultant fire destroyed the ship. *Held.* The charterers were liable for the loss. Even though a reasonable man could not have foreseen the consequences of such negligence, because the loss was a direct consequence of the negligent act, liability was established.

Overseas Tankship (U.K.) Ltd *v.* Morts Dock and Engineering Co. Ltd (The Wagon Mound) 1961)

While a ship was taking on oil in Sydney, Australia, the appellant's servants negligently allowed some oil to spill into the sea. The wind and tide carried the slick to a wharf where the respondent's servants were using welding equipment to repair another ship. Upon seeing the slick, welding stopped, but after consultations with the wharf manager, work was restarted (on the basis that in the past flying sparks had never ignited floating oil). However, some molten metal ignited a cloth which was floating on the oil, this set the oil alight and the respondent's wharf was badly damaged. *Held.* The court followed the precedent of **Re Polemis**

and Furness Withy and Co. (1921) and the appellants were held liable. Upon appeal to the Judicial Committee of the Privy Council, the Polemis decision was not considered to be good law and that the foreseeability principle should be the prime test. Thus, the decision of the lower court was reversed, and the appellants were held not to be liable.

Note: This decision is not binding (only persuasive) on English Courts. Even so, the rule was followed in **Hughes *v.* Lord Advocate (1963)** – by the House of Lords, and in **Doughty *v.* Turner Manufacturing Co. Ltd (1964)** – by the Court of Appeal.

BURDEN OF PROOF IN NEGLIGENCE

The burden of proof in negligence is upon the plaintiff on all three points. The proof must go beyond the realm of pure conjecture into that of reasonable inference.

Wakelin *v.* L.S.W. Railway Co. (1886)
While on a railway crossing during a dark night, the plaintiff's husband was killed. It was alleged by the plaintiff that the accident occurred because the train had not whistled. *Held.* This was pure conjecture, and the facts of the case were equally consistent with suicide.

RES IPSA LOQUITUR

As mentioned above, the general rule is for the plaintiff to prove negligence – not for the defendant to disprove it. On occasions, this rule will cause the plaintiff considerable hardship because the cause of an accident may only be known to the defendant who caused it. This hardship is overcome, to a considerable extent, by the principle "*Res Ipsa Loquitur*" – "The thing speaks for itself".

The maxim applies where:

(a) It is so improbable that such an action would have happened without the negligence of the defendant; and
(b) The defendant had control over the events; and
(c) The defendant has means of knowledge denied to the plaintiff.

In such cases the facts speak for themselves and the mere occurrence of an accident in the absence of an explanation provides prima facie evidence of negligence.

Byrne *v.* Boadle (1863)
A barrel of flour fell out of the defendant's warehouse on to a passer-by, and injured him. At the time the barrel fell, there was no evidence to show that the defendant was negligent. *Held.* In the absence of a suitable explanation by the defendant, the facts indicated that negligence had occurred and thus the plaintiff's action was successful.

Applications of this doctrine were also made in:

Scott *v.* London and St Katherine Docks Co. (1865) – Where six bags of sugar fell from a warehouse on to a passer-by.

McGowan *v.* Stott (1923) – where a car mounted a pavement and knocked a pedestrian down from behind.

Skinner *v.* L.B. & S.C. Railway (1850) – where two trains on the same railway line collided.

Mahon *v.* Osborne (1939) – where a swab was left in a patient's body by a surgeon.

Grant *v.* Australian Knitting Mills (1936) – where chemicals in clothing caused dermatitis.

NEGLIGENT STATEMENTS

The previous section in this chapter described the law which relates to negligent acts. In this section, a review is carried out of the law as it relates to negligent statements.

Some of the fundamentals have already been looked at in the Contract Chapter, under the heading of Classification of Misrepresentations. In that section, it was seen that if one party made a fraudulent misrepresentation and as a result, another party was induced into acting upon it, there are grounds for a legal action: **Derry *v.* Peek (1889)**. It was seen that where such a misrepresentation has been made, an action will only be successful where the representation has been made in writing and signed by the representor: Statute of Frauds Amendment Act 1828. This Statutory provision does not apply, though, where the misrepresentation has been given negligently, as the case below illustrates:

Anderson (W.B.) and Sons *v.* Rhodes (Liverpool) (1967)
The parties here were wholesalers at a fruit and vegetable market. Rhodes began to sell vegetables to a newly formed company, originally for cash, then on a credit basis. The market operated on a seven day credit period, but this was grossly exceeded by the new company. The position was known to and accepted by the manager of Rhodes, who at no time advised

the salesman and buyer of Rhodes. Reid, their buyer, acted as an agent with regards to deals between the plaintiff and the newly formed company and was paid commission for setting up the deals. Reid made an oral statement that the new company was creditworthy. As a result, supplies were made to the new company on a credit basis. Subsequently, it became insolvent and could not pay its debts. The plaintiff sued Rhodes for the negligent statement of its buyer, Reid. *Held*. The action was successful and damages were awarded. Liability arose because:

(1) The defendant owed a duty of care in respect of their buyer's statement.
(2) The defendant was vicariously liable for the negligence of the manager, who was fully aware of the poor financial position of the new company.
(3) As Reid's statements were negligent, no defence was available within the provisions of the Statute of Frauds Amendment Act, 1828.

Where financial loss results from a negligent representation, it was necessary at one time, if a legal action was to be successful, for the plaintiff to establish that there was a fiduciary or contractual relationship between himself and the party against whom he was commencing the legal action. If this could not be shown, the action would fail, as seen in:

Candler *v*. Crane, Christmas & Co. (1951)
The defendant, a firm of auditors, had been requested to prepare a set of accounts for a company customer knowing that they would be used by Candler as a basis for deciding whether or not to invest in the company. After analysing the figures that had been produced, Candler decided to make an investment. Unfortunately, the company was wound up within twelve months and Candler lost his money. He alleged that there had been negligence in preparing the accounts, especially with regards to the valuation of leases in the balance sheet. He thus sued for negligence. *Held*. By the Court of Appeal, in a majority judgement. As there was no contractual or fiduciary relationship between the parties to the legal action, the auditors owed no duty of care to the plaintiff. Thus, the action failed.

When Denning delivered his judgement in this case, he stated that in some circumstances, even though two parties are neither in a contractual nor fiduciary relationship, a defendant may incur liability on a negligent statement to a party who sees and relies on the statement. It was not until twelve years later that the Candler decision was disapproved (and Denning's statement applied) in **Hedley Byrne & Co. Ltd *v*. Heller and Partners Ltd (1963)**, a case described in the Contract Chapter. Here, it was pointed out that, in normal circumstances, a representor incurs a liability to the recipient of a negligent reply to a status enquiry. However, in this case, the plaintiff's action failed because of an appropriately worded disclaimer clause – although, today, such disclaimer clauses will be subject to the test of reasonableness in accordance with the provisions of the Unfair Contract Terms Act, 1977. But, the key principle to evolve was that a duty of care was owed by a representor even where there was no contractual or fiduciary relationship between the two parties.

In an Australian case, **Commercial Banking Company of Sydney Ltd *v.* R. H. Brown & Co. (1972)**, the bank made a fraudulent misrepresentation (in that they knew that their customers were in financial difficulties, but gave a favourable reply). Even though the bank included a disclaimer, the court held that this did not protect the bank because its reply was fraudulent – it would only protect the bank where a reply was framed negligently. As this was an Australian case, it is merely persuasive as English courts and, thus, the effect that this decision will have on equivalent legal cases in this country is unknown.

In a more recent case, it was pointed out that it was not necessary, in order to establish liability for a negligent statement, to show that the representor was aware of the identity of the person who would rely on the statement. For, the Courts would apply the test of foresight to a given set of circumstances and where it was positively applied, a liability would arise:

J. E. B. Fasteners Ltd *v.* Marks Bloom & Co. (1981)
The defendant, a firm of chartered accountants, audited the books of B.G. Fasteners Ltd for the year ended 31.10.1974. On the basis of the figures and information contained therein, the plaintiff purchased all the shares of B.G. As the accounts did not give a true and fair view of B.G.'s financial position, the plaintiff suffered financial loss as a result of the purchase and the company began an action in negligence. *Held.* As the real objective of the plaintiff was to purchase the services of two of B.G.'s directors, the action failed – for, J.E.B. would have purchased the shares in B.G. in any case. The judge went on to say that auditors owed a duty of care to persons who were complete strangers at the time of audit. By foresight, auditors should be aware that third parties, such as bankers or potential investors (or, as here, those considering a take-over), may rely on the published figures and other information as being accurate and giving a true and fair representation of a company's financial position at the date specified.

There may be special occasions where it is unnecessary for a plaintiff to show that he was the person who relied on the representation, as illustrated by the decision in:

Ross *v.* Caunters (1979)
A will was prepared by a solicitor, who forgot to advise the testator that his signature should not be witnessed by a beneficiary's spouse. Unfortunately, the spouse of a beneficiary acted as one of the witnesses, thus debarring the beneficiary from taking under the will. As a result, the solicitor was sued in negligence for economic loss. *Held.* The solicitor owed a duty of care to the beneficiary and thus the action was successful.

As a final point under this heading, at one time, it was considered that only persons who were in business or who had or claimed to have special skills (such as accountants, solicitors, surveyors, etc.) could incur liability on a negligent statement. However, this opinion is not now so, as the contrasting decisions in the cases below show:

Mutual Life Assurance Co. Ltd *v.* Evatt (1971)
Evatt had invested some of his money in a company, P. Ltd, and wanted advice as to whether to retain or increase his investment in the company. P Ltd and Mutual (the appellant) were both subsidiaries of the same holding company and the only relationship between Evatt and Mutual was that, at the time, Evatt was one of Mutual's policy holders. Evatt sought Mutual's investment advice which was given without a disclaimer. As a result of the advice, Evatt purchased some more shares. In due course, the shares fell in value and Evatt claimed that the advice he had been given was negligent. *Held.* By the Judicial Committee of the Privy Council. Mutual's appeal was successful. For, it was established that it was no part of an assurance company's business to give investment advice and so Evatt lost his money. The Hedley Byrne case, which was cited in the judgement, established that liability for negligent representations would arise only where the party making the representations held themselves out as being skilled in the appropriate subject matter.

Esso Petroleum Co. Ltd *v.* Mardon (1976)
Mardon was considering whether or not to take over a lease of an Esso petrol station. To enable him to make a decision, he asked how much petrol per year he could anticipate selling. One of Esso's senior sales representatives, who was not in business or employed to give such advice, replied. On the basis of the statements, Mardon took over the lease. It was later established that the statements were inaccurate and Mardon sued for damages in negligence. *Held.* As the statement was shown to be negligent, the sales representative was liable and so was Esso, as his employer, by vicarious liability.

Notes: (1) This decision developed the law of negligence, for it established that there would be a liability for misrepresentation even though two parties were only in a pre-contractual situation at the time the misrepresentation was made.

(2) When the misrepresentation was made, it occurred at a time before the Misrepresentation Act, 1967 was law. Hence, its provisions could not be applied. Today, most legal actions based on similar circumstances would look to this piece of statute rather than the ratio decidendi of the Mardon case in order to decide whether or not to commence a legal action. The main reason why this statute would invariably be used is because the act obliges the person who has made a statement to prove that there had been no negligence on his part – whereas, previously, the onus of responsibility was on the plaintiff to prove negligence.

CONTRIBUTORY NEGLIGENCE

Before 1945, if the plaintiff was guilty of any negligence which contributed towards the cause of the accident, he recovered nothing. However, the situation was changed by section 1(1) of The Law Reform (Contributory Negligence) Act, 1945: "Where any person suffers damage as a result partly of his own fault and partly of the fault of any other person or persons, a claim in respect of that damage shall not be defeated by reason of the fault of the person suffering the damage, but the damages recoverable in respect thereof shall be reduced to such an extent as the court thinks just and equitable having regard to the claimant's share in the responsibility for the damage." This is known as the doctrine of contributory negligence and allows the court to apportion the liability between the plaintiff and the defendant. It does not mean that the plaintiff's claim will fail – only that the damages will be reduced by an amount which relates to the plaintiff's apportioned fault.

There are many legal cases which illustrate this point and the majority relate to road accidents.

Nettleship *v.* Weston (1971)

A non-professional driving instructor agreed to give a lady a series of driving lessons. But before the first lesson took place he made sure the lady's insurance policy covered injury to passengers. During one lesson, the lady crashed the car and injured Nettleship. He wished to claim on Weston for damages, but she pleaded volenti – he freely took the risk of injury. *Held*. By the Court of Appeal – as Nettleship had enquired about and saw the policy which covered injury to passengers, he could not have consented freely to the risk of injury. Thus, his claim was successful.

O'Connell *v*. Jackson (1971)
Here a moped rider, who was not wearing a crash helmet, sustained severe head injuries in a road accident. Although the accident was caused by the defendant, the plaintiff's injuries would have been less severe if he had been wearing a crash helmet. Thus, the damages were reduced (by 15%).

Pasternack *v*. Poulton (1973)
Here a car passenger failed to wear a seat belt. The car was later involved in an accident and the plaintiff suffered facial injuries. Although contributory negligence was proven, damages were only reduced by 5% because she had not been actively encouraged to wear the seat belt by the defendant.

Purnell *v*. Shields (1973)
Here a man was thrown out of a van and killed after it had been involved in a collision. Because he was not wearing a sealt belt, the action brought by his wife resulted in the damages being reduced by 20%.

It should be remembered that actions for negligence have, as their objective, punishment of the defendant. But where the defendant has insured himself against the negligent action, the end product of a successful claim of contributory negligence, is that the payment by his insurance company to the plaintiff is reduced.

Since the above cases in the early 1970s, different judges have commented on the doctrine of contributory negligence. For O'Connor J. found that failure to wear a car seat belt did not amount to contributory negligence, especially where the injury is caused by the gross negligence of another, (**Smith *v*. Blackburn (1974)**), and so the insurers were obliged to pay proper compensation. This opinion was followed in **Chapman *v*. Ward. The Times 8.10.1974** and **James *v*. Parsons (1974).**

In contrast Lord Denning later disapproved of these decisions. For, where road accident injuries would have been lessened or prevented through the wearing of a seat belt, any claim by a plaintiff for damages would be reduced if it was shown that the seat belt had not been worn. **Froom *v*. Butcher (1975)**. In this case, Lord Denning enlarged the definition of contributory negligence. He also quantified the amount by which damages should be reduced.

(a) Where failure to wear a seat belt would have made no difference – no reduction to the damages.

(b) Where less severe injuries would have resulted – a 15% reduction in damages.

(c) Where the injuries would have been prevented altogether – a 25% reduction in damages.

He also intimated that special groups of people (e.g. pregnant women, very fat people, etc.), would have to be considered on a different basis.

In general, where a case involves contributory negligence, the judge must first of all assess the damages on the basis that the plaintiff was completely innocent of any negligence. He must then decide to what extent the plaintiff was negligent (in the form of a percentage) and then make the necessary reduction.

When considering all the above today, it should be remembered that the wearing of seat belts for drivers and front seat passengers became legally compulsory with a few minor exceptions on 1st February 1983.

SHOCK

In some situations, the courts will not consider that illness caused by nervous shock is too remote and may award damages to claims. For such claims to be successful one of the following points must be proven:

1. By his action the defendant intended to shock the party who is making the claim. **Wilkinson *v.* Downton (1897)**; or
2. The shock arose as a direct consequence of the plaintiff's negligent action and the action was foreseeable.

The meaning of the word foreseeable, in this context, is best illustrated by reference to case law.

(a) Causing fear for one's own safety.

Dulieu *v.* White (1901)
White, while driving negligently, crashed into some premises in which Dulieu, a pregnant woman, was working. As a result of the shock, caused by the crash, she gave birth prematurely and the child was found to be mentally retarded. *Held.* White was liable to pay damages. By driving in this way, it could be foreseen that someone would be shocked.

(b) Threatening or injuring one's children or other relations.

Hambrook *v.* Stokes (1925)
A lady, having just left her children, noticed a runaway lorry moving in the direction she thought her children were. As a result, she suffered shock and subsequently died. Her husband brought an action for loss of services. *Held.* As the lorry moved because of the negligent application

of the handbrake and death resulted as a direct consequence of her experience, the claim was successful.

This decision should be compared with the one in:

King *v.* Phillips (1953) where a taxi-cab reversed into a small boy riding a tricycle. Although the mother could not see her son as she was seventy yards away at the time, she heard a scream and suffered shock as a result. *Held.* Strangely, her action was unsuccessful, for the damage was too remote. In these circumstances, a driver could not foresee that he would shock a mother some seventy yards away.

Hinz *v.* Berry (1970)
A married lady witnessed an accident, caused by a negligent driver. In the accident, her husband was killed and children injured. She subsequently became depressed and morbid. *Held.* By the Court of Appeal, she was entitled to damages. Had she not seen the accident, probably her condition would not have developed.

(c) Horrific accidents involving strangers.

Chadwick *v.* British Railways Board (1967)
Following a serious railway accident caused by the negligence of an employee, a volunteer helped with the rescue operation. As a result of this experience, he suffered shock. After his death his administratix claimed damages. *Held.* The defendants were liable even though the fear was not for the person's own safety nor that of one of his relations.

(d) Witnessing an event, even though physical injury to a third party could never arise.

Owens *v.* Liverpool Corporation (1939)
As a funeral cortege was proceeding to the cemetery, a negligently driven tram collided with the hearse and overturned the coffin. As a result, several of the mourners suffered shock. *Held.* By the Court of Appeal, the defendants were liable.

From the above cases, it can be summarised that where a claim is successful, damages may be awarded, but these will only be given when it can be shown that:

1. The defendant owed a duty of care to the plaintiff.

Bourhill *v.* Young (1943)
Young, a motor cyclist, drove negligently past a tram, in which a pregnant lady was travelling. Young then collided with a car and was killed. The lady heard the accident, and after getting off the tram witnessed the scene. Although Young's body had been removed, she sighted pools of blood which caused her nervous shock and subsequently she gave birth to a still born child. *Held.* Young's personal representatives were not liable – for Young owed no duty of care to her.

and

2. The shock resulted as a direct consequence of seeing or hearing what happened (see **Hambrook *v.* Stokes (1925)** above) rather than being told about it by a witness – **Benson *v.* Lee (1972)**, or reading it in a newspaper. **Guay *v.* Sun Publishing Co. (1953)**.

Since the House of Lord's decision in **McLoughlin *v.* O'Brian (1981)**, this statement needs modifying. In this case, the negligence of the defendant caused a road accident in which the plaintiff's husband and two of her children were badly injured and her daughter killed. The plaintiff was about two miles away from the scene of the accident when it occurred. When advised of the accident, she visited the survivors in hospital and as a result of seeing their injuries and hearing of the death of her daughter, she suffered nervous shock. As a result, she brought an action in negligence against the defendant. *Held.* The Court of Appeal's decision was reversed by the House of Lords and the plaintiff's action succeeded. For, the defendant should have foreseen that his negligence would cause a spouse to suffer nervous shock.

EXAMINATION QUESTIONS

Question 1
James has carried on business as a retail grocer for over twenty years in the same shop in Grantchester. Recently a supermarket has opened in the same street and, as a result, James has lost many of his customers. Advise him if he has any legal remedy in these circumstances and, if so, against whom.
(Chartered Institute of Bankers)*

Question 2
(a) When is M vicariously liable for a tort committed by N?
(b) N is a chauffeur employed by M, and when driving M's car to the railway station to meet M, the driver negligently injured O. Who can O sue for damages for this accident?

Would your answer differ if N was a taxi driver who had arranged with M to meet him at the station and drive him home in N's taxi?
(Chartered Institute of Bankers)

Question 3
A petrol tanker owned by X and driven by his employee Y was delivering petrol to Z's garage. While waiting for the tanker to be unloaded, Y lit a cigarette and threw away the ignited match. This caused an explosion, which did considerable damage to the garage premises. Is X liable to Z for this damage?
(Chartered Institute of Bankers)

Question 4
Describe the general defences available in a tort action.
(A.E.B. O-Level)

Question 5
Explain the defence of *volenti non fit injuria* in the law of tort. Illustrate your answer with examples.
(A.E.B. O-Level)

Question 6
Richard and Stephen were spectators at a motor car race. A car driven by Thomas failed to negotiate a sharp bend and left the racing track. It collided with Richard, who was seriously injured. Stephen went to assist Thomas by attempting to pull him out of his car, which was on fire. Stephen was seriously injured when doing this rescue work. The cause of the accident was the exceptionally fast speed at which Thomas was driving.

Discuss the legal rules which decide whether Richard and Stephen can claim damages for their injuries.
(Chartered Institute of Bankers)

Question 7
Arthur was a lawful spectator at an ice hockey match. During the course of the game one of the players hit the puck into the crowd and Arthur was injured in the face. May he sue for this injury?
(Chartered Institute of Bankers)

Question 8
Lift & Co. Ltd, stevedores, employed John and also hired the services of Henry, a crane driver, from his employers, Winch & Co. Ltd. While the crane was lifting a bale out of the hold of a ship, John negligently gave a signal indicating where the bale should be lowered, without checking to

see that it was safe to do so. Henry lowered the bale at that place, and injured Peter who was working there. Has Peter a right to sue Lift & Co. Ltd or Winch & Co. Ltd for damages?
(Chartered Institute of Bankers)

Question 9
John was walking along the street when a sack of cement fell from the upper storey of the Warble Warehouse. The sack hit Jack knocking him to the ground and he broke his arm. Advise John.
(A.E.B. O-Level)

Question 10
(a) Evan agreed to a 10 round boxing match with Frank, the loser to pay the winner £100. Evan won and has been paid this sum. He now finds out that his jaw was fractured in the fight.

Can Evan sue Frank for this injury?

(b) Phillip left his car, forgetting to lock it and apply the hand brake. Quentin saw the car move off slowly and jumped in to stop it, but injured himself.

Can Quentin sue Phillip for his injury?
(Chartered Institute of Bankers)*

Question 11
" 'Rescue cases' raise issues of duty, remoteness and consent." Discuss this statement.
(A.E.B. A-Level)

Question 12
What are the essential features of the tort of negligence?
(Chartered Institute of Bankers)

Question 13
Sheila finds a caterpillar in a bottle of milk purchased from Dainty Dairies Ltd.

(a) In what tort can Sheila sue and for what remedy?
(b) Describe the criminal action that can be taken against Dainty Dairies Ltd.
(c) Explain which courts would be involved in (a) and (b).
(A.E.B. O-Level)

Question 14
Jack is engaged to marry Jill, a wealthy heiress. They are to be married

in a remote country church. On his way to the wedding Jack's car breaks down and he asks Kapp, a garage owner, to repair it, explaining fully to him the urgency of his journey. Kapp does the repair work so badly that the car only travels another ten miles before breaking down again. Jack fails to reach the church and the ceremony is postponed. Jill is so hurt and angry that she now refuses to marry him. Jack has been made the laughing stock of his acquaintances and he is emotionally distressed. Advise him as to his legal position.
(Chartered Institute of Bankers)

Question 15
John drove his car negligently and collided violently with a car driven by Frank. At the time of the collision Gertrude was in the lounge of her home overlooking the road. She saw the collision clearly through the window and fainted. She became seriously ill as a result of what she had seen of this collision. Is John liable to compensate her for this illness?
(Chartered Institute of Bankers)

Question 16
What is meant by *res ipsa loquitur*?
(A.E.B. O-Level)

Question 17
At the end of Peter's garden runs a main railway line. Two trains collided and Peter, who heard the crash, immediately went to help the victims. He assisted in the rescue work for several hours and the experience caused him to suffer severe nervous shock. Is the railway company liable to him for this illness?
(Chartered Institute of Bankers)

Question 18
Dora, who was pregnant, accepted the offer of a lift for herself and her daughter, Cathy, from Brenda, a friend. Brenda stopped at a garage for some petrol. Dora and Cathy went into the office to pay while Brenda turned the car. Brenda did not look to see if anything was behind the car and reversed it into Cathy, who had come out of the office while her mother was talking to the cashier. Dora heard Cathy's screams and fainted. When Dora recovered she was told that Cathy was seriously injured and this further shock led to a miscarriage. Dora seeks your advice as to her legal position. What would that advice be?
(A.E.B. A-Level)

CHAPTER 10

DEFAMATION

DEFINITION

Defamation has been defined by Professor Winfield as "The publication of a statement which tends to lower a person in the estimation of right-thinking members of society generally; or, which tends to make them shun or avoid that person."

In the definition, the term "statement" has been interpreted to include words (written or printed), statements, gestures, effigies, caricatures, talking films (**Youssoupoff *v.* Metro Goldwyn Mayer Ltd (1934)**) and statues (**Monson *v.* Tussauds (1894)**). Furthermore, by section 1 Defamation Act, 1952, words and images broadcast for general reception by wireless or television are now treated as publications in a permanent form, and, as such, can be considered as potentially libellous. The same interpretation has since been applied to words and gestures used in the performance of a play in public by s. 4, Theatres Act, 1968.

CATEGORIES OF DEFAMATION

The tort of defamation has been divided into two major categories – libel and slander. These may be compared as follows:

LIBEL	SLANDER
A statement made in a permanent form – by writing, print, pictures, etc.	A statement made in a transitory form, usually by speech or gesture.
Not only is it a tort which can be sued on, it may also be a crime which can result in a prosecution.	It is a civil wrong only, and as such, the person making the statement can only be sued – he cannot be prosecuted.
It is actionable per se – so it is not necessary to show that financial loss has been sustained.	It is only actionable by proving financial loss except in a limited number of circumstances.

The final comparison indicates quite clearly why it is essential to establish whether a statement is a libel or a slander. For libel is actionable by itself, whereas loss has to be proved for slander.

Where a plaintiff's action is successful, he will be awarded damages by way of compensation. The level of damages awarded in an action for libel is decided upon by a jury, and, surprisingly, they do not have to indicate how they have arrived at the figure they chose. If the defendant feels that the amount is too high, then the matter may be referred to the Court of Appeal – as it was in **Blackshaw *v.* Lord and the "Daily Telegraph" Ltd (1983)**, where damages of £45,000 had been awarded to the plaintiff in a lower court. As the case was "not one of those rare and exceptional cases where the court would order a new trial or substitute a lower award", the appeal was dismissed.

PROOF OF DEFAMATION

For a plaintiff's action to be successful, he must prove the following points:

1. THE STATEMENT WAS AN UNTRUE FACT

A true statement cannot constitute the tort of defamation (e.g. where a newspaper correctly prints an article describing a person as being mentally ill and this is true because he is a resident of an institution, then the statement cannot be defamatory).

2. THE STATEMENT WAS DEFAMATORY

It is the responsibility of the judge to decide on the facts of a case as to whether the statement can be considered defamatory. If he decides it can be, then it is the jury's responsibility to say whether, in the circumstances, the statement is or is not defamatory.

Under this heading, a special category of defamation – innuendo – needs to be considered. For, on occasions, words that seem, on the face of them, to be innocent, may actually be defamatory because they have a secondary or hidden meaning. Such a statement is known as an *innuendo*.

Various precedents illustrate what this term means and how it has been applied by the courts.

Cassidy *v.* "Daily Mirror" Newspapers Ltd (1929)

A photograph of a man and a woman was published in a newspaper and underneath it was printed "Mr C. and Miss B. whose engagement has been announced". As Mr C. was already married, his wife sued the newspaper. She alleged that the words were innuendo – for they tended to indicate that she (although legally his wife), was not married to him and so was immorally cohabiting with him. *Held*. Even though the words were innocently printed (because Mr C. had told the newspaper photographer that Miss B. was his fiancée and the paper could announce his engagement), the plaintiff's action succeeded and £500 of damages were awarded. For certain of the plaintiff's friends thought after reading the newspaper, that she *was* cohabiting.

Tolley *v*. J. S. Fry & Sons Ltd (1931)
An amateur golf champion sued the defendants, who were chocolate manufacturers, because they had published an advertisement incorporating a caricature of Mr Tolley with a bar of their chocolate sticking prominently out of his pocket. Furthermore, they had printed a limerick underneath the advertisement which included both the golfer's name and the chocolate manufacturer's name. The golfer alleged an innuendo, because people would assume that he had consented to the use of his name in exchange for a financial reward, and this would have prostituted his reputation as an amateur golfer. *Held*. The advertisement was capable of being interpreted this way and so the plaintiff's action succeeded.

A case in which the words were not considered as defamatory was:

Byrne *v*. Deane (1937)
As a result of a complaint to the police, certain gaming machines were removed from a golf club. Not long afterwards, a verse appeared on a wall near to where a machine had been located, in which one line was "May he byrne in hell and rue the day!" Byrne brought an action against the Deanes (who were the proprietors of the club), alleging that the words were defamatory and that the Deanes were responsible for the words being there. *Held*. The action failed because the following test was unsuccessfully applied – "Did the words complained of tend to lower the plaintiff in the estimation of right-thinking members of society?" Here this could not be proved to the satisfaction of the court.

With regards to publications, where a plaintiff alleges innuendo, other rules have since been formulated:

(1) He must provide the court with names of people who had received the publication and had the requisite knowledge to link the article with the plaintiff. This condition may be difficult, if not impossible to comply with, especially where:

(a) the plaintiff is someone who has moved around the country; and,
(b) the article which contains the alleged innuendo has been pub-

lished in a local newspaper which is only distributed in the area to which the plaintiff has recently moved: **Fulham *v.* Newcastle Chronicle and Journal (1977).**

(2) He must prove that the words were published to a specific person, who, at the time of publication, believed that they related to the plaintiff. If the link between the plaintiff and the publication becomes apparent at a later date, the statement cannot be defamatory: **Grappelli *v.* Derek Block (Holdings) Ltd (1981).**

3. THE STATEMENT REFERRED TO THE PLAINTIFF

It must be proved that the statement referred to the plaintiff. Where the plaintiff is actually named, then this presents no difficulty, but where only a general description is given, then the plaintiff must prove that it refers to him. **J'Anson *v.* Stuart (1787).**

Generally speaking, a class of persons cannot be defamed unless the class is so small that the statement can be taken to refer to each and every one of them, e.g. Directors of a company. In this latter situation, all directors can bring an action.

Where a defendant has made a defamatory statement about a fictitious character or a person other than the plaintiff, he will still be liable to the plaintiff if a reasonable person would interpret the statement as referring to the plaintiff.

E. Hulton & Co. *v.* Jones (1910)

A newspaper article about life in Dieppe made reference to a character called Artemus Jones. Although described as a Church Warden and a resident of Peckham, he was stated to have lived with a French mistress while in Dieppe. The character was entirely fictitious, but, unfortunately, a well-known barrister and journalist had the same name. He sued the paper for libel as many of his friends thought the article referred to him. *Held.* The plaintiff's action succeeded and damages were awarded.

Newstead *v.* "London Express" Newspaper Ltd (1940)

The newspaper published an article about a thirty-year-old Camberwell man named Harold Newstead, who had been convicted of bigamy. Unfortunately, there were two people of that name and age living in Camberwell at that time. The person about whom the article did not refer sued the newspaper. *Held.* The defendants were liable and damages were awarded against them.

Note: If the above two cases were heard today, it may be possible to use section 4 Defamation Act, 1952, as a defence; i.e. the defendant had made an offer of amends, as described in Defence 5 below. However, this is only possible when it can be shown that the defendant (or his servants or agents) had taken all reasonable care regarding the publication.

Hayward *v.* Thompson and Others (1981). During the period 1970 to 1975, Hayward donated £200,000 to the Liberal Party. In 1978, an article was published in a newspaper which stated that "the names of two or more people 'connected with' an alleged murder plot had been given to the police and one was a wealthy benefactor of the Liberal Party" – although the article did not name him. A week later, a second article was published which named the benefactor. An action in libel was taken against the editor, proprietors and journalists who were responsible. *Held.* Although the second article in itself was not libellous, the first was. The two articles could be linked together and so the plaintiff's action was successful. Fifty thousand pounds in damages was awarded. The newspaper subsequently appealed against the decision, but the action was dismissed.

4. THE WORDS WERE PUBLISHED

Publication is described as the communication of the defamation to some person other than the plaintiff or the defendant's spouse. Thus, if someone tells another person that he is a rogue, and no one else is present, the statement is not defamatory. In contrast, if the same statement is made in the presence of others, it is defamatory if it is untrue.

A defendant will only be liable for a publication which he makes himself, or which he asks others to make. In some instances, liability will depend upon whether or not the defendant ought to have foreseen that his actions would lead to publication; e.g.

(a) A post card sent through the post will be presumed to have been read by post office staff (but not letters contained in sealed or unsealed envelopes).

(b) Publication, as it relates to spouses of the parties to an action in defamation, is a more complex issue. In the first instance, it does not matter whether the defendant's spouse read or did not read an item of mail before or after it had been posted. For whatever circumstances prevail, neither would amount to publication. However, with regards to the plaintiff, the position is different, for, the law presumes that the plaintiff's spouse will open mail addressed to her partner and so publication is presumed. Quite clearly, the presumption can be rebutted.

(c) Revelation of the contents of an author's letter may be held as publication, but there are occasions when such a publication will be held as privileged.

It should be noted that any repetition of a defamatory statement is considered as a new publication – and it is no defence for the person who repeats the statement to say that he did not originate it. Thus, when a defamatory statement is published in a newspaper or book, not only is the writer liable but also the printer or publisher.

With regard to booksellers and newspaper vendors, they, too, will be liable, unless they can prove:

(a) The statement was not known to be libellous.
(b) The lack of knowledge could not be attributed to negligence.
(c) The circumstances were such that they would not have suspected that the paper (or book) was libellous.

5. PROOF OF DAMAGE

In all cases of slander, the plaintiff must prove he has suffered special damage, however disgraceful the imputation and however certain it may be that it will damage his reputation. The special damage required in actions for slander must be the loss of some definite, material advantage, e.g. following publication, third parties no longer wished to enter into contracts with the plaintiff.

There are several exceptions to this general ruling and the following are actionable per se:

(a) An imputation that the plaintiff has committed a criminal offence, punishable by imprisonment.

(b) An imputation that the plaintiff is suffering from a disease likely to make others avoid him socially. (Say a contagious disease.)

(c) An imputation against a female of unchastity or adultery – Slander of Women Act, 1891.

(d) Words calculated to disparage the plaintiff in any office, profession, calling, trade or business, held or carried on by him at the time of the publication – section 2, Defamation Act, 1952.

DEFENCES AGAINST ACTIONS FOR DEFAMATION

1. JUSTIFICATION

An action based on the publication of a defamatory statement will not be successful where the defendant can prove that the statement is substantially or wholly true. Thus, it is not essential that every detail in the statement is true, provided the statement, as a whole, is accurate.

Alexander *v*. The North Eastern Railway Co. (1865)
The defendant published a notice which indicated that Alexander had been convicted of travelling on the railway without a railway ticket and refusing to pay the proper fare. The stated penalty was £9 or twenty-one days imprisonment. The latter detail was incorrect, for it should have read fourteen days. *Held*. The statement, as a whole, was true, and even though the term of imprisonment had been misstated, it did not make the notice libellous. The defence of justification was successful.

Furthermore, section 5 Defamation Act, 1952, provides that in an action for libel or slander in respect of words containing two or more distinct charges against the plaintiff, a defence of justification shall not fail by reason only that the truth of every charge is not proved, if the words not proved to be true do not materially injure the plaintiff's reputation having regard to the truth of the remaining charges.

To use a defence of justification in court is considered a dangerous one because an unsuccessful attempt to establish it may be treated as an aggravation of the original injury and so higher damages may have to be paid.

2. FAIR COMMENT

To be successful with this defence, it is necessary to establish the following points:

(a) The statement was comment (or expression), not fact.
It is generally difficult to distinguish between comment and fact.

(b) The comment was fair,
There are three considerations here:

1. *The comment must be truly stated*. For, no comment can be fair which is based upon details which are invented or misstated. At one time, it was necessary to prove that everything was true. However, by section 6 Defamation Act, 1952, in an action for defamation in respect of words consisting partly of allegations of fact and partly of expressions of opinion, a defence of fair comment shall not fail by reason only that the truth of every allegation of fact is not proved if the expression of opinion is fair comment having regard to such facts as are proved.

2. *The comment must be honest*. Here, the test is "Would an honest man, however prejudiced he may be, however exaggerated or obstinate his views, have said that which this criticism has said of what is criticised?"

Where the answer is "yes", the comment is considered honest. However, where activated by malice, a comment is considered unfair.

3. *Imputations of Corrupt Motives*. A person's moral character is not a permissible subject of adverse comment. For anyone who suggests that a person is dishonest, corrupt, immoral, untruthful, etc. must either justify the comment by proving it to be true, or show that the imputation is correct, or may be reasonably inferred from the comments made.

(c) The Subject Matter was of Public Interest.
Comments relating to the conduct of Parliament, local authorities, and trade unions fit under this heading. It may also refer to situations where a plaintiff has voluntarily submitted himself and his affairs to public criticism. Examples of this are where someone makes a public speech, or publishes a book, or presents a play – for such subject matters are, by their very nature, available for public comment.

3. ABSOLUTE PRIVILEGE

This defence protects certain statements made in circumstances where the public interest in securing a free expresion of facts or opinion outweighs the private interests of the person about whom the statement was made.

Even where a statement is false or malicious, no action can be taken if it is made:

(a) By statement in Parliament. Bill of Rights, 1689.

(b) In reports published by Parliament, for example, Hansard, Government White Papers, etc.

(c) In state communications, e.g. Communications between Officers of State which are in the ordinary course of their duty. The same privilege may apply to subordinates of the Officers of State (**Chatterton *v.* Secretary of State for India (1895)**). Where it does not apply, qualified privilege may be pleaded. (See below.)

(d) In judicial proceedings. This includes statements by a judge, jury, witnesses or advocates during proceedings which must be judicial.

(e) In fair, accurate and contemporaneous reports of public proceedings which must be judicial.

(f) In reports by a Parliamentary Commissioner.

(g) In a communication between solicitor and client.

4. QUALIFIED PRIVILEGE

There are some occasions where the public interest does not demand the complete immunity of absolute privilege, but when, nevertheless, some extended right of freedom of speech is desirable. On these occasions, the law will admit a plea of qualified privilege.

The defence will only be admitted when the statement was made without malice and with the honest belief that it was truthful. Where a statement is activated by malice (or is published more widely than it need have been), then this type of protection is not available.

This type of defence is available in the following circumstances:

(a) *Legal or Moral Duty*
This applies where the person making the statement was acting under a legal or moral duty to do so and the person about whom the statement was made either had a legal or moral duty to receive it. It is essential for both elements to be present.

Watt *v.* Longsdon (1930)
The defendant received a defamatory letter about the plaintiff alleging that he was a thief, a liar and immoral, which, in fact, was untrue. The plaintiff was employed by a company of which the defendant was a director. The defendant then showed the letter to his chairman and also to the plaintiff's wife. *Held.* Although showing the letter to his chairman was protected by qualified privilege, there was no protection against showing the letter to the plaintiff's wife. The defendant had no duty or interest to show it to her.

Sometimes the following test is used: "Would the great mass of right-minded men in the position of the defendant have considered it their duty, under the circumstances, to make the communication?" For this reason, an employer may answer questions about the character of an existing or former employee who is seeking another job. Thus, a reference may be given. **Jackson *v.* Hopperton (1864)**. An action against any referee will only be successful where it can be proved that the statement was made with malice, even if it was untrue.

(b) *Protection of a Person's Private Interests*
Even when there is no duty to make the statement, it is, nevertheless, privileged if it is made in the protection of some lawful interest of the person making it. As above, it is essential for the two-way element to be present.

(c) *Statements to the Authorities*
Letters of complaint to the police or local government officials or petitions to Parliament are included under this heading.

(d) *Reports of Parliamentary Proceedings, Judicial Proceedings or Public Meetings*

5. APOLOGY

Where a libellous action is based on a statement contained in a newspaper or periodical or broadcast over the radio or television, a defendant may plead:

(a) The publication was made without malice or gross negligence; and
(b) A full apology was published at the earliest opportunity; and
(c) Compensation has been paid into court.

This is a rarely used form of defence, for it debars using any of the other forms of defence.

6. UNINTENTIONAL DEFAMATION

This protection is now available under section 4 Defamation Act, 1952. Prior to this, the statement propounded by Russell L.J. in 1929 was applied whereby "Liability for libel does not depend on the intention of the defamer, but on the fact of defamation." The law was amended by section 4 of the above Act, which provided that "a person who has published words alleged to be defamatory of another person may, if he claims the words were published by him innocently in relation to that other person, make an offer of amends".

An offer of amends means:

(a) An offer of a suitable correction and apology; and
(b) Where copies of the defamatory statement have been distributed, an offer to take reasonable steps to notify those who have received the distributed copies that the words are alleged to be defamatory.

Two alternative situations may ensue:

1. Where the offer of amends is accepted and complied with then no legal proceedings for libel or slander shall be taken against the person making the offer.
2. Where the offer of amends is not accepted, then it is a defence to show that:

   (a) The words were published by the defendants innocently in relation to the plaintiff; and
   (b) An offer was made as soon as practicable after the defendant had received notice that they were or might be defamatory to the plaintiff; and

(c) The offer has not been withdrawn.

The onus of responsibility is on the defendant to prove these points.

These are situations which newspapers find themselves in from time to time. Should litigation result, the vital question to be answered is whether the words have been published innocently. This protection is available where the publisher has exercised all reasonable care and thereby can be held to have acted innocently and either:

(a) Did not intend to publish them of and concerning the party aggrieved, and did not know of circumstances by virtue of which they might be understood to refer to him. **Newstead *v.* "London Express" Newspapers Ltd (1940)**; or

(b) Where the words were not defamatory on the face of them and the publisher did not know of the circumstances by virtue of which they might be understood to be defamatory of the party aggrieved. **Cassidy *v.* "Daily Mirror" Newspaper Ltd (1929)**.

EXAMINATION QUESTIONS

Question 1

What is the meaning of defamation?
(Chartered Institute of Bankers)

Question 2

Is a defamatory statement made during a televised interview libel or slander? Give reasons for your answer.
(Chartered Institute of Bankers)

Question 3

(a) When is a statement defamatory?
(b) When is a defamatory statement (i) libellous; (ii) slanderous?
(Chartered Institute of Bankers)

Question 4

A defamatory statement is either a libel or a slander. Why is it important to make the distinction?
(Chartered Institute of Bankers)

Question 5

Explain the importance of (a) innuendo and (b) publication, in the law of defamation.
(A.E.B. A-Level)

Question 6

A local newspaper reported correctly that Tom Boy, a Liverpool sailor, aged 30, had been convicted of theft. This was not true of another man of the same name, age and occupation also from Liverpool. This other man claimed that he has been defamed by the newspaper. What is the legal position?
(Chartered Institute of Bankers)*

Question 7

Mr X wrote in his desk diary that his employee Y was a liar and a thief. This was untrue. Mrs X accidently read this entry. Can Y sue Mr X for damages for defamation? Would your answer differ if Mrs Y had read it?
(Chartered Institute of Bankers)

Question 8

A letter containing defamatory material about Michael is written by Basil to Stephen. Stephen leaves the letter open on his desk where it is read by Stephen's private secretary. Advise Michael.
(A.E.B. O-Level)

Question 9

Albert told Bertha that Charles had contracted venereal disease while at university three years ago. This statement is a wicked lie. Can Charles sue Albert for making this defamatory statement?
(Chartered Institute of Bankers)

Question 10

(a) What is meant by an "innuendo" in the law of defamation? What purpose does an innuendo serve? What kinds of innuendo are there? When must an innuendo be pleaded?

(b) In what circumstances are statements subject to absolute privilege? What is the effect of a successful plea of absolute privilege? How does this differ from the effect of a plea of qualified privilege?
(I.C.S.A.)

Question 11

In the course of a debate in the House of Commons, James called Ian, another Member of Parliament, "a scoundrel who has cheated innocent people out of large sums of money". This statement was reported in "The Clarion", a newspaper, in an editorial which hinted that Ian had connections with criminals. "The Clarion" frequently attacked Ian's party and its views. James later repeated this statement to the member-

ship committee of the club to which both he and Ian belonged. Advise Ian.
(A.E.B. A-Level)

Question 12

X applied for employment with Y Co Ltd, and Z furnished a written testimonial on his behalf. X failed to obtain the appointment and alleges that this was due to untrue statements made by Z in the testimonial. Consider his prospects of successfully suing Z for damages for defamation.
(Chartered Institute of Bankers)

Question 13

(a) In a public lecture Bishop said to the audience, "Roe, the present Chairman of the Wet Fish Board would be at home in any prison he visits. I expect him to be in one very shortly." Advise Roe on his legal position.

(b) Abbott was one of the 25 members of the "Estoverians", a local organisation. Prior, the editor of a local paper, wrote in an article, "It is well known that Estoverians are all loose-living, self-indulgent and immoral." Abbott is greatly distressed by this and fears his business may suffer. Advise him as to his legal position.
(A.E.B. A-Level)

CHAPTER 11

NEGOTIABLE INSTRUMENTS

INTRODUCTION

Many years ago, the most common medium used to settle trading debts was a bill of exchange. The parties to such bills adopted certain rules and regulations which defined their relative responsibilities and liabilities and these became known as the "Law of the Merchants". Eventually, this law was codified as the Bills of Exchange Act, 1882. This statute has recently celebrated one hundred years of existence and, in fact, has stood the test of time very well, for only minor amendments have been made to it during its life time.

Since the last century, the cheque (a special type of bill of exchange), has started to be used more and more as a medium of settling debts and today it predominates. It became obvious that the provisions for cheques made in the Bills of Exchange were no longer adequate and that a further statute was needed to up-date the law relating to this type of instrument. The result was the Cheques Act, 1957.

To what extent these statutes will cover future developments remains to be seen. But almost certainly new statutes will be needed as more and more transactions are settled by plastic cards (e.g. credit cards) and computers (e.g. the SWIFT system of settling international banking indebtedness, where it is available).

As we will see in this chapter, bills of exchange and cheques are special types of negotiable instruments. In the first instance, though, it is necessary to appreciate the difference between a chose in possession and a chose in action. It is particularly important to know what the term "chose in action" means, because a negotiable instrument is a type of chose in action.

PERSONAL PROPERTY

The term "personal property" applies to any type of property which is not freehold. In law, it is conveniently divided into two categories:

1. *Chose in possession, and*
2. *Chose in action.*

CHOSE IN POSSESSION

This relates to tangible, moveable objects such as books, stamp collections, cars, etc., whereby a person can actually possess them and/or get enjoyment from them. In most cases, ownership is transferred merely by delivery. However, with certain types of chose in possession, a register of owners is maintained, and to effect a transfer legally, the name of the registered owner must be changed in the special register – e.g. transfers of ships, cars, etc.

CHOSE IN ACTION

In contrast, there are certain types of property which are not recognisable as tangible objects. These include debts, shares in a company, contractual rights, etc. With these types, the owners' right to it can only be obtained by means of an action. Although choses in action can be classified (e.g. into patents, copyright, trademarks, etc.), the only type that is described in this book is a negotiable instrument. This is a very special type of chose in action, for it can be transferred (negotiated) without the usual formalities needed for the transfer of most types of choses in action.

ASSIGNMENT OF A CHOSE IN ACTION

In general, when a chose in action is transferred (assigned), one party, the transferee, will want to have the rights of the other transferred to him. The transfer of rights is achieved by way of an assignment and applies to most types of chose in action.

If a transferee wants to take a legal assignment, he must conform with s. 136 Law of Property Act, 1925. Thus, for an assignment to be legal, it must be:

1. In writing and signed by the assignor (transferor), and be,
2. Absolute and not by way of a charge only, and
3. Express notice should be given to the debtor (trustee or other person) who holds funds for the assignor.

Even though assignments suffer from certain defects, they are still frequently carried out, e.g. transfers of leasehold land are effected by way of an assignment. The major defects are:

1. Both legal and equitable assignments take place subject to equities. Thus, if, at the time of assignment, there was a defect in title, then because the assignor had no title, the assignee will have no title. (The way in which negotiability overcomes this problem is described later.)

2. An equitable assignee cannot enforce his rights without the concurrence of the legal owner.

3. An equitable assignee cannot give a good discharge without the concurrence of the legal owner.
4. If s. 136 has not been complied with, then the assignee cannot sue in his own name for he will only have acquired equitable rights.

Because of these defects, merchants did not like to take an assignment in settlement of a debt owed to them. Instead, they were looking for a form of payment which would not be affected by any of the above defects, and so they developed what came to be known as negotiable instruments.

DEVELOPMENT OF NEGOTIABLE INSTRUMENTS

After economies had evolved out of the barter system, all debts were settled by precious metals, as this was a convenient and trusted medium of payment. However, because of the additional risks of carrying out precious metal settlements, merchants looked for other less risky methods. Assignment of debts was one method, but it suffered from the series of defects mentioned above. Furthermore, the common law, which existed at that time, was considered to be very cumbersome, and did not always protect the merchants' best interests. Thus, the merchants developed their own systems and procedures, and out of this came a document which was transferable and could be passed between parties free from equities. It became known as a negotiable instrument. Customary law relating to such instruments was recognised as early as the 14th century and in the United Kingdom, the "Law of the Merchants" was fully incorporated into the common law during the period 1756 to 1788.

Eventually, the law relating to negotiable instruments was formally codified by an act known as the Bills of Exchange Act, 1882. This has stood the test of time, and, although there have been several minor amendments since it became law, there has only been one new major statute. This was the Cheques Act, 1957, and was written in recognition of the fact that cheques rather than bills of exchange were predominantly used to settle debts, and that some of the practices which the B.E.A. 1882 applied to bills (and cheques) were not strictly relevant for modern usage of cheques. For example, prior to 1957, all cheques had to be endorsed before they could be paid into a bank account, even if the payee was putting them into his own account. After the Cheques Act had been passed, this practice was no longer deemed necessary for cheques, except in certain situations. Thus, the amount of time previously spent by collecting and paying bankers in ensuring that this procedural step had been carried out, and having to process the return of cheques which had not been endorsed, was immediately saved.

Note: This chapter will contain many references to various sections of the Bills of Exchange Act, 1882. Where they appear, then the full title is not repeated, just the respective section is quoted, e.g. Section 29 or s. 29. The Cheques Act is referred to as C.A.

CHARACTERISTICS OF NEGOTIABLE INSTRUMENTS

1. The holder of a negotiable instrument, for the time being, can sue on the bill in his own name.

2. The transferee takes any negotiable instrument free from equities and from the rights of third parties, provided he has no notice of these (if they exist) at the time of transfer to him.

3. If a transferee takes a bill in good faith and, for value, he can acquire a better title than the transferor had. Thus, the transferee can be a holder in due course (see later), and will be unaffected by previous defects in title, provided he was not aware of any defect at the time the bill was transferred to him.

4. It is not necessary for a new holder to give notice to previous holders in order to establish a good title. In this respect, the procedure differs from most types of assignments for they have to comply with s. 136 Law of Property Act, 1925.

5. Title to a negotiable instrument is transferable by delivery (if a bearer instrument) or by endorsement and delivery (if an order instrument). (For the difference between bearer and order see below.)

EXAMPLES OF NEGOTIABLE INSTRUMENTS

Although the list below is not a comprehensive one, it does, in fact, give an indication of the most important types.

(a) Bills of Exchange.
(b) Cheques – provided they have not been crossed "not negotiable".
(c) Promissory notes – promises to pay at a future date.
(d) Treasury Bills
(e) Bearer Bonds.

EXAMPLES OF INSTRUMENTS WHICH ARE NOT NEGOTIABLE

This list would be much longer than the above if the full range was quoted. But the ones which many believe to possess the characteristics of negotiability, but which, in fact, do not, are:

(a) Insurance Policies
(b) Deeds of a House
(c) Postal Orders
(d) Money Orders
(e) Share Certificates.

DISTINCTION BETWEEN NEGOTIABLE AND NON-NEGOTIABLE INSTRUMENTS

If a negotiable instrument, such as a bearer bond, is transferred by someone other than the owner to another person, and this person takes it in good faith and for value without notice of defect in title, the bearer bond cannot be recovered by the true owner. **London Joint Stock Bank *v.* Simmons (1892)**. In contrast, if the instrument had not been negotiable, because it was, say, a share certificate, and it was transferred in the same way, then the true owner can recover it when the unlawful transfer is discovered.

The most commonly used negotiable instruments are bills of exchange and cheques and the remainder of this chapter is devoted to them.

BILLS OF EXCHANGE

EXAMPLE OF A BILL OF EXCHANGE

EXAMPLE 1

64, Sherwood Road,
Whitchurch.
4.3.1988

£1,000
At sight pay T. Foy or order the sum of one thousand pounds for value received.

S. Reddington,
32 Lever Grove,
Chester

M. Wroe

PARTIES TO A BILL OF EXCHANGE

There are three parties in the above example. They are:

M. Wroe – he is known as the drawer of the bill. It is he who writes out and signs the bill.

S. Reddington – he is known as the drawee of the bill. The bill is drawn upon him and it is he who is actually going to be asked to pay the sum of a thousand pounds.

Note: This is the simplest type of bill of exchange, for it is drawn payable at sight. It means that, as soon as S. Reddington sees the bill, he must pay it. The situation which develops if he refuses to pay will be described later.

T. Foy – he is known as the payee of the bill. The bill is drawn in his favour and it is he who will eventually receive the payment of one thousand pounds – unless he passes the bill on to someone else by negotiation (i.e. transfer).

Note: By a procedure described as endorsement, T. Foy can transfer (negotiate) the bill to another person.

THE USE OF BILLS OF EXCHANGE

EXAMPLE 2

Taverna Pedro.
Barcelona.
1.3.1987

£1,000
Pay J. Adereti or order the sum of one thousand pounds at sight.

Mrs R. Adu, C. Cuadrado
146, Queen Victoria Street,
Lagos, Nigeria

Let us say that Cuadrado, the proprietor of Taverna Pedro in Barcelona, trades with Mrs Adu and Adereti, both of whom are Nigerian and live in Lagos. Mrs Adu buys wine from him, which clearly she must pay for and, Adereti, sells Cuadrado cocoa, which he, in due course, will want to be paid for.

Centuries ago, the method of settling these separate debts would have been for Mrs Adu to send one thousand pounds worth of gold to Cuadrado in Spain, while Cuadrado, perhaps on the same boat that was doing the reverse trip, would send one thousand pounds of gold to Adereti in Nigeria. In those days, this procedure was very cumbersome (and risky – pirates!) and to eliminate the problem, the merchants developed a medium of settlement which did not, of itself, have an intrinsic value. This medium of settlement (effectively a piece of paper) which developed was the bill of exchange. The beauty of it was that it enabled Cuadrado (in Spain) to instruct Mrs Adu (in Nigeria) to pay a sum of money to Adereti (another resident of Nigeria). In a way, two separate debts were being settled with one piece of paper. In practice, Cuadrado would draw the bill and send it by post to Adereti, the payee. As this was a sight bill, it would be in his own interest to present the bill to Mrs Adu for payment as soon as possible after he had received it. Then, assuming she pays, all inter-party indebtedness would be cancelled.

DEFINITION OF A BILL OF EXCHANGE

By s. 3(1), a bill of exchange is an unconditional order in writing, addressed by one person to another, signed by the person giving it, requiring the person to whom it is addressed to pay, on demand, or at a fixed, or determinable future time, a sum certain in money to or to the order of a specified person or to bearer.

This definition, as it stands, is difficult to understand, but if it is applied to Example 1, the constitutent elements of the definition should be understood.

An Unconditional Order

A bill must have no conditions attached to it. If Example 1 had read "Pay T. Foy on condition that he delivers a Barclays Bank P.L.C., certificate for 500 ordinary shares . . ." this would be conditional and invalidate the document as a bill.

Furthermore, the bill must be an order, not a mere request. For it was held in **Hamilton *v*. Spottiswoode (1849)** that a document containing the words "We hereby authorise you to pay on our account to the order of . . . £6,000" was not a valid bill.

In Writing

A bill can be completed in pen, pencil, ink, in handwriting or typescript and it is still valid. Nowhere in the definition does it state what the bill should be written on. Over the years, this has enabled jokers and aggrieved parties to complete bills of exchange (and cheques) on items such as cows, eggs, planks, fish, etc., and these are still legally valid.

Addressed By One Person To Another

A bill must be directed from one person (known as the drawer – M. Wroe) to another person (known as the drawee – S. Reddington). These parties must be different people, for, where they are the same (e.g. in a banker's draft where the bank is both drawer and drawee), special rules are applied to them as outlined in the Bills of Exchange and Cheques Act.

Signed By the Person Giving It

As will be seen later on, no person can be liable on a bill unless they have signed it. Because of this, primary liability, initially, must rest with the giver of the bill (the drawer – M. Wroe), and so he must sign it (or his agent). A minor may draw a bill of exchange, but if he refuses to pay it when presented to him, payment cannot be enforced against him even if the bill is for necessaries. **Re Soltykoff (1891)**.

Requiring the Person to Whom It Is Addressed To Pay

According to the previous clause, by signing the bill, the drawer assumes primary liability. This clause, though, refers to the drawee (S. Reddington), for a bill is addressed to him. A sight bill will be sent to him for payment alone. Most tenor bills (i.e. bills which are drawn for payment in the future), have to be presented upon him for acceptance in the first place. Upon acceptance, he assumes primary liability – and the drawer then becomes secondarily liable – i.e. liable only if the drawee defaults. (See Example 5 for a tenor bill.)

Bills may be addressed to more than one person (e.g. S. Reddington, H. Reddington and M. Reddington). Bills drawn in this way must be accepted by all of them, unless one or several have authority to act for all. In contrast, a bill drawn in the alternative (e.g. S. Reddington or H. Reddington or M. Reddington), is invalid . . .s. 6(2).

A minor can be the drawee of a bill, but if he does not honour it, it cannot be enforced against him even if it represents a payment for necessaries. **Re Soltykoff (1891)**.

To Pay On Demand

The payee, T. Foy (or holder), of the bill must present it to the drawee of the bill (S. Reddington) for payment. When presented to him, the drawee must pay it at that time, and if he does not or will not pay, then the holder may take recourse against the drawer or any prior endorser, provided the holder carries out certain procedures which should follow after dishonour.

Note: Example 1 is a sight (demand) bill.

To Pay at a Fixed or Determinable Future Time

In this situation, the bill is payable in the future, either at a fixed time (e.g. payable 31.12.1993) see Example 4, or a determinable future time (e.g. three months after acceptance by the drawee), see Example 5. These terms are fully described later. So, on the due date the payee (or holder) must present the bill on the drawee for payment and, if he does not or will not pay, then the holder will ask the drawer or any prior endorser to pay, subject to the holder having carried out the necessary procedures concerning dishonour.

A Sum Certain in Money
A bill must be drawn in units of currency (e.g. pounds and pence, U.S. dollars and cents, etc.), to be valid. It cannot refer to tons of coal, stock exchange securities, etc.

It can contain an interest clause such as ". . . £10,000 plus interest at the rate of 10% per annum between the date of acceptance and payment" or be payable in stages such as "Pay £15,000 in equal instalments on 28.2.87, on 28.3.87 and on 28.4.87." According to Section 9(2), if the words and figures on a bill differ, then the words have priority. Furthermore, it is permissible to indicate from which account the holder should be paid, e.g. No. 1 account, No. 2 account, Office Account, etc.

To or To the Order of A Specified Person or to Bearer
Payment under the terms of the bill must be made to someone, and this can either be to:

(a) One particular person only – which means it cannot be transferred; e.g. "Pay T. For only".

(b) To a person's order (see your own cheque book if you have one) – which allows the Bill to be transferred by endorsement and delivery, e.g. Pay T. Foy or order – then endorsed by T. Foy and transferred by him.

(c) To bearer – which allows the Bill to be transferred merely by delivery – e.g. "Pay bearer" or "Pay T. Foy or bearer".

(d) To joint payees (e.g. T. Foy and A. Foy) or alternative payees (e.g. T. Foy or A. Foy). Section 7(2).

NON-EXISTENT/FICTITIOUS PARTIES TO A BILL

The majority of Bills of Exchange will be drawn on and payable to real people. Occasionally, though, the drawee or payee may be either fictitious or non-existent. This situation, as regards the payee, has been provided for in s. 7(3), which indicates that such Bills may be treated as payable to bearer. However, this does not answer the question of what is meant by "non-existent" and "fictitious", and to appreciate the difference, reference can be made to case law.

Non-existent Payee
This is someone of whose existence the drawer is unaware when he makes out the bill. The decision in **Clutton v. Attenborough (1897)** illustrates the principles which may be applied. A fraudulent clerk made out a

cheque to a person whose name he had invented and obtained his employer's signature as drawer. *Held.* The payee was a non-existent person and thus the cheque was payable to bearer. This was so, even though the drawer believed the payee was real.

Fictitious Payee

This is someone of whose existence the drawer is aware, but who was not intended by the drawer to receive payment. Consider the decision in **Bank of England *v.* Vagliano Brothers (1891)**. The Vagliano Brothers were in the habit of accepting Bills of Exchange drawn by foreign correspondents in favour of P. & Co. of Constantinople. Vagliano's fraudulent clerk forged the drawer's signature and the payee's endorsement (P. & Co.) and cashed the bills at the Bank of England. *Held.* The bills were bearer bills (irrespective of the forged endorsements) because the drawer (i.e. the clerk) never intended P. & Co. to receive payment. Therefore, the payee was fictitious, even though the name was actually borne by someone.

ACCEPTANCE OF A BILL OF EXCHANGE

It is the drawee who will be asked to accept a Bill of Exchange. However, it should be remembered that not all bills have to be sent for acceptance. For sight bills are only presented for payment and bills drawn payable at fixed future times do not legally have to be sent for acceptance – although in practice, the majority are, in order to get the drawee's liability on the bill. This latter point is of major importance, for until the drawee has accepted the bill, he is not liable on it. For primary liability originally lies with the drawer. After acceptance, the drawee assumes primary liability and the drawer can only be considered as secondarily liable – i.e. if the drawee does not pay on the due date, then a claim can be made on the drawer, provided the necessary procedures for dishonour have been followed by the holder.

Some bills are drawn payable at, say, thirty days after sight, i.e. at a determinable future time. Thus, until this type of bill has been sighted (accepted), the date of payment cannot be established. The minimum requirement for a valid acceptance is the signature of the drawee, and, although acceptance is usually effected on the face of the bill, it can be carried out on the reverse. Section 17(2).

TYPES OF ACCEPTANCE

By s. 19, an acceptance may either be general or qualified.

GENERAL ACCEPTANCE

This type of acceptance assents, without qualification, to the order of drawer. Thus, the drawee makes no attempt to alter the terms of the bill. Examples of general acceptances are (a) the drawee's signature only, (b) his signature plus the word accepted. The date may also be added to either of the examples.

QUALIFIED ACCEPTANCE

This type of acceptance varies the effect of the bill as drawn and may be done in any of the following ways:

(a) *Conditional*, e.g. "Accepted payable on delivery of a certificate for 1,000 Barclays Bank P.L.C. ordinary shares,"

(b) *Partial*, e.g. An acceptance to pay part only of the amount for which the bill was drawn. So, if Example 5 had been accepted for £250, this would be a partial acceptance.

(c) *Local*. An acceptance to pay at a particular specified place. So, if Example 5 was "accepted payable at Barclays Bank P.L.C., Victoria Street, Liverpool, and there only" or "accepted . . . and not elsewhere" – this would be a local acceptance. It should be noted, though, that where a bill is accepted payable at Barclays Bank P.L.C., Victoria Street, Liverpool, then this is a general acceptance.

(d) *Time*. An acceptance to pay either at a later date or an earlier date than that for which the bill was drawn. Clearly, the former is more likely, for it would be most unusual for a drawee to reduce the tenor of a bill. So if, for example with regards to Example 1, S. Reddington accepted the bill payable six months after sight or 20 days after sight, either would be an acceptance qualified as to time.

(e) *Parties*. Earlier it was stated that a bill could be drawn on more than one party. If some accepted but not all of them, then this is a qualified acceptance – unless one or several of the parties has been given the authority to accept for all of them.

In practice, an unqualified (general) acceptance would be looked for. If this was not given by the drawee, the bill should be treated as dishonoured for non-acceptance and the appropriate action taken by the holder of the bill – i.e. he must give notice of dishonour to all previous parties if their liability is to be retained. The same action should be taken if a bill, although accepted, is dishonoured for non-payment – again to preserve rights against the prior parties. If the bill is a foreign one, then the additional action of protest needs to be carried out. (For explanations of the terms "dishonour" and "protest", see later.)

ENDORSEMENT (INDORSEMENT)

The procedures necessary to complete a valid endorsement and the various types of endorsement are defined in sections 32–35 inclusive. Basically, to be valid, the endorsement must be of the entire bill and be signed by the endorser on the bill itself. The first person who may endorse a bill is the payee. In carrying out this action, the payee is known as the endorser, while the person the bill is passed on to is known as the endorsee. In theory, this sequence of events could continue indefinitely, but, in practice, endorsements are rarely seen today. The standard types of endorsement are:

(a) *Blank*. Here, no endorsee is specified, and, therefore, the bill becomes payable to bearer after endorsement. For example, it would simply involve T. Foy (in Example 1) putting his signature on the back of the bill.

(b) *Special*. Here, the payee (or endorser) specifies the person to whom, or to whose order, the bill is to be payable. In our example, T. Foy may want to pass the bill on to W. Holmes (or W. Holmes or order). Thus, he would write one of these alternatives on the back of the cheque and then add his signature. This now means that if W. Holmes wants to pass the bill on to someone else, he must add his signature to the instrument, endorsing it by using any of the three available methods, e.g. (a), (b) or (c).

(c) *Restrictive*. Here, the endorsement will indicate that the bill is to be transferred to one party only and, therefore, when given, it prohibits further transfer (negotiation) of the bill. As an example, T. Foy may endorse the bill "Pay P Hayes only" and then add his signature. Further examples are "Pay Lloyds Bank P.L.C. for the account S. Entwistle" or "Pay Lloyds Bank for collection".

(d) *Conditional*. According to s. 33, the payer of an instrument which is or appears to be conditionally endorsed may safely disregard the condition because payment to the endorsee is valid irrespective of whether the condition has been met or not. This affords protection to the drawee for he can pay an instrument endorsed "Pay A. Gerrard or order on his marriage to B. Phillips, signed T. Foy" and there will be no recourse to the drawee (S. Reddington) even if the marriage has not taken place. A further example of a conditional endorsement is when the payee or a holder, after endorsing the bill, adds the words "sans recours" (without recourse).

TIME OF PAYMENT OF A BILL

Sections 10 to 14 define and describe the computation of time of payment and this will depend upon how the bill was drawn in the first place.

DEMAND BILLS

A bill is payable on demand where it is expressed to be payable on demand or at sight, or upon presentment, or where no time for payment is expressed. The following is an example of such a bill.

EXAMPLE 3

18, Mary St,
Wigan
4.4.87

£500
On demand,* Pay T. Coleman or order five hundred pounds, value received.

P. Beresford F. Case
28, The Parade, Southport

*Or at sight, or on presentment, or where nothing is mentioned. (These are alternatives.)

Such bills should be presented for payment "within a reasonable" time of issue or alternatively negotiated in order to retain the liability of the drawer. Thus, if Coleman wishes to retain Case's liability on the bill, he should present it to Beresford for payment within a reasonable time of issue or endorse it and deliver it to someone else. If the bill has been endorsed by Coleman (and other parties), the endorsee should either endorse it again or present it to Beresford for payment within a reasonable time if the liability of the drawer and prior endorsers is to be retained.

BILLS PAYABLE AT A FUTURE TIME

These types of bills are commonly referred to as tenor or usance bills. Sometimes they require acceptance to establish the due date of payment, whereas others do not require acceptance because they are drawn payable at a fixed future date. (In practice, though, these are often sent for acceptance because until someone signs a bill of exchange, they cannot be liable on it. Therefore, a holder will often present such a bill to the drawee for acceptance to establish the drawee's liability on the bill.)

FIXED FUTURE TIME

An example of such a bill is:

EXAMPLE 4

33 Bridge St,
St Helens.
14.2.87

£500
On 31st December 1993, Pay M. Stokoe or order five hundred pounds, value received.

J. Dorgan — I. Hargreaves
84, Hospital Rd,
Southport

DETERMINABLE FUTURE TIME

Examples of such bills are those drawn payable at, say:

(a) 90 days after date (i.e. date of the bill) or,
(b) 3 months after sight. (See Example 5) or,
(c) 90 days after the death of O. Benson or,
(d) On the death of M. Murphy.

Note: The last two illustrations are valid because they are events which are certain to happen.

EXAMPLE 5

16, Worcester Rd,
Bolton
5.8.87

£500
Pay P. Carney or order three months after sight the sum of five hundred pounds, value received.

G. Walker — W. Farrell
84 Moss Bank Way, Southport

Where bills are drawn payable at, say:

(a) 90 days after M. Egan's marriage, or,
(b) 90 days after M. S. Titanic arrives in New York.

They are invalid, because the events might or might not happen. Therefore, there is no certainty here, and, in law, they are considered as contingencies. Even if the event does happen, it does not cure the defect.

COMPUTATION OF TIME OF PAYMENT

As we saw in the previous section, some bills are drawn payable upon demand (or at sight or upon presentment), while others are payable at fixed or determinable future times. It is s. 14 which indicates how the time of payment is computed for bills drawn payable in the future.

By s. 14(1), if a bill falls due for payment on a Saturday, Sunday or Bank Holiday (i.e. days when most banks and factories are closed), then the bill falls due for payment on the next working day and should be presented on that day.

By s. 14(2), the date of the drawing of the bill, or its acceptance or the happening of a specified event (e.g. death of a stated person) should be excluded in computing the due date of payment: e.g. if a bill is drawn payable 30 days after sight, and acceptance takes place on 1st January, the bill becomes due for payment on 31st January (not 30th January).

On a small number of occasions, a bill drawn payable at a fixed period after sight may not be accepted when presented for acceptance: s. 14(3) deals with this situation. For, if the bill is not accepted, time will begin to run from the date of noting or protesting, whichever of these actions has been carried out.

Finally, by s. 14(4), the word "month" means calendar month. Therefore, a bill payable "three months after date" and dated 4.1.87 is due for payment on 4.4.87. Care should be exercised when bills are drawn (or sighted) on the 29th, 30th or 31st of a month. For what happens if a bill drawn payable three months after sight is accepted on the 30th of November? It is not payable on the 30th of February because no such date exists. Such bills will be payable on the 28th of February in normal circumstances (or 29th of February in leap years) subject to these being working days.

BEARER/ORDER BILLS

Bearer Bills

A bill is payable to bearer when it is expressed to be so payable, or where the only or last endorsement is in blank, as the following examples illustrate.

(1) Pay bearer.

(2) Pay M. Beeby or order . . . which has simply been endorsed by M. Beeby's signature.

(3) Pay R. Walker or order . . . which has been endorsed "Pay D. Bessant, R. Walker (signature)" and then endorsed by D. Bessant using his signature alone.

Such bills are negotiated merely by delivery s. 31(2).

Order Bills

An order bill is expressed to be so payable (e.g. "Pay N. Burrows or order") or which is expressed to be payable to a particular person (e.g. "Pay N. Burrows") and does not contain words prohibiting transfer or indicating an intention that it should not be transferable. Such bills are negotiated by endorsement and delivery s. 31(3).

There are certain types of bill which are neither bearer nor order. These are bills which, after a person's name contain words which prohibit transfer or indicate an intention that the bill should not be transferable, viz.

(1) Pay J. Gray only.
(2) Pay B. Wrigley personally.

HOLDER

By s. 2, this is the payee or endorsee of a bill who is in possession of it, or the bearer thereof. Thus, neither the drawer nor drawee can ever be a holder. The first holder will be the payee of an order bill, and if a bill is specially or restrictively endorsed, the endorsee will become the holder. If an order bill is endorsed in blank, or was originally drawn to bearer, then the bearer of the bill, who is in possession of it, is the holder.

HOLDER FOR VALUE

By s. 27(2), a holder for value is the holder of a bill upon which value has, at some time, been given – not necessarily by the holder himself.

Value (consideration or valuable consideration) was defined in **Currie *v.* Misa (1875)** and its meaning has been described in the Contract chapter.

The concept of value must be compared with a situation where a bill is transferred without consideration, e.g. when it is being given as a present or a gift.

To help understand the terms "holder" and "holder for value", consider the following illustrations. In these and all later descriptions relating to bills of exchange, it will be assumed that all bills have been signed by the respective parties and, when endorsed, this has been carried out specially.

A will be the drawer
B will be the drawee
C will be the payee
E (F, G, etc.) will be the endorsers who, if the bill is further transferred, become endorsees
V means value has been given
P means the bill has been transferred as a present or gift.

1. $A \xrightarrow{P} B \xrightarrow{P} C \xrightarrow{P} D \xrightarrow{P} E$

E here can only be a holder as value has never been given.

2. $A \xrightarrow{V} B \xrightarrow{V} C \xrightarrow{P} D \xrightarrow{P} E$

E here is a holder for value, as value has, at sometime, been given, but not by E.

3. $A \xrightarrow{V} B \xrightarrow{V} C \xrightarrow{V} D \xrightarrow{P} E$

E is a holder for value, for the reasons stated in 2.

4. $A \xrightarrow{V} B \xrightarrow{V} C \xrightarrow{P} D \xrightarrow{V} E$

E is a holder for value, as value has, at some time, been given on the bill. But note in this example that value has also been given by E himself. We will see in the next section that because E has given value, he may have become a holder in due course.

HOLDER IN DUE COURSE

By s. 29, this is someone who has taken a bill.

Complete and regular on the face of it under the following conditions:

1. That he became the holder of it before it was overdue and,
2. Without notice that it had previously been dishonoured, if such was the fact and,

3. That he took the bill in good faith and for value, and,
4. At the time the bill was negotiated to him he had no notice of any defect in the title of the person who negotiated it.

An explanation of this definition is necessary, for it goes to the heart of negotiability. Taking each point in sequence:

Introduction. All essential details must appear on the bill so that it fully complies with the terms of the definition contained in s. 3(1). Furthermore, it must not bear a forgery of a signature either on the front of it or the back. Front and back are considered as the face!

Point 1. It is impossible to become a holder in due course if at the time a person comes into possession of it, it is either overdue (i.e. out of date) or it is stale (i.e. it is a sight bill and has been in circulation for an unreasonable length of time).

Point 2. If a person takes a bill knowing it to have been previously dishonoured (this can happen where a sight bill has previously been presented to the drawee and he has refused to pay it, and a reason for dishonour has been noted on the bill. Then the bill is transferred to another party who can see the note on the bill), it follows that the transferee in these circumstances cannot be a holder in due course.

Point 3. When taking the bill, value must be given for it by the current holder. Furthermore, it must not have been obtained by way of fraud or illegal action, for either of these are considered to be bad faith.

Point 4. The bill must be negotiated to the holder (i.e. endorsed and delivered to him if the bill is payable to order or simply delivered if the bill is payable to bearer). At the same time, the negotiation should have taken place without the holder having any notice of a defect in title.

Note: "Defect in title" must be differentiated from "no title".

Defect in Title

When a bearer bill or an order bill, which has been properly endorsed by the holder, is stolen or lost and then passed on to subsequent parties, then a defect in title has occurred. (Note here there is no forgery). If such bills are negotiated, then, provided subsequent parties are unaware of this defect at the time the bill is transferred to them (and satisfy all the other considerations of section 29), they can become a holder in due course.

No Title
If an order bill is stolen prior to endorsement, and the thief forges an endorsement, then no one can acquire a good title to this instrument because it would not be complete and regular on the face of it. Thus, any subsequent party to the bill has "no title" and can never become a holder in due course. (Persons who take such bills are known as wrongful possessors and only have limited rights on the bill.)

The advantages of someone being able to set himself up as a holder in due course are the ability to:

1. Sue on the bill in his own name; and
2. Enforce payment against all prior parties; and
3. Hold the bill free from defects in title (of other parties); and
4. Pass on a perfect title.

An illustration of the powers of a holder in due course and the limited rights of a wrongful possessor is given in the Cheques section of this chapter.

It should be noted that a payee can never become a holder in due course. **R. E. Jones Ltd *v.* Waring and Gillow Ltd (1926)**. The reason for this is that a bill is issued to a payee not negotiated to him – and, as explained earlier, to become a holder in due course, a bill must be negotiated to the holder.

COMPARISON OF HOLDER, HOLDER FOR VALUE AND HOLDER IN DUE COURSE

Consider the four examples shown in the section relating to Holder for Value, on the assumption that B dishonours the bill by non-payment and the appropriate notice of dishonour has been given.

In Example 4, E was a holder in due course and so he has the right to sue all parties on the bill.

In Examples 3 and 2, E was a holder for value. As such, he has the right to sue all parties on the bill prior to the last giving of value. Thus, in Example 3, E may sue C, B or A. Whereas in Example 2, E may only sue B or A. Two points are immediately apparent from this comparison:

(a) A holder for value, because he has not given value himself, will be in a weaker position than a holder in due course, as the latter will have more parties to sue.

(b) The positioning of the last giving of value dictates the number of parties from whom the holder for value can recover. If the last giving of value was way back along the chain, the ability to recover would be severely restricted.

In Example 1, E cannot sue anyone – no one received value, all the parties having received the bill as a present. E is simply a holder and not a holder for value.

LIABILITY OF PARTIES TO A BILL

The Drawer – section 55(1)
By drawing the bill, he engages that:

1. On due presentment, the bill will be accepted and paid according to its tenor.
2. If the bill is dishonoured, he will compensate the holder or any endorser who is compelled to pay it, provided the proper dishonour proceedings have been followed.
3. He is precluded from denying to a holder in due course the existence of the payee and his capacity to endorse.

The Drawee (Acceptor) – section 54
Immediately upon acceptance, the drawee becomes primarily liable. By accepting, he engages that:

1. The bill will be paid according to its tenor (i.e. the terms and time as drawn).
2. He is precluded from denying to a holder in due course the existence of the drawer. the genuineness of his signature, and his capacity to draw the bill and also the capacity of the payee to endorse, but not the genuineness of the payee's endorsement.

The Endorser(s) – section 55(2)
These are persons, including the payee, who endorse an order bill to effect a transfer of it. By endorsing, he engages that:

1. On due presentment the bill will be accepted and paid according to its tenor and that if it is dishonoured, he will compensate the holder and any subsequent endorser who is compelled to pay it, provided the proper dishonour proceedings have been followed and,
2. He is precluded from denying to a holder in due course the genuineness and regularity in all respects of the drawer's signature and all previous endorsements, and,
3. He is precluded from denying to his immediate or subsequent endorsee that the bill is a valid bill to which he has good title.

Order of Liability

1. Prior to acceptance, the drawer is primarily liable.

2. After acceptance, the drawee becomes primarily liable. The drawer and endorsers being joint and several sureties for payment. However, to retain their liability in the event of dishonour by non-payment by the drawee, the appropriate notice of dishonour must be given.

INLAND AND FOREIGN BILLS

By s. 4(1), an inland bill is a bill which is, on the face of it, purporting to be:

(a) both drawn and payable within the British Isles, or,
(b) drawn within the British Isles upon some resident therein – even if payable abroad.

Any other bill is a foreign bill.

Thus, in respect of part (a), if a bill is drawn by a U.K. resident and payable within this country, the bill is defined as an inland bill. It does not matter about the drawee's residential status.

In respect of part (b), an inland bill is defined as one where the drawer and drawee are resident in the U.K. even though the bill is payable abroad.

The distinction between a foreign bill and an inland bill is an important one, because by s. 51, a foreign bill must be noted or protested if dishonoured by non-acceptance or non-payment, whereas it is not essential to carry out this legal action for an inland bill. For both types of bill, notice of dishonour must be given using the method described below.

DISHONOUR OF A BILL

A bill is considered as dishonoured if it is not accepted or, if given a qualified acceptance; or is not paid. Sections 43 to 47 refer to these matters and indicate that dishonour occurs:

1. When a bill is duly presented for acceptance or payment at the proper place and acceptance or payment is refused or cannot be obtained, *or*

2. Where presentment for acceptance or payment is excused, and in the case of the latter, the bill is overdue and unpaid.

Once a bill has been dishonoured, the holder can acquire an immediate right of action against the drawer and all prior endorsers, if any, to the bill. But to be in a position to enforce the right, notice within the time limits defined by s. 49 must be given to all prior parties to the bill (for both inland or foreign bills), while for foreign bills noting or protesting must additionally be carried out. Where the above procedures have been carried out for non-acceptance, it is not necessary to repeat them for non-payment unless acceptance has been given in the meantime.

There is no strict form which notice of dishonour should take, but the following details must be given:

1. The bill must be clearly identified.
2. The reason for dishonour (i.e. non-acceptance or non-payment) must be stated.
3. Notice must be given immediately after dishonour has occurred, or within a reasonable time; e.g. A, B, C, D, E, F and G are parties to a bill. (The letters have the same meaning as in previous examples.) If B dishonours the bill for non-payment, then G, the holder, should advise all prior parties (with the exception of B, the drawee), in order to retain their liability. In law, it should be noted that G need only advise the next party back in the chain, i.e. F, then F should advise E, etc. The problem is that if F does not advise any of his previous parties, G will only have recourse to F. So, to maximise his claims, G should advise everyone. Remember, also, that if G recovers from F, then F can recover from any prior party. So, in theory, the final claim could be by A (the drawer) upon B (the drawee).

FOREIGN BILLS

In order to retain the liability of the drawer and endorsers, notice of dishonour must be given as outlined above. **ADDITIONALLY**, for a FOREIGN BILL, the bill must be "*noted*" or "*protested*".

"Protest" is recognised internationally and is often a prerequisite to bringing an action on a bill in a foreign law court.

"PROTEST"

(a) "Protest" occurs where either the bill is protested:
   (1) By a solicitor who has been granted powers as a notary public, or
   (2) By a householder and two witnesses.
   – A specimen Householder's protest is to be found in Schedule 1 of the Bills of Exchange Act. Such a protest is used where no notary public is available.

(b) "Protest" takes the following form:
   The bill having been dishonoured when presented by the holder

is re-presented by the notary public (or householder and witnesses) and when dishonoured, a formal notice, signed by the notary, is drawn up, which must contain a copy of the bill, specifying at whose request the bill was protested, place, date and reason for protest, and answer obtained (if any).

Protest is normally at the place of dishonour and may be made irrespective of the availability of the original bill. (Protest is excused in circumstances similar to those that excuse notice of dishonour.)

(c) Time limit for protesting:
   (1) On the day of dishonour or the next business day only: (Bills of Exchange (Time of Noting) Act, 1917), or
   (2) At any time after "noting" has taken place – see below.

"NOTING"

To save time and initial expense, the Act allows "noting" to take place prior to protesting – so long as the "noting" takes place on the day of dishonour or the next business day.

Here, the bill is re-presented by a notary public (*Note:* there is no provision for a Householder's "noting"!) who notes on the bill or on a slip of paper attached, the date and answer obtained (if any) – when he returns to his office, he will record what was said and done in one of his registers. At any time later, the bill, having been noted, can be formally protested.

DISCHARGE OF A BILL

The methods by which Bills may be discharged are contained in ss. 59 and 61 to 64. They are:

1. *Payment in Due Course*. This is the most usual method and involves payment by or on behalf of the drawee. The expression means "payment made at or after the maturity of the bill to the holder thereof in good faith and without notice that his title to the bill is defective."
2. *When the Acceptor (Drawee) is the Holder at Maturity*. As we saw earlier, bills can be transferred from one party to another. It is assumed here that the current holder is the drawee of the bill – and clearly he will not present it on himself for payment. This method is known as a merger.
3. *Express Waiver*. Here, the holder must absolutely and unconditionally renounce his right against the acceptor at or after the bill's maturity. The renunciation must be in writing unless the holder has returned the bill to the acceptor (drawee).

4. *Cancellation*. The cancellation must be carried out by the holder or his agent. Furthermore, it must be intentional and apparent. For example:
   (1) When someone tears a cheque up – then clearly it satisfies both requirements.
   (2) When a bank (as a customer's agent) cancels a bill, it satisfies both requirements.

   Note: If the bill was torn accidentally (say when opening an envelope containing the bill), then a statement to this effect can be made on the back of the bill, thereby confirming that the bill had not been deliberately cancelled, but cancelled in error.
5. *Alteration of a Bill*. To be discharged under this heading, the alteration must be a material one. Two such examples are changing an inland bill to a foreign one, or varying the rate of interest as specified in an interest clause.

NEGATING LIABILITY

Either the drawer or any holder can negate their liability (i.e. avoid liability) by adding the phrase "sans recours" against their signature. If a bill is dishonoured by non-acceptance or non-payment by the drawee, the holder cannot enforce the bill against any party who has negated his liability in this way.

Clearly, as the primary liability rests with the drawee, then he is the one person who cannot add this phrase by his signature.

CHEQUES

INTRODUCTION

A cheque is really a special type of Bill of Exchange and therefore the law which applies to Bills in general applies to cheques. There are several differences, some of which stem from the definition.

DEFINITION

A cheque is a "bill of exchange drawn on a banker and payable on demand" s. 73. As with Bills of Exchange, there will always be three parties:

drawer –the bank customer
drawee –the bank

payee –the beneficiary

All those parts of the Bills of Exchange Act which apply to demand bills also apply to cheques. More specifically, sections 73–81 refer solely to cheques, while the Cheques Act, 1957, applies to cheques (and certain analogous instruments, e.g. banker's drafts, dividend warrants, etc.).

CROSSING ON CHEQUES

Although there is no statutory provision for the crossing of bills, there is a statutory provision for crossing cheques. Crossings by themselves do not affect the transferability of an instrument, but they do provide a measure of protection, mainly for the drawer, but also for a holder. Where a drawer issues one of his crossed cheques to a payee, the payee cannot encash it unless he is someone described as the known agent of the "drawer". In all other circumstances, a payee must have the cheque credited to his bank account or someone else's after endorsement. Thus, if there is a forgery or fraud, the banking system can be used to trace into whose bank account the cheque was paid.

TYPES OF CROSSINGS ON CHEQUES

GENERAL CROSSING

By s. 76(1), a general crossing exists where a cheque has, on the face of it:

(a) The words "and company" or any abbreviation of these words (e.g. and Co.) between two parallel transverse lines, either with or without the words "not negotiable", or,

(b) Two parallel lines alone, either with or without the words "not negotiable".

Examples

NOT NEGOTIABLE

NOT NEGOTIABLE
A/C PAYEE ONLY

A/C PAYEE

& CO.

SPECIAL CROSSING

By s. 76(2), a special crossing exists where a cheque has, on the face of it, the name of a banker, either with or without the words "not negotiable".

In this case, the cheque is crossed specially to one banker and only that banker can collect the cheque. If a cheque is presented to a paying banker which bears the crossing stamps of two different banks, the paying banker will return it unpaid, unless one bank is acting as agent for the other (e.g. National Westminster Bank acting as an agent for the Bank of Credit and Commerce), or unless the second crossing bank gives an indemnity on the reverse of the cheque.

Examples

MB BANK PLC

MB BANK PLC NOT NEGOTIABLE

MB BANK PLC A/C PAYEE

MB BANK PLC A/C PAYEE ONLY NOT NEGOTIABLE

EFFECT OF CROSSING A CHEQUE

A banker may only cash a crossed cheque for either the drawer or his known agent. In all other cases, crossed cheques must be collected by one bank so that they can be presented through the bank clearing system to the drawer's bank (paying banker). When carrying out these actions, a collecting banker must act within terms of s. 4 C.A. 1957, and a paying banker must act within the terms of s. 60, and/or s. 80 and/or s. 1 C.A. 1957, if they ever want to seek the protections contained therein. (See later sections of this chapter for how these apply.)

OTHER WORDS WHICH MAY BE WRITTEN IN A CROSSING

ACCOUNT PAYEE

This term may sometimes be abbreviated to "A/C Payee" or be in the form of "Account Payee Only". These words are not directly provided for by statute and are not for the attention of the paying banker. However, they are of great significance to the collecting bank, for if the bank collects such items for an account other than that of the true payee, they may be held negligent and thus lose the protection of s. 4 C.A. 1957.

NOT NEGOTIABLE

As we saw earlier, both bills of exchange and cheques are negotiable instruments, and as such, a transferee, who can set himself up as a holder in due course, can acquire a good title to such instruments, even if his transferor or a prior transferor did not have one – say, where there was a defect in the title because the cheque at some time had been stolen. A holder in due course can enforce a bill (or cheque) against any party who has signed the bill. This includes parties subsequent to and prior to the theft (which will include both the drawer and drawee). Clearly, these parties would be happier if they could protect their positions against claims by parties who became holders after a theft. In respect of cheques, protection can simply be achieved by writing "not negotiable" across the face. For, if these words have been used, it means that the transferee cannot acquire a better title than his transferor had, and if a transferee holds under a defective title (because of the theft), a later holder takes the instrument subject to this defect. Thus, in these circumstances, a holder can never set himself up as a holder in due course, and therefore he cannot enforce the cheque against all prior parties, only those subsequent to the theft but not those prior to the theft – so the drawer would be excluded from liability.

For bills of exchange, the effect of a "not negotiable" crossing is to restrict its transferability. **Hibernian Bank Ltd *v.* Gysin and Hanson (1939)**.

> *Note:* When a cheque is crossed "not negotiable", it does not mean that the transferee can never acquire a good title. What it means is that the transferee can never acquire a better title than his transferor had. Thus, if the transferor had a good title, he passes this good title on and the holder can sue all prior parties on the cheque. If the transferor was holding under a defect of title, such as through a theft, the subsequent transfer is taken subject to these defects. This means that the person holding the cheque can only sue parties on the cheque who became parties subsequent to the theft.

EXAMPLE OF THE POWERS OF A HOLDER IN DUE COURSE

Morgan draws a cheque on his account for one hundred pounds. The cheque is drawn in favour of Williamson and is issued in payment for goods. Williamson specially endorses the cheque to Wells in payment for goods, and Wells specially endorses the cheque to Smith in payment for goods. Because of a subsequent disagreement between Morgan and Williamson, Morgan decides to stop payment of the cheque. Smith presents the cheque through his banker to Morgan's bankers and the cheque is returned marked "Payment Stopped". The question arises of what is Smith's position regarding the cheque? The answer is that provided Smith can satisfy all the conditions of s. 29, which almost certainly he can do so here, he will be a holder in due course and can thus enforce the cheque against any prior party, subject to him giving the appropriate notice of dishonour. Thus, he can enforce the bill against the drawer (Morgan) or the endorsers (Williamson or Wells).

Taking the example one stage further, let us assume that after Smith has endorsed it in blank it is stolen by a thief. The cheque is then specially endorsed in favour of Jones for goods, who, in turn, specially endorses it to Edwards for goods. On the assumption that Smith is aware of the theft, he will ask Morgan to put a stop on the cheque (and issue a duplicate – although Morgan would not, in practice, be wise to do so at this stage). Edwards will pass the cheque through his bankers to Morgan's bankers who will return it unpaid marked "Payment Stopped". Again, the question arises of what is Edwards' position, even though the theft (a defect in title) has taken place. The answer is that that if Edwards was not aware of the defect in title at the time the cheque was transferred to him, and he satisfies all other terms of s. 29, he can sue all prior parties on the cheque, including the drawer. Edwards, the holder, can set himself up as a holder in due course because a cheque is a negotiable instrument. This is the advantage of using a negotiable instrument for it enables a holder in due course to exist, even where there has been a defect in title. But several points should be noted:

1. If the cheque had been crossed "not negotiable", then Edwards could never have become a holder in due course. He would acquire limited rights on the cheque and the main one would be to sue parties subsequent to the defect, i.e. Jones or the thief, if the latter could be found.
2. Edwards would be in the same position as 1. if he had been advised of the defect at the time the bill was transferred to him.
3. If the bill contained a forgery (say, of Smith's signature), then no one could set themselves up as a holder in due course, but, as in 1, a person holding the bill still has limited rights – and this includes the ability to sue any party subsequent to the forgery.
4. If a drawer wants to protect himself against the possible subsequent theft of his cheques (or fraudulent activity), he should always cross his cheques "not negotiable". This means that if a defect in title is created, then the chain of claims is broken – so, a person possessing the bill cannot enforce it against the drawer.

PERSONS WHO MAY CROSS A CHEQUE

These are defined in section 77, all of which are self explanatory. Thus,

1. A cheque may be crossed generally or specially by the drawer.
2. Where a cheque is uncrossed, the holder may cross it generally or specially.
3. Where a cheque is crossed generally, the holder may cross it specially.
4. Where a cheque is crossed generally or specially, the holder may add the words "not negotiable".
5. Where a cheque is crossed specially, the banker to whom it is crossed may again cross it specially to another banker for collection.
6. Where an uncrossed cheque or a cheque crossed generally is sent to a banker for collection, he may cross it specially to himself.

From the above, it can be seen that anyone (i.e. drawer, endorser or holder) may convert an uncrossed cheque into a crossed cheque. However as a crossing is a material part of a cheque (by section 78), it cannot be cancelled by anyone, as there is no legal provision for this action. However, when a banking customer writes "Please pay cash" or "Crossing cancelled" within the parallel lines (crossing) on the face of the cheque – although this contravenes the provisions of Bills of Exchange Act, the bank, in paying out only the drawer or his known agent, cannot suffer any loss.

PROTECTIONS AVAILABLE TO BANKERS PROCESSING CHEQUES

When a banker processes a cheque, he will be acting as either collecting banker or paying banker or both. A collecting banker is someone who takes credits over his counter, and places his bank crossing stamp on cheques paid in with customer credits before passing them through the clearing system. A paying banker is a drawee banker and is someone who receives a debit in-clearing each day from Head Office and must decide whether (or not) he is prepared to pay each of the cheques. If he decides to pay, he will add his paid-stamp to the cheque, which effectively discharges the cheque by cancellation. Both types of banker have onerous responsibilities and, because of the massive numbers of cheques being processed daily, they need some form of protection for when they innocently become party to a fraud. Protections are available against this and other risks in both the Cheques Act, 1957, and Bills of Exchange Act, 1882, and they are briefly covered below.

COLLECTING BANKER

RISKS TO THE COLLECTING BANKER

These fall under three main headings:

1. *Conversion.* This occurs when a collecting banker takes a cheque from a person who has no title or a defective title. Here, the bank may be liable to the true owner for conversion, which has been defined as "an act of wrongful interference, without lawful justification with any chattel in a manner inconsistent with the rights of another, whereby that other is deprived of the use and possession of it".
2. *Failure to Comply with Collection Procedures.* This would occur if a bank did not send its out-clearing to Head Office at the end of a particular working day or follow recognised procedures. As a result of this negligent action, a customer may sustain a loss.
3. *Failure to Give Notice of Dishonour.* When a banker, who has collected a cheque for his customer, has it returned to him unpaid, he should immediately advise the customer. For if the bank does not, the customer will assume it has been paid, and, relying on the assumption that it has been paid, alter his position – say, by spending or committing the money.

PROTECTIONS FOR A COLLECTING BANKER

When a claim is made on a collecting bank by its customer, there are three possible courses of action.

1. To set itself up as a holder for value or holder in due course.
2. To plead contributory negligence – here a claim is made that the drawer by his actions, must bear part (or all) of the loss because he contributed to it. **Lumsden and Co. *v.* London Trustee Savings Bank (1971).**
3. To use section 4 Cheques Act, 1957.
   This is the most commonly used defence, and the provision is that where a banker:
   (a) in good faith, and
   (b) without negligence,
   Either receives payment for a customer of any instrument to which this section applies, or, having credited a customer's account with the amount of such an instrument, he receives payment himself, he incurs no liability to the owner of the instrument merely by reason of the fact that the customer had no title or a defective title to the instrument, and the banker will not be regarded as negligent, even though the instrument is unendorsed or irregularly endorsed.

In analysing the meaning of s. 4, it is found that the term "good faith" is defined in s. 90 as "a thing done honestly whether negligently or not". In fact, a banker's good faith will rarely be questioned. The major problem for a banker is to disprove that he has been negligent. This term is not defined in statute and so case law must be used to interpret its meaning. There is much litigation on this matter and when one bank has lost a legal action all banks will revise their procedures. In this context, "without negligence" is defined as "whether the transaction of paying in any given cheque, coupled with the facts antecedent and present was so out of the ordinary course that it ought to have aroused doubts in the banker's mind and caused him to make enquiry". **Commissioners of Taxation *v.* English, Scottish and Australian Bank Ltd (1920)**. Not only should the bank make an enquiry but it should also receive an answer which would satisfy a prudent businessman.

Briefly, negligence can be classified under three headings:

1. Negligence when opening a bank account:

   Examples:

   Failure to obtain a reference. **Ladbroke *v.* Todd (1914)**.
   Failure to follow up a reference. **Guardians of St John's Hampstead *v.* Barclays Bank Ltd (1923)**.
   Failure to obtain employer's name. **Lloyds Bank Ltd *v.* E. B. Savory and Company (1933)**.

2. Negligence concerning the control of an account:

   Examples:

   Collecting cheques for the account of a company official, where the cheques were made payable to the company. **A. L. Underwood Ltd *v.* Bank of Liverpool and Martins Ltd (1924)**.
   Collecting cheques for the private account of an agent where the cheques were drawn by him on his principal's account. **Morrison *v.* London County and Westminster Bank Ltd (1914)**.

3. Negligence concerning a particular transaction.

   Example:

   Failure to enquire about a third party cheque which was presented for credit of an unsatisfactory account. **Motor Traders Guarantee Corporation *v.* Midland Bank Ltd (1937)**.

PAYING BANKER

The paying banker is under a legal obligation to honour its customers cheques provided:

(a) There is sufficient credit balance or unutilised overdraft limit available. *NB:* The bank can deduct the value of any cheque paid in to the account but not yet cleared (i.e. uncleared effects).

(b) The cheque is properly drawn (i.e. correctly signed, dated, words and figures agree, payee's name quoted, etc.) and presented at the bank where the account is held.

(c) There is no legal bar to payment (such as where the customer has stopped payment or notice has been received of the customer's death, etc.).

RISKS TO THE PAYING BANKER

These may be said to fall under two main headings:

1. WRONGFUL DISHONOUR OF CHEQUES

This may arise because a banker either:

(a) Debits his customer's account with a stopped cheque or post dated cheque, or,
(b) Debits his customer's account with someone else's cheque, or,
(c) Fails to credit his customer's account with money that he has paid in.

Whichever of these happens, the customer's credit balance will be artificially low. If, as a result of one of the above actions, the paying banker dishonours any of the customer's other cheques, then the customer has a right of action against his banker. This will be for both breach of contract and also possibly libel. With regard to the former, the level of damages awarded will depend upon whether the customer is a trader or a non-trader, as illustrated below.

Trader (or professional person)

(a) **Damages for breach of contract**. Assuming the financial loss was reasonably foreseeable (i.e. actual loss would not need to be proved), the trader would recover his loss and also reasonable compensation for injury to his credit.

(b) **Damages for libel** (i.e. tort of defamation). These may be awarded depending upon the words which the banker uses as a reason for returning the cheque. The interpretation of the words "refer to drawer" has changed over the years. In **Flach *v*. London and S. W. Bank Ltd (1915)**, they were not held to be libellous but interpreted as "We are not paying – go back to the drawer and ask why." But in an Irish case, **Pyke *v*. Hibernian Bank Ltd (1950)** they were held to be libellous as they meant "no funds". Subsequently, in **Jayson *v*. Midland Bank Ltd (1968)**, they were held to be libellous – although the plaintiff's action did not succeed here because the bank was held justified in returning the cheques. Thus, the words were used correctly. Furthermore, the words "not sufficient" have been held to be libellous. **Davidson v. Barclays Bank Ltd (1940).** Here, £250 damages were awarded.

NON-TRADER; e.g. HOUSEHOLDER

(a) **Damages for breach of contract.** Unless special damage can be proved, damages will be merely nominal; e.g. in **Gibbons v. Westminster Bank Ltd (1939)**, a lady whose cheque for rent had wrongly been dishonoured, was awarded nominal damages of £2 as she did not prove special damages (damage for libel not claimed), and

(b) **Damages for libel.** (As in (b) above). In a Supreme Court of New Zealand case (persuasive but not binding in English law) – **Baker v. Australia and New Zealand Bank (1959)** a non-trader was awarded £2 nominal damages for each cheque wrongly returned unpaid and £100 total damages for libel in respect of the answer "present again" – the court decided it had a defamatory meaning "in implying that the customer had defaulted as to time for performance of the legal and ethical obligation to provide for payment by the bank on presentment of a cheque issued for immediate payment": *NB:* The damage took into account the bank had made no apology.

In any situation like the above where the bank is at fault, it should:

1. Make profuse apologies to the customer, and,
2. Make necessary correcting entries to the bank accounts, and
3. Write to the payee, stating that the problem that has developed does not truly reflect the customer's credit-worthiness and that if the cheque is re-presented, it will immediately be paid.

2. CONVERSION

This has been defined earlier and arises where the paying banker pays someone other than the true payee.

PROTECTIONS FOR A PAYING BANKER

These are provided for in three sections of the Bills of Exchange Act and one of the Cheques Act.

Section 59. If a banker pays a cheque to the holder in good faith and without notice of any defect in title, he is entitled to debit his customer's account for the amount, provided it is:

(a) in accordance with the customer's instructions, and

(b) in the ordinary course of business (an example of a payment made, not "in the ordinary course of business", is when a paying banker advises a collecting banker that a direct remittance has been paid before the bank officially opens at 9.30 in the morning).

Section 80. This relates to the payment of crossed cheques, and protects a banker, provided payments are made:

(a) in good faith, and,
(b) without negligence, and
(c) in accordance with the crossing.

Section 60. This relates only to the payment of open or crossed cheques which have forged or unauthorised endorsements on them, and protects a banker, provided payments are made:

(a) in good faith, and,
(b) in the ordinary course of business.

Section 1. C.A. This relates to the payment of open and crossed cheques (and certain analogous instruments but not bills of exchange) which have no endorsement or an irregular endorsement on them, and protects a banker provided that the cheque is:

(a) drawn on a banker; and is paid,
(b) in good faith, and,
(c) in the ordinary course of business

COLLECTING BANKER WHO IS ALSO A PAYING BANKER

This occasionally happens and occurs when customers pay in for the credit of their account cheques drawn by other customers of the same bank. The precedent established in **Carpenters Company *v.* British Mutual Banking Company (1938)**, indicates the standards expected of a banker. For where such a bank is being sued for conversion, to defend itself successfully it must prove that it complied with the protective sections for both a collecting banker (section 4. C.A. 1957), and a paying banker (section 1. C.A. 1957 or s. 60, or s. 80). Hence, if a banker was only successful in its defence as either paying banker or collecting banker, it would still remain liable to the true owner.

EXAMINATION QUESTIONS

Question 1

1. A bill of exchange is an instrument of the class called "negotiable". Give other examples of negotiable instruments.
2. State the main characteristics of a negotiable instrument.

(Chartered Institute of Bankers)

Question 2

Ernest is employed by International Unity, a firm of merchant bankers, as a securities clerk. A customer of the firm deposited for safe custody a company share certificate and a bearer bond issued by the Ruritanian Government. Without lawful authority, Ernest took these documents from the safe and sold them to Peter.

1. Are these documents negotiable instruments?
2. Can their owner recover them from Peter?

(Chartered Institute of Bankers)

Question 3

(a) Starcos, in Greece, has just purchased machinery for £10,000 from Timothy in England. Angus, in Scotland, owes Starcos £15,000. Draft an appropriate document by which Starcos may settle his debt to Timothy without transferring funds from Greece.

(b) Explain fully what is the essential difference between negotiable instruments and other assignable contracts.

(Chartered Institute of Bankers)

Question 4

State the three essential parties to a bill of exchange.

(Chartered Institute of Bankers)

Question 5

(a) By s. 19 of the Bills of Exchange Act, 1882, an acceptance of a bill is either (a) general or (b) qualified. State briefly the meanings of a general acceptance and a qualified acceptance of a bill.

(b) Study carefully this bill:

> £1,000 WRENDON
> 31st August, 1988
>
> 90 days after date pay to John Clever or order the sum of one thousand pounds of value received.
>
> William Sykes
>
> To Arthur Fagin,
> 10, High Street,
> Grantchester

Indicate whether the acceptance is general or qualified if Arthur Fagin writes thereon:

1. His signature only.
2. His signature plus the word "accepted".
3. His signature plus the words "accepted for £900".
4. His signature plus the words "accepted payable at 100 days after date".
5. His signature plus the words "payable at Wessex Bank, Grantchester".
6. His signature plus the words "payable at Wessex Bank, Grantchester only".

(Chartered Institute of Bankers)

Question 6

Draft an example of:

1. A bill payable after acceptance;
2. A bill payable after date;
3. An order bill payable on demand.

(Chartered Institute of Bankers)

Question 7

A drew a bill of exchange dated 1st September 1987 on B for £500, payable to C or order 6 months after date. B accepted it and C endorsed it to D on 1st January 1988.

(a) On what date is the bill due for payment?
(b) On that date who is liable to pay the £500 and to whom?

(c) What are the rights and liabilities of the parties if the bill is dishonoured for non-payment?

(Chartered Institute of Bankers)

Question 8

Are the following bills payable to order:

1. "Pay AB £500".
2. "Pay AB only £500".
3. "Pay AB personally £500".

(Chartered Institute of Bankers)

Question 9

Andrew drew a bill of exchange upon Bernard, payable to Charles, who negotiates it to David. What features would you look for to decide whether the bill is:

1. Payable to order?
2. Payable to bearer?
3. An inland bill?
4. A foreign bill?

(Chartered Institute of Bankers)

Question 10

(a) Define the term "holder in due course" of a bill of exchange.

(b) Andrew drew a cheque for £50 payable to Bertram as payment for a camera. Bertram specially endorsed the cheque to Charles as a wedding gift. Charles specially endorsed this cheque to Donald in payment of his rent. Donald paid the cheque into his bank and it was returned marked "refer to drawer". State with reasons who is liable to Donald on the cheque.

(Chartered Institute of Bankers)*

Question 11

(a) Albert drew a cheque for £500 payable to Ben in payment for a motor cycle. Ben specially endorsed the cheque to Carol as a gift. She specially endorsed the cheque to Dora in payment for furniture. Dora paid the cheque into her bank account. It was dishonoured and marked "Refer to Drawer". Whom may Dora sue on the cheque?

(b) Desmond drew a bill upon Thomas payable to Patrick on demand. Desmond delivered it to Patrick, who presented it to Thomas for payment. Thomas refused payment. State the rights (if any) of Patrick on the bill.

(Chartered Institute of Bankers)

Question 12

Arthur Frawd is a factory manager employed by XYZ Co. Ltd. In the course of his work he lawfully received a cheque made payable to "XYZ Co. Ltd, or order". He endorsed it "XYZ Co. Ltd", and signed this endorsement "A. Frawd, Manager". He then paid this cheque into his private account. In due course the cheque was cleared. Advise XYZ Co. Ltd what their legal position is according to the civil law.
(Chartered Institute of Bankers)

Question 13

What is the liability of an endorser of a bill of exchange?
(Chartered Institute of Bankers)

Question 14

Study carefully this bill of exchange:

> MUDBURY
> £10,000 1st April 1987
>
> Three months after date pay William Sykes or order ten thousand pounds for value received.
>
> To Paul Grabbitt Albert Jorrocks

1. Name the parties to the bill and state their respective roles.
2. How does Paul Grabbitt become the acceptor?
3. How does William Sykes become the holder?
4. How does William Sykes become the endorser?
5. Who presents the bill for acceptance, to whom, and when?
6. Who presents the bill for payment to whom and when?
7. How may the bill be discharged?

(Chartered Institute of Bankers)*

Question 15

> £4,000 LONDON 1st October 1987
>
> On demand pay John Jorrocks or order the sum of four thousand pounds for value received.
>
> To Thomas Snodgrass Alec Smart

Study this bill carefully and answer these questions:

1. Is it a bearer bill?
2. Is it an order bill payable on demand?
3. Name the drawer.
4. Name the drawee.
5. Name the payee.
6. Name the holder.
7. What is the legal position if the drawee is a fictitious person?
8. What is the legal position if the payee is a fictitious person?
9. Is it an inland bill?
10. After the bill has been issued what steps should the payee take?

(Chartered Institute of Bankers)

Question 16

(a) State, giving your reasons, whether the undermentioned instruments are valid bills of exchange (assume that they are valid in all other respects):

1. An instrument drawn on A who is an infant;
2. An instrument drawn by B who is an infant;
3. An instrument drawn on "C or D";
4. An instrument drawn in favour of "E or F";
5. An instrument which stipulates, "Pay cash or order £1,000";
6. An instrument which stipulates, "Pay John Jones £1,000 on the death of my wife";
7. An instrument which stipulates, "Pay John Jones £1,000 and charge my account with the payment".

(b) By s. 31(3) of the Bills of Exchange Act, 1882, "a bill payable to order is negotiated by the endorsement of the holder completed by delivery". Give examples of:

1. An endorsement in blank;
2. A special endorsement;
3. A restrictive endorsement.

(Chartered Institute of Bankers)

Question 17

1. A cheque is a crossed cheque when two parallel lines are drawn across it. What are the four types of crossings which may appear on a cheque?

2. What is the legal effect of a crossing (on a cheque) plus the words "Mudbury Bank P.L.C."?

3. What is the legal effect of a crossing (on a cheque) plus the words "not negotiable"?
(Chartered Institute of Bankers)

Question 18

(a) An open cheque has the words "not negotiable" written across it. What effect do these words have?

(b) If a drawer crosses a cheque adding the words "not negotiable" can there ever be a holder in due course of that cheque?

(c) Is it the collecting banker or the paying banker who is affected by the crossing "a/c payee"?

(d) Why is a banker's draft not a cheque?

(e) Write an example of a special crossing.

(Chartered Institute of Bankers)

Question 19

(a) What is a cheque?

(b) Maurice and Norman made a contract with each other whereby Maurice was to pay Norman £100. Maurice had no cheque book with him, but on a plain piece of paper he wrote out and signed a form of "cheque" drawn on his bank. He also wrote on the face of it "to be retained", and he orally promised Norman that he would send him a cheque on one of his bank's printed forms. The original "cheque" was presented by Norman but dishonoured. Consider whether Norman can sue Maurice on this document by treating it as a dishonoured cheque.

(c) Albert, a clerk employed by the firm of Brown and Co. fraudulently represented to the partners in that firm that plumbing work had been completed for the firm by Card. Card is a non-existent person. Brown and Co. drew a cheque to the order of Card in payment for the work and handed it to Albert for dispatch to Card. Albert endorsed the cheque in the name of Card and paid it into his own bank account; his bank accepted it in good faith. Albert's account was credited with the amount of the cheque, and in due course the cheque was paid by Brown and Co. to Albert's bankers. Can Brown and Co. recover from Albert's bank the amount of the cheque?

(Chartered Institute of Bankers)

Question 20

P draws a bearer cheque for £50 in favour of Q in payment of a debt. R steals it and hands it as a gift to S, who in turn hands it to T in exchange for a motor scooter. T gives the cheque to his wife, U, as a birthday present. State the legal rights of Q, R, S, T, and U in respect of this cheque.

(Chartered Institute of Bankers)

Question 21

(a) Explain in relation to bills of exchange what is meant by the following:

(1). A blank indorsement, a special indorsement, a conditional indorsement;
(2). A holder in due course;
(3). Acceptance for honour.

(b) E signed a cheque and crossed it "not negotiable". He told his secretary to fill in a certain amount and to fill in X's name as payee. The secretary filled in a larger amount than she had been authorised to do, made the cheque payable to F and give it to F in settlement of a debt of her own. F cashed it. E seeks to know his rights, if any, against F. Advise E.

(I.C.S.A.)

Question 22

Discuss the special obligations owed by a banker to his customer in respect of cheques. To what extent, if at all, does the law afford special protection to bankers?

(I.C.S.A.)

TABLE OF LEGAL CASES

APPENDIX OF ANSWERS

In this section, a cross sample of questions is answered. These questions can be identified in the main body of the book by an asterisk which has been printed by the side of the respective question number.

It will be seen that the selection of answered questions has been limited to those that have been set by the various professional bodies. On this matter, I wish to make it clear that the model answers are my own, and reflect what I would have written if I had been answering the question in that particular examination. As a condition of publication, I have been asked to point this matter out and to confirm that none of the answers have been officially approved by the respective Institutes.

With regard to published questions set by the Associated Examining Board and the Joint Matriculation Board as a condition of publication I have had to agree not to provide specimen answers. As a result of this promise, you will find that none of their questions have been answered in the text. This means that there are many questions which your tutor can ask you to answer for which a specimen solution has not been provided. By being asked to write an answer yourself, it will certainly give your tutor an indication of whether he/she feels you will do well in the examination, or whether you will have to do further work in order to reach the required standard. It will also provide an opportunity for the tutor to comment on your technical knowledge and examination style. All I can suggest is that if you want to be successful in your Law examination, you should attempt to answer all the questions – not just those which the tutor specifically asks you to answer and submit for assessment.

CHAPTER 3

Q.12.
When a judge is uncertain of the meaning of a word contained within a statute, he will initially look to the preamble (introductory statement) of the statute and also to any definitions that are contained within the various sections or other notes that are printed at the bottom of each page. If no explanation is provided in these places then reference can be made to the Interpretation Act, 1889. Where this approach also fails to provide an explanation, then certain general rules may be applied. These are:

1. *The literal rule:* Here, the word will be given its normal literal and grammatical meaning, even if hardship results. But where to use such an interpretation would lead, for example, to absurdity, it would not be followed.
2. *The golden rule:* In some situations, interpretation of a single word in isolation could lead to

absurdity, but if looked at in the context of the whole enactment, the interpretation is reasonable: Re Sigsworth (1935). In these circumstances, the golden rule would be applied.

3. *The mischief rule:* If after applying rules (1) and (2), there is still uncertainty, the judge may consider looking at the original law to see what wrong (mischief), the statute sought to remedy and apply a meaning to the word to satisfy these circumstances: Gorris *v*. Scott (1874).

4. *The Ejusdem Generis Rule:* Where particular words are followed by general words, the general words will be interpreted in relation to the particular words. In Powell *v*. Kempton Park Racecourse Co. (1899), the courts interpreted "other places for betting purposes" in the context of "house or office" as meaning covered accommodation and not an open air enclosure.

5. *Ut res magis valeat quam pereat:* Every word in a statute must be there for a purpose and none of them must be repetitious or redundant. If words appear to be either of these, the court must interpret them in such a way to avoid this happening.

6. *Expressum facit cessare tacitum:* Where something is expressed, then there is no room for implication. So if a statute imposed rates on houses and buildings but did not refer to land, then rates would only apply to land upon which properties had been built.

Finally, in addition to these major rules, a series of minor ones exist. In general, some of the minor rules contradict each other, while in other situations, they provide exceptions to the general rules.

CHAPTER 4

Q.6.

(a) There is no simple answer to the question "when does an offer lapse?" For each situation will have to be judged on its own merit and so the answer will depend upon the circumstances.

But there is evidence to show that an offer made by letter must be accepted by letter (or by a quicker method) while an offer made by telegram must be accepted by telegram. Thus, the method of accepting an offer must reflect the urgency with which the offer was made.

There are other situations whereby offers will not lapse even after a month has expired since the offer was made, but the period will not extend indefinitely. Ramsgate Victoria Hotel Ltd *v*. Montefiore (1866). Here, Montefiore offered to take some shares in the plaintiff company in a letter dated 8th June 1864. The company did not immediately confirm its acceptance of the offer, but subsequently on 23rd November 1864, they wrote to advise him that a number of shares had been allocated to him. Because of the time delay, Montefiore refused to take up the allocated shares, and the plaintiff attempted to enforce the contract against him. *Held*. Because of the company's unreasonable delay in accepting the offer, the court considered that the offer had lapsed. Thus the plaintiff's action failed.

(b) In the law of contract, there is something called a counter offer. When it has been given, it acts as a rejection of the original offer. It arises when the offeree introduces new terms which the offeror does not have the chance of examining. To explain how the principle operates, consider the circumstances of Hyde *v*. Wrench (1840). Here, Wrench offered to sell a farm to Hyde for £1,000 on 6th June. On 8th June, Hyde offered £950. On 27th June, Wrench refused the offer for £950, then two days later, Hyde said he would be prepared to pay £1,000. Wrench refused this second offer, even though it was the equivalent of the original asking price, and Hyde attempted to enforce the contract. *Held*. There was no enforceable contract as the counter offer of 8th June was considered to be a rejection of the original offer. Without the agreement of Wrench, the offer was not capable of being revived.

Applying the courts decision in the Hyde case to the circumstances presented in the question, then there would be no valid contract – unless A was prepared to revive the contract at the price of £1,500.

Q.30.

To discharge a debt in general, the debtor must fully pay the amount he has agreed to be liable for under the terms of the contract. Where a debtor attempts to pay a lesser amount on the due date, even with the other party's agreement, then it is still possible for the "other party" to pursue a legal action through the courts to claim the difference at a later date. This principle was established in the classic precedent Pinnel's Case (1602). Pinnel sued Cole in debt for £8 10 shillings which fell due for payment on a bond on 11th November 1600. Cole, in his defence, said that, at Pinnel's request, he only repaid £5 2 shillings and 6 pence which had been accepted in full settlement of the debt. *Held*. Pinnel's action was successful and in the judgement, it was established that payment of a lesser sum on the due date could not, in general, be considered as satisfaction for the whole debt.

Applying the decision of the Pinnel's case to this question, then Kenneth could compel James to pay the difference. The answer would be different if Kenneth had accepted James' watch in full settlement of the debt, even if the watch was worth less than £50. For in these circumstances Kenneth would not be able to recover the balance through the court, because the offer and acceptance of a watch is considered to be sufficient "new" consideration, even though it is "inadequate". For, it should be remembered that in any contract, consideration must be present (unless the contract is executed under seal) but consideration need not be adequate.

Q.48.
In general, when two parties are negotiating a contract, the principle "caveat emptor" (let the buyer beware) applies. During the negotiating stage, various statements may be made which are described as representations – these are inducements by one party to get the other party to enter into a contract which he may not otherwise do so. In fact, there may be some details that the vendor is aware of but he remains silent, thereby not bringing certain matters to the attention of the "other party". Provided these actions do not amount to positive misrepresentation, then the "other party" would have no grounds for attempting to rescind the contract. In this situation, Harold has made certain positive statements and because they were true at the time they were made, they cannot be described as misrepresentations.

But in the present circumstances, one further matter developed – and this was that between the time the contract was initially negotiated and the date the contract was signed, there had been a material change in circumstances. For although all the statements origianlly made at the time the contract was negotiated were true, because of a change of circumstances not all of them were completely true at the time the contract was signed. Where such changes occur, then there is a responsibility on the vendor, Harold, to advise Ian of the up to date position then his action would amount to fraudulent misrepresentation. Should Ian wish to do so, then he may sue Harold for damages and on the basis that his action would be successful, the court would have to decide the amount of damages to be awarded to him based on the prevailing circumstances. Moreover, if he so desired, Ian could attempt to have the contract rescinded, and, in fairly similar circumstances, in With *v.* O'Flanagan (1936), the action for rescission succeeded.

In this set of circumstances, Ian could be advised to sue Harold for damages and then the court would have to decide how much he was entitled to. Alternatively, Ian could be advised to take an action to rescind the contract thereby enabling him to recover his consideration monies and perhaps buy a better business.

Q.72,
(a) A contract is a private contractual agreement between parties to it and under the terms of the contract, the parties acquire rights against each other which are enforceable in the courts. From this stems a general rule that only parties (privies) to a contract can sue and be sued on the contract. Because, to allow third parties to acquire rights under a contract that did not involve them, would be inequitable. The method of applying this principle is clearly illustrated by the decision made in Dunlop *v.* Selfridge (1915). Here, Dunlop sold some of their tyres to Dew & Co who were wholesalers. Under the terms of the sale contract it was agreed that the tyres would not be sold at less than Dunlop's list price. Selfridges ordered two of Dunlop's tyres from Dew & Co. Even though Selfridges had agreed not to sell any of the tyres at less than list price, one was sold at below this figure. Dunlop then tried to get an injunction preventing Selfridges from selling tyres, in the future, at less than list price and also claimed damages. *Held.* There was no contract between Selfridges and Dunlop and so the action failed – only parties who are privy to a contract may sue. (*Note:* As a result of s. 26 Resale Prices Act, 1976, then such matters would be resolved in a different way today.)

(b) Here a contract has been entered into between John and the publishers of a magazine. Thus, if the principle of privity of contract is applied, then only actions between John and the publishers may be pursued in the courts. As it is John's wife who is attempting to pursue legal action, then in normal circumstances, because she is not a privy to the contract, she cannot sue on it. But to this general rule, there are certain exceptions, which if they can be established would permit a third party to sue on a contract. One of these exceptions relates to the law of agency – for provision has been made which allow a principal (even if undisclosed) to sue on a contract which has been entered into by his agent. Thus, if it could be established that Jane was John's agent in negotiating the contract, Jane could sue on it. This would seem unlikely and if this is assumed, then only John can sue on the contract. It would appear to be simpler for John to pursue a legal action.

CHAPTER 5

Q.2.
(a) The definition of a partnership is to be found in s. 1(1) Partnership Act, 1980, which provides that a partnership is "the relationship which subsists between persons carrying on a business in common with a view to profit".

For any relationship to satisfy the definition, certain criteria have to be met:

1. "Persons" – partnership must consist of more than one person (and normally less than twenty). This requirement is satisfied here as there are three parties.
2. "A business in common" – the parties must act together for their common good and the agreement between A, B and C certainly has a business nature to it – rather than say a wholly charitable nature.

3. "Profit" – any relationship of this type will be formed to generate an income and operate on a profitable basis.

Thus, the relationship between A, B and C is a partnership in the legal sense.

(b) If A, B and C subsequently decide to incorporate themselves (and there is nothing to prevent them from doing this), they may attempt to do it in one of the following ways:

1. By Royal Charter – This method is infrequently seen today and would only be used by charities, educational bodies or professional institutes, for example. It would certainly not be appropriate nor permitted for this entertainment venture.
2. By Statute – Again this method is infrequently seen and today would only be used by bodies such as public utilities, nationalised industries or county councils. Therefore, it would not be appropriate for this entertainment venture.
3. Under the Companies Act – This is the most common method used today and to achieve incorporation, A, B and C would have to comply with the requirements of the Companies Act, 1985

The company would be registered as a private limited company, and although it could be limited by guarantee or be unlimited, almost certainly it would be registered as a company limited by shares.

The legal consequences of incorporation in this way are:

(a) A company is separate legal entity from the people who own it (the shareholders) and the people who manage it (the directors).
(b) A company enjoys perpetual succession and upon the death of a shareholder or director, the company does not cease to exist. This is in complete contrast to a partnership which is automatically determined – even though the surviving partners may continue in business using the same trading name if provision has been made for continuation.
(c) The liability of the members (shareholders) in the event of liquidation, is limited to the amount of their shareholding – unlike a partnership, whereby the partners are liable to the full extent of their private resources in the event of the partnership becoming bankrupt.
(d) The powers of the Company are contained within its Memorandum and those of the directors in its Articles and formal procedures are needed to change these. In contrast, partners usually informally agree to what their respective powers and responsibilities are and only simple procedures are needed to effect a change.

CHAPTER 6

Q.2

(a) English law classifies property under two main headings – Real and Personal. Although real property cannot be further classified, personal property can, as the following diagram illustrates:

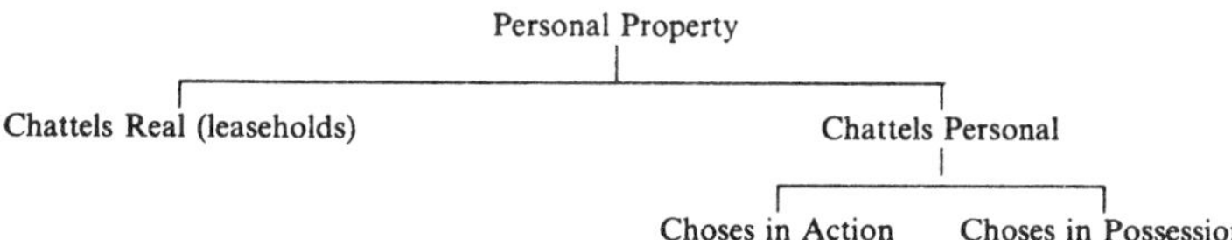

A brief explanation of the various types of property is:

1. Real Property – This consists of freehold land and buildings and the rights over such freehold land.
2. Personal Property – This consists of anything which is not real property. It may be subdivided as follows:

Chattels – Real. Leasehold land is included under this heading.

Chattels – Personal. This is subdivided as follows:

(a) Choses in Action. This is property which cannot be physically held, but it can be owned and transferred (e.g. a debt may be transferred by assignment). Clearly, a transferee cannot physically hold a chose in action, but he acquires certain rights which can be enforced by legal action. Typical examples of such choses are: debts, patents, trade marks and negotiable instruments.
(b) Choses in Possession. This is property which can be possessed and can be transferred, usually by delivery. Sometimes, more formal procedures are needed to effect a transfer

(e.g. when transferring ownership of a car, a registration document must be completed and forwarded to the Vehicle Licensing Authority in Swansea). Other examples of such choses are: caravans, televisions, jewellery, etc.

(b) Using the above explanations then:
1. A house if freehold is real property, but if it is leasehold, it is a chattel real.
2. A caravan is personal property – and is a chose in possession.
3. A horse is personal property – and is a chose in possession.
4. A debt is personal property – and is a chose in action.
5. A cheque is personal property – and is a chose in action.

Q.13.
When someone takes a legal mortgage, they have strong powers for rights, against the thing (in rem) taken as security, have been acquired. Where an equitable mortgage has been taken, the rights of the mortgagor depend upon what type of equitable mortgage has been taken, i.e. whether it has been taken under seal or hand. Where the mortgage has been taken under seal, the mortgagee's powers and remedies are the same as those of a legal mortgagee, but where the mortgage has been taken under hand, the powers of the mortgagee are restricted.

Legal Mortgage. The mortgagee's range of remedies is:

1. *To sue the mortgagor on a personal convenant to repay* (a remedy also available to an equitable mortgagee): This effectively ignores that security has been taken and is really a demand upon the mortgagor to pay from another source.
2. *To enter into possession:* This remedy is rarely used because of the various responsibilities placed on the mortgagee as soon as he takes possession of the property as he will be responsible for any default or missions as if he was the owner.
3. *To foreclose:* This remedy is rarely used because the court needs to be used to effect it. At the first hearing, an order nisi will be issued by the court, if it approves the mortgagee's action. The mortgagee will then be requested to come back to court, say in six months time, so that the matter can be reviewed. At this stage the court will either grant an order absolute (making the mortgagee the legal owner of the land) or instruct that the land should be sold. It is more usual for a sale order to be given (if this happens the mortgagee has really wasted six months time for it would have been simpler and quicker for the mortgagee to have exercised his power of sale at the outset as this remedy would already have been conferred upon him by the Law of Property Act, 1925 (see remedy 5 below) as amended by clauses in the mortgage form).
4. *To appoint a Receiver:* This remedy would be appropriate where the property was a block of flats from which a rental income could be derived and the income used to reduce the debt.
5. *To Sell:* This is the remedy which is usually exercised. A mortgagee would have to comply with the Law of Property Act, 1925, before effecting a sale (i.e. he may have to wait three months after demanding repayment and the mortgagor defaulting in whole or part) unless the mortgage deed permitted the mortgagee to effect an immediate sale following demand on the mortgagor and default. When exercising the power of sale remedy a mortgagee:
   (a) Should act in good faith and not sell to himself: Cuckmere Brick Co. Ltd *v*. Mutual Finance Ltd (1971).
   (b) Need not wait for property prices to rise before effecting a sale: Bank of Cyprus (London) *v*. Gill (1979).
   (c) Must not sell at an unfavourable time: Standard Chartered Bank Ltd *v*. Walker and Walker (1982).

NB: In practice, to sell a property with vacant possession (which a mortgagee will always with to do, so as to gain the highest market price), he will always have to go to court to obtain a "possession order".

Equitable Mortgage

Under Seal. The powers of such mortgagees are the same as for legal mortgagees and are acquired because of special clause(s) contained within the mortgage from (e.g. Power of Attorney and/or Declaration of Trust clauses).

Under Hand. A mortgagee may sue on a personal convenant to repay, but more usually, he will look to a clause in the form of equitable mortgage in which the mortgagor will have promised to execute a legal mortgage if he is ever called upon to do so. If the mortgagor complies with such a request, the powers of a legal mortgagee (outlined above) are acquired, but if he does not or will not, then the assistance of the court will be needed to effect a sale. This would be a costly and time consuming exercise.

CHAPTER 7

Q.2.

(a) For an express private trust to be valid there must be three certainties. These were laid down in Knight *v.* Knight (1840) as:

Certainty of Words. There must be a clear intention to create a trust which is binding in law. If words are used wheich merely request or hope that a person will act, then the courts will not consider the trust to be valid.

Certainty of Subject Matter. The property of which the trust relates must be clearly defined, e.g. My £500 of I.C.I. Stock; My house addressed 16 Dee Road, Chester. Any document containing phrases such as "some portion of my property" or "a decent sum" would fail.

Certainty of Objects. Objects here means beneficiaries and they should be clearly identified in the document. If all beneficiaries are not clearly identified, then this does not mean that the whole trust fails. Wishaw *v.* Stephens (1970). But if none are adequately identified, then upon the donor's death the property which had been detailed in the supposed "trust document" would form part of the deceased's estate and would have to be dealt with in accordance with (other) terms of the donor's will or the rules of intestacy rather than forming part of a trust.

(b) For a trust to be valid, even when contained in a will, the three certainties described in part (a) above must be satisfied. Clearly there is certainty of words and certainty of objects in the case study described in this question. Unfortunately though there is no certainty of subject matter and, as such, the trust will fail.

CHAPTER 8

Q.12.

1. The disposition contained within a will may be of two types: devises or legacies. The distinction between the two is that:

   A devise is a disposition which relates to freehold land. It may be specific (e.g. My freehold house, "Rose Cottage, Heswall") or residuary (e.g. The rest of my realty).

   A legacy is a disposition which relates to any other kind of property, including leasehold land. Legacies may be subdivided under the following main headings.

   (a) *General Legacy.* This relates to a gift which cannot be distinguished from any other of the same type: for example, a car, a clock, five thousand pounds (which may also be called a pecuniary legacy). If several, say, cars exist at the time of death, the legatee may choose which one he wants.

   (b) *Specific Legacy.* This relates to a gift which is expressly described: for example My Rover car, my holding of £5,000 of 3½% War Stock. If the item had been disposed of prior to the testator's death, the legatee receives nothing.

   (c) *Demonstrative Legacy.* This is really a special type of general legacy, but it goes a little further in the sense that there is an indication of which fund should be used to meet the legacy. If the fund had been extinguished prior to the testator's death, the legacy is still available, but as a general legacy.

   (d) *Residuary Legacy.* Whatever remains after the above legacies have been settled, is described as the residuary estate and a will should indicate who the legatee is that will take this residue. If the will does not make this provision, the residue has to be dealt with in accordance with the rules of intestacy.

2. From the above description, it can be seen that:

   (a) Charles is a general legatee – who may also be described as a pecuniary legatee.
   (b) David is a general legatee.
   (c) Edward is a specific legatee.
   (d) Frank is a demonstrative legatee.

CHAPTER 9

Q.1.
The law of tort is concerned with those situations where the conduct of one party causes or threatens harm to the interests of other parties. The aim of this law is to compensate for the harm suffered by those whose interests have been invaded by the conduct of others. The law divides harm up under two headings.

Injuria Sine Damno. This applies where wrongs are committed which cause no actual loss or damage, but legal actions are still available (e.g. trespass).

Damnum Sine Injuria. The applies where wrongs are committed but for which the law provides no remedy. A typical example of where this rule applies is in the situation described in this question. For if a shopkeeper's trade is seriously affected because a competitor, such as a supermarket chain, opens up a local branch, then the shopkeeper cannot use the courts in an attempt to be paid compensation or stop the supermarket from opening up, or continuing to trade.

Q.10.
(1) There is nothing to prevent Evan suing Frank for the injury that he has caused. The chances of his action being successful are very remote because Frank would almost certainly set up a good defence of "volenti not fit injuria", i.e. Evan had consented to the harm that was done to him. For anyone who involves themselves in dangerous physical sports such as wrestling, boxing, judo, etc. must accept that at some time, they may have a limb dislocated or broken and that by participating in such sports they have impliedly consented to such things happening. To support this viewpoint, the details and decision in Simms *v*. Leigh Rugby Football Club (1969) should be considered. Here a rugby player broke his leg after crashing into a concrete wall following a tackle. The player sued the rugby club which used volenti as a defence. Furthermore, it was also established that the wall had been erected in accordance with the rugby league's guidelines. *Held*. The defence of volenti was successful.

(2) The first legal point to be decided in this situation is whether Philip was negligent in not locking his car door and not applying the hand brake correctly. For if this cannot be established, then there is no liability in tort. If it is established that the action was negligent, then Quentin would be seen to have involved himself in a rescue situation. Whether his action for damages would be successful or not depends upon the surrounding circumstances. If the car had been left in a built up area or by a shopping centre and by moving off was in danger of injuring the public in general, then Quentin's action for damages would succeed as the court would follow the leading precedent on this matter: Haynes *v*. Harwood and Son (1935). But, if, say, the car had been left in a remote area and after moving away was in no danger of injuring anyone, then Quentin's action would be unlikely to succeed as the court would apply the precedent of Cutler *v*. United Dairies (London) Ltd (1933).

CHAPTER 10

Q.6.
In order to succeed in an action for damages, a plaintiff must establish that:

1. The statement was an untrue fact.
2. The statement was defamatory.
3. The statement referred to the plaintiff.
4. The words were published.

These points need to be applied to the circumstances of the question. Firstly, there can be no dispute about publication, for the statement appeared as an article in a newspaper. Secondly, where untrue, publication of an article indicating that someone is a thief would be considered as defamatory – for, such a statement would "tend to lower that person in the estimation of right-thinking members of society generally; or tend to make others shun or avoid that person". Finally, it is necessary to consider if the statement was an untrue fact which referred to the plaintiff. From the details of case study, this would appear to be so – but it would still be necessary for Boy to show that the general public would think that the statement referred to him. In order to establish this point, reference could be made to two precedents: E. Hulton & Co. *v*. Jones (1910) and Newstead *v*. London Express Newspaper Ltd (1940). The latter case is very similar to the one described in the question. For here, a newspaper published an article about a thirty-year-old Camberwell man, named Harold Newstead, who had been convicted of bigamy. Unfortunately, there were two people of that name and age living in Camberwell at the time. The person about whom the article did not refer, sued the newspaper. *Held*. The newspaper was liable because the court considered that the statement was defamatory as regards the plaintiff. So his claim for damages was successful.

If such situations arise today, then it may be possible for a newspaper to seek a defence under s. 4

Defamation Act, 1952. To use it, then it would be necessary for the newspaper to show that prior to publication, it took all reasonable steps to avoid such a claim ever being made against it, and that when the aggrieved party had made a claim against the newspaper, it had made an offer of amends, i.e. an offer to publish an apology in a subsequent edition of the newspaper which would clearly indicate that the original article did not relate to the plaintiff.

CHAPTER 11

Q.10.

(a) The definition of a holder in due course is to be found in section 29 Bills of Exchange Act, 1882. It provides that:

> "A holder in due course is a holder who has taken a bill complete and regular on the face of it, under the following conditions:
>
> That he became the holder of it before it was overdue, and without notice that it had previously been dishonoured, if such was the fact. That he took the bill in good faith and for value, and that at the time the bill was negotiated to him he had no notice of any defect in the title of the person who negotiated it."

(b) In this situation, the following chain has been established:

$$\text{Andrew} \xrightarrow{\text{value}} \text{Bertram} \xrightarrow{\text{gift}} \text{Charles} \xrightarrow{\text{value}} \text{Donald.}$$

In these circumstances, Andrew has signed the cheque as drawer, while Bertram and Charles have signed the cheque as endorsers. Because of their actions in signing the bill, each has a liability on the cheque itself.

When Donald receives the returned cheque, he must immediately notify his transferor (Charles) in order to preserve his rights of recourse against Charles. The notification of dishonour should comply with s. 49 B.E.A., 1882. In practice, Donald will also advise Bertram about dishonour and thus pursue his rights of recourse against him. *Note:* It is not necessary to advise the drawer (Andrew) of dishonour, for his banker, the paying banker will have advised him that the cheque has been dishonoured.

But, whether Donald can or cannot recover from prior parties on the cheque depends upon his ability to establish himself as either a holder, holder for value or holder in due course. In the circumstances of this question, is it seen that Donald himself has given value and provided he can satisfy all the other requirements of s. 29 B.E.A. (see part (a) above), he can enforce the cheque against any prior party, i.e. Charles or Bertram subject to him having given the appropriate notice of dishonour to these prior parties. Alternatively, Donald will be able to enforce the cheque against Andrew, as drawer, although as Andrew's bank has almost certainly returned the cheque for lack of funds, this right is unlikely to be worth pursuing.

Q.14.

1. (a) Albert Jorrocks – He is the drawer of the bill and as such he makes out and signs the bill. After drawing this bill, he will send it to the payee, William Sykes – This procedure would certainly happen here as the bill has been drawn payable at a fixed future time, and thus, it is not necessary to send the bill for acceptance.
   (b) William Sykes – He is the payee of the bill and as such, he will either hold on to bill until it matures and present it on the drawee, Grabbitt, on the due date or transfer it to another party by endorsement (signature) and delivery.
   (c) Paul Grabbitt – He is the drawee of the bill and as such, he will be asked to honour the bill on its maturity date. If Sykes held on to the bill until this date, he would request payment. However, if he endorsed the bill to another party, Grabbitt would have to pay the person (holder) who presented it to him.
2. Paul Grabbitt would become the acceptor if the bill was presented to him for acceptance. To accept the bill, the minimum requirement would be for Grabbitt to place his signature on the bill, s. 17 B.E.A., 1882, although in practice, he would usually add the word accepted and the date (as this bill is drawn payable at a fixed future date, acceptance is not an essential requirement).
3. A holder is defined in s. 2 B.E.A., 1882, as the payee or endorsee of the bill who is in possession of it, or the bearer thereof. Thus, the first person who could be the holder of this bill is Sykes, the payee and he would become the holder upon receipt of the bill, sent to him by Jorrocks.
4. Sykes becomes the endorser if he signs his own name on the bill in order that he may transfer it to another party. The endorsement may be in blank (i.e. just his signature), special (e.g. Pay D. Jones, W. Sykes (signature) or restrictive (pay A. Griffiths only, W. Sykes (signature)).
5. Where a bill has to be sent for acceptance, usually it will be the drawer (Jorrocks) who sends the

bill to the drawee (Grabbitt). By asking for the bill to be returned to him, the drawer will always be in a position of knowing whether or not a bill has been accepted. Bills should be sent for acceptance within a reasonable time of them being drawn and upon their return to the drawer, they will be forwarded to the payee.

Note: Section 18 B.E.A., 1882, fully defines "the time of acceptance" and the description given above relates to the simplest alternative.

6. The payee, Sykes (or the holder, if the bill has been transferred), is responsible for presenting the bill on the drawer (Grabbitt) for payment on the maturity date. This bill will mature on 1st July 1987 and if that was a non-working day, on the next available working day.
7. The most common way by which bills are discharged is payment in due course by the drawer (Grabbitt). The less common methods by which bills may be discharged are:

   (a) By Grabbitt becoming the holder at maturity.
   (b) By Sykes (or a holder) expressly waiving his rights on the bill.
   (c) By Sykes (or a holder) cancelling the bill – say by ripping the bill up into several pieces.

INDEX